"If you want to understand and eng̱ this new field of sustainable HRM, strong grounding in the academic literature, Sugumar Mariappanadar provides detailed discussions of the challenges facing proponents of sustainable economic development worldwide and offers practical examples of the steps being taken to improve our common future. It's the best book of its kind available today."

—Susan E. Jackson, Rutgers University, USA

"This is a comprehensive book that will enhance your understanding and enable you to design and implement HRM practices for achieving organizational financial performance without compromising on stakeholders' wellbeing. It illustrates various domains of Sustainable HRM with sound theories to shape HRM practices with pro-organizational, social and environmental values."

—Klaus J. Zink, University of Kaiserslautern, Germany

Sugumar Mariappanadar guides readers with clarity of purpose and direction through and beyond the layers of controversy – and opportunity – that HRM thinking and practices labelled as 'sustainable' can offer. The author's open and engaging style draws readers in, informs them comprehensively about strategic contexts for sustainable HRM, and allows them spaces to reflect critically on their own values in relation to current HRM practice and research. With this book, Dr Mariappanadar will both prompt and satisfy the curiosity of students and of practitioners of HRM as they prepare for an increasingly complex future.

—Keith Jackson, SOAS University of London,
UK; Kobe University, Japan

"This inspirational book makes an exciting scholarly contribution to an increasingly important debate on the intersection between the management of human resources and the creation of sustainable organisations. Expertly analysed, it will appeal to students, scholars, policy makers and the wider business and social science community".

—Thomas Lange, Middlesex University, UK

"Sugumar Mariappanadar has written a thoughtful and strategic book which will certainly become essential reading in its field. It marries high level incisive scholarship with enlightening cases of companies which have adopted proactive policies in term of HRM sustainability. I am sure it will generate many new ideas about the manner to sustainably conduct people management, in itself a key element in achieving global sustainability"

—Philippe Debroux, Soka University, Japan

MANAGEMENT, WORK AND ORGANISATIONS

Series editors: **Gibson Burrell**, School of Management, University of Leicester, UK
Mick Marchington, Manchester Business School, University of Manchester and Strathclyde
Business School, University of Strathclyde, UK
Paul Thompson, Strathclyde Business School, University of Strathclyde, UK

This series of textbooks covers the areas of human resource management, employee relations, organisational behaviour and related business and management fields. Each text has been specially commissioned to be written by leading experts in a clear and accessible way. The books contain serious and challenging material, take an analytical rather than prescriptive approach and are particularly suitable for use by students with no prior specialist knowledge.

The series is relevant for many business and management courses, including MBA and post-experience courses, specialist masters and postgraduate diplomas, professional courses and final-year undergraduate courses. These texts have become essential reading at business and management schools worldwide.

Titles include:

Maurizio Atzeni
WORKERS AND LABOUR IN A GLOBALISED CAPITALISM

Stephen Bach and Ian Kessler
THE MODERNISATION OF THE PUBLIC SERVICES AND EMPLOYEE RELATIONS

Emma Bell
READING MANAGEMENT AND ORGANIZATION IN FILM

Paul Blyton and Peter Turnbull
THE DYNAMICS OF EMPLOYEE RELATIONS (3rd edition)

Paul Blyton, Edmund Heery and Peter Turnbull (editors)
REASSESSING THE EMPLOYMENT RELATIONSHIP

Sharon C. Bolton
EMOTION MANAGEMENT IN THE WORKPLACE

Sharon C. Bolton and Maeve Houlihan (editors)
SEARCHING FOR THE HUMAN IN HUMAN RESOURCE MANAGEMENT

Peter Boxall and John Purcell
STRATEGY AND HUMAN RESOURCE MANAGEMENT (4th edition)

J. Martin Corbett
CRITICAL CASES IN ORGANISATIONAL BEHAVIOUR

Susan Corby, Steve Palmer and Esmond Lindop
RETHINKING REWARD

David Farnham
THE CHANGING FACES OF EMPLOYMENT RELATIONS

Ian Greener
PUBLIC MANAGEMENT (2nd edition)

Keith Grint
LEADERSHIP

Irena Grugulis
SKILLS, TRAINING AND HUMAN RESOURCE DEVELOPMENT

Geraldine Healy, Gill Kirton and Mike Noon (editors)
EQUALITY, INEQUALITIES AND DIVERSITY

Damian Hodgson and Svetlana Cicmil (editors)
MAKING PROJECTS CRITICAL

Marek Korczynski
HUMAN RESOURCE MANAGEMENT IN SERVICE WORK

Karen Legge
HUMAN RESOURCE MANAGEMENT: ANNIVERSARY EDITION

Patricia Lewis and Ruth Simpson (editors)
GENDERING EMOTIONS IN ORGANIZATIONS

Patricia Lewis and Ruth Simpson (editors)
VOICE, VISIBILITY AND THE GENDERING OF ORGANIZATIONS

Sugumar Mariappanadar
SUSTAINABLE HUMAN RESOURCE MANAGEMENT

Alison Pullen, Nic Beech and David Sims (editors)
EXPLORING IDENTITY

Jill Rubery and Damian Grimshaw
THE ORGANISATION OF EMPLOYMENT

Hugh Scullion and Margaret Linehan (editors)
INTERNATIONAL HUMAN RESOURCE MANAGEMENT

John Walton and Claire Valentin (editors)
HUMAN RESOURCE DEVELOPMENT

For more information on titles in the Series please go to **www.macmillanihe.com/series/
management,-work-and-organisations/14037**

Sustainable Human Resource Management

Strategies, Practices and Challenges

Sugumar Mariappanadar

First published 2019 by
RED GLOBE PRESS

Red Globe Press in the UK is an imprint of Springer Nature Limited,
registered in England, company number 785998, of 4 Crinan Street,
London, N1 9XW.

Red Globe Press® is a registered trademark in the United States,
the United Kingdom, Europe and other countries.

ISBN 978–1–137–53049–3 Softcover

This book is printed on paper suitable for recycling and made from fully
managed and sustained forest sources. Logging, pulping and manufacturing
processes are expected to conform to the environmental regulations of the
country of origin.

A catalogue record for this book is available from the British Library.

A catalog record for this book is available from the Library of Congress.

It takes a village to raise a child – An African proverb

I dedicate this book to the memory of my mother and father and to my brothers and sisters for their endless contributions and sacrifices in developing the person I am today. My lovely wife, Valsa, who believed in me and supported me during challenging times to complete this book. Our two beautiful daughters, Tara and Dipti, who made me constantly believe that I can accomplish this piece of work. Last but not least, to all my friends who facilitated my critical thinking to perceive the world differently.

Contents

List of figures and tables   xi
Acknowledgements   xiii
List of contributors and biographies   xiv

Part I   Introduction to Sustainable HRM

**1   Human resource management in the twenty-first century:
      Sustainable HRM**   7
Sugumar Mariappanadar

   1.1 What is human resources?   8
   1.2 Traditional human resource management   9
   1.3 Challenges for strategic HRM in the twenty-first century 10
   1.4 Sustainable HRM   12
   1.5 Corporate sustainability and sustainable HRM   16
   1.6 The importance of sustainable HRM for the twenty-first century 19
   1.7 Barriers to sustainable HRM   22
   1.8 Conclusion   22
   References   23

Part II   Framing Sustainable HRM

2   Institutional contexts for developing sustainable HRM   31
Sugumar Mariappanadar

   2.1 Introduction   31
   2.2 Macro-level institutional contexts   33
   2.3 Background for meso- and micro-level contexts   48
   2.4 Conclusion   56
   References   57

3   **A paradox perspective for sustainable Human Resource Management**   **61**
    Christine Parkin Hughes

    3.1 Introduction   61
    3.2 Tension between sustainability and HRM   62
    3.3 The paradox perspective   65
    3.4 Key organisational paradoxes   67
    3.5 Key paradoxes for HRM   69
    3.6 Strategies to cope with paradox   70
    3.7 Conclusion   73
    References   74

Part III Developing Values and Strategies for Sustainable HRM

4   **Sustainable HRM practices: Values and characteristics**   **81**
    Sugumar Mariappanadar

    4.1 Introduction   81
    4.2 Organisational values for sustainable HRM   83
    4.3 Characteristics of control and strategic HRM systems   85
    4.4 Characteristics of business strategy for sustainable development   87
    4.5 Organisational design and process characteristics of sustainable HRM   90
    4.6 Sustainable HRM strategies   91
    4.7 Characteristics of sustainable HRM practices   93
    4.8 Paradoxes or tensions between using strategic and sustainable HRM practices   98
    4.9 Conclusion   100
    References   100

5   **Sustainable HRM theories: Simultaneous benefits for organisations and stakeholders**   **104**
    Sugumar Mariappanadar

    5.1 Introduction   104
    5.2 Perspectives of simultaneous effects of HRM practices   106
    5.3 Theory of negative externality of HRM   108
    5.4 The theory of harm of work   113
    5.5 The costs framework for harm of HRM practices   117
    5.6 The theory of synthesis effects of HRM practices   121
    5.7 Conclusion   123
    References   125

6   **Sustainable HRM for environmental management: Green HRM**   **128**
     Sugumar Mariappanadar
     6.1 Introduction   128
     6.2 Background of environmental management system   130
     6.3 The role of HRM in environmental management system   136
     6.4 Green HRM   137
     6.5 A framework of synthesis of green HRM for environmental
          sustainability   142
     6.6 Conclusion   149
     References   150

Part IV Sustainable HRM: Implementation, Measurement and
Reporting

7   **Implementing sustainable HRM practices**   **157**
     Sugumar Mariappanadar
     7.1 Introduction   157
     7.2 A framework of typologies of sustainable HRM   157
     7.3 Embedding characteristics of sustainable HRM typologies to
          HRM functions   172
     7.4 A scheme of classification of sustainable HRM for corporate
          sustainability   173
     7.5 Resource regeneration strategy for sustainable work performance 174
     7.6 Overcoming barriers to implementing sustainable HRM practices   177
     7.7 Paradoxes in implementing strategic and sustainable HRM practices 181
     7.8 Conclusion   182
     References   183

8   **Bridging sustainable HRM theory and practice: The Respect,**
     Openness and Continuity model   **188**
     Peggy De Prins
     8.1 The triple P translated: Introduction of the ROC model   189
     8.2 First sustainable HRM block: Respect   192
     8.3 Second sustainable HRM block: Openness   198
     8.4 Third sustainable HRM block: Continuity   205
     8.5 Summary and conclusions   211
     References   212

9   **Measurements for sustainable HRM practices**   **216**
     Sugumar Mariappanadar
     9.1 Introduction   216
     9.2 Measurements for sustainable HRM   218
     9.3 Measures for the harm of work   228

9.4 Measure for sustainable leadership   236
9.5 Measure for green HRM practices   237
9.6 Conclusion   239
References   241

10   **Sustainability reporting and sustainable HRM**   **245**
     Elaine Cohen, Iris Maurer, Sugumar Mariappanadar and Michael
     Müller-Camen

     10.1 Introduction   245
     10.2 Sustainability reporting by corporations   246
     10.3 The global reporting initiative framework   247
     10.4 From reporting standards to the assessment of sustainability
           performance   262
     10.5 Current sustainable HRM theories to enrich performance
           indicators of GRI   268
     10.6 Conclusion   269
     References   269

Part V Developing the Future of Sustainable HRM

11   **Sustainable HRM roles and competencies**   **275**
     Sugumar Mariappanadar and Robin Kramar

     11.1 Introduction   275
     11.2 Introduction to HR roles and HR competencies   277
     11.3 Strategic HR roles and competencies   278
     11.4 Sustainable HR roles and competencies   280
     11.5 Types of sustainable HR roles   283
     11.6 Rationale for the integration and fusion of sustainable HR roles 293
     11.7 Competencies for sustainable HR roles   297
     11.8 Competencies for integration and fusion of sustainable HR roles 302
     11.9 Conclusion   302
     References   303

12   **Global sustainable HRM practices**   **307**
     Robin Kramar and Sugumar Mariappanadar

     12.1 Introduction   307
     12.2 Globalisation and multinational enterprises   309
     12.3 Limitations of strategic HRM in addressing stakeholders'
           expectations   310
     12.4 Global sustainable HRM   313
     12.5 Transference and implementation of global sustainable HRM 317
     12.6 Conclusion   323
     References   324

Index   326

List of figures and tables

Figures

1.1 Synthesis paradox framework of sustainable HRM 14

2.1 An institutional contexts framework for sustainable HRM 32

2.2 A macro-level contexts model for sustainable HRM 35

2.3 A sample materiality matrix with key issues for developing the focus of sustainable HRM 40

3.1 Strategies to manage tensions 71

4.1 An integrated model of sustainable HRM system 82

4.2 Possible paradoxes created due to different organisational values between strategic and sustainable HRM practices in organisation decision making 99

5.1 A framework of sustainable HRM theories from the harm of work and the synthesis effects perspectives 106

5.2 The costs framework for harm of HRM practices 118

6.1 The framework of synthesis of green HRM for environmental sustainability 143

7.1 A configurational model of job contexts for the typologies of sustainable HRM 160

7.2 A scheme of classification of sustainable HRM (after Gollan & Xu's (2014) framework) 173

7.3 Sustainable work performance framework (after Dorenbosch, 2014) 175

8.1 The Respect Openness Continuity (ROC) model of sustainable HRM 189

9.1 The role of measurements in facilitating sustainable HRM practices 217

11.1 Link between sustainable HRM characteristics and sustainable HR roles for sustainable HRM performance outcomes 276

11.2 Rationale behind the role identity construction for sustainable HR 294

Tables

2.1	Key definitions for understanding GRI reporting as a context for developing sustainable HRM	39
2.2	The ten UN Global Compact principles	45
4.1	Definition for sustainable organisational values	84
4.2	Characteristics of control, strategic and sustainable HRM systems	88
7.1	List of typologies of sustainable HRM practices	163
8.1	Theoretical antecedents and overview of practical approaches to implementing sustainable HRM	191
9.1	The stakeholder harm of work index	224
9.2	Items for the health harm of work scale	232
9.3	Items for the social harm of work scale	235
10.1	GRI disclosures and performance indicators and HRM relevance	250
10.2	HRM-related indicators of B-corp and economy of the common good	265
11.1	Dedicated sustainable HR roles and Competencies	297
11.2	Integrated and fusion of sustainable HR roles and competencies	299
12.1	Definition of ethical values relevant for global sustainable HRM	314

Acknowledgements

I am indebted to Swinburne University of Technology for funding my early years of research in the field of sustainable HRM, and for the funding and support I subsequently received from Australian Catholic University to pursue my research in this field. I acknowledge Ina Aust's contribution for rekindling my research passion in the field of sustainable HRM in 2009, and for her initial input into the proposal of this book to the publisher, Macmillan. I am fortunate that some of the International Sustainable HRM Network members subsequently joined me in revising the original book proposal and assisted me in completing the book, in particular Professor Robin Kramar, Professor Michael Muller-Camen, Professor Peggy De Prins and Dr. Christine P. Hughes. I have benefited immensely from Robin's expert guidance in the writing journey of completing this book. I thank Ursula Gavin, Editor, and Peter Atkinson and the editorial team of Macmillan for their continued support in completing this book. Finally, I have learned and benefited considerably from critical and encouraging comments from international reviewers of the book chapters.

List of contributors and biographies

Dr. Sugumar Mariappanadar

Sugumar Mariappanadar, is a member of the Centre for Sustainable HRM and Wellbeing, Peter Faber Business School, Australian Catholic University, Australia. He has published many journal articles in the field of sustainable HRM since 2003. He has also designed and teaches sustainable HRM as a course in both the postgraduate and undergraduate programs.

Professor Robin Kramar

Robin Kramar is an Adjunct Professor at the University of Notre Dame, Sydney. She has a commitment to improving the employee experience in the workplace and has done research in this area for more than forty years.

Professor Michael Müller-Camen

Michael Müller-Camen is Professor of Human Resource Management at Vienna University of Economics and Business (WU), Professor (part-time) of International Human Resource Management at Middlesex University Business School, London and Distinguished Professor at the Open University of Hong Kong. Michael has developed a reputation as one of the leading academics in the newly emerging areas of Sustainable HRM and Green HRM.

Dr. Peggy De Prins

Peggy De Prins holds a PhD in social sciences. Since the early nineties she has been conducting scientific research in the area of HRM and labour sociology. Key subjects in her research are sustainable HRM, labour relations and employee engagement. She is currently employed as associate professor at the Antwerp Management School (Belgium).

Dr. Christine Parkin Hughes

Christine Parkin Hughes currently works at the Business School, University of Exeter as the Programme Director: DA Chartered Manager, and BSc Applied Business Management. Christine's research interests centre on sustainable and responsible business with a focus on the human factor.

Elaine Cohen

Elaine Cohen, is a CSR Consultant and Sustainability Reporter based in Israel. Elaine contributes to the community as a Board Member of a Women's Empowerment non-profit and offering sustainability services to non-profits.

Iris Maurer

Iris Maurer is a Teaching and Research Associate at the Institute for Human Resource Management at Vienna University of Economics and Business (WU). Iris' research interests include Sustainability Reporting and Sustainable Human Resource Management.

part I
Introduction to Sustainable HRM

Introduction

I am engaged in my job, passionate about my career and committed to the organization. However, I am progressively struggling with increased physical and mental tiredness, work-life imbalance due to my work related commitments to improve organizational performance. Also, I am not sure how as a non-specialized environmental management employee I can contribute to ecosystem sustainability. Hence, I more often feel that my life happiness and enjoyment are not complete. – A common dilemma encountered by employees in the modern workplace

Can you or your family and friends, as employees, relate to the stated work–life–environment dilemma and the irreversible consequences the dilemma has on you, your family, the natural environment and society?

Stop thinking that you and your family and friends have personally not done enough to cope with the work–life–environment dilemma.

Start thinking what you, as an agent of an organization, can do more of at the organizational level to benefit the ecosystem as well as to enhance employees' quality of life both within the workplace and outside of work.

This book aims to help HR and management professionals, including academics, researchers and practitioners at all levels in an organization, to act as 'agents' in order to make the workplace environmentally sustainable and enhance stakeholders' (employees, their families, society etc.,) well-being while simultaneously attempting to improve organizational performance. Strategic HRM has made a significant contribution in offering a mental schema for HR and management professionals. This schema engages HR as a human capital to gain competitive advantage for the organization and contribute to shareholders' benefits. However, stakeholders' growing pro-social and sustainable environmental expectations have become major disruptors to the current dominant business strategy, which seeks to satisfy only the pro-organizational expectation of shareholders. Consequently, many organizations have embraced corporate sustainability in terms of the triple bottom line (TBL) requirements. That is, corporate sustainability is about management approaches used by organizations to integrate and achieve TBL (i.e. economic/financial, human/social and natural environmental outcomes) as part of their business strategy (UN Global Compact, 2014).

The academic field of HRM has responded to the challenges of this disruptor that has resulted from stakeholders' changing expectations regarding business performance in terms of both financial and non-financial benefits. The field of sustainable HRM was developed as one that explicitly recognized that engaging HR is important for achieving sustainability outcomes as part of a corporate business strategy. Sustainable HRM acknowledges the importance of the employee/human capital and the impact of management practices in achieving corporate sustainability business strategy outcomes. In Europe, the UK, the USA and the Asia-Pacific region, the literature on sustainable HRM has grown to include both influential books and seminal articles in leading academic journals, including *Human Resource Management, Human Resource Management* Review, the *International Journal of Human Resource Management, Management Revue*, the *German Journal of Human Resource Management*, the *International Journal of Manpower*, and the *Asia-Pacific Journal of Business Administration*.

Following on from these publications, in the early 2000s, sustainable HRM as an idea evolved into a theoretical domain and discipline within the field of HRM. Furthermore, sustainable HRM, as a subject, has been introduced as courses at universities and business schools around the world to train future managers. These courses seek to enable students to reframe the existing business strategy, which focuses primarily on outcomes that benefit shareholders and senior executives, with improving organization–stakeholder relationships in order to achieve corporate sustainability in its broad sense. The primary motivation for this book on sustainable HRM for the twenty-first century is to provide a sustainability-oriented vision of HRM so as to synthesise the competing and inconsistent economic/financial, human/social and environmental outcomes of sustainability business strategy. This book explores the sustainability-oriented aspects of HRM functions and practices in large companies in a globalised world and focuses on integrating sustainability principles both in HRM theory and in the practical decision making of all managers *performing the role of managing people*. In sustainable HRM, the notion of success is extended beyond the single financial-performance bottom line, to consider simultaneously human, social and ecological sustainability based on the paradox perspective.

In this book, an attempt is made to show how the complexities of sustainable HRM can lead to potential paradoxes and tensions in the implementation of new practices and processes, and how these can be constructively dealt with by HR and line managers. The aim of the book is to extend the existing dominant strategic HRM approach for financial performance to a strategic focus on synthesizing positive economic/financial, environmental and human/social outcomes of corporate sustainability. To achieve this aim the book takes an analytical approach to HRM instead of a prescriptive approach for HRM functions (i.e. employee selection, training etc.) by substituting the word 'sustainable' for 'strategic' as the principal HRM function. That is, as well as referring to the existing literature on sustainable HRM, new theoretical frameworks are also provided to engage HR into synthesizing the three apparently inconsistent and competing outcomes of organizational corporate sustainability so as to advance the field of HRM generally, and sustainable HRM in particular. Furthermore, it is important to note that in this book sustainable HRM includes a 'strategic' focus for HRM even though the title of the discipline of sustainable HRM does not itself include the word 'strategic'. Hence, 'sustainable' HRM uses a strategic approach to engage HR to achieve the three sustainability (economic/financial, human/social and environmental) outcomes of corporate sustainability business strategy.

In achieving this objective, Part I of the book gives the various definitions of sustainable HRM and explains how it builds on and extends strategic HRM. Furthermore, the importance of sustainable HRM for managing employees in the twenty-first century is discussed to help HR and management professionals achieve the TBL sustainability outcomes. In Part II the institutional contexts are discussed for developing sustainable HRM and why this is important for the HRM profession. As well, a paradox perspective for sustainable HRM is presented as a means of effectively dealing with the tensions in synthesising the complementary but apparently inconsistent outcomes of corporate sustainability.

In Part III, theoretical foundations grounded in organizational values as a means of developing sustainable HRM strategies are provided so that HRM practices can align with the corporate sustainability business strategy. Furthermore, theories on the harm of work and 'green HRM' are also discussed. These theories will enhance students' understanding of the importance of sustainable HRM practices and to recognise the impacts of both sustainable and unsustainable practices on stakeholders (i.e. organizations, employees, family members, the community and employees/practitioners involved in environmental management).

Part IV explains the practical aspects of implementing sustainable HRM in people management using a three-dimensional configuration model for sustainable HRM strategies, the Respect Openness Continuity (ROC) model, and measurement of sustainable HRM performance and reporting. Finally, in Part V the future of sustainable HRM, including sustainable HR roles and global sustainable HRM, are explored. As mentioned, the five sections of the book are based on an analytical approach and supported by research evidence. This will enhance researchers' ability to pursue future research and forms the basis for practitioners who seek to synthesise the inconsistent outcomes of HRM (i.e. economic/financial, human/social and environmental) in order to contribute to a corporate sustainability business strategy. The aim of this book is to engage readers to appreciate the paradox or tension of the competing and inconsistent outcomes of corporate sustainability, and attempt to synthesize rather than integrate (i.e. comprise on) the outcomes in management decision making.

To extend the field of HRM from strategic HRM to sustainable HRM, research and insights from diverse fields, including strategic HRM, sustainable HRM, green HRM, corporate sustainability, corporate social responsibility and institutional theory have been used. In addition, examples and cases from HRM practices are used to provide inspiration for this book. Furthermore, a comprehensive review of the literature relating to each of the topics in the book and new theoretical and practical insights to extend the new and emerging field of sustainable HRM are also provided. This is important for practitioners, researchers and students of HRM as well as management who need to know the latest developments in the field of HRM so that they can attempt to further develop sustainable HRM practices for organizations. Hence, the readership of this book will be primarily professionals involved in HRM, management and sustainability-related tasks in organizations and/or advanced students with some prior knowledge of organizational behaviour and HRM at the undergraduate level as well as MBA students.

The book is complemented by a suite of supplementary materials available on the companion website at www.macmillanihe.com/mariappanadar-sustainable-hrm. This includes learning objectives, a glossary of key terms, exercises and PowerPoint lecture slides.

References

Compact Global UN (2014). *Overview of the UN Global Compact.* http://nbis.org/nbisresources/sustainable_development_equity/un_global_compact.pdf. Accessed on 22 September 2015.

1

Human resource management in the twenty-first century: Sustainable HRM

Sugumar Mariappanadar

In the human resource management (HRM) field there are many courses that provide insight into the management issues that affect the financial bottom line of companies. However, there is limited understanding of how implementation or overuse of certain HRM practices may have sustainable and unsustainable impacts on organisational outcomes and stakeholders (employees, their families, society's sustainable environmental management expectations) respectively. Sustainable HRM focuses on practices which enhance both profit maximisation for the organisation and also simultaneously improving human, social and environmental sustainability. This reflects the synthesis perspective.

The aim of this chapter is to introduce the field of sustainable HRM to advance the understanding of human resource management in achieving sustainability outcomes for organisations and promote the synthesis effect. To achieve this aim four areas are covered. Firstly, the evolution of HRM practices is briefly discussed to highlight the additional value sustainable HRM adds to strategic HRM which is a relatively recent development in the field of HRM. This discussion on evolution also provides a short overview on different perspectives used in strategic HRM. Secondly, multiple definitions for sustainable HRM are discussed. Thirdly, a synthesis paradox framework of sustainable HRM is proposed to achieve corporate sustainability by satisfying the competing expectations of stakeholders (e.g. organisation, society's sustainable environmental management expectations, employees

7

and their family members). Fourthly, the importance of sustainable HRM in the twenty-first century is discussed. Finally, the barriers to the development and implementation of sustainable HRM are indicated.

1.1 What is human resources?

Many people question the ethical aspect of the usage of the term human resources (HR) in managing people in organisations. The proponents of the ethical aspect of human resources argue that 'human' cannot be downgraded and equated to resources, such as energy, finance, technology, raw material and so on, because unlike other resources which contribute to organisational performance 'humans' should not be exploited in the same way to achieve their desired goals. However, Boxall and Purcell (2016) indicate that 'human resources' is not about 'people' as a resource but it is about 'employee competencies' (e.g. attitude, skills, motivation, etc.) which are the resources used by organisations to achieve their strategic goals. This simply means that humans/employees who own or possess valuable resources/competencies (job knowledge, skills, motivation, attitudes, etc.) choose to use those resources for achieving organisational goals. At the same time employees could also gain benefits for themselves and society, and preserve the health of the ecosystem. However, these human resources (i.e. employee competencies) are only available at the employees' discretion. Employees might choose to use their human competencies to their best ability in order to benefit an organisation only when the organisation entices them with various transactional and transformative HR practices.

However, employees are not bound to an organisation regardless of the organisation's attractive or cohesive practices, whereas every individual employee has the right to voluntarily leave an organisation if they choose to do so. The International Labour Organization (ILO) Convention on human rights and industrial relations provides protection to employees from any human rights violation by organisations. Hence, in this book, 'human resources' is referred to as 'people' and human resources is also referred to the potential resources as competencies (e.g. job knowledge, skills, motivation, attitudes, individual differences, etc.). People bring these competencies to an organisation and can develop them for the benefit of an organisation (shareholders), employees (internal stakeholders), society's sustainable environmental management expectations (external stakeholders). However, the term 'human' is used to refer to 'people' working in organisations. For example, the term 'human' is used in the 'human aspect' of sustainable development to indicate the positive and/or negative impacts of work experiences of employees as people in organisations.

1.2 Traditional human resource management

HRM is a broad term that refers to the activities associated with the management of the people who do the work of organisations. This view of HRM extends the definition of Boxall and Purcell (2016) who define HRM in terms of activities associated with managing employees. However, increasingly work is being done by people who are engaged to do the work of organisations on contracts other than employment contracts. The nature of HRM is broadened by recognising that HRM is associated with more than just managing full-time and part-time employees, but also involves managing people who are contractors, consultants and volunteers.

Kramar and colleagues (2017) in explaining traditional HRM have indicated that the personnel work undertaken before the 1980s was predominantly administrative and operational such as record-keeping, routine administration, recruitment and selection, training, salary and wage administration, safety, and supervisor and management development (Deery & Dowling, 1988). These activities were undertaken at the expense of the original 'welfare' aspects undertaken in earlier years (O'Neill & Prentice, 1982). During this period, in large organisations with formal industrial relations arrangements, staff were involved in short-term policy making and dealing with trade unions (Tyson, 1987).

According to these writers, the productivity of workers, and therefore the product, service, financial and other outcomes of an organisation are influenced by the way in which people are managed (Kramar et al., 2017). During the two world wars (1914–1918 and 1939–1945) research was conducted to improve the productivity of munitions workers and at the same time improve morale. In Australia, the Department of Labour and National Service (DLNS) trained people as welfare workers. These staff were charged with the responsibility of developing systematic formal procedures and improving working conditions in munitions and some private sector organisations. These welfare workers were the forerunners of personnel specialists and personnel departments which were established during the 1950s and 1960s (Andrewartha, 1998). These departments expanded and became more formalised during the 1960s and early 1970s as employers searched for ways to increase employee productivity, employee motivation, operation reliability and efficiency (Dunford, 1992).

Subsequently, in the early 1980s, the emergence of the concepts and processes of strategic management had a profound impact on personnel work and people management (Kramar et al., 2017). The idea that people are resources to be managed to achieve organisational objectives fostered the development of HRM policies, systems and strategies which promoted business strategy, cultural change and strategic planning (Tichy et al., 1984). Consequently, the work of managing people in a strategic way requires HRM professionals to also have extensive knowledge and skills on business management (Storey, 1992). Hence, in the next section strategic HRM is discussed to explain the evolution of traditional HRM to strategic HRM.

1.3 Challenges for strategic HRM in the twenty-first century

Noe et al. (2014) defined HRM as the policies, practices and systems that influence employees' behaviour, attitudes and performance to achieve organisational goals and strategies. As discussed earlier the traditional HRM function was used by management professionals as a tool to deal with staff function, employee record-keeping and file maintaining for organisations. However, the HRM function has evolved into being a strategic partner by engaging employees to achieve business strategies (Ulrich & Dulebohn, 2015). Strategic HRM is an approach to management which encompasses those HR strategies designed to improve financial outcomes and measure the impact of these strategies on organisational performance (Boxall et al., 2007). A very popular definition of strategic HRM is expressed as the pattern of planned human resource deployments and activities intended to enable an organisation to achieve financial goals (Wright & McMahan, 1992; Boxall & Purcell, 2016). Strategic HRM therefore assumes HRM activities need to be integrated with organisational strategic objectives and organisational context. It also assumes effective HRM activities improve organisational performance (Schuler & Jackson, 2005) and that different HRM activities and functions reinforce each other, that is, they need to be aligned to achieve organisational goals (Jackson & Seo, 2010).

The concept of strategic HRM is not static, but has evolved in many ways. These include the development of theoretical frameworks informing strategic HRM, views about the specific contributions it could make to organisational performance and the specific 'bundles' of HR practices which make a strategic contribution. These bundles include high performance work practices (HPWPs) such as selective recruitment and selections, extensive employee development and participation in decision making, and these practices need to be internally consistent to achieve organisational goals (Combs et al., 2006). Therefore, the central concern of strategic HRM has been the contribution of HRM to organisational performance by demonstrating a positive relationship between HR policies and financial organisational outcomes (Nikandrou & Papalexandris, 2007). There are two competing theoretical perspectives that are used to explain how strategic HRM has simultaneous impacts on organisational performance and employees. They are the mutual benefits perspective and the critical HRM perspective which are discussed next.

1.3.1 The mutual benefits perspective

This perspective holds the view that the effects of HRM or bundle of HPWPs benefit both the organisation as well as employees. This perspective is based on two theories. Firstly, the behavioural perspective (Wright & McMahan, 1992) indicates that HRM practices are used in organisations to manage employee behaviours to enhance organisational performances. Secondly, the social exchange theory (Blau, 1964) indicates that employees perceive organisational support leads to organisational commitment and job satisfaction which mediates or intervenes in the improved organisational performance (Peterson, 2004).

Appelbaum and colleagues (2000) used the Ability–Motivation–Opportunities (AMO) theory to explain how HRM activities are used in organisations to improve employees' abilities, provide opportunities to participate and increase motivation which increased job satisfaction. Subsequently, the increased job satisfaction and organisational commitment improved organisational performance. Furthermore, research findings in strategic HRM literature indicated that HRM contributes to organisational performance by developing many positive mediating factors including improving productivity, positive social outcomes and reduced turnover (Brammer et al., 2007). These positive mediating or intervening outcomes contribute to greater cost efficiencies through increased productivity, reduced turnover, better and lower recruitment and training costs, and hence that has a positive impact on financial outcomes (Peterson, 2004).

Strategic HRM gained popularity in research by emphasising and revealing the relationship between financial, competitive performance and HRM practices (Huselid, 1995; Pfeffer, 1998) and the recurring claims that HRM practices must be able to demonstrate their contribution to business outcomes and organisational value (Ulrich, 1998; Ulrich & Brockbank, 2005). Also, in the strategic HRM literature many researchers have found that linking appropriate HRM practices with business strategies has produced positive impacts on firm performance (e.g. Lee et al., 2010). Strategic HRM prospered with the thinking that HRM practices contribute to improving organisational performance and also benefit employees. Hence, the mutual benefits perspective indicates that strategic HRM has simultaneous benefits for both organisations and employees. However, this mutual benefits perspective of strategic HRM also has critics which are discussed next.

1.3.2 Critical HRM perspective

The strategic HRM approach, however, is fraught with difficulties, including failing to consider a variety of stakeholder requirements and the simultaneous effects of organisational benefits focused HRM have in creating negative impacts on stakeholders, in particular employees and their families. The critical HRM perspective endorses this outcome of strategic HRM and it is explained by the sceptical and pessimistic views (Peccei, 2004). In the sceptical view it is argued that employee benefits and organisational performance benefits are two distinct goals which are influenced by different sets or bundles of HRM practices (Boxall & Purcell, 2016). Furthermore, the pessimistic view highlights that organisational benefits could be achieved at the cost of reduced employee benefits and hence these two are not only distinct but are also conflicting outcomes (Legge, 1995).

For example, Godard (2001) indicated in his study on alternative work practices associated with HPWPs that a higher level of adaptation to such work practices leads to more stressful work. Hence, an institutional level intervention is required to minimise such negative impacts created by HPWPs. Furthermore, when organisations focus on improving financial performance there is evidence that employees in such organisations experience an increased level of work intensification and job strain (Ramsay et al., 2000). The critical HRM perspective highlights three negative impacts of strategic HRM practices on employees. These negative impacts are more beneficial to organisations than employees, practices which are not beneficial to employees and which can even be harmful to employees. Hence, there is tension (see Figure 1.1) between improving organisational performance and employee well-being (i.e. social aspect of sustainability), and environmental performance (Jackson & Seo, 2010).

1.4 Sustainable HRM

All HPWPs are not intrinsically harmful or unsustainable but some HPWPs have unsustainable impacts on employees either because of the way those HPWPs are implemented in an organisation or because of the overuse of such practices by managers. Hence, a third perspective within the simultaneous effects of HPWPs has emerged in the literature to explain sustainable HRM (Mariappanadar, 2003; Ehnert, 2009). This third perspective adds value to the earlier two perspectives by suggesting that HPWPs are most likely to have unsustainable impacts on employees (in terms of well-being) while maximising organisational performances. However, attempts can be made by organisations using the institutional level intervention to minimise simultaneous unsustainable impacts of work on stakeholders (i.e. employees, their families, and society's sustainable environmental management expectations).

In the literature, terms such as HR sustainability (Gollan, 2000), sustainable HRM (Mariappanadar, 2003, 2014a, 2016; Ehnert et al., 2015), sustainable management of HR (Ehnert, 2009) and sustainable work systems (Docherty et al., 2002) are used to link sustainability to HRM practices. The sustainable HRM focus extends beyond strategic HRM, suggesting HRM practices should be designed to further organisational consideration of stakeholders' well-being outcomes while still achieving financial outcomes for the organisation (Kramar, 2014).

As indicated, there are many published definitions of sustainable HRM which address the social and environmental aspects of sustainable development. For example, the earliest definition of sustainable HRM was provided by Mariappanadar (2003) which was about the management of human resources to meet the optimal needs of the company and community of the present without compromising the ability to meet the needs of the future. Subsequently, Ehnert (2009) highlighted conservation of HR capabilities required by organisations to operate effectively in dynamic business environments. Engaging employees in achieving the economic aspect of sustainability is predominantly dealt by strategic HRM practices. Hence, in extending strategic HRM practices the definitions of sustainable HRM focused on highlighting the individual economic/financial, human/social and environmental aspects of sustainability. For example, Mariappanadar's (2014a) definition of sustainable HRM, 'as those HR systems or bundles that enhance both profit maximization for the organization and also "reduce the harm" on employees, their families and communities' (p. 313). Ehnert and her colleagues (2015) defined sustainable HRM as 'the adoption of HRM strategies and practices that enable the achievement of financial, social and ecological goals, with an impact inside and outside of the organization and over a long-term time horizon while controlling for unintended side effects and negative feedback (externalities/harm)' (p. 3).

These two definitions reflect the use of HR in achieving individual aspects of sustainability outcomes. However, these two definitions do not highlight the tension/paradox which organisations experience while engaging employees to synthesise and achieve the complementary but varied economic/financial, human/social and environmental outcomes of sustainability. Hence, the definition of synthesis effect of sustainable HRM is explained to highlight how HRM practices could accept and manage the diverse outcomes of corporate sustainability without ignoring the tension created by these diverse economic/financial, human/social and environmental outcomes of sustainability.

1.4.1 Synthesis paradox perspective of sustainable HRM

Figure 1.1 highlights that sustainable HRM is about engaging employees to achieve the diverse outcomes (economic/financial, human/social and environmental) of sustainability, which inherently create paradoxical tensions (refer to the dotted-line arrow in Figure 1.1). Paradox is about contradictory but interrelated elements that exist simultaneously and persist over time (Smith & Lewis, 2011). The concept of paradox is used to highlight the role of sustainable HRM in achieving the contradictory outcomes of sustainability (Ehnert, 2009; Kozica & Kaiser, 2012) which facilitates theory enrichment to understand the complexities of the twenty-first century business realities (see also Chapter 3). Furthermore, the paradox perspective in sustainable

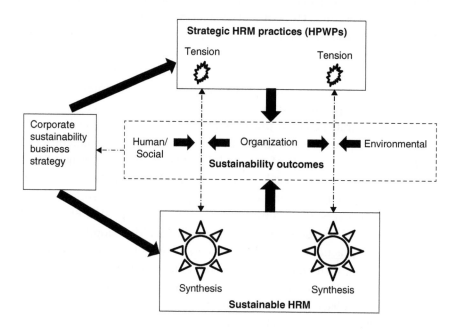

Figure 1.1   Synthesis paradox framework of sustainable HRM

HRM highlights the tension and dilemmas that organisations encounter in achieving diverse but interrelated economic/financial, human/social and environmental sustainability outcomes. Hence, paradox in sustainable HRM is about understanding the coexistence of outcomes (i.e. both/and) and not about 'either/or' options in achieving sustainability outcomes (Lewis, 2000).

For example, the focus of sustainable HRM is to enable organisations to implement HRM practices with means-end rationality-based characteristics to achieve economic outcomes for organisations, and also contribute to their human/social responsibility. This social responsibility has normative characteristics to achieve human/social and natural environmental outcomes as a means of satisfying stakeholders' expectations. Therefore, in the process of achieving the focus of sustainable HRM, HR professionals and line managers experience tension/paradox due to the normative characteristics-based human/social and natural environmental outcomes which limit and constrain the economic outcome of an organisation while pursuing a sustainability business strategy.

In the paradox literature synthesis is a strategy suggested to be used in managing the tension or dilemma created by a paradox situation (Ehnert, 2009). Hence, sustainable HRM is built on the 'synthesis paradox' perspective of HRM (see Figure 1.1) to explore the tension in achieving diverse outcomes of sustainability instead of suppressing or ignoring the tension. That is, organisations must achieve financial outcomes using HRM practices with minimal negative impacts or the harm of work imposed on the stakeholders (employees, their families, and society's sustainable environmental management expectations). This synthesis paradox perspective of sustainable HRM is shaped by holistic corporate sustainability (Van Marrewijk, 2003), the ethics of care for stakeholders (Greenwood, 2002), the negative externality (Mariappanadar, 2012, 2014b) and the need for corporate survival to long-term business success (Wilkinson et al., 2001).

Sustainable HRM from the synthesis paradox is about *HR systems or bundles of HRM practices that engage employees to synthesise increased organisational performance outcome while simultaneously reducing the unsustainable impacts on the natural environment as well as on employees and their families (i.e. stakeholders).* The synthesis effect (refer to the dotted-line arrow in Figure 1.1) of reducing the unsustainable impacts on stakeholders (e.g. employees, their families, and society's sustainable environmental management expectations) while improving organisational performance highlights that these three polarities are not mutually exclusive but are rather mutually reinforcing in achieving sustainability.

The reason for choosing the synthesis effects-based definition for sustainable HRM in this book compared to the other definitions in the literature to align with corporate sustainability is because it highlights the tension/paradox in the organisation–stakeholder relationship which organisations should manage effectively in achieving corporate sustainability. The synthesis effects of HRM are different from the commonly used integration effect to manage tension/paradox in workplaces (see Clegg et al., 2002). The integration effect is about balancing the expectations as a 'compromise' to manage the tension between the two groups. However, the synthesis effects of sustainable HRM accept the tension in the business–stakeholder relationship so that both a business and its key stakeholders' expectations are simultaneously managed to produce positive outcomes for all stakeholders while implementing corporate sustainability business strategies. Hence, based on this broad definition of sustainable HRM and the other definitions discussed earlier in this chapter, it is evident that sustainable HRM is not a theoretical construct (i.e. an attribute of HRM) but it is a 'theoretical domain' or a field of study.

1.5 Corporate sustainability and sustainable HRM

As indicated previously, sustainable HRM has evolved as a field to support business operations to achieve corporate sustainability goals. That is, strategic HRM as a discipline predominantly focuses on helping organisations to achieve improved performance, whereas sustainable HRM evolved as a discipline to strategically engage employees in business operations to achieve sustainability which includes broader stakeholder expectations. The business world has broadly adopted sustainable development outcomes as part of corporate sustainability business strategy to gain competitive advantage (McWilliams & Siegel, 2011). Hence, in the next section a brief description of corporate sustainability is explained to provide insight into how sustainable HRM extends strategic HRM to engage employees for achieving simultaneously the diverse outcomes of corporate sustainability business strategy. This is important because the different chapters in the book explore how employees can be strategically involved in various business operations to achieve corporate sustainability outcomes.

Corporate sustainability as a business strategy is implemented by organisations to achieve three outcomes of sustainability (economic/financial, human/social and environmental) which are known as the triple bottom line (TBL) concept (Elkington, 1997). These three sustainability outcomes are interrelated and influence each other in multiple ways while an organisation is implementing business strategy for sustainability. Furthermore, Van Marrewijk (2003) explained that corporate sustainability is about demonstrating the inclusion of social and natural environmental concerns in business operations and in interactions with stakeholders. Most managers have accepted corporate sustainability as a precondition for doing business in the twenty-first century (Dyllick & Hockerts, 2002). Furthermore, large organisations have adopted corporate sustainability due to external pressures for practices supporting sustainability by global organisations (e.g. World Commission on Environment and Development (WCED), Global Reporting Initiative (GRI) for sustainability to integrate stakeholder (i.e. employees, their families, supply chain, environment and society) relationship in their business strategy. Stakeholder theory implies that organisations have obligations to individuals and groups, both internal and external to organisations, including shareholders, employees, customers and the wider community (Wheeler & Sillanpaa, 1997).

It is important to understand the meaning of each of the economic/ financial, human/social and environmental aspects of corporate sustainability so that sustainable HRM practices can strategically engage HR with these sustainability outcomes. Keeble and his colleagues (2003) used case studies to indicate that the economic aspect of sustainability highlights the prosperity that the organisation creates in a community through a strong alignment of management practices to company profitability. The social aspect is about organisations creating equitable benefits to the community through organisational processes aligned to improved social infrastructure. Furthermore, Keeble and his colleagues (2003) also found that employee job security, employment conditions, engagement of stakeholders, training and development, upholding human rights and quality of life have the strongest alignment to social sustainability. Therefore, these aspects of the social dimension of corporate sustainability facilitate equitable benefits for the community to enhance quality of life for the citizens through paid work. Hence, in this book, the social aspect is referred to with the emphasis on the 'human/employees' aspect of corporate sustainability. Finally, the environmental aspect indicates the role of governance in environmental management to prevent and manage business practices that have potential long-term damage to the natural environment. Based on the components identified by the case study it is revealed that the economic/financial, human/social and environmental aspects of corporate sustainability are diverse but they complement each other for sustainable development of societies. The synthesis effects-based definition of sustainable HRM provides a strong theoretical basis to engage employees at all levels in an organisation to achieve these three diverse corporate sustainability outcomes.

1.5.1 Bundles of sustainable HRM practices for corporate sustainability business strategy

A 'bundle' of complementary HRM practices shapes the pattern of interactions between and among managers and employees (MacDuffie, 1995). A bundle of HRM practices is explained based on the integrationist perspective and the isolationist perspective. The integrationist perspective explains that individual HRM practices have mutually supportive properties and organisations gain by integrating these practices into a consistent bundle to achieve organisational goals. However, the isolationist perspective is based on the need to investigate the unique and independent effects of individual HRM practices on organisational outcomes (Kalmi & Kauhanen, 2008). A study found that the integrated bundle of HRM practices has more explanatory power on employee well-being and work intensification compared to the isolated effect (Ogbonnaya et al., 2017). Hence, it is appropriate to use a bundle of internally consistent (Bowen & Ostroff, 2004) sustainable HRM practices as a system to achieve varied economic/financial, human/social and environmental outcomes of corporate sustainability.

For example, during employee selection there is merit in assessing during employment testing for competencies that include a high level ability to synthesise, integrate and abstract the diverse but complementary outcomes of corporate sustainability. A central aspect of this competency is to seek employees' abilities in seeing the HRM decision choices not as an 'either/or' choice, but the reconciliation of contradictions and, if possible, being able to dynamically balance these contradictions in achieving corporate sustainability. Employee training and development should be used to gain knowledge and capabilities in synthesising contradictory economic/financial, pro-social and pro-environmental outcomes of corporate sustainability. Finally, performance management and employee rewards and compensation should be used to provide feedback on how well an employee has synthesised the diverse outcomes of corporate sustainability and reinforce acceptable employee behaviour with rewards and compensation. Hence, it is important that a bundle of internally consistent sustainable HRM practices is advocated for sustainable HRM rather than individual HRM practices to engage HR to synthesise the diverse outcomes of corporate sustainability.

1.6 The importance of sustainable HRM for the twenty-first century

Salzmann and colleagues (2005) have defined the business case for sustainability as a strategic and profit driven corporate response to natural environmental and social issues caused through the organisation's primary and secondary activities. Stakeholder-based HRM explains that employees are moderately important stakeholders and they can exercise influence over management only through a well-established alliance with the organisation's top management or by state regulators or socially responsible investors who provide cheaper finance for business operations (Guerci et al., 2014). Employees are moderately salient stakeholders, so that the business case for sustainable HRM is explained in terms of *the role of the HR system or a bundle of HRM practices with pro-environmental and human characteristics to facilitate eco-efficiency and socio-efficiency based on the relationship between financial performance of an organisation and its natural environmental and human (social) performances.*

Socio-efficiency (Dyllick & Hockerts, 2002) of sustainable HRM is about minimising the negative social impacts of work on employees (i.e. occupational health issues, health and social harm of work, etc.). The business case for sustainable HRM for socio-efficiency can be drawn from two hypotheses from the corporate social responsibility (CSR) literature: the social impact hypothesis and available funds hypothesis. The social impact hypothesis suggests that meeting the needs of various non-owner stakeholders (e.g. employees) increases financial performance (Cornell & Shapiro, 1987). Waddock and Graves (1997) used the social impact hypothesis to indicate that the actual costs for implementing sustainable HRM for corporate environmental and social (employee) performances are minimal compared to the potential benefits to an organisation. The available funds hypothesis (Waddock & Graves, 1997) indicates that good management practices use sustainable HRM to facilitate corporate social performances to highlight the organisation–stakeholder relationship in the financial performance of an organisation.

Sustainable HRM can also provide for eco-efficiency (Dyllick & Hockerts, 2002) which is about engaging employees in environmental management practice to enhance economic value for an organisation in relation to its aggregated ecological impact, for example, managing employees to achieve eco-efficiency indicators, which include water, energy and resource efficiency and resource wastage, by an environmental management system (e.g. ISO14001) in an organisation. The business case for sustainable HRM based on eco-efficiency and socio-efficiency primarily focuses on financial performance (economic outcomes) of an organisation.

1.6.2 Beyond business case for sustainable HRM

The business case for sustainable HRM discussed earlier highlights the eco-efficiency and socio-efficiency, however, Dyllick and Hockerts (2002) indicated that organisations must go beyond the business or economic case for sustainability and use the 'nature case' and the 'societal case' for sustainability. Similarly, sustainable HRM should be implemented by organisations for the benefit of employees and for preserving the health of the ecological system without considering the relative improvement to economic benefits for organisations. Therefore, the nature case and the societal or employee case for implementing sustainable HRM for corporate sustainability business strategy are about 'effectiveness' and not 'efficiency'.

Boudreau and Ramstad (2005) provided definitions for HRM efficiency and effectiveness for sustainability. HRM efficiency is applied to sustainability to highlight the 'resources' used to bring HRM practices into compliance or to provide incentives that reflect community, natural environmental or social goals. HRM effectiveness relating to sustainability focuses on how HRM practices affect 'human capacity and aligned actions' that go beyond traditional job and performance requirements for sustainability outcomes. Furthermore, HRM effectiveness could also be a proxy for organisational performance such as human/social and natural environmental performances (Guest & Conway, 2011). Hence, *sustainable HRM from beyond business case perspective focuses on achieving HRM effectiveness by improving social and natural environmental performances without being constrained by HRM efficiency from the economic term.* That is, effectiveness of sustainable HRM in achieving human/social and natural environmental performance of an organisation can be understood in terms of factors or indicators such as non-substitutability of capital and irreversibility (Dyllick & Hockerts, 2002).

Non-substitutability of capital is derived from the traditional economic theory which assumes that all input resources of production can be converted into monetary value. This suggests that human resources (i.e. employee competencies) can be substituted from the labour market based on a 'hire and fire' organisational policy. This policy is relevant for HR efficiency and not for HR effectiveness. That is, a new employee substituted for a previous employee whose work engagement suffered due to work intensification (an organisational process issue) will be able to be engaged in work and improve performance, thus explaining HR efficiency. However, the HR effectiveness of sustainable HRM from the normative guidelines is about an organisation creating equitable benefits for employees by providing conducive employment conditions (e.g. standard daily working hours) for work engagement through organisational processes. However, in the example discussed, the organisation failed to provide sustainable work conditions to the terminated employee, hence, there is no social case for sustainable HRM in this example. Regarding non-substitutability of natural capital with economic capital, technology innovations can find substitutes for natural products, such as medium density fibreboard (MDF) doors instead of timber doors for houses for preserving forest resources, but it is unlikely that any future innovation can provide the climate stabilising function of forests. Hence, the normative limit of sustainable HRM highlights that organisations have moral and ethical reasons to protect employees and the health of the ecosystem irrespective of indicators that support economic or monetary value for such actions.

In the work context, irreversibility is about employees' work recovery experience. Work recovery experience (Sonnentag et al., 2010) focuses on the need for recovery after a stressful job situation to improve quality of life through employee well-being. There is evidence in the high performance work practices literature that work intensification is associated with improved job satisfaction but through role overload it leads to greater fatigue, stress and work–life imbalance (see Boxall & Macky, 2014). The jobs designed by strategic HR function to achieve the best fit with business strategies to improve financial performance, leading to work intensification and subsequent negative impacts on employee health and well-being. For example, Akerstedt and colleagues (2002), in their study on sleep disturbances and work-related lifestyle factors, found that smoking and drinking more than three cups of coffee a day was related to more difficulties awakening (insomnia) for employed men. Difficulties awakening were also predicted by high work demands and low social support. The social cost for employees as stakeholders is the long-term negative effect of cardiovascular disease due to excessive smoking and drinking coffee to cope with high work demands (Woodward & Tunstall-Pedoe, 1999). Hence, the negative impacts of work intensification can have irreversible employee health and quality of life issues when work intensification impedes on employees' normal work recovery experience. Organisations have ethics of care to protect employees' health as social effectiveness (i.e. goal) irrespective of limited scientific evidence to establish that lack of work recovery experience due to overwork or work intensification has long-term health issues among employees.

Irreversibility from the nature case for sustainability can be explained by the ecocentric perspective to preserve the health of the ecosystem compared to the anthropocentric perspective for environmental management which focuses on maximising organisational benefits, and in that process, it aims to limit the impact on the natural environment. Ecocentrists are concerned about the human dominance in exploiting nature, hence, the proponents of the ecocentric paradigm use ethical responsibility to effect change in human values, ethics, attitudes and lifestyles to appreciate equality of the intrinsic value of humans and non-humans as components of the ecosystem (Imran et al., 2014). Ecocentric values aim to preserve wilderness areas, protect the integrity of biotic communities and to restore ecosystems to a healthy state of equilibrium while utilising the natural resources for economic activities (Purser et al., 1995).

1.7 Barriers to sustainable HRM

The existing dominant strategic HRM-based mental schema used by HR professionals acts as a barrier to framing the organisation–stakeholder relationship to synthesise economic/financial, human/social and environmental outcomes of corporate sustainability business strategy in the twenty-first century. Furthermore, strategic HRM which focuses on organisational performance has a limited theoretical basis to engage managers in organisations to overcome the barrier to synthesise the three competing outcomes of corporate sustainability. Hence, in the sustainable HRM literature, initially the expression of HRM for sustainability was used to indicate the paradigm shift of strategic HRM from using HR to improve the organisational performance focused approach to achieving stakeholders' human (i.e. social) and society's sustainable environmental management expectations. Subsequently, as the published literature on HRM for sustainability grew and so the interest by line managers and HR professionals, hence the need for developing the discipline of sustainable HRM within the field of HRM became important. That is, tweaking the current dominant traditional and strategic HR practices for sustainability is not going to be helpful for the future of this discipline.

1.8 Conclusion

Attempts are made in this chapter to lay foundations to establish sustainable HRM as a new discipline, highlighting the next developmental stage in the field of HRM to handle the ambiguities and complexities which future organisations should grapple with in order to achieve corporate sustainability. Furthermore, understanding of the organisation–stakeholder relationship using new and contemporary theories in the sustainable HRM literature is useful in reframing the dominant strategic HRM-based mental schema of managers. Hence, the evolution of sustainable HRM from traditional HRM through strategic HRM is explained to understand the transition in focus in managing employees in the field of HRM. The synthesis effect of sustainable HRM is discussed along with other definitions of sustainable HRM in the literature to align with the business and stakeholders' expectations of business performances in the twenty-first century. Finally, the business case and beyond business case perspectives are used to explain the importance of sustainable HRM in achieving economic/financial, natural environmental and human/social outcomes of corporate sustainability.

References

Andrewartha, G. (1998). The future role of human resource management. *Australian Human Resource Management, 2,* 1–16.

Åkerstedt, T., Knutsson, A., Westerholm, P., Theorell, T., Alfredsson, L., & Kecklund, G. (2002). Sleep disturbances, work stress and work hours: A cross-sectional study. *Journal of Psychosomatic Research, 53*(3), 741–48.

Appelbaum, E., Bailey, T., Berg, P. & Kalleberg, A. (2000). *Manufacturing Advantage: Why High-Performance Work Systems Pay Off.* Ithaca, NY: Cornell University Press.

Blau, P. M. (1964). Justice in social exchange. *Sociological Inquiry, 34*(2), 193–206.

Boudreau, J. W. & Ramstad, P. M. (2005). Talentship, talent segmentation, and sustainability: A new HR decision science paradigm for a new strategy definition. *Human Resource Management, 44*(2), 129–36.

Bowen, D. E., & Ostroff, C. (2004). Understanding HRM–firm performance linkages: The role of the 'strength' of the HRM system. *Academy of Management Review, 29,* 203–21.

Boxall, P., & Macky, K. (2014). High-involvement work processes, work intensification and employee well-being. *Work, Employment and Society, 28*(6), 963–84.

Boxall, P. & Purcell, J. (2016). *Strategy and Human Resource Management* (4th edn). London: Palgrave.

Boxall, P. F., Purcell, J. & Wright, P. M. (eds) (2007) *The Oxford Handbook of Human Resource Management.* Oxford: Oxford University Press.

Brammer, S., Millington, A. & Rayton, B. (2007). The contribution of corporate social responsibility to organizational commitment. *The International Journal of Human Resource Management, 18*(10), 1701–19.

Clegg, S. R., Da Cunha, J. V. & E Cunha, M. P. (2002). Management paradoxes: A relational view. *Human Relations, 55*(5), 483–503.

Combs, J., Liu, Y., Hall, A. & Ketchen, D. (2006). How much do high-performance work practices matter? A meta-analysis of their effects on organizational performance. *Personnel Psychology, 59*(3), 501–28.

Cornell, B. & Shapiro, A. C. (1987). Corporate stakeholders and corporate finance. *Financial Management, 16*(1), 5–14.

Deery, S. & Dowling, P. (1988). The Australian personnel manager and industrial relations practitioner: Responsibilities, characteristics and attitudes. *Australian Personnel Management, Macmillan, South Melbourne*, 15–32.

Docherty, P., Forslin, J. & Shani, A. B. (eds) (2002) *Creating Sustainable Work Systems: Emerging Perspectives and Practice.* London: Routledge.

Dunford, R. (1992). *Organisational Behaviour in Australia.* Sydney: McGraw-Hill.

Dyllick, T. & Hockerts, K. (2002). Beyond the business case for corporate sustainability. *Business Strategy and the Environment, 11*(2), 130–41.

Ehnert, I. (2009). *Sustainable Human Resource Management: A Conceptual and Exploratory Analysis from a Paradox Perspective.* London: Springer.

Ehnert, I., Parsa, S., Roper, I., Wagner, M. & Muller-Camen, M. (2015). Reporting on sustainability and HRM: A comparative study of sustainability reporting practices by the world's largest companies. *The International Journal of Human Resource Management, 27*(1), 88–108.

Elkington, J. (1997). *Cannibals with Forks: The Triple Bottom Line of Twentieth Century Business.* Oxford: Capstone.

Godard, J. (2001). High performance and the transformation of work? The implications of alternative work practices for the experience and outcomes of work. *Industrial & Labor Relations Review, 54*(4), 776–805.

Gollan, P. J. (2000). Human resources, capabilities and sustainability. In: D. Dunphy, J. Benveniste, A. Griffiths, & P. Sutton (eds) *Sustainability: Corporate Challenge for the 21st Century* (pp. 55–77). St. Leonards, NSW: Allen and Unwin.

Greenwood, M. R. (2002). Ethics and HRM: A review and conceptual analysis. *Journal of Business Ethics, 36*(3), 261–78.

Guerci, M., Shani, A. B. R. & Solari, L. (2014). A stakeholder perspective for sustainable HRM. *Sustainability and Human Resource Management* In: I. Ehnert, W. Harr & K. J. Zink (eds) *Sustainability and Human Resource Management* (pp. 205–23). Berlin, Heidelberg: Springer.

Guest, D. & Conway, N. (2011). The impact of HR practices, HR effectiveness and a 'strong HR system'on organisational outcomes: A stakeholder perspective. *The International Journal of Human Resource Management, 22*(8), 1686–702.

Huselid, M. A. (1995). The impact of human resource management practices on turnover, productivity, and corporate financial performance. *Academy of Management Journal, 38*(3), 635–72.

Imran, S., Alam, K., & Beaumont, N. (2014). Reinterpreting the definition of sustainable development for a more ecocentric reorientation. *Sustainable Development, 22*(2), 134–44.

Jackson, S. E. & Seo, J. (2010). The greening of strategic HRM scholarship. *Organization Management Journal, 7*(4), 278–90.

Kalmi, P. & Kauhanen, A. (2008). Workplace innovations and employee outcomes: Evidence from Finland. *Industrial Relations: A Journal of Economy and Society, 47*(3), 430–59.

Keeble, J. J., Topiol, S., & Berkeley, S. (2003). Using indicators to measure sustainability performance at a corporate and project level. *Journal of Business Ethics, 44*(2–3), 149–58.

Kozica, A. & Kaiser, S. (2012). A sustainability perspective on flexible HRM: How to cope with paradoxes of contingent work. *Management Revue, 23*(3), 239–61.

Kramar, R. (2014). Beyond strategic human resource management: Is sustainable human resource management the next approach? *The International Journal of Human Resource Management, 25*(8), 1069–89.

Kramar, R., Bartram, T., De Cieri, H., Noe, R. A., Hollenbeck, J. R., Gerhart, B. & Wright, P. M. (2017). *Human Resource Management in Australia: Strategy, People, Performance* (5th edn). Sydney: McGraw-Hill.

Lee, F. H., Lee, T. Z. & Wu, W. Y. (2010). The relationship between human resource management practices, business strategy and firm performance: Evidence from steel industry in Taiwan. *The International Journal of Human Resource Management, 21*(9), 1351–72.

Legge, K. (1995). What is human resource management? *Human Resource Management* (pp. 62–95). London: Palgrave.

Lewis, M. W. (2000). Exploring paradox: Toward a more comprehensive guide. *Academy of Management Review, 25*(4), 760–76.

MacDuffie, J. (1995). Human resource bundles and manufacturing performance: Organisational logic and flexible production systems in the world auto industry. *Industrial and Labor Relations Review, 48*, 197–221.

Mariappanadar, S. (2003). Sustainable human resource management: The sustainable and unsustainable dilemmas of downsizing. *International Journal of Social Economics, 30*(8), 906–23.

Mariappanadar, S. (2012). The harm indicators of negative externality of efficiency focused organizational practices. *International Journal of Social Economics, 39*(3), 209–20.

Mariappanadar, S. (2014a). Stakeholder harm index: A framework to review work intensification from the critical HRM perspective. *Human Resource Management Review, 24*(4), 313–29.

Mariappanadar, S. (2014b). Sustainable HRM: A counter to minimize the externality of downsizing. In: I. Ehnert, W. Harry & K. J. Zink (eds) *Sustainability and Human Resource Management* (pp. 181–203). Berlin, Heidelberg: Springer.

Mariappanadar, S. (2016). Health harm of work from the sustainable HRM perspective: Scale development and validation. *International Journal of Manpower, 37*(6), 924–44.

McWilliams, A. & Siegel, D. S. (2011). Creating and capturing value: Strategic corporate social responsibility, resource-based theory, and sustainable competitive advantage. *Journal of Management, 37*(5), 1480–95.

Nikandrou, I. & Papalexandris, N. (2007). The impact of M&A experience on strategic HRM practices and organisational effectiveness: Evidence from Greek firms. *Human Resource Management Journal, 17*(2), 155–77.

Noe, R. A., Hollenbeck, J. R., Gerhart, B. & Wright, P. M. (2014). *Human Resource Management* (9th edn). New York: McGraw-Hill.

O'Neill, G. L. & Prentice, E. R. (1982). Twenty years of IPMA publication. *Asia Pacific Journal of Human Resources, 19*(4), 16–20.

Ogbonnaya, C., Daniels, K., Connolly, S. & Van Veldhoven, M. (2017). Integrated and isolated impact of high-performance work practices on employee health and well-being: A comparative study. *Journal of Occupational Health Psychology, 22*(1), 98.

Peccei, R. (2004). *Human Resource Management and the Search for the Happy Workplace.* Inaugural Address, 15 January 2004. Erasmus Research Institute of Management, Rotterdam.

Peterson, D. K. (2004). The relationship between perceptions of corporate citizenship and organizational commitment. *Business & Society, 43*(3), 296–319.

Pfeffer, J. (1998). *The Human Equation: Building Profits by Putting People First.* Harvard Business Press. Boston, Massachusetts

Purser, R. E., Park, C., & Montuori, A. (1995). Limits to anthropocentrism: Toward an ecocentric organization paradigm?. *Academy of Management Review, 20*(4), 1053–89.

Ramsay, H., Scholarios, D. & Harley, B. (2000). Employees and high-performance work systems: Testing inside the black box. *British Journal of Industrial Relations, 38*(4), 501–31.

Salzmann, O., Ionescu-Somers, A. & Steger, U. (2005). The business case for corporate sustainability: Literature review and research options. *European Management Journal, 23*(1), 27–36.

Schuler, R. S. & Jackson, S. E. (2005). A quarter-century review of human resource management in the US: The growth in importance of the international perspective. *Management Revue, 16*(1), 11–35.

Smith, W. K. & Lewis, M. W. (2011). Toward a theory of paradox: A dynamic equilibrium model of organizing. *Academy of Management Review, 36*(2), 381–403.

Sonnentag, S., Kuttler, I. & Fritz, C. (2010). Job stressors, emotional exhaustion, and need for recovery: A multi-source study on the benefits of psychological detachment. *Journal of Vocational Behavior, 76*(3), 355–65.

Storey, J. (1992) HRM in action: The truth is out at last. *Personnel Management,* 28–31 April.

Tichy, N., Fombrun, C. J. & Devanna, M. A. (eds) (1984). *Strategic Human Resource Management.* New York: Wiley.

Tyson, S. (1987). The management of the personnel function. *Journal of Management Studies, 24*(5), 523–32.

Ulrich, D. (1998). A new mandate for human resources. *Harvard Business Review, 76,* 124–35.

Ulrich, D. & Brockbank, W. (2005). *The HR Value Proposition*. Boston, MA: Harvard Business Press.

Ulrich, D. & Dulebohn, J. H. (2015). Are we there yet? What's next for HR? *Human Resource Management Review, 25*(2), 188–204.

Van Marrewijk, M. (2003). Concepts and definitions of CSR and corporate sustainability: Between agency and communion. *Journal of Business Ethics, 44*(2), 95–105.

Waddock, S. A. & Graves, S. B. (1997). The corporate social performance-financial performance link. *Strategic Management Journal, 18*(4) 303–19.

Wheeler, D. & Sillanpaa, N. (1997). *The Stakeholder Corporation: A Blueprint for Maximizing Stakeholder Value*. London: Pitman.

Wilkinson, A., Hill, M. & Gollan, P. (2001). The sustainability debate. *International Journal of Operations & Production Management, 21*(12), 1492–502.

Wright, P. M. & McMahan, G. C. (1992). Theoretical perspectives for strategic human resource management. *Journal of Management, 18*(2), 295–320.

Woodward, M., & Tunstall-Pedoe, H. (1999). Coffee and tea consumption in the Scottish Heart Health Study follow up: Conflicting relations with coronary risk factors, coronary disease, and all cause mortality. *Journal of Epidemiology & Community Health, 53*(8), 481–87.

part II

Framing Sustainable HRM

2

Institutional contexts for developing sustainable HRM

Sugumar Mariappanadar

2.1 Introduction

Organisations have incentives for maximising profits and shareholders' values by acting opportunistically. Why would an organisation act in socially responsible ways using sustainable HRM to improve sustainable outcomes for stakeholders such as employees, their family, society's sustainable environmental management expectations and the supply chain? These are important economic/financial, natural environmental and human/social issues that sustainable HRM aims to address so as to achieve corporate sustainability. Institutional theory provides an important theoretical basis to understand the contexts for an organisation's strategic choice to use sustainable HRM to benefit the stakeholders as well as their shareholders. Institutional theory is defined as how organisations develop strategic choices of organisational practices as responses to its macro-, meso- and micro-level contexts (see Figure 2.1). Hence, there are two parts to the definition of institutional theory; the first part indicates the 'meaning' or the 'ideational' aspect of interpreting the business environmental or context cues which an organisation processes to act. The latter part of the definition explains the structural aspect or 'how' an organisation adopts or responds (strategic choices) to its context/environment. That is, institutional theory includes the context as well as the organisational response to those contexts. Therefore, an institutional contexts framework for sustainable HRM (Figure 2.1) is proposed based on the contingency theory which explains the interplay between contexts and management styles that shape organisational practices.

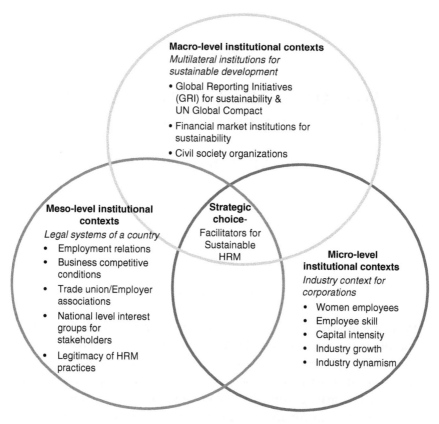

Figure 2.1 An institutional contexts framework for sustainable HRM

In the institutional contexts framework for sustainable HRM (Figure 2.1), initially an attempt is made to explore three different contexts to which organisations respond to develop sustainable HRM. The macro-level contexts focus on three sets of institutions. They are GRI for sustainability and United Nations (UN) Global Compact (2000) as a set of institutions that provide sustainability guidelines for organisations. A set of institutions in the financial market for sustainable development (e.g. Dow Jones Sustainability Group Index, the FTSE4Good Index) and a set of civil society organisations (e.g. Amnesty International) that impact on organisations' corporate social responsibility (CSR) are the institutions in the macro-level contexts. There are many more international institutions that shape an organisation's sustainability development credentials but only those institutions that are relevant to shaping sustainable HRM are discussed. The legal and political systems of a country indicate the meso-level environment of the institutional context. Finally, organisations within a type of industry join to advance collective interests, often with the objective of having these interests codified as informal practices, formal rules or both within an industry. This represents the micro-level institutional setting. Therefore, the three institutional contexts highlight the three levels of business environmental context which demand organisations to respond similarly or differently to that of other organisations in an industry to develop sustainable HRM policies and practices. Finally, the strategic choices which large corporations would adopt or refrain from developing sustainable HRM as responses to the three institutional contexts or pressures (the intersection of three circles) are discussed.

2.2 Macro-level institutional contexts

The institutional contexts framework for sustainable HRM (Figure 2.1) is further expanded from using a macro-level contexts model for sustainable HRM which is shown in Figure 2.2. Figure 2.2 depicts various institutions for sustainable development that act as the macro-level contexts for the development of sustainable HRM as an emerging new discipline within the field of HRM. Arrow-A in Figure 2.2 indicates that global institutions for sustainable development, such as the Brundtland or WCED (1987) report and ILO, have contributed to the development of economic/financial, human/social and natural environment as the three pillars of sustainable development. Arrow-B in Figure 2.2 indicates that global institutions for sustainable development (e.g. the Brundtland or WCED (1987) report; ILO) have contributed to the development of multilateral sustainable development organisations (i.e. Arrow-B) to provide guidelines to shape sustainable development practices of large corporations. Subsequently, the multilateral sustainable development institutions (e.g. GRI for sustainability and UN Global Compact), financial market institutions for sustainability and civil society organisations are the important macro-level contexts that shape corporate sustainability business strategy to achieve economic/financial, human/social and environmental outcomes (Arrow-C). Arrow-D in Figure 2.2 indicates that sustainable HRM is an offshoot development of social sustainability which is one of the three pillars of sustainable development. Furthermore, sustainable HRM facilitates organisations to develop policies and practices for specialised and non-specialised HR relating to sustainability to achieve corporate sustainability outcomes to support the three pillars of sustainable developments.

In this section initially, the background of global institutions (e.g. Brundtland report, Rio Summit, 1992; World Summit on Sustainable Development,

2005; ILO) that brought sustainable development to the world's attention is discussed. Secondly, the operational aspect of sustainability is explained using GRI and UN Global Compact guidelines which have important roles in disclosing and shaping future sustainable HRM practices of corporations through sustainability reporting. Thirdly, the voluntary disclosures of sustainability reporting by corporations are used by financial market-based institutions to provide assurances of corporations' sustainability credentials to investors. Fourthly, the role of civil society organisations (e.g. international non-governmental organisations (NGOs)) as an organisational field or context for developing sustainable HRM policies and practices to implement corporate sustainability business strategy is explored. Finally, the social sustainability perspective of sustainable development is used to explain sustainable HRM so as to shape HRM policies and practices of an organisation to engage HR to achieve economic/financial, human/social and natural environmental outcomes of corporate sustainability.

2.2.1 Background for sustainable development

In this section, the role of global institutions, such as the WCED (1987) for the UN, Rio Summit (1992), World Summit on Sustainable Development (WSSD, 2005), ILO, the Organisation for Economic Co-operation and Development (OECD) and UN Human Rights on sustainable development, is explained as a background for sustainable development. These global institutions rely on voluntary initiatives regarding monitoring, accountability and enforcing of sustainable development. They rely on voluntary initiatives because of three reasons: a lack of support from businesses for more authoritative regulations, negative experiences with previous attempts to regulate transnational companies through codes of conduct, and a lack of capacity at the international institutions level to monitor and enforce compliance. However, voluntary initiatives also have two specific benefits. Firstly, the need to operationalise the universal principles of sustainable development implies trial and error and mutual learning from experiences of networks of companies and NGOs, also in the context of a highly dynamic business environment. This makes it impossible to define ex ante operationalised criteria and hence requires more flexible and less hierarchical governance strategies. Secondly, it is believed that voluntary initiatives may enhance sustainable development above levels that could be negotiated upon in the case of a regulatory framework among other things due to the stimulation of dialogue and learning (Kell, 2005).

Sustainable development is 'development which meets the needs of the present without compromising the ability for future generations to meet their

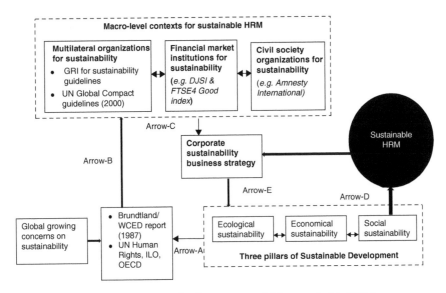

Figure 2.2 A macro-level contexts model for sustainable HRM

own needs' (WCED, 1987, p. 43). The sustainable development was popularised in *Our Common Future* report. This report was published by the WCED (1987), and also known as the Brundtland report. Brundtland was a Norweign prime minister who chaired the WCED for the UN to address growing concerns over the 'accelerating deterioration of human, environment and natural resources, and the consequences of that deterioration for economic and social developments'. Subsequently, the Brundtland report provided the impetus for the landmark Rio Summit (1992) that laid the foundation for the global institutionalisation of sustainable development (Drexhage & Murphy, 2010).

The *Earth Summit*, also known as Rio Summit, adopted the *Rio Declaration on Environment and Development* – Agenda 21, which is a global plan of action for sustainable development. Since the Rio Summit the Earth Summit +5 (1997) in New York and the 2002 WSSD in Johannesburg reviewed the progress and reported a few positive results, but implementation efforts for sustainable development were unsuccessful at the national and international levels. The challenge in implementing the initiative of the Rio Summit was attributed to the lack of attention, commitment and resources required for sustainable development actions by multilateral agreements between countries and also multiple stakeholders including government, businesses and NGOs.

A major shift happened from the focus of natural environmental issues to human/social and economic development at the WSSD negotiations in 2002.

Hence, at an international level, the sustainability development has evolved to have environmental, economic/financial and human/social goals as three pillars of sustainable development (see Arrow-A). One of the common characteristics accepted by all sustainability development specialists is that the three pillars of sustainable development are interlinked and interdependent. For example, the social sustainability specialists such as Littig and Griessler (2005) believe that equal treatment of the three pillars is important, based on the conclusion that human needs cannot be adequately met just by providing an ecologically stable and healthy environment but also ought to take care of the economic and social needs of the society.

Furthermore, from a different global institution, the Tripartite Declaration of Principles Concerning Multinational Companies and Social Policy of the ILO refers to 28 international Labour Conventions and Recommendations and sets out principles in the field of employment to achieve sustainable development. Some of the principles relating to the field of employment are employment promotion, equality of opportunity and treatment, security of employment, training, conditions of work and life (wages, benefits and conditions of work, safety and health, quality of life), industrial relations (freedom of association and right to organise) and collective bargaining and consultations (examination of grievances, settlement of industrial disputes). Many of these ILO principal recommendations have shaped the business practices of multinational companies to achieve sustainable development (Zink, 2005).

In summary, it is clear that the Brundtland report (1987), Rio Summit (UN Summit, 1992), WSSD Summit (2005), ILO and UN Human Rights are the global organisations that brought sustainable development into the limelight for creating other multilateral organisations to promote, shape and operationalise sustainable development among multinational corporations (see Arrow-B). Furthermore, these are the institutions that have played important roles in developing sustainable HRM as part of sustainable development initiatives by multinational corporations (MNCs).

The next section explains 'work' as an institutional arrangement that provides citizens with a platform to balance the economic/financial, human/social, environmental and cultural aspects of social sustainability. In this context, sustainable HRM as a recent development within the HRM field has evolved to explore and understand the institutional level work practices (work arrangements) that shape the characteristics and the role of work which have sustainable and unsustainable impacts on citizens' quality of life while balancing the economic/financial, human/social, ecological and cultural elements of social sustainability. The next section also explains social sustainability as foundation principles for the development of sustainable HRM, and hence sustainable

HRM is depicted in the macro-level contexts model for sustainable HRM (Figure 2.2) as an offshoot development of social sustainability (see Arrow-D).

2.2.2 Social sustainability and sustainable HRM

There are varied definitions for social sustainability but I chose to provide two important definitions that provide us the opportunity to link social sustainability to sustainable HRM. Firstly, according to Becker et al. (1999), 'sustainability describes a topic of research that is basically social, addressing virtually the entire process by which societies manage the material conditions of their reproduction, including social, economic, political and cultural principles that guide the distribution of environmental resources' (p. 4). Secondly, Littig and Griessler's (2005) definition suggests:

> Social sustainability is a quality of societies. It signifies the nature-society relationships, mediated by work, as well as relationships within the society. Social sustainability is given, if work within a society and related institutional arrangements satisfy an extended set of human needs and shaped in a way that nature and its reproductive capabilities are preserved over a long period of time and the normative claims of social justice, human dignity and participations are fulfilled. (p. 72)

Furthermore, Littig and Griessler (2005) provided a few sociological indicators to assess the social dimensions of sustainability. The first set of core indicators relate to satisfaction of basic needs and the quality of life. The second set of core indicators is about social justice (equal opportunity for quality of life and participation in society). Finally, the third set of indicators is about the aspect of social coherence which includes involvement in activities as volunteers as well as measures for solidarity and tolerant attitudes towards migrants, the unemployed and so on.

The two definitions of social sustainability and the sociological indicators discussed here clearly highlight that work is an institutional arrangement for citizens to satisfy social, economic, political and cultural needs for themselves which may also have unsustainable impacts on stakeholders. Hence, these two definitions and the sociological indicators of social sustainability are considered as foundation principles for sustainable HRM. For example, Mariappanadar (2003) initially explained sustainable HRM is about 'the management of human resources to meet the optimal needs of the company and community of the present without compromising the ability to meet the needs of the future'. Furthermore, Mariappanadar (2014a) and Mariappanadar and Kramar (2014) highlighted the synthesis effect focus of sustainable HRM when an organisation uses HR systems or a bundle of practices for profit maximisation (economic aspect) and also has the responsibility to reduce the harm of such practices on stakeholders (employees, their family, and society's sustainable environmental management expectations) to improve quality of life of employees and citizens.

A comprehensive sustainable HRM definition suggests: 'the adoption of HRM strategies and practices that enable the achievement of financial, social and ecological goals, with an impact inside and outside of the organisation and over a long-term time horizon while controlling for unintended side effects and negative feedback (externalities)' (Ehnert et al., 2015, p. 3). This definition highlights two components of sustainable HRM: (1) the recognition of multiple, potentially contradictory, economic, ecological and social goals for human sustainability (Docherty et al., 2009; Wilkinson et al., 2001) or ecological sustainability (Jackson et al., 2011). (2) Complex interrelations between HRM systems and their internal and external business environments with particular emphasis on relationships which allow the long-term reproduction of resources (Ehnert, 2009) and which control externalities or harm on stakeholders (Mariappanadar, 2003; 2012, 2014b). Therefore, these definitions of sustainable HRM align well with the integration of human/social, economic/financial and cultural aspects of social sustainability as explained by Littig and Griessler (2005). That is, sustainable HRM plays an important role in mediating the employer–stakeholders relationship in a society so as to preserve social justice, stakeholders' well-being and human dignity. Therefore, the evolution of sustainable HRM as a new field within HRM is not just altruistic for stakeholders because it is also for the future good of the organisation.

2.2.3 Multilateral organisations for sustainability

2.2.3.1 GRI guidelines as a context for sustainable HRM

It is indicated in the macro-level contexts model for sustainable HRM (Figure 2.2) that global institutes such as the WECD (WECD, 1987), and United Nations Office of the High Commissioner for Human Rights, have contributed along with governments, businesses and civil societies to develop multilateral organisations such as GRI for sustainability and UN Global Compact to address sustainable development. Initially, an attempt is made to explain GRI and how it has acted as a context for developing, shaping and operationalising sustainable HRM as a field. Similarly, the role of the UN Global Compact in shaping the sustainable HRM field is discussed subsequently. In Chapter 10 more detailed information on sustainability reporting using GRI and UN Global Compact are discussed.

GRI for sustainability is a tool for voluntary reporting of economic/financial, natural environmental and human/social performance by global businesses and other organisations. The GRI guidelines are now regarded as the de facto global standard for sustainability reporting (Hahn & Lülfs, 2014). GRI is not just about setting global standards for sustainability reporting but it also becomes an organisational field (Scott, 1995) or an institutional context for the field of HRM to develop a new field of study or change an existing one. To explain GRI guidelines as a context for sustainable HRM an attempt is made to simplify the complex processes that are involved in preparing GRI disclosure reports. Key definitions are provided in Table 2.1 to help understand the steps involved in GRI sustainability reporting according to the published guidelines. For example, the initial step in preparing a sustainability report

Table 2.1 Key definitions for understanding GRI reporting as a context for developing sustainable HRM

GRI concept	Definition
Category	The three pillars or categories of sustainable development are economic, environmental and social.
Subcategory	Social category has four subcategories; they are labour practices and decent work, human rights, society and product responsibility.
Aspect	This refers to the list of subjects covered under each category or subcategories, e.g. occupational health and safety is a subject under the labour practices and decent work subcategory, and freedom of association and collective bargaining is a subject within the human rights subcategory.
Material	Data or facts about the aspect and management approach.
Material aspects	This reflects the data or facts on a list of key issues that highlight significant economic, environmental and social impacts on an organisation; or the data or facts on a list of key issues that substantively influence the assessments and decisions of stakeholders.
Management approach	Policies, practices or specific actions that an organisation has used to identify, analyse and respond to actual or potential data or facts (material) about impacts on a list of subjects within the economic, environmental and social categories.
Indicators	This provides information on the economic, environmental and social performance or impacts of an organisation related to its material aspects.
Governance disclosure	Information regarding the way governance of sustainability and remuneration are interlinked.

Source: The definitions are based on GRI 4 guidelines (2014)

for an organisation is to initiate discussions with both internal and external stakeholders and identify material aspects (i.e. issues) that are important for the organisation and for the stakeholders. Based on these consultations with different stakeholders (e.g. employee blogs and forums, community advisory panels, market research of reputation issues, scan industry trends, etc.) an organisation prepares a materiality matrix/analysis to identify key issues (i.e. material aspects) that are relevant for sustainability.

In the second step, the organisation must identify management approaches (e.g. policies, practices and specific actions), in this case the sustainable HRM policies and practices, which have actual or potential positive and negative impacts on the list of identified key issues that are important for a company as well as for the stakeholders based on the materiality analysis. In this step, the company should use materiality to determine the threshold at which a set of aspects or issues (see Figure 2.3 for a sample materiality matrix) that are sufficiently important for an organisation to develop management approaches mitigate negative impacts or enhance positive impacts on stakeholders as well as for organisations and subsequently disclose it in the GRI report.

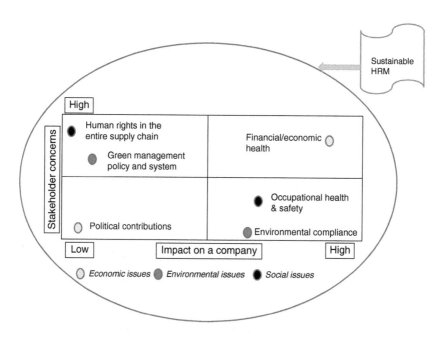

Figure 2.3 A sample materiality matrix with key issues for developing the focus of sustainable HRM

Now let us understand how GRI sustainability reporting guidelines for materiality analysis act as an organisational field or an institutional context for developing sustainable HRM (see Figure 2.3) as a corporate response to sustainability. As discussed earlier in Chapter 1, sustainable HRM is explained differently by varied authors. However, based on the sample material issues provided in Figure 2.3, it is evident that sustainable HRM policies and practices should be able to engage both specialised and non-specialised HR relating to sustainability to manage all economic/financial, human/social and natural environmental issues to reduce the negative effects to achieve corporate sustainability outcomes. Hence, the appropriate definition of sustainable HRM for implementing corporate sustainability business strategy is the synthesis paradox-based definition. That is, sustainable HRM from the synthesis paradox is about HR systems or bundles of HRM practices that engage employees to synthesise increased organisational performance outcome while simultaneously reducing the unsustainable impacts on natural environment as well as human/social well-being of stakeholders. This definition of sustainable HRM for implementing corporate sustainability business strategy is different from the definition by Ehnert and her colleagues (2015) because their definition of sustainable HRM aligned to just one of the social subcategories which is labour practices and decent work of GRI. Thus, the synthesis effects-based sustainable HRM is more comprehensive in highlighting how HR must be engaged in implementing corporate sustainability business strategy to achieve contradictory but complementary economic/financial, human/social and environmental outcomes of sustainability. Furthermore, this comprehensive definition of sustainable HRM is used to develop contents in Chapter 3 (on paradox), Chapter 4 (characteristics of sustainable HRM practices) and Chapter 7 (strategies for implementing sustainable HRM) in this book to engage HR to implement corporate sustainability business strategy.

Materiality on the threshold for reporting highlights the need for objective measurements or data for positive and negative impacts of management practices on the stakeholders as well as on organisational performances. The measurement of materiality in GRI for sustainability reporting becomes another institutional context for developing sustainable HRM. That is, sustainable HRM as a field has evolved to develop many theoretical frameworks to understand both sustainable and unsustainable impacts of management practices on stakeholders and organisational performance so as to improve materiality on threshold to improve the quality of reported information in GRI. However, the need for disclosing materiality of economic, human/social and environmental outcomes using objective data in the GRI disclosure has created institutional pressures for developing objective measures for sustainable HRM which are discussed in more detail in Chapter 9. Furthermore, materiality of sustainable HRM practices is also related to the auditability principle of GRI reporting (Moneva et al., 2006). Auditability is based on the traditional accounting principles of verifiability of reported information. Therefore, the materiality or the objective measurements for the quality of information on reporting is important to enable stakeholders (e.g. employees, their families and society) to make sound and reasonable assessments of an organisation's performance on corporate sustainability. The final step is about governance which highlights that the sustainability report should be considered and acted on by the highest governance body (the Board of Directors, usually) within an organisation in building a sustainable business. The GRI guidelines for this step indicate that sustainability reporting is no longer a low-key matter for an organisation but it has far-reaching impacts on the organisation.

In summary, it is evident from the explanation provided in this section that three important elements of GRI guidelines have acted as contexts for the evolution of sustainable HRM. They are, firstly, the material matrix/analysis of economic/financial, human/social and natural environmental issues that are important for stakeholders as well as to the organisation. Secondly, scientific measures (quantitative and qualitative) to assess materiality of issues to improve the quality of reported information in GRI and finally governance. Hence, the sustainability reporting guidelines, along with management approaches about policies, practices and specific actions, form important institutional contexts or organisational fields that provided adequate impetus to develop a new field of sustainable HRM within HRM to support corporate sustainability initiatives of organisations.

2.2.3.2 UN Global Compact guidelines as a context

The Global Compact was initiated by the United Nations and it is based on a set of ten principles related to human rights, labour, the natural environment and anti-corruption (see Table 2.2). The principles are drawn from the Universal Declaration of Human Rights, the Fundamental Principles on Rights at Work from the International Labour Organization, the Rio Declaration on Environment and Development, and The United Nations Convention Against Corruption (UNGC, 2006). Furthermore, UN Global Compact offers platforms for companies and international NGOs to discuss issues related to sustainable development and implementation, and through interaction and co-operation of networks of businesses and NGOs can learn from each other's experiences. Since its launch on 26 July 2000, the Global Compact has grown to some 3,800 participants, of which more than 2,900 are companies from one hundred countries (Runhaar & Lafferty, 2009).

The Global Compact makes important contributions to sustainability development and implementation in different ways (Runhaar & Lafferty, 2009). Similar to the GRI guidelines discussion earlier in the chapter, the principles of UN Global Compact as contexts for development of sustainable HRM practices (see Table 2.2) are discussed in this section. Firstly, these principles can lead to the incorporation of normative principles for sustainable HRM. For example, Deutsche Telekom used four principles relating to labour conditions as a framework for the corporation's responses to sustainability pressures by developing corporate sustainability business strategies (see Arrow-C). Secondly, the Global Compact promotes learning processes across companies where a network of companies can share experiences that they can use to further shape their sustainable HRM initiatives and strategies. For example, Telenor and Deutsche Telekom disclosed that they organised once a year a network meeting to discuss these principles of Global Compact to learn from peer companies how to develop sustainable HRM practices for the benefit of employees, their family, natural environment and society.

Thirdly, the interactions within network companies may give rise to co-operation between companies, or between companies and other stakeholders (e.g. NGOs), regarding the formulation and implementation of sustainable HRM initiatives and strategies. For example, Business for Social Responsibility is a global non-profit organisation that helps more than 1,400 member companies to achieve commercial success in ways that respect ethical values, people, communities and the environment (Zink, 2005). Furthermore, British Telecom in their disclosure reported that the company is committed to elimination of discrimination (e.g. equal pay) in all countries in which they operate. Finally, the Global Compact report can be used for public relations purposes by companies, both in positive ways, by making sustainable development initiatives more transparent or in negative ways, such as 'blue washing'. For example, Telenor, British Telecom and Deutsche Telekom have indicated that the common driver for UN Global Compact reporting is company's reputation. It is evident that the Global Compact is actually utilised by companies but it depends on company- and context-specific factors that influence the decision to use the UN Global Compact as normative principles for shaping a company's sustainable practices (see Arrow-C). Hence, the ten principles of the UN Global Compact have acted as contexts for corporations to respond to these principles to facilitate creation and development of sustainable HRM to engage HR for implementing corporate sustainability business strategy.

There are three well-known financial market-based contexts for sustainable development. They are the Dow Jones Sustainability Group Index (DJSI), the FTSE4Good Index and the World Business Council for Sustainable Development. The DJSI was established in 1999 to develop opportunities and manage economic/financial, natural environmental and human/social risks, which investors consider as crucial for a company's competitive advantage. A study conducted by Beloe et al. (2004) revealed that in the DJSI requirements concerning sustainability aspects are further reaching than in other sustainability indexes, and hence an attempt is made to explain in this section just about DJSI and not about the other sustainability indexes.

For a company to be included in the DJSI it has to fulfil the criteria imposed in three elements (economic, environment and social) of sustainable development by GRI and the UN Global Compact. The DJSI is based on an assessment conducted using a corporate sustainability questionnaire by RobecoSAM, a sustainable investment management company. Zink (2005) suggested that a corporate sustainability questionnaire measured information on economic/financial, human/social and natural environmental elements of sustainable development by involving stakeholders and used at the highest management level in developing and shaping sustainable HRM policies and practices to implement corporate sustainability business strategy.

There is evidence that a company's reported practices and strategies on the sustainability criteria will shape firms' investment and financing decisions, and provide stakeholders with a good perspective for observing corporate sustainability management. For example, López et al. (2007) found in the empirical study on the differences between companies in the DJSI group and the non-DJSI group that differences exist in various profitability measures. Hence, the finding indicates that the investors value a company's strategies on sustainable development. Therefore, a corporation's responses to sustainability pressures (see Arrow-C) created by the DJSI as a financial market-based driver act along with GRI sustainability reporting and UN Global Compact reporting to shape a company's sustainable HRM initiatives.

In summary, the DJSI in the stock market is an important financial market institutional context that shapes sustainable HRM research and practices as part of sustainable development reporting. The DJSI is an important context for the development of sustainable HRM because more and more individual and institutional investors are showing interest in investing companies with sustainable development strategies. Due to this enhanced interest among

Table 2.2 The ten UN Global Compact principles

Area	Principles
Human rights	1. Businesses should support and respect the protection of internationally proclaimed human rights; and
	2. Make sure that they are not complicit in human rights abuses.
Labour conditions	3. Businesses should uphold the freedom of association and the effective recognition of the right to collective bargaining.
	4. The elimination of all forms of forced and compulsory labour.
	5. The effective abolition of child labour; and
	6. The elimination of discrimination in respect of employment and occupation.
Environment	7. Businesses should support a precautionary approach to environmental challenges.
	8. Undertake initiatives to promote greater environmental responsibility; and
	9. Encourage the development and diffusion of environmentally friendly technologies.
Anti-corruption	10. Businesses should work against all forms of corruption, including extortion and bribery.

Source: UN Global Compact (2006)

investors, many companies have a growing interest to become listed in the Dow Jones Group index as well as in other sustainability indexes to prove their company's sustainability credentials and this interest has facilitated the growth of sustainable HRM as a new discipline to engage employees to implement a corporate sustainability business strategy.

2.2.5 Civil society organisations as a context for sustainable HRM

Civil society organisations are voluntary organisations and are characterised by individuals coalescing around common ideas, needs or causes to promote collective action (Olson, 1971). Furthermore, Williams et al. (2011) defined civil society organisations as a broad range of bodies, including charities, faith groups, voluntary associations, advocacy bodies, social movement organisations, campaigning groups and other NGOs, although not trade unions or professional bodies. Civil society organisations include NGOs, and NGOs are defined as private, not-for-profit organisations that aim to serve particular societal interests by focusing advocacy and/or operational efforts on social, political and economic goals, including equity, education, health, environmental protection and human rights (Teegen et al., 2004). It is evident from Teegen's definition of NGOs that NGOs act as the third sector for governance and value creations using advocacy and operational roles in a context where there are reduced regulations by governments and increased demand for self-regulations by private sector companies. For example, the dominant joint regulations by trade unions and collective bargaining have markedly diminished in developed economies and hence there is a growing interest for broader social purpose NGOs to influence management policies and practices including HRM, as suggested by the 'social embeddedness' of HRM (Paauwe & Boselie, 2007). Hence, in this section, civil society organisations that include NGOs act as an organisational field to shape sustainable HRM as a corporation's responses to sustainability pressures for implementing corporate sustainability business strategy (see Arrow-C). The corporation's responses to NGOs' sustainability pressures for shaping the corporation's sustainable HRM are discussed based on the principle of 'social embeddedness' of HRM.

An attempt is made to use the three principles for an effective system of regulatory control which were suggested by Hood et al. (2001) to explain how international NGOs could act as an institutional context to shape a company's sustainable HRM policies and practices to implement corporate sustainability business strategy. The first principle of regulation control includes setting of standards, goals, targets and guidelines as an intrinsic feature of regulatory systems. International NGOs can directly and/or indirectly influence multinational corporations to set standards for sustainable HRM while implementing corporate sustainability business strategy. For example, international NGOs like Amnesty International set standards on working conditions, such as setting standards or a tolerance level for unsustainable impact of HRM practices on stakeholders (e.g. employees, their family, and society's sustainable environmental management expectations). As discussed earlier, high performance work practices (a strategic HRM practice) have the simultaneous effect of improving organisational performance while creating unsustainable impacts on the stakeholders (Appelbaum et al., 2000). Hence, NGOs have an important direct role in setting the tolerance level for unsustainable impact on stakeholders while the corporation is pursuing profit maximisation. Alternatively, NGOs can influence employment standards indirectly by lobbying with social institutions for sustainability regulators like GRI and the UN Global Compact for changes to HRM policies to reduce unsustainable impacts on stakeholders as part of corporate sustainability reporting.

The second principle for system-based regulatory control relates to the capacity for information-gathering or monitoring to produce knowledge about current or changing states of the system. That is, NGOs can develop capabilities in measuring the unsustainable impacts of certain HRM practices and provide that information to companies to create awareness of unsustainable impacts of HRM practices on stakeholders. This is similar to RobecoSAM's role in DJSI as discussed earlier, which measures corporate sustainability using a questionnaire on corporate sustainability and provides that report to DJSI to include those companies in the Dow Jones Group Index. Similarly, the capability to measure and disseminate information on unsustainable impacts imposed by certain HRM practices on stakeholders can act as an effective regulation for companies to reduce these risks so as to improve companies' corporate sustainability reputations.

Finally, the principle of behaviour modification for companies highlights the difference between 'compliance' and 'deterrence' approaches to changing the behaviour of companies. The compliance approach is a positive role for civil regulation because it highlights that NGOs as a civil society organisation have an important role to play in building and maintaining healthy societies, by helping to regulate business activity and thus creating more structured and stable employment conditions (Williams et al., 2011). The deterrence approach relies on the credible threat of sanctions by customers and litigation to deter companies from breaching the rules. Therefore, NGOs as civil society organisations complement civil regulation or provide an alternative to state laws as an institutional context (see Arrow-C) to shape sustainable HRM to improve corporate sustainability. Civil regulations by NGOs are gaining more importance among MNCs because NGOs are perceived to play a complementary role along with businesses and governments in achieving sustainable development for society. However, Williams and colleagues argue that it is not a substitute for joint regulations (e.g. trade unions, industry associations) and state regulations in shaping MNCs' sustainable HRM practices.

In summary, economic/financial, human/social and natural environmental sustainability are discussed as foundation principles for sustainable HRM. Furthermore, GRI and the UN Global Compact guidelines for sustainability reporting, financial market institutions for sustainability and civil societies are explained as the important macro-level contexts that have operationalised (see Arrow-C) the development and shaping of sustainable HRM practices for MNCs to enhance their HR capabilities to implement corporate sustainability business strategy. Hence, sustainable HRM as a new discipline will help researchers and practitioners to develop knowledge and skills to facilitate corporate sustainability initiatives as part of sustainable development.

2.3 Background for meso- and micro-level contexts

In this section an attempt is made to explain how MNCs respond to both the meso- and micro-level institutional contexts to develop sustainable HRM. This is done to help understand the ethical context for sustainable HRM based on MNCs' CSR towards stakeholders. It was decided to discuss MNCs to explain meso- and micro-level contexts of sustainable HRM because MNCs are stateless players, although most MNCs remain deeply rooted in the national business system of their home country. Furthermore, international competition among MNCs is rooted in the specific arrangements of their home country systems and those systems reflect that country's version of economic development. For example, US capitalism is based on shareholder perspective and European capitalism is predominantly based on stakeholders (i.e. Germany and France). When MNCs spread their operations from the USA and European countries to other countries, they tend to spread their country of origin version of economic development or capitalism which creates strong pressure for its dissemination to other countries (Ferner, 1997). Hence, it will be interesting to explain how MNCs respond to host country meso- and micro-level contexts while considering convergence and divergence in organisational practices to that of the home country.

2.3.1 Ethics of care and corporate social responsibility

The moral view of the stakeholder perspective (Greenwood, 2002) of HRM assumes that the care of the interests of various stakeholders may involve a trade-off between the economic advantage of the shareholders and the interest of others. Furthermore, the ethics of care (Gilligan, 1982; Botes, 1998; Mariappanadar, 2012) in the HRM context refers to the ethical choices MNCs face when seeking to maximise profit as well as reduce the unsustainable aspects of HRM practices on stakeholders, such as society's sustainable environmental management expectations, employees, their families, and future HR supply, so as to maintain harmonious relations between the corporation involved and the stakeholders. That is, when MNCs' HRM practices are strategically driven by the internal referenced efficiency then they are most likely to disregard the ethics of care. However, MNCs have social responsibilities to take care of stakeholders, which is explained by holistic corporate sustainability (Van Marrewijk, 2003). Holistic corporate sustainability suggests that each person or corporation has a universal responsibility towards all other beings. Furthermore, CSR is the obligation a corporation assumes to maximise its positive effect while minimising its negative effect on society.

It is important to first understand what a socially responsible corporate behaviour is because it is not a straightforward exercise (Roberts, 2003). For example, it may be a socially responsible behaviour to pay employees a decent living wage relative to local costs of living as determined by some independent organisations. Alternatively, a socially acceptable behaviour for sustainable HRM can be that MNCs do not ruin the local ecological systems and negatively affect health and social well-being outcomes for the stakeholders (e.g. employees, their family and society's sustainable environmental management expectations). On the other hand, it can be defined using more subjective criteria of a corporation's acceptable behaviour matching that of the stakeholders' expectations.

Socially responsible corporate behaviour shifts historically, for example, during the industrial revolution it was a socially responsible behaviour to reduce the standard working hours from fourteen to ten hours. However, recently, anything more than eight hours of work probably seems unacceptable in advanced countries, at least unless huge overtime wages are paid to employees. Therefore, the meaning of socially responsible corporate behaviour for sustainable HRM is different in different places or to different people and at different times. However, two important things form the basis for understanding acceptable socially responsible corporate behaviour of large corporations (Campbell, 2007). Firstly, large corporations must not knowingly do anything that could negatively impact on their stakeholders such as employees, customers, suppliers, society's sustainable environmental management expectations, and investors. Secondly, if large corporations do cause negative impacts on their stakeholders then they should voluntarily rectify them in response to some sort of normative pressure from institutional contexts, legal threats, regulatory rulings and court orders. These two aspects align well with the principles of GRI sustainability reporting and UN Global Compact guidelines which were discussed in the macro-level contexts in this chapter. Therefore, the understanding of CSR gained from this part will be used to explain initially how national contexts (e.g. employment relations, trade union influence, etc.) and subsequently micro-level industry or sector contexts shape sustainable HRM using CSR.

2.3.2 Meso-level national context

Taylor and Lewis (2014) have suggested that there are clear differences in national contexts between the USA and European countries that promote sustainable HRM. Hence, the national context plays an important role in understanding if sustainable HRM practices practised by MNCs are based on convergence or divergence of a MNC's home country HRM practices. The objective in this section is to explain the role of national contexts in shaping sustainable HRM but not about cross-cultural sustainable HRM practices, which is dealt with in Chapter 12.

To understand the national context for sustainable HRM it is important to use different factors that influence HRM policies and practices in different national contexts (Budhwar & Khatri, 2001). Budhwar and Katri suggested dynamic business environment, national institutions, business sectors, trade union influence, interest of different stakeholders and societal culture are some of the factors worth considering for HRM examination in different national or regional contexts. Subsequently, Budhwar and Sparrow (2002) developed an integrated framework for factors determining cross-national HRM practices and in which they suggested national institutions for educational and vocational set-up is also an important factor to be considered for the national context. Campbell (2007) called this educational institution factor a 'legitimacy' condition for the national context. Hence, in this section different national contexts, such as business competitive condition (dynamic business environment), employment relations, trade union influence, employee involvement in decision making and legitimacy (national vocational/university education programmes) of HRM practices are discussed to explain the role played by national contexts in developing and shaping sustainable HRM.

2.3.2.1 Business competitive conditions

Campbell (2007) indicated different economic and institutionalised conditions that might act as facilitators or inhibitors for corporations to shape acceptable socially responsible corporate behaviour for sustainable HRM. Certain business competitive market conditions act as facilitators for MNCs to practise sustainable HRM, such as good financial performance in a relatively healthy economic environment, and healthy competition in their business. However, certain other business competitive market conditions act as inhibitors for MNCs to practise sustainable HRM, such as weak financial performance in a relatively unhealthy economic environment, and intense competition in their business. Furthermore, a business with reduced profit has fewer resources to spare for sustainable HRM behaviour compared to businesses with increased profit margins. Therefore, managers in such a business would act opportunistically (i.e. with self-interest and guile) and may behave in a socially irresponsible way to improve their business' financial performance without considering the simultaneous unsustainable impacts on the sustainable natural environmental expectations and human/social well-being of stakeholders. Furthermore, MNCs with too little or too high competition may act as inhibitors for sustainable HRM. That is, normal competitive conditions can assure modest profit for a corporation whereas intense competition erodes a firm's profit and it might behave opportunistically and disregard the simultaneous unsustainable impacts on stakeholders. In contrast, when there is too little competition or monopoly, MNCs may have very little interest in socially responsible behaviour, such as sustainable HRM, because their reputation or customer loyalty will not be likely to affect their profitability.

2.3.2.2 *Employment relations*

Industrial relations is about the employment relationship between employers and employees, employees and their unions, employers and their associations and government that make regulations governing employment. In developed economies, since 1980 there is less and less need for a traditional system of industrial relations in a society because more employees are employed in service sectors and fewer in the manufacturing sector. This has led to declining worker unionisation levels in many developed economies and a new type of employer-employee relations called 'employment relations' originated in the literature. There are two dominant reasons for this change from collective agreements (centralised industrial relations) to more decentralised employment relations. Firstly, it is believed that employment relations are increasingly characterised by mutual commitment and common interests in developing competitive work processes (Blyton & Turnbull, 2004) so as to achieve mutual benefits for employees as well as for employers. Secondly, globalisation and internationalisation of corporations are also a reason for deregulation of labour markets and hence centralised industrial relations reduced in relevance and paved the way for individualised employment relations. However, the critics of employment relations argue that deregulation of labour markets due to globalisation has marginalised employees instead of benefiting employees because of the change in relative power position between individual employees and their powerful employers. It is important to be aware that the centralised industrial relations institution will continue to exist in spite of labour market liberalisation pressures from MNCs in particular in large public sector companies in Europe, Australia, Asia and the USA.

Considering the critical view of marginalisation of employees through employment relations, is it possible for MNCs to consider developing sustainable HRM? Deakin and Whittaker (2007) indicated that the concept of CSR could serve as a bridge between issues of governance, on one hand, and principles of equity and fairness in employment and in society on the other. Hence, CSR as a set of mechanisms has managerial, voluntary (instead of regulatory) and financial dimensions to it. Furthermore, in the Anglo-Saxon systems unions have limited options to become highly involved in the corporate governance and CSR debate as a business partner. This change in values among trade unions has happened because of institutional investors' pressure which has become more significant in reducing trade union influence in being the voice of employees in MNCs so as to achieve competitive advantage and improve shareholder value. For example, in the Australian context, two mining company case studies have revealed the link between CSR and employment relations (Jones et al., 2007). They revealed that CSR has the potential to affect employment relations in three ways: by changing the type of relationships within existing collective bargaining arrangements, to foster dialogue over developing 'partnership' between employees and management, and by encouraging the adoption of high performance work practices. However, Béthoux et al. (2007) have indicated that if CSR is to have an empowering and emancipatory effect on employees, it will have to operate as a complement to, and not a substitute for, a centrally administered industrial relations system.

I now go on to explain how the CSR aspect of employment relations can promote sustainable HRM practices in MNCs. Using Deakin and Whittaker's (2007) explanation of CSR as a bridge between governance and equity and fairness in employment can facilitate development of sustainable HRM practices in MNCs through employment relations. For example, MNCs' CSR initiatives, such as treating their employees with equity and fairness; their obligations to employee health and safety; how customers and suppliers are treated; the extent to which they abide by the law; and how it treats the community and ecology and so forth are some expectations of employment relations that facilitate sustainable HRM. It is important to be aware that the dimensions of CSR of MNCs towards sustainable development, which include sustainable HRM, will evolve over a period of time. Hence, new dimensions of CSR for sustainable HRM will be developed and included in employment relations as expectations from the stakeholders on sustainable HRM change over a period of time which MNCs are obliged to satisfy.

2.3.2.3 Trade union and employee association

MNCs that are involved in collective bargaining with trade unions, and those trade unions that have joined the MNCs as strategic partners to promote socially responsible behaviour for sustainable development, will act in socially responsible ways for developing sustainable HRM practices. For example, Danish business associations highlighted to their member businesses the importance of partnering with labour unions and state officials to shape the labour market and social policies to improve the sustainable HR base (Mariappanadar, 2003; Ehnert, 2009) by retraining workers to improve their skills, support retrenched workers during periods of unemployment and help them find new jobs (Martin, 2006). Furthermore, institutionalised dialogue with unions, employees, community groups, investors and other stakeholders strongly influence MNCs to behave in socially responsible ways. However, in an age of increasing economic globalisation MNCs pressurise governments to adopt neoliberal policies, notably deregulations. Deregulations are premised on the assumption that institutional constraints (e.g. trade unions and other stakeholders) on MNCs tend to undermine competition and market efficiency, and ultimately improve economic performance (Campbell, 2007). In contrast, Mariappanadar and Kramar (2014) revealed that large companies in the Asia-Pacific region, which had active trade union engagements, increased economic performance for firms and simultaneously reduced employee harm of work.

2.3.2.4 Regional/national NGOs

Doh and Guay (2006) indicated that MNCs' perceptions about the legitimacy of social issues is dependent on NGOs' activism towards the resolution of specific issues involving the social responsibilities of corporations. Furthermore, they indicated that the legitimacy of NGO activism in resolving CSR issues is different in countries within Europe compared to the USA because of the early political structure of the country. NGOs represent stakeholder perspectives and they play an important role to act as a counterweight to business and global capitalism (Naim, 2000), although others indicate that there are risks of privatising public policies through NGOs that deal with environmental, labour and social issues thereby leading to a loss in democratic accountability (Kapstein, 2001). In many European countries (Wilson, 2003), Australia and India, NGOs have a formal and institutionalised place in the policymaking process. However, the NGOs' influence is limited in the USA because of the federal structure (Doh & Guay, 2006). Hence, NGOs have important influences on MNCs to behave in socially responsible ways such as developing and shaping sustainable HRM to minimise unsustainable impacts on stakeholders while increasing organisational performances.

2.3.2.5 Legitimacy of HRM practices

This is an important institutional condition for institutionaliation, which is about how MNCs' socially responsible behaviour for sustainable HRM practices is dependent on the context where normative calls for such corporate behaviour are institutionalised within that industry sector. For example, managers develop schema (mental constructs) about CSR for sustainable HRM practices by absorbing the messages that are delivered to them at business schools and through the professional publications they pay close attention to (e.g. business magazines, etc.). Hence, publications on sustainable HRM that are used in teaching a course curriculum will be able to shape the existing and prospective managers' schema on CSR relating to stakeholders such as prospective employees (HR base), current employees, their family members, society's sustainable environmental management expectations (green HRM). However, the normative institutions vary significantly across countries in ways that affect corporate behaviour (Dobbin, 1994). For example, it is common in the USA to have mass employee lay-offs during difficult economic times but in Japan many firms are reluctant to engage in mass employee lay-offs even during the recent recession because the normative status of employees as stakeholders in Japanese society is deeply entrenched in their business culture.

In summary, it is clear from the discussion on the meso-level national contexts such as employment relations, that local NGOs, trade unions, business schools and business competitive conditions can shape socially responsible corporate behaviour for developing sustainable HRM. For example, evidence in the economics literature indicates that when MNCs treat their employees fairly, such as providing them with a decent living wage, and engage in other forms of social justice, national economic growth and development improve (Putnam & Goss, 2002; Campbell, 2007).

2.3.3 Micro-level industry context

There are many ways an industry can be defined. Commonly an industry is linked to a group of organisations that offer similar products or services. There are classification schemes, such as the Standard Industrial Classification in each country, which are also used in defining industries. In contrast to the externally established categorisations of industries, organisations' own understanding of who is part of an industry and who is not can also be used to define an industry. However, one common strand emerges in all definitions of an industry, that is, a similar or homogeneous group of organisations with similar organisational practices or similar products or services (Messner, 2015). Furthermore, industry contexts are those characteristics (e.g. percentage of female workers, skill level requirements, capital intensity) that shape similar (i.e. isomorphism) or different (i.e. idiosyncratic) strategic choices of organisational practices to that of other corporations within an industry group. Therefore, in this section we will focus on those characteristics of industry contexts that pressurise MNCs to develop sustainable HRM practices as organisational practices.

In the field of HRM, researchers have explored the role of industry contexts in understanding corporations' responsiveness to work and family issues (Morgan & Milliken, 1992), labour productivity to improve financial performance of corporations (Datta et al., 2005) and many other issues. For example, Morgan and Milliken, in their work and family issues study, used percentage of female employees in an industry that triggers strategic choice from organisations within an industry to resolve work-family conflicts, if an organisation is keen to attract and retain women employees. Also, average employee skill level and the higher training costs are other industry contexts that pressurise MNCs to develop appropriate organisational practices.

The industry characteristics used by Datta and colleagues (2005) in the strategic HRM literature are different to those of Morgan and Milliken's (1992) study on work-family conflict. For example, Datta and colleagues used capital intensity, industry growth, industry differentiation and industry dynamism as industry characteristics (contexts) that facilitate the relationship between high performance work practices and labour productivity. In this study they found that all these industry contexts have significant effects in facilitating the relationship between high performance work practices and labour productivity. Resolving work-family issues along with other harm to the stakeholders and simultaneously improving corporation financial performance are the core aspects of sustainable HRM as discussed in the earlier part of this chapter. Hence, there are strong inclinations for organisations to use industry characteristics, such as the percentage of female employees, average employee skill requirements, higher training costs, capital intensity, industry growth, industry differentiation and industry dynamism, as industry contexts. Organisations develop sustainable HRM strategies, policies and practices as strategic choices or responses to these industry characteristics.

Many researchers (Goodstein, 1994; Ahuja et al., 2007; Kostova et al., 2008) have used institutional theory to explain organisations' strategic choices as responses to pressures from industry characteristics or contexts. The strategic choice perspective highlights the ability of organisations to interpret and select industry characteristics or contexts for developing sustainable HRM practices. Hence, institutional theory provides the theoretical basis (Suddaby, 2010) to understand strategic choices of organisations in determining how and why organisations attend, and attach meaning, to some elements of industrial characteristics or contexts for developing and shaping sustainable HRM practices.

2.4 Conclusion

In this chapter institutional theory is used to explain the macro-, meso- and micro-level contexts and strategic choices as responses to those contexts. The first part of the institutional theory was used to highlight 'why' MNCs attribute importance to certain elements of the contexts to develop corporate sustainability business strategy. Subsequently, shaping sustainable HRM practices to engage HR to implement corporate sustainability business strategy. To support this part of the institutional theory an attempt is firstly made to explain the roles of various global institutions (e.g. UN Rio Summit, ILO, etc.) that promote sustainable development to achieve economic/financial, natural environmental and human/social goals of the society as a background. Secondly, this chapter explains that sustainable HRM advocates HR as a key resource which plays an important role in implementing corporate sustainability business strategy to achieve economic/financial, human/social and natural environmental outcomes of sustainability. Furthermore, it is highlighted in this chapter that sustainable HRM is developed based on the social sustainability perspective of sustainable development. Thirdly, it is explained that the foundation principles of sustainable HRM, as part of sustainable development, are operationalised by the guidelines set for reporting on sustainability as a macro-level context by multilateral institutions such as GRI for sustainability and the UN Global Compact. Along with sustainability reporting, financial market institutions for sustainable investments and civil society organisations are discussed as macro-level contexts to develop an organisation's corporate sustainability business strategy, and subsequently shape sustainable HRM practices to implement this business strategy.

Fourthly, the ethical and CSR perspectives are used as background theoretical information to explain the meso- and micro-level contexts for sustainable HRM. Fifthly, it is highlighted in this chapter that the meso-level national context includes business competitive conditions, employment relations, trade union influence and university courses that shape socially responsible corporate behaviour among MNCs for developing sustainable HRM practices. Lastly, the micro-level industry context for developing and mouflding sustainable HRM practices among MNCs is explained as strategic choices or responses to industry characteristics or contexts, such as the percentage of female employees in an industry, higher training costs, capital intensity, industry growth, industry differentiation and industry dynamism.

References

Ahuja, M. K., Chudoba, K. M., Kacmar, C. J., McKnight, D. H. & George, J. F. (2007). IT road warriors: Balancing work-family conflict, job autonomy, and work overload to mitigate turnover intentions. *MIS Quarterly, 31*(1), 1–17.

Appelbaum, E., Bailey, T., Berg, P. & Kalleberg, A. (2000). *Manufacturing Advantage: Why High Performance Work Systems Pay Off.* New York: Cornell University Press.

Becker, E., Jahn, T., & Stiess, I. (1999). Exploring uncommon ground: Sustainability and the social sciences. In: E.Becker & T. Jahn (eds) *Sustainability and the Social Sciences: A Cross-disciplinary Approach to Integrating Environmental Considerations into Theoretical Reorientation* (pp. 1–22). London: Zed Books.

Beloe, S., Scherer, J. & Knoepfel, I. (2004). *Values for Money: Reviewing the Quality of SRI Research.* SustainAbility.

Béthoux, É., Didry, C. & Mias, A. (2007). What codes of conduct tell us: Corporate social responsibility and the nature of the multinational corporation. *Corporate Governance: An International Review, 15*(1), 77–90.

Blyton, P. & Turnbull, P. (2004). *The Dynamics of Employee Relations.* New York: Palgrave Macmillan.

Botes, A. C. (1998). *Ethics of Justice and Ethics of Care.* Johannesburg: Rand Afrikaans University.

Budhwar, P. S. & Khatri, N. (2001). HRM in context applicability of HRM models in India. *International Journal of Cross Cultural Management, 1*(3), 333–56.

Budhwar, P. S. & Sparrow, P. R. (2002). An integrative framework for understanding cross-national human resource management practices. *Human Resource Management Review, 12*(3), 377–403.

Campbell, J. L. (2007). Why would corporations behave in socially responsible ways? An institutional theory of corporate social responsibility. *Academy of Management Review, 32*(3), 946–67.

Datta, D. K., Guthrie, J. P. & Wright, P. M. (2005). Human resource management and labor productivity: Does industry matter? *Academy of Management Journal, 48*(1), 135–45.

Deakin, S. & Whittaker, D. H. (2007). Re-embedding the Corporation? Comparative perspectives on corporate governance, employment relations and corporate social responsibility. *Corporate Governance: An International Review, 15*(1), 1–4.

Dobbin, F. (1994). *Forging Industrial Policy.* New York: Cambridge University Press.

Docherty, P., Kira, M. & Shani, A. B. (2009). What the world needs now is sustainable work systems. *Creating Sustainable Work Systems. Developing Social Sustainability* (1–21).

Doh, J. P. & Guay, T. R. (2006). Corporate social responsibility, public policy, and NGO activism in Europe and the united states: An Institutional-Stakeholder perspective. *Journal of Management Studies, 43*(1), 47–73.

Drexhage, J. & Murphy, D. (2010). Sustainable development: From Brundtland to Rio 2012. *United Nations Headquarters, New York*, 9–13.

Ehnert, I. (2009). *Sustainable Human Resource Management: A Conceptual and Exploratory Analysis from a Paradox Perspective*, Heidelberg, London, New York: Springer.

Ehnert, I. (2014). Paradox as a lens for theorizing Sustainable HRM: Mapping and coping with paradoxes and tensions. In: I. Ehnert, W. Harry & K. J. Zink (eds) *Sustainability and Human Resource Management: Developing Sustainable Business Organizations* (pp. 247–72). Berlin, Heidelberg: Springer.

Ehnert, I., Parsa, S., Roper, I., Wagner, M. & Muller-Camen, M. (2015). Reporting on sustainability and HRM: A comparative study of sustainability reporting practices by the world's largest companies. *The International Journal of Human Resource Management, 27*(1), 1–21.

Ferner, A. (1997). Country of origin effects and HRM in multinational companies. *Human Resource Management Journal, 7*(1), 19–37.

Gilligan, C. (1982). *A Different Voice: Psychological Theory and Women's Development*. Cambridge, MA: Harvard University Press.

Goodstein, J. D. (1994). Institutional pressures and strategic responsiveness: Employer involvement in work-family issues. *Academy of Management Journal, 37*(2), 350–82.

Greenwood, M. R. (2002). Ethics and HRM: A review and conceptual analysis. *Journal of Business Ethics, 36*(3), 261–78.

Hahn, R. & Lülfs, R. (2014). Legitimizing negative aspects in GRI-oriented sustainability reporting: A qualitative analysis of corporate disclosure strategies. *Journal of Business Ethics, 123*(3), 401–20.

Hood, C., Rothstein, H. & Baldwin, R. (2001). *The Government of Risk: Understanding Risk Regulation Regimes*. Oxford: Oxford University Press.

Jackson, S. E., Renwick, D. W., Jabbour, C. J. & Muller-Camen, M. (2011). State-of-the-art and future directions for green human resource management: Introduction to the special issue. *German Journal of Human Resource Management: Zeitschrift für Personalforschung, 25*(2), 99–116.

Jones, M., Marshall, S. & Mitchell, R. (2007). Corporate social responsibility and the management of labour in two Australian mining industry companies. *Corporate Governance: An International Review, 15*(1), 57–67.

Kapstein, E. (2001). The corporate ethics crusade. *Foreign Affairs, 80*(5), 105–19.

Kell, G. (2005). The global compact. selected experiences and reflections. *Journal of Business Ethics, 59*(1–2), 69–79.

Kostova, T., Roth, K. & Dacin, M. T. (2008). Institutional theory in the study of multinational corporations: A critique and new directions. *Academy of Management Review, 33*(4), 994–1006.

Littig, B. & Griessler, E. (2005). Social sustainability: A catchword between political pragmatism and social theory. *International Journal of Sustainable Development, 8*(1–2), 65–79.

López, M. V., Garcia, A. & Rodriguez, L. (2007). Sustainable development and corporate performance: A study based on the Dow Jones sustainability index. *Journal of Business Ethics, 75*(3), 285–300.

Mariappanadar, S. (2003). Sustainable human resource management: The sustainable and unsustainable dilemmas of downsizing. *International Journal of Social Economics*, *30*, 906–23.

Mariappanadar, S. (2012). Harm of efficiency oriented HRM practices on stakeholders: An ethical issue for sustainability. *Society and Business Review*, *7*, 168–84.

Mariappanadar, S. (2014a). Stakeholder harm index: A framework to review work intensification from the critical HRM perspective. *Human Resource Management Review*, *24*(4), 313–29.

Mariappanadar, S. (2014b). Sustainable HRM: A counter to minimize the externality of downsizing. In: I. Ehnert, W. Harry & K. J. Zink (eds) *Sustainability and Human Resource Management* (pp. 181–203). Berlin, Heidelberg: Springer.

Mariappanadar, S. & Kramar, R. (2014). Sustainable HRM: The synthesis effect of high performance work systems on organisational performance and employee harm. *Asia-Pacific Journal of Business Administration*, *6*(3), 206–24.

Martin, C. J. (2006). Corporatism in the post-industrial age: Employers and social policy in the little land of Denmark. In: Campbell, J. L., Hall, J. A. & Pedersen, O. K. (eds) *National Identity and the Varieties of Capitalism: The Danish Experience* (271–94). Montreal: McGill-Queen's University Press.

Messner, M. (2015). Does industry matter? How industry context shapes management accounting practice. *Management Accounting Research, Forthcoming.*

Moneva, J. M., Archel, P. & Correa, C. (2006). GRI and the camouflaging of corporate unsustainability. *Accounting Forum*, *30*(2), 121–37.

Morgan, H. & Milliken, F. J. (1992). Keys to action: Understanding differences in organizations' responsiveness to work-and-family issues. *Human Resource Management*, *31*(3), 227–48.

Naim, M. (2000). Lori's War. *Foreign Policy*, *118*, 29–55.

Olson, M. (1971). *The Logic of Collective Action: Public Goods and the Theory of Groups*. Cambridge, MA: Harvard University Press.

Paauwe, J. & Boselie, P. (2007). HRM and societal embeddedness. In: Boxall, P., Purcell, J. & Wright, P. (eds) *The Oxford Handbook of Human Resource Management*. Oxford: Oxford University Press.

Putnam, R. D. & Goss, K. A. (2002). Introduction. In: R. D. Putnam (ed.) *Democracies in Flux: The Evolution of Social Capital in Contemporary Society* (pp. 3–20). Oxford: Oxford University Press.

Rio Summit (1992). *Rio Declaration on Environment and Development*. http://www.unesco.org/education/nfsunesco/pdf/RIO_E.PDF. Accessed on 7 October 2015.

Roberts, J. (2003). The Manufacture of corporate social responsibility: Constructing corporate sensibility. *Organization*, *10*, 249–65.

Runhaar, H. & Lafferty, H. (2009). Governing corporate social responsibility: An assessment of the contribution of the UN Global Compact to CSR strategies in the telecommunications industry. *Journal of Business Ethics*, *84*(4), 479–95.

Scott, W. R. (1995). *Institutions and Organizations* (Vol. 2), Thousand Oaks, CA: Sage.

Suddaby, R. (2010). Challenges for institutional theory. *Journal of Management Inquiry*, *19*(1), 14–20.

Taylor, S. & Lewis, C. (2014). Sustainable HRM in the US: The influence of national context. In: I. Ehnert, W. Harry & K. J. Zink (eds) *Sustainability and Human Resource Management: Developing Sustainable Business Organizations* (pp. 297–314). Berlin, Heidelberg: Springer.

Teegen, H., Doh, J. P. & Vachani, S. (2004). The importance of nongovernmental organizations (NGOs) in global governance and value creation: An international business research agenda. *Journal of International Business Studies, 35*(6), 463–83.

UNGC (UN Global Compact) (2006). About the Global Compact: The Ten Principles, UN Global Compact Office, New York. https://www.unglobalcompact.org/what-is-gc/mission/principles. Accessed on 5 October 2015.

Van Marrewijk, M. (2003). Concepts and definitions of CSR and corporate sustainability: Between agency and communion. *Journal of Business Ethics, 44*, 95–105.

WCED (World Commission on Environment and Development) (1987). *Our Common Future.* Oxford: Oxford University Press.

Williams, S., Abbott, B. & Heery, E. (2011). Civil regulation and HRM: The impact of civil society organisations on the policies and practices of employers. *Human Resource Management Journal, 21*(1), 45–59.

Wilkinson, A., Hill, M., & Gollan, P. (2001). The sustainability debate. *International Journal of Operations & Production Management, 21*(12), 1492–1502.

Wilson, G. (2003). *Business and Politics: A Comparative Introduction.* London: Chatham House.

World Summit on Sustainable Development (2005). *United Nations Sustainable Development Summit.* United Nations. http://www.un.org/sustainabledevelopment/summit/. Accessed on 7 October 2015.

Zink, K. J. (2005). Stakeholder orientation and corporate social responsibility as a precondition for sustainability. *Total Quality Management and Business Excellence, 16*(8–9), 1041–52.

3

A paradox perspective for sustainable Human Resource Management

Christine Parkin Hughes

3.1 Introduction

If sustainable social and economic growth, both now and in the future, is to be achieved, people throughout the world need to be in position to work and be managed sustainably within the workplace (Jackson, 2012). Human resource management (HRM) is fundamental to the success of organisational strategy and thus plays an integral part in the sustainability of an organisation (e.g. Boudreau & Ramstrad, 2005; Clarke, 2011; Ehnert & Harry, 2012; Mariappanadar, 2012; Voegtlin & Greenwood, 2016). Yet the tensions that are inherent throughout the organisational context, and in particular within HRM, are not abating – rather, they are intensifying (Aust et al., 2015).

Working practices tend to be driven by efficiency and performance-focused approaches grounded in profit maximisation, with increasing control over workers' lives beyond the organisation, which can negatively impact on family, community and society (Mariappanadar, 2012); whereas sustainability embodies the potential for societal advancement towards a more equitable and wealthy world in which the natural environment and cultural achievements are preserved far into the future (Dyllick & Hockerts, 2002). Therefore, translating sustainability into a meaningful concept for the organisational context is onerous, not least because it directly challenges short-termism and the fascination with profit maximisation (Elkington, 1999; Rappaport, 2005; Starkey & Tempest, 2008). Indeed, it requires a shift in focus to where the very definition of organisational success moves from purely financial and shareholder outcomes to one encompassing multi-stakeholderism and an intergenerational perspective (Boudreau & Ramstad, 2005; Benn et al., 2014; Mariappanadar, 2014; Zink, 2014). Consequently, the corporate model requires modification in order to contribute to the continuing health of the planet; the development of a just and humane society; and the creation of work that brings dignity and self-fulfilment to the worker (e.g. Kirsch, 2011; Benn et al., 2014; Burns, 2014). However, managing both owner and employee needs and internal and external stakeholder requirements is not straightforward (Bratton & Gold, 2017), and has significant implications for the alignment of HRM with sustainability, rendering both those responsible for managing the human resource and the human resource itself as victims of ambiguity (Legge, 1978; Aust et al., 2015).

This chapter introduces the basic tenets of the paradox perspective and provides an overview of the key paradoxical tensions at the organisation level and those which are of particular relevance to sustainable HRM. It considers approaches to managing the tensions through *acceptance* and *resolution* strategies (further broken down into those of *separation* and *synthesis*). It builds on Chapters 1 and 2, which consider the context and challenges faced by sustainable HRM and where the synthesis approach is discussed in more detail. The understanding from this chapter forms a foundation from which to develop sustainable HRM functions and practices that can effectively handle the tensions and the impact on stakeholders, which is explored in the following chapters of this book, particularly Chapters 4–7. It is worth noting that the position taken here is that tensions do not need to represent true paradox in order to be viewed from a paradox perspective.

3.2 Tension between sustainability and HRM

Given the often broad conceptualisation of sustainability and the multiple explanations it evokes, any definition is bound to remain abstract, contestable and ideologically controversial, creating difficulties for its enactment within organisations (e.g. Marshall & Toffel, 2005; Colbert & Kurucz, 2007; Benn et al., 2014; Perey, 2015; Parkin Hughes, Semeijn & Caniëls, 2017). It is a philosophy, an attitude, a lens through which to view the world. Therefore, rendering 'sustainability' into a germane concept for the organisational context, especially in terms of the HR function, remains problematic. It is a 'convenient slogan' in the challenging task of aligning the conflicting goals of bringing prosperity to all people while preserving the capacity of the world to cope (Fleurbaey, 2015:34). It has become a 'fashionable buzzword' and it does not necessarily follow that proliferation of the term denotes an increase in the understanding of it (Laasch & Conaway, 2015:61).

When attention is given to the socio-environmental effects of organisational actions and management practice, the focus tends to be on the consequence of economic development, sustainable financial outcomes and the achievement of competitive advantage – not on the consequences of management practices for the natural environment or for the individual and society in terms of work–life balance, happiness, health and well-being in their own right (e.g. Pfeffer, 2010; Kramar, 2011; Mariappanadar, 2012; Benn et al., 2014; Perey, 2015). Certainly, economic viability is generally considered the foundation stone of an organisation, with the long-term sustainability of the organisation dependent on remaining financially feasible and competitive, and economic considerations underpinning most strategic decision making (e.g. Norman & MacDonald, 2003; Clarke, 2011; Dawson & Zanko, 2011; Jones, 2011; Kramar, 2011; Christofi et al., 2012).

It seems the reality is that organisations and the people within them are experiencing the 'shadow side of HRM' (Kramar, 2013:2), through increasing working hours, work intensification, high turnover, downsizing, restructuring and the general attempt to do more with less to satisfy stakeholder expectations (e.g. Clarke, 2011; Mariappanadar, 2012; Kleiner & Pavalko, 2014). Indeed, analysis by the Chartered Institute of Personnel and Development (CIPD, 2014) of various surveys (including the Skills and Employment Survey, Workplace Employment Relations Study, European Social Survey and European Working Conditions Survey) suggests that employees believe they are working harder than ever before, with increasing job insecurity and greater work intensity.

Clearly, there is tension between the execution of efficiency drivers and maintaining the human condition, capability and relational rationality (Ehnert, 2009; Garavan & McGuire, 2010; Benn et al., 2014; Laasch & Conaway, 2015). Take, for instance, the emerging use of microchip implants for employees in organisations such as Three Square Market, a technology company in the USA, and Epicenter, the Swedish start-up hub, which raises a number of pertinent discussions surrounding efficiency on the one hand and privacy and the ethical and responsible management of people on the other. HR managers remain in an ambiguous position, having to demonstrate, for example, that they are contributing to the well-being of employees, yet at the same time contributing strategically to the financial outcomes and 'adding value' to the organisation, with employees potentially being viewed as a payroll cost and disposable resource rather than a long-term investment. Hence, paradoxically, HRM enacts strategic logic in managing people and their expectations – both individually and collectively – yet remains married to the traditional financial definition of organisational success and economic rationalism (e.g. Pfeffer, 1998; Boudreau & Ramstad, 2005; Garavan & McGuire, 2010; Kramar & Syed, 2012).

The prevalence towards a more organisational-centric strategic perspective reveals a tendency for a mechanistic, rational world view that has enabled managers to design policies which act as levers to shape behaviour and produce the outcomes which are desired because of the requirements of the owners of the organisation rather than the needs of the employees (Kramar, 2011). Although mission statements, rhetoric and other discourse can claim that people are the most important resource, the reality is characterised by a managerialist focus, impersonal economic rationalism, work intensification and a resource of willing slaves (e.g. Wilmott, 1993; Vaughan, 1994; Biglan, 2009; Redman & Wilkinson, 2009; Kramar & Syed, 2012; Mariappanadar, 2012; Bratton & Gold, 2017). Indeed, particularly in times of instability, uncertainty and recession, unitary-couched rhetoric may actually impart a business-case HR culture which promotes the supremacy of particular stakeholders at the expense of the employees, their families, the wider society and the natural environment (Greenwood, 2002; Kramar & Syed, 2012; Mariappanadar, 2012; Hahn et al., 2017). Such fundamental complexities within the field inevitably result in more challenging engagement with sustainability, particularly at senior level (Majed, 2014).

Plainly, therefore, HRM does not always sit comfortably with, and at times directly challenges, notions of sustainability, which arguably are to commit to the creation of better workplaces for the sake of people, society, economy and ecology (e.g. Greenwood, 2002; Docherty et al., 2009; Kramar, 2011). Managing the tensions between various outcomes is of practical and theoretical importance, yet there is a growing theory–practice gap (Aust et al., 2015). Even so, the literature regarding the sustainable management of people is developing and endeavours to investigate the relationship between people management practices and outcomes beyond those which are predominantly financial. Yet it remains 'piecemeal, diverse and fraught with difficulties' (Kramar, 2013:7), mostly failing to progress beyond the mapping of the tension dichotomies to explore the underlying theoretical assumptions (Aust et al., 2015), and is at best positioned at the pioneering stage.

More recently there is a burgeoning conversation which considers and applies a paradox lens to the challenge of realising sustainable practice in business – it is a riposte to the prevailing instrumental view which focuses on profit maximisation and dismisses the inherent tensions in corporate sustainability (see, e.g. Smith & Lewis, 2011; Gao & Bansal, 2013; Aust et al., 2015; Van der Byl & Slawinski, 2015; Schad et al., 2016; Hahn et al., 2017). It represents an integrative rationale, reasoning that organisations should engage with different demands, even if they apparently oppose each other.

3.3 The paradox perspective

The drive for achieving sustainability is intrinsically burdened with tensions between different dimensions at different levels that dwell at different temporal and spatial scales, and so is fundamentally paradoxical (e.g. Ehnert, 2009; Gao & Bansal, 2013; Hahn et al, 2017). The basic premise of the paradox perspective is one of acknowledgement, not defensiveness (Smith & Lewis, 2011). It does not seek compromise, balance or shared values to resolve the tensions between HRM and sustainability, as espoused by some more traditional notions of sustainable development. Rather, the paradox perspective explicitly recognises that satisfying all stakeholders is inevitably unrealistic. In reality, the stakeholders need to coexist despite having conflicting objectives, and therefore any tensions need to be managed through approaches which recognise key stakeholders and embrace the challenges to be able to work through them.

3.3.1 Defining the Paradox Perspective

The paradox perspective is an unsettled notion which has yet to establish a shared definition and framework, despite being considered a core theme of postmodern organisational design and an important theoretical lens through which to study contemporary organisations (Child & McGrath, 2001; Ehnert, 2009; Hahn et al., 2017). However, the literature does tend to agree that it is *a set of contradictory and incompatible poles all supported by apparently sound arguments* (e.g. Poole & Van de Ven, 1989; Guerci & Carollo, 2016; Schad et al., 2016). Smith and Lewis add that the long-term success of an organisation requires 'continuous efforts to meet multiple divergent demands' (2011:381). They recognise that decision makers could respond defensively or proactively to paradoxical tensions, but argue that generative outcomes can be achieved where the awareness of tensions elicits a management strategy which is grounded in accommodating them, rather than actively avoiding and ignoring them. Hahn and colleagues have sympathy with this view and, when explaining the paradox perspective in terms of organisational sustainability, they suggest that it:

> embraces tensions to simultaneously accommodate competing yet unrelated economic/financial, natural environmental, and human/social concerns that reside at different levels and operate in different logics and time frames and in different spatial scales. (Hahn et al., 2017:2)

Tensions do not necessarily need to represent a true paradox to be viewed from a paradox perspective. The paradox perspective does not yet occupy a large space within the HRM field. However, the embedded ambiguities of the HRM role were outlined in Legge's seminal work of 1978. Later, Evans (1999) introduced the notion of duality, dilemma and paradoxes and the opposing forces within the organisation. These were built on through the work of Ehnert (2009), which explicitly focused on the sustainability–HRM paradoxes.

It is argued that a successful manager is one who can accept the tensions and is capable of embracing all the constitutive poles at the same time, rather than focusing on just one, thereby denouncing cognitive limits and creating a space for reflexivity, innovation, change and possibly organisational survival (e.g. Lewis, 2000; Smith & Lewis, 2011; Guerci & Carollo, 2016). A virtuous learning cycle can emerge when an awareness is developed of the diverse and contradictory pulls, both internally and externally, to the organisation, even if it appears counterintuitive at outset. Conversely, a vicious cycle is arguably more likely to arise when a narrower approach is adopted in the search for 'fit', resulting in other outcomes being left unexplored. Ultimately, organisations and managers who successfully work with desirable but mutually exclusive courses of action are most likely to succeed in the long term; whereas those who are unable to deal with opposing courses of action are more likely to fail (see Cameron, 1986; Handy, 1994; Probst & Raisch, 2005; Guerci & Carollo, 2016).

3.3.2 Normative, Descriptive and Instrumental Aspects of a Paradox Perspective

Hahn and colleagues (2017) attempt to further consolidate and clarify the emerging use of the paradox perspective by delineating its components. Focusing on corporate sustainability, they offer a framework which considers three mutually supportive and interconnecting aspects of a paradox perspective: descriptive, instrumental and normative. In cyclical form, each aspect impacts and informs on the other. These three elements reflect on the normative foundations of a paradox perspective on corporate sustainability, frame the descriptive categories which capture how organisations make sense of and therefore respond to those paradoxical tensions, and consider the implications as a result of the paradoxes and their underlying mechanisms.

The *normative* aspect is about the attribution of value and advocates the need to recognise intrinsic value in overarching societal and natural environmental systems. It is fundamental because it is grounded in the principle that organisations have a wider responsibility which extends beyond economic performance and shareholder gains. It recognises that responsibility is multifarious and elusive and is determined by the relationships between the multiple stakeholders, with each world view perceiving the nature of the relationships differently (Gray et al., 2014). It is a complex concept which is as much about what has *not* been done as that which has. And, as Jones (2011:2) succinctly purports, 'Responsibility is about doing good, not because of a rational business case, but because of a capacity to do so.'

The *descriptive* aspect represents how tensions are variously espoused, made sense of and given meaning to. Then – depending on which of the many responses this garners – how they impact on the strategy. There is currently little research or evidence on the particular forms of these responses; however, such plurality perhaps provides the opportunity to reconstruct knowledge and break down perceived barriers between the perspectives of different stakeholders – particularly when considering the more holistic notions of sustainability, signalling a disruption to the reliability of their understanding as well as leading to the reconstruction of their sense making (Weick, 1995; Perey, 2015).

The *instrumental* aspect refers to the consequences of the tensions and the different ways and mechanisms by which these can be managed. It seeks to establish connections with multiple outcomes, at the organisational level and beyond, explicitly incorporating wider underpinning socio-environmental dimensions across the short- to long-term spectrum. It does not recognise a hierarchy between the dimensions, nor is it necessarily looking for balance – simply the annulment of predetermined primacy.

3.4 Key organisational paradoxes

Hahn and colleagues (2015) suggest that there are four key paradoxes within an organisational-level context:

1. Personal versus organisational sustainability agendas
2. Short-term versus long-term orientation
3. Isomorphism versus change
4. Efficiency versus resilience

3.4.1 Personal versus Organisational Sustainability Agendas

This refers to the tensions between personal values and preferences for sustainability which may be in conflict with the organisational sustainability agenda. For instance, a manager may hold a firm view that social and environmental concerns should be acted on within the organisation, whereas the organisational structure, culture, strategic direction and administrative procedures may act as constraints, preventing the manager from doing so. And, should a manager act contrary to the organisation, it could be at the risk of some form of penalty such as facing disapproval by the organisation.

3.4.2 Short-Term versus Long-Term Orientation

The publication of the World Commission in Environment and Development's Brundtland Report was a historic moment, triggering a new wave of debate and sustainability-related activity. It defined sustainable development as: 'development that meets the needs of the present without compromising the ability of future generations to meet their own needs' (WCED, 1987:8). Fleurbaey (2015) argues that the notion of giving future generations the *ability* captures the essence of sustainability better than any other explanation before or since. If, for instance, organisations engage in the regeneration and development of the resources that they consume today and will need in the future, it can lead to sustainable organisational behaviour and thus be called sustainability (Ehnert & Harry, 2012). Indeed, inherent in the meaning of *sustain* is the idea of maintenance, of enduring systems over long, if not indefinite, spans of time (Perey, 2015). Similarly, Doppelt (2010:58) suggests that sustainability is simply about 'protecting our options', arguing that a new economic paradigm is needed which 'can be maintained for decades and generations'. So there is a need for intergenerational equity, where the current decision-making time horizon does not undervalue the interests of future generations. However, what is best for the organisation in the long term is not necessarily best in the short term and vice versa. Therefore, there is a tension – particularly when trying to justify sustainability undertakings in terms of economic drivers such as productivity and profitability.

3.4.3 Isomorphism versus Change

Achieving sustainable development requires individual organisations, whole industries and entire economies to reconsider and change how they function and behave. However, calls for innovation and evolution towards sustainability are in direct opposition to maintaining established modes of 'best practice'. On the one hand organisations are expected to act as drivers of change for sustainable development, yet they are under institutional burdens compelling them to conform with norms for legitimate behaviour, thereby leading to isomorphism. Another challenge is the paradox raised by advocates of processual and emergent change, which recognises that historical, political and contextual processes unfold as change progresses, but are notoriously difficult to identify at the strategic planning stage, and nigh-on impossible to predict exactly how they will unfold – a principal cause of change failure (Grieves, 2010:388). However, change does happen. After all, it is increasingly difficult to consider organisations as simply a matter of economic expediency. Indeed, the history of industrial legislation in Great Britain from around the 1750s (the first industrial revolution) is populated by the development of the Factory Acts, natural environmental legislation, social legislation and the involvement of pressure groups (Grieves, 2010).

3.4.4 Efficiency versus Resilience

There are divergent demands between efficiency drivers pursuing the ability to operate with minimum time and waste on the one hand and the need for resilience on the other. Efficiency is born out of standardisation, homogenisation, centralisation and reductionism; whereas, paradoxically, resilience is born out of diversity, adaptability and innovation, particularly in times of uncertainty. Therefore, as organisations attempt to increase efficiency, both intra- and interorganisational diversity and resilience are reduced (Hahn et al., 2015).

3.5 Key paradoxes for HRM

Demonstrating some clear intersections with the organisational-level tensions suggested by Hahn and colleages (2015), Ehnert (2009) previously identified three key paradoxes which are particularly relevant for HRM.

1. Efficiency versus substance
2. Performance versus regeneration
3. Short-term versus long-term

3.5.1 Efficiency versus Substance Paradox

This paradox focuses on the classic HR challenge of deploying people efficiently and effectively to achieve organisational objectives and remain competitive on the one hand and the need to train, develop and maintain a competent, motivated and future-ready workforce on the other. However, developing a motivated workforce which can fulfil future needs can take significant time and investment, and there is often a culture of continuous change and restructuring which makes the future very difficult to predict with any certainty, as recognised in the isomorphism versus change discussions above.

3.5.2 Performance versus Regeneration Paradox

This paradox considers the dual economic rationality versus relational rationality, id est, the ability of employees to perform, regenerate and develop themselves. It is necessary for an employee to invest time and energy into the processes of work. Similarly, rest and recuperation are also necessary to be able to maintain body, mind and soul, and the ability to remain productive over the long term.

3.5.3 Short-Term versus Long-Term Paradox

In a similar vein to the explanation provided for the organisational level in Section 3.4 above, differing perspectives of what constitutes long and short term and the varying value attributed to them can be problematic. Ehnert (2009) suggests that HR practitioners are confronted with the persistent tension between short-term profit making and long-term organisational viability. In HR terms, this manifests itself as needing to develop efficient and effective human resources in the short term while preserving the human condition and maintaining access to appropriately skilled and motivated people for the long term.

3.6 Strategies to cope with paradox

Given that paradoxical tensions are acknowledged, theorists tend to couch the approaches to cope with them in terms of three broad strategies (see also Figure 3.1):

1. Acceptance (also referred to as opposition)
2. Resolution through separation (temporal or spatial)
3. Resolution through synthesis

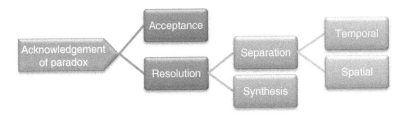

Figure 3.1   Strategies to manage tensions

See also Mariappandar's Synthesis Paradox Framework in Chapter 1; Poole and Van de Ven's
Four Methods for Working with Paradox (1989:565); Enhert's Representation of Coping
(2009:231); and Managing Tensions by Hahn et al., (2015:300).

3.6.1 Acceptance

As Poole and Van de Ven explain, this strategic response is to accept the tension and 'learn to live with it' (1989:566). It requires that a way is found to consider simultaneously the divergent demands without the need to separate them or by giving one the priority over the others. Tension is expected and accepted, and room is made for it.

For example, an acceptance strategy may be used to manage tensions between conflicting long- and short-term reward management outcomes. Managers could complement those business practices which are beneficial in terms of short-term financial outcomes with concurrent practices which are not harmful economically, environmentally or socially over longer periods of time. Given the overriding myopic culture of short-termism within business, inducing managers to simultaneously also take more notice of long-term considerations – without penalty – can enable organisations to combine short- and long-term outcomes through the implementation of organisational practices. For instance, following the financial crash and the accusations of irresponsible business practices, some organisations (e.g. TNT, DSM) reconfigured their reward management systems in terms of the bonuses awarded, to incorporate long- and short-term elements as well as financial and non-financial targets. By encouraging managers to accept the importance of short-term earnings, while simultaneously recognising the need for non-financial and long-term objectives, it means that both the poles in the paradox are acknowledged and remain intact, despite their fundamental contradictions (Hahn et al., 2015).

Similarly, when considering the divergent demands of personal and organisational sustainability agendas, an acceptance strategy will allow an innovative space for creative tension, accommodating open dialogue and diverse information exchange, both internally and externally to the organisation. It will act as a driver for cognitive organisational disruption, reorientation and reframing. The challenge of this strategy is to accept that tension is inevitable and create conditions which facilitate and nurture this process, rather than penalise it. For instance, Intel and eBay have adopted the acceptance strategy by creating a space for 'green teams'. These teams have few bureaucratic constraints, are self-organised and are cross-departmental. By creating a space for divergent personal and organisational sustainability agendas, these two organisations have managed the tension without needing to favour one over the other. Indeed, as Hahn and colleagues observed, 'Paradoxically, by allowing employees to deviate from the organisational agenda the firm can increase employee loyalty and satisfaction' (2015:305).

3.6.2 Resolution

Here, organisations attempt to transform the tensions into a more manageable situation through separation or synthesis strategies. A *separation* strategy requires that different factions are spatially and/or temporally separated, thereby avoiding possible clashes of agenda and other interferences if brought into close proximity, and realising the rewards of various approaches without having to reconcile them (Smith & Tushman, 2005). For example, opposing short- and long-term issues are separated and divided appropriately between different parts of the organisation. In a top-down approach, for instance, managers and non-managers at lower levels of the organisation are more likely to be concerned with their responsibilities for day-to-day operational aspects of the business, while senior management may have the capacity to consider the longer-term, more sustainable strategic operations, which can then be implemented and embedded throughout the fundamental day-to-day operations of the organisation. Separation could allow the organisation to continue to concentrate on traditional products and services for established markets, but also pursue more sustainable options in different market segments where institutional change has already happened, thereby avoiding tensions caused by close proximity and the risk to legitimacy.

Alternatively, tensions may be managed by a resolution through a *synthesis* strategy (a framework for synthesis is discussed more fully in Chapter 1). This approach is grounded in involvement and participation, calling for organisations to actively mediate between the opposing agendas through the introduction of formal process and procedures. It empowers mangers to pursue, for example, both short- and long-term issues in the same arena (in terms of time or place), through the application of enabling governance structures. This distributes authority and engenders participative decision making which can directly shape organisational practices. For instance, an alternative governance structure which is more tolerant of not meeting short-term financial objectives could be introduced through the overarching strategic aims, thereby allowing both long- and short-term objectives to be pursued. This more flexible institutional approach can often be seen in organisations which intentionally blur the lines between for-profit and not-for-profit outcomes, such as hybrid organisations and social enterprises (see Dart, 2004; Haigh & Hoffman, 2012). Indeed, these organisations may grow their own talent or actively attract and select employees who are yet to be socialised into the more traditional ways of conducting business, thereby strengthening the synthesis culture (Battilana & Dorado, 2010).

3.7 Conclusion

Progressive HRM should develop practices and behaviours which achieve the objectives of systematic and future sustainability. It is clear that the relationship between sustainability and the HR function is complex and often paradoxical. Yet, despite the increasing interest in the links between sustainability and HRM, the field has yet to provide comprehensive insights into that relationship and the tensions within it, or take the opportunity to apply a paradox perspective in any significant way.

The paradox perspective is a fundamental lens through which to theorise sustainable HRM by explicitly recognising the tensions between different desired, yet interdependent and conflicting, outcomes. Decision makers do not have to choose between competing outcomes; rather, by embracing divergent demands of HRM and sustainability, tensions can be acknowledged, accommodated and worked through, creating the opportunity for superior business contributions. Furthermore, in contrast to business-case logic, a paradox perspective recognises that socio-economic outcomes are valuable in their own right, and challenges the primacy of economic drivers over socio-environmental concerns.

This chapter introduced the basic tenets of the paradox perspective and provided an overview of the key paradoxical tensions at the organisation level, and of those which are of particular relevance to sustainable HRM. It then considered approaches for dealing with paradoxical challenges through *acceptance* and *resolution* strategies.

References

Aust, I., Brandl, J. & Keegan, A. (2015). State-of-the-art and future directions for HRM from a paradox perspective: Introduction to the special issue. *German Journal of Human Resource Management, 29*(3–4), 194–213.

Battilana, J. & Dorado, S. (2010). Building sustainable hybrid organizations: The case of commercial microfinance organizations. *Academy of Management Journal, 53*(6), 1419–40.

Benn, S., Dunphy, D. & Griffiths, A. (2014). *Organizational Change for Corporate Sustainability.* Abingdon: Routledge.

Biglan, A. (2009). The role of advocacy organizations in reducing negative externalities. *Journal of Organizational Behavior Management, 29*(3–4), 215–30.

Boudreau, J. W. & Ramstad, P. M. (2005). Talentship, talent segmentation, and sustainability: A new HR decision science paradigm for a new strategy definition. *Human Resource Management, 44*(2), 129–36.

Bratton, J. & Gold, J. (2017). *Human Resource Management* (6th edn). Basingstoke: Palgrave Macmillan.

Burns, G. W. (2014). Gross national happiness: A case example of a Himalayan Kingdom's attempt to build a positive nation. In: H. Águeda Marujo & L. Neto (eds) *Positive Nations and Communities: Cross-Cultural Advancements in Positive Psychology* (Vol. 6, pp. 173–91). Dordrecht: Springer.

Cameron, K. S. (1986). Effectiveness as paradox: Consensus and conflict in conceptions of organizational effectiveness. *Management Science, 32*(5), 539–53.

Child, J. & McGrath, R. G. (2001). Organizations unfettered: Organizational form in an information-intensive economy. *Academy of Management Journal, 44*(6), 1135–48.

Christofi, A., Christofi, P. & Sisaye, S. (2012). Corporate sustainability: Historical development and reporting practices. *Management Research Review, 35*(2) 2012, 157–72.

CIPD (Chartered Institute of Personnel and Development). (2014). *Megatrends: The Trends Shaping Work and Working Lives: Are We Working Harder Than Ever?.* London: CIPD.

Clarke, M. (ed.) (2011). *Readings in HRM and Sustainability.* Prahran: Tilde University Press.

Colbert, B. A. & Kurucz, E. C. (2007). Three conceptions of triple bottom line business sustainability and the role for HRM. *Human Resource Planning, 30*(1), 21.

Dart, R. (2004). The legitimacy of social enterprise. *Non-Profit Management and Leadership, 14*(4), 411–24.

Dawson, P. & Zanko, M. (2011). Social innovation at work: Sustainable OHS in HRM. In: M. Clarke (ed.) *Readings in HRM and Sustainability* (pp. 83–100). Prahran: Tilde University Press.

Docherty, P., Kira, M. & Shani, A. B. (eds) (2009). *Creating Sustainable Work Systems.* Abingdon: Routledge.

Doppelt, B. (2010). *Leading Change Toward Sustainability: A Change-Management Guide for Business, Government and Civil Society.* Sheffield: Greenleaf Publishing.

Dyllick, T. & Hockerts, K. (2002). Beyond the business case for corporate sustainability. *Business Strategy and the Environment, 11*(2), 130–41.

Ehnert, I. (2009). *Sustainable Human Resource Management: A Conceptual and Exploratory Analysis from A Paradox Perspective.* Heidelberg: Physica-Verlag.

Ehnert, I. & Harry, W. (2012). Recent developments and future prospects on sustainable HRM. *Management Review, 23*(3), 221–38.

Elkington, J. (1999). *Cannibals with Forks: The Triple Bottom Line of 21st Century Business.* Oxford: Capstone Publishing.

Evans, P. A. (1999). HRM on the edge: A duality perspective. *Organization, 6*(2), 325–38.

Fleurbaey, M. (2015). On sustainability and social welfare. *Journal of Environmental Economics and Management, 71*(34–53).

Gao, J. & Bansal, P. (2013). Instrumental and integrative logics in business sustainability. *Journal of Business Ethics, 112*(2), 241–55.

Garavan, T. N. & McGuire, D. (2010). Human resource development and society: Human resource development's role in embedding corporate social responsibility, sustainability, and ethics in organizations. *Advances in Developing Human Resources, 12*(5), 487–507.

Gray, R., Adams, C. & Owen, D. (2014). *Accountability, Social Responsibility and Sustainability: Accounting for Society and the Environment.* London: Pearson Higher Ed.

Greenwood, M. R. (2002). Ethics and HRM: A review and conceptual analysis. *Journal of Business Ethics, 36*(3), 199–214.

Grieves, J. (2010). *Organizational Change: Themes and Issues.* Oxford: Oxford University Press.

Guerci, M. & Carollo, L. (2016). A paradox view on green human resource management: Insights from the Italian context. *The International Journal of Human Resource Management, 27*(2), 212–38.

Hahn, T., Pinkse, J., Preuss, L. & Figge, F. (2015). Tensions in corporate sustainability: Towards an integrative framework. *Journal of Business Ethics, 127*(2), 297–316.

Hahn, T., Figge, F., Pinkse, J. & Preuss, L. (2017). A paradox perspective on corporate sustainability: Descriptive, instrumental, and normative aspects. *Journal of Business Ethics,* 1–14.

Haigh, N. & Hoffman, A. J. (2012). Hybrid organizations: The next chapter of sustainable business. *Organizational Dynamics, 41*(2), 126–34.

Handy, C. (1994). *The Age of Paradox.* Cambridge, MA: Harvard Business School Press.

Jackson, K. (2012). An essay on sustainable work systems: Shaping an agenda for future research. *Management Revue, 23*(3), 296–309.

Jones, G. (ed.) (2011). *Current Research in Sustainability.* Prahran: Tilde University Press.

Kirsch, C. (2011). Systems theory and organisational change for a sustainable future. In: G. Jones (ed.) *Current Research in Sustainability.* Prahran: Tilde University Press.

Kleiner, S. & Pavalko, E. K. (2014). Double time: Is health affected by a spouse's time at work?. *Social Forces, 92*(3), 983–1007.

Kramar, R. (2011). Human resources: An integral part of sustainability. In: G. Jones (ed.) *Current Research in Sustainability*. Prahran: Tilde University Press.

Kramar, R. (2013). Beyond strategic human resource management: Is sustainable human resource management the next approach?. *The International Journal of Human Resource Management, 25*(8), 1069–89.

Kramar, R. & Syed, J. (2012). *Human Resource Management in a Global Context: A Critical Approach*. London: Palgrave Macmillan.

Laasch, O. & Conaway, R. N. (2015). *Principles of Responsible Management: Global Sustainability, Responsibility, and Ethics*. Stamford, CT: Cengage.

Legge, K. (1978). *Power, Innovation, and Problem-Solving in Personnel Management*. London: MacGraw-Hill.

Lewis, M. W. (2000). Exploring paradox: Toward a more comprehensive guide. *Academy of Management review, 25*(4), 760–76.

Majed, H., (2014). *Overcoming the Engagement Barrier: 2degrees Sustainable Business Trends Tracker Executive Summary*. Oxford: 2degrees Network.

Mariappanadar, S. (2012). Harm of efficiency oriented HRM practices on stakeholders: An ethical issue for sustainability. *Society and Business Review, 7*(2), 168–84.

Mariappanadar, S. (2014). Stakeholder harm index: A framework to review work intensification from the critical HRM perspective. *Human Resource Management Review, 24*(4), 313–29.

Marshall, J. D. & Toffel, M. W. (2005). Framing the elusive concept of sustainability: A sustainability hierarchy. *Environmental Science and Technology, 39*(3), 673–82.

Norman, W. & MacDonald, C. (2003). Getting to the bottom of the 'triple bottom line'. *Business Ethics Quarterly, 14*(2), pp. 243–62.

Parkin Hughes, C., Semeijn, J. & Caniëls, M. (2017). The sustainability skew. *Current Opinion in Environmental Sustainability, 28*, pp. 58–63.

Perey, R. (2015). Making sense of sustainability through an individual interview narrative. *Culture and Organization, 21*(2), 147–73.

Pfeffer, J. (2010). Building sustainable organisations: The human factor. *Academy of Management Perspectives, 24*(1), 34–45.

Pfeffer, J., & Jeffrey, P. (1998). *The Human Equation: Building Profits by Putting People First*. Harvard, MA: Harvard Business Press.

Poole, M. S. & Van de Ven, A. H. (1989). Using paradox to build management and organization theories. *Academy of Management Review, 14*(4), 562–78.

Probst, G. & Raisch, S. (2005). Organizational crisis: The logic of failure. *The Academy of Management Executive, 19*(1), 90–105.

Rappaport, A. (2005). The economics of short-term performance obsession. *Financial Analysts Journal, 61*(3), 65–79.

Redman, T. & Wilkinson, A. (2009). *Contemporary Human Resource Management: Texts and Cases*. Essex: Prentice-Hall.

Schad, J., Lewis, M. W., Raisch, S. & Smith, W. K. (2016). Paradox research in management science: Looking back to move forward. *Academy of Management Annals*, *10*(1), 5–64.

Smith, W. K. & Lewis, M. W. (2011). Toward a theory of paradox: A dynamic equilibrium model of organizing. *Academy of Management Review*, *36*(2), 381–403.

Smith, W. K. & Tushman, M. L. (2005). Managing strategic contradictions: A top management model for managing innovation streams. *Organization Science*, *16*(5), 522–36.

Starkey, K. & Tempest, S. (2008). A clear sense of purpose? The evolving role of the business school. *Journal of Management Development*, *27*(4), 379–90.

Van der Byl, C. A. & Slawinski, N. (2015). Embracing tensions in corporate sustainability: A review of research from win-wins and trade-offs to paradoxes and beyond. *Organization and Environment*, *28*(1), 54–79.

Vaughan, E. (1994). The trial between sense and sentiment: A reflection on the language of HRM. *Journal of General Management*, *19*(3), 20–32.

Voegtlin, C. & Greenwood, M. (2016). Corporate social responsibility and human resource management: A systematic review and conceptual analysis. *Human Resource Management Review*, *26*(3), 181–97.

WCED (World Commission on Environment and Development). (1987). *Our common future*. Oxford: Oxford University Press.

Weick, K. E. (1995). *Sensemaking in Organizations*. London: Sage Publications.

Wilmott, H. (1993). Strength is ignorance; Slavery is freedom: Managing culture in modern organizations. *Journal of Management Studies*, *30*(4), 515–53.

Zink, K. (2014). Social Sustainability and Quality of Working Life. In: I. Ehnert, H. Wes & K. Zink (eds) *Sustainability and Human Resource Management: Developing Sustainable Business Organisations*. Berlin: Springer.

part III

Developing Values and Strategies for Sustainable HRM

4

Sustainable HRM practices: Values and characteristics

Sugumar Mariappanadar

4.1 Introduction

An integrated sustainable HRM system model is depicted in Figure 4.1 to achieve the learning objectives of this chapter. An integrated sustainable HR system is explained as one in which HRM practices are holistically interdependent and connected with business (i.e. business strategy) and organisational design contexts to achieve competitive advantage for an organisation (Von Glinow et al., 1983). Subsequently, the business strategy influences in shaping organisational design, sustainable HRM strategies and the characteristics of sustainable HRM practices to achieve the synthesis effects of HR practices. The synthesis effects of sustainable HRM practices have been explained as an organisation's attempts to maximise performance by using HR practices while reducing negative impacts on stakeholders (i.e. employees, society's sustainable environmental management expectations etc.) as well as facilitating future HR regeneration (Ehnert, 2009; Mariappanadar & Kramar, 2014; Mariappanadar, 2014a).

Organisational value systems shape individual employees' reactions to work. As sustainable HRM is an institutional-level theory, it is important to develop organisational value systems that promote sustainable HRM systems and characteristics of sustainable HRM practices. These will subsequently have impact on employees' attitudes and behaviours to achieve sustainable outcomes for all stakeholders involved. Furthermore, Vandenberghe and Peiro (1999) have indicated that the organisational values not only have impact on existing employees' reactions to work but also on the new and prospective employees to achieve sustainable outcomes. Hence, in the integrated sustainable HRM system model (Figure 4.1) it is indicated that sustainable

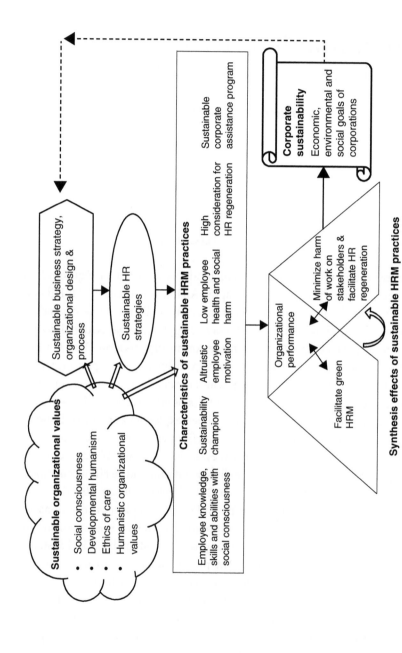

Sustainable organizational values

- Social consciousness
- Developmental humanism
- Ethics of care
- Humanistic organizational values

Sustainable business strategy, organizational design & process

Sustainable HR strategies

Characteristics of sustainable HRM practices

| Employee knowledge, skills and abilities with social consciousness | Sustainability champion | Altruistic employee motivation | Low employee health and social harm | High consideration for HR regeneration | Sustainable corporate assistance program |

Organizational performance

Facilitate green HRM

Minimize harm of work on stakeholders & facilitate HR regeneration

Synthesis effects of sustainable HRM practices

Corporate sustainability
Economic, environmental and social goals of corporations

Figure 4.1 An integrated model of sustainable HRM system

organisational values have important roles in influencing and shaping business strategies, organisational design, sustainable HRM strategies and the characteristics of sustainable HRM practices for organisations to achieve corporate sustainability through the synthesis effects of HRM practices. The parts of the integrated model are discussed next.

4.2 Organisational values for sustainable HRM

The core values of strategic HRM are to align organisations' HRM practices to strategies, industry or the developmental stage of an organisation to achieve increased financial outcomes for shareholders. However, Colakoglu et al. (2006) have highlighted that organisations that do well on financial performance metrics may not be doing equally well on other types of natural environmental and social metrics that focus on other stakeholders. For example, efficiency and cost-cutting measures may prove to be beneficial for shareholders and customers (if the low cost is reflected in the price of goods and services), but employees might have to work longer for the increased efficiency. This transfer of price to employees and their families as stakeholders due to increased organisational efficiency for cost-cutting measures is also explained as negative externality of HRM practices (Mariappanadar, 2012b; Mariappanadar, 2014a). Hence, the need to identify and develop organisational values that promote sustainable HRM from the multiple-stakeholders perspective is paramount for corporate sustainability as well as for a sustainable society. Corporate sustainability is about the management approaches used by organisations in achieving the three pillars (i.e. economic/financial, human/social and natural environmental outcomes) of sustainable development (UN Global Compact, 2014). That is, if an organisation is keen to achieve corporate sustainability outcomes based on the three pillars of sustainable development then the HRM strategy will be integrated to achieve human/social and natural environmental outcomes for stakeholders along with economic outcomes for shareholders.

It is believed that a combination of utilitarian instrumentalism of HRM and developmental humanism as organisational values facilitate HRM practices to achieve the synthesis effects of HRM practices (Mariappanadar, 2003). Organisational value such as developmental humanism, without disregarding the importance of utilitarian instrumentalism of strategic HRM management, is likely to yield better economic performance for organisations by stressing the significance of employee development, learning and commitment, along with stakeholders' well-being (Mariappanadar, 2003; Ehnert, 2009; Kira & Lifvergren, 2014). Furthermore, social consciousness, altruistic employee motivation, pro-social value orientation in decision making, ethics of care for stakeholders for reduced harm of work on employees, high consideration for HR regeneration and humanistic organisational value for workplace wellness and workers' wellness are some of most recent organisational values indicated in the sustainable HRM literature. Table 4.1 shows the

Table 4.1   Definitions of sustainable organisational values

Sustainable organisational value	Definition
Social consciousness	The highest level of organisational consciousness that focuses on systems, policies and practices to include the characteristics of care, compassion and altruism in HR practices (Chiva, 2014).
Ethics of care	In the HRM context this refers to the ethical choices organisations face when seeking to maximise profit as well as reduce the harmful aspects of HRM practices on the stakeholders, such as employees, their families and communities, so as to maintain harmonious relations between the employer involved and the stakeholders (Mariappanadar, 2012a).
Utilitarian instrumentalism	Emphasises the quantitative and calculative business strategic aspects of managing HR, just as rationally as any other factor of production (Mariappanadar, 2003).
Developmental humanism	This is about not disregarding the importance of strategic HR management, perceiving employees as an asset and stressing the significance of their development, learning and commitment to yield better economic performance as well as satisfied staff (Mariappanadar, 2003).
Humanistic organisational values	Emphasises the possibilities of integrating humanistic values with general moral principles such as employee well-being and employee personal growth with strategic management goals such as maximum productivity and long-range economic rationality (Alvesson, 1982).
Altruistic employee motivation	Witnessing another person in need may elicit empathic concern (e.g. sympathy, compassion) and that produces an altruistic motivation to reduce the distress of the person in need (Dovidio et al., 1990).
Pro-social value orientation	Pro-socials, compared to employees who are individualists and competitors, provide greater positive weight and equality to others' outcomes, exhibit greater reciprocity with others depending on the degree of co-operation, and are strongly inclined to exhibit the same level of co-operation as they expect from others (Van Lange, 1999).

definitions of these sustainable organisational values. These are the organisational values that shape sustainable business strategy, organisational design, sustainable HRM strategies and characteristics of sustainable HRM practices that are discussed in the integrated sustainable HRM system model. Before progressing to explain the characteristics of the integrated sustainable HRM system it will be useful to highlight the characteristics of mainstream HRM which include strategic HRM practices and critical HRM. This will facilitate our understanding of how the characteristics of sustainable HRM based on the organisational values that are discussed in this section will extend the mainstream and critical HRM practices.

4.3 Characteristics of control and strategic HRM systems

Greenwood (2002) highlighted that mainstream HRM (i.e. control and strategic HRM systems) is dominantly advocated by the US-based researchers and it focuses on individualistic enterprise ideology with the strategic focus of HRM, unitarists (mutual benefits), highly prescriptive, practitioner-oriented and reinforces power inequities. Finally, HRM as a valuable tool is developed and used based on empirical investigation. However, critical HRM originated dominantly from the UK and continental Europe and it highlights that HRM is rhetorical and HRM is used as a tool to manipulate and control employees and stakeholders to achieve the needs of organisations, and it is pluralist (i.e. employees, stakeholders and organisations have different purposes and goals).

4.3.1 Ethical issues of control and strategic HRM systems

The critical HRM perspective highlights the ethical deficiency of control (i.e. Taylorist perspective of management) and strategic HRM systems. The control HRM system is about authoritarian and hierarchical organisation which is developed based on Taylorist ideas to improve efficiency and reduce labour costs for achieving competitive advantage. The Taylorist perspective of the control system is characterised by relying on past categories, acting on automatic pilot, precluding attention to new information and tends to lead to mechanically employing cognitively and emotionally rigid, rule-based behaviours for managing efficiency. However, the strategic HRM system is based on commitment or self-actualisation, intrinsic motivation, shaping high performance employee behaviours and attitudes by aligning psychological links between organisational and employee goals, developing employee competencies with enriched work contents and participative management to achieve economic performance of an organisation.

It was suggested that to improve the ethical credentials of control and strategic HRM practices, organisations must treat individuals with 'respect' and do not have the right to interfere with individual employee 'freedom'. Treating employees with respect includes the rights of an employee such as the right to freedom, the right to well-being and the right to equality (Rowan, 2000). The right to freedom includes not only negative freedom, such as the right to not be physically restrained, but also positive freedom such as the right to not be coerced or hindered by the effect of external forces such as work practices that impede employees' personal, health and social aspects of quality of life. The right to well-being can be understood as the right of individuals to pursue their own interests and goals and organisations must also recognise individual's interests. Finally, right to equality implies that everyone has rights to freedom and well-being equally.

4.3.2 Developments in control and strategic HRM systems to address ethical issues

The mainstream HRM resorted to considering CSR as an initiative to address the ethical issues raised by critical HRM (Preuss et al., 2009), at the same time forestalling the efforts of employees for organised labour (i.e. trade unions). CSR is defined as actions that appear to further some human/social good, beyond the interests of the organisation and that is required by law (McWilliams & Siegel, 2001, p. 117). Others define CSR as being of a voluntary nature and it is not an altruistic activity but it can be strategic for an organisation so that CSR can be a business case for the organisation (Porter & Kramer, 2002; Vogel, 2005; Husted & de Jesus Salazar, 2006). Jamali and colleagues (2015) have indicated that CSR is about understanding how organisations interpret and translate CSR principles into managerial actions and practices through the systematic leveraging of organisational resources, including human resources practices.

Apart from CSR, when organisations' HRM practices are strategically driven by the internal referenced efficiency (i.e. profits) they can disregard ethics of care (Mariappanadar, 2012a). The ethics of care in the HRM context refer to the ethical choices organisations face when seeking to maximise profit as well as reduce the harmful aspects of HRM practices on the stakeholders, such as employees, their families, and society's sustainable environmental management expectations, so as to maintain harmonious relations between the employer involved and the stakeholders. Hence, it is evident that organisational values that promote CSR and ethics of care through sustainable HRM have highlighted organisations' interests in considering multiple stakeholders in managerial actions and practices to achieve corporate sustainability. Sustainable HRM has evolved as a discipline within the HRM field to address the ethical and stakeholder issues.

Table 4.2 shows the comparison of the characteristics of HRM systems between the control HRM system, the strategic HRM system (Arthur, 1994; Chiva, 2014) and the sustainable HRM system. The comparison attempts to indicate how the strategic HRM system, which is characterised as high performance work practices (Arthur & Boyles, 2007), can be shaped to become a sustainable HRM system using the indicated organisational values and characteristics. The characteristics of a sustainable HRM system are depicted under three parameters, which are business strategy, organisational design and HRM practices. These unique characteristics facilitate HR professionals to diagnose the type of HRM system they are currently operating in (Von Glinow et al., 1983; Rodriguez & Ventura, 2003) so as to shape or develop a sustainable HRM system. Next, the organisational values that shape each of the parts in the integrated sustainable HRM system are discussed.

4.4 Characteristics of business strategy for sustainable development

Lengnick-Hall and colleagues (2009), in their review of strategic HRM literature, have indicated that there is increased emphasis on the moderated effect of business strategy on the relationship between HPWPs and competitive performance. Arthur (1994) found that different companies in the US steel minimills have used control HRM systems to achieve cost reductions and other companies have adopted strategic HRM systems to achieve differentiation as a strategic business objective for competitive advantage. However, for an organisation to embrace sustainable development as part of their strategic objective they must increase the social consciousness of the organisation. The social consciousness of an organisation explains the connections between employer–employee and organisation–stakeholder (Pandey & Gupta, 2008). Furthermore, in this level of consciousness an organisation values human/ social wealth, aims to make partnerships with different stakeholders and defines success based on human/social wealth and satisfying expectations of different stakeholders. Therefore, an organisation with sustainable development as a strategic business objective will be a socially conscious organisation

Table 4.2 Characteristics of control, strategic and sustainable HRM systems

Criteria for HRM system	Characteristics of Control HRM system	Characteristics of strategic HRM system	Characteristics of Sustainable HRM system
Business strategy			
Strategic business objective	Cost reduction for competitive advantage	Differentiation for competitive advantage	Competitive advantage through sustainable development
Organisational design and process			
Human-based system	Organisation centred	Person and organisation centred	Organisation, employee and stakeholder centred
Structural complexity	Simple system	Highly complex system (integration and differentiation)	Highly complex system (integration and differentiation)
Process	A reactive system	Developmental orientation	A self-reflective system
Boundary	A reactive strategic linkage (a closed system)	A proactive linkage (a partially open system)	Direct environmental sensitivity (an open system)
Characteristics of HRM practices			
HRM attributes instrumental in improving organisational performance			
Employee competencies (Knowledge, skills and abilities – KSA)	Align employee competencies with those of an organisation (a clan system) in selection, training	Employee competencies are aligned with organisational and employee interests for mutual benefits in selection, performance appraisal, training and retaining	Employee competencies with social consciousness will align with mutual interest of employees, organisation and stakeholders in selection, performance appraisal, training and retaining

Employee motivation	Extrinsic motivation	Intrinsic and extrinsic motivation	Individual and altruistic motivation
Employee participation – employee empowerment	Employee empowerment is low due to high work standardisation	Organisational citizenship	Sustainability champion

HRM attributes of negative side effects of work while improving organisational performance

Health and social harm of work	High level of health and social harm of work on employees and their families	High level of health and social harm of work on employees and their families	Low level of health and social harm of work on employees and their families
Future supply of skilled HR	Low consideration for HR regeneration	Low consideration for HR regeneration	High consideration for HR regeneration globally
Employer sponsored support services for employees	Employee assistance programme for individual employees to cope with the consequences of work-related stress	Employee assistance programme for worker wellness to facilitate employees to cope with work-related stress and improve organisational outcomes	Sustainable corporate assistance programme – achieving workplace wellness along with worker wellness

HRM attributes for reducing ecology footprint of business by environmental management system (EMS)

The alignment of HRM orientation to management of environmental issues related to an organisation's economic activities	Control and dominate natural world to achieve ever-greater progress	Egocentric oriented action to optimise and exploit the social and natural environment for competitive advantage of an organisation	Pro-environmental oriented action to maintain and preserve the health of the ecosystem by reducing ecological footprint

with the characteristics of the utilitarian notion of profitability to improve market share of the firm as well as satisfy the utilitarian expectations of different stakeholders (see Table 4.2).

For example, Banco do Brasil (Bank of Brazil) indicated in their annual report (2012) that the bank has continuous dialogue with their stakeholders and uses market studies and reports to indicate trends in the bank's sustainability performance. The trends are provided to the bank Board to use the sustainability performance as a context for their business strategy. The example clearly indicates that Banco do Brasil is a socially conscious organisation which uses sustainable development as a context for their business strategies to gain competitive advantage as well as satisfy the utilitarian expectations of the company's stakeholders. Furthermore, the sustainable development (socio-environment) credibility of the bank is evidenced by its acceptance of the listing in the New York Stock Exchange DSJI.

4.5 Organisational design and process characteristics of sustainable HRM

The characteristics of organisational design along with business strategy shape the characteristics of HRM practices of an integrated HRM system perspective (Von Glinow et al., 1983). Therefore, organisational design must also have sustainability characteristics for it to subsequently shape sustainable HRM strategies and practices (see Table 4.2). The characteristics of organisational design of a sustainable HRM system are based on the human–based system, organisational structure, process and boundary (Von Glinow et al., 1983). The characteristics of the human-based system are expected to be centred on an organisation, employees and stakeholders. That is, the organisational design of a sustainable HRM system should be not only concerned about employers' expectations of employees meeting organisational goals but also be considerate of an individual employee's needs as well as stakeholders' expectations (e.g. labour unions, civil societies). The organisational structure characteristics of sustainability-based organisational design is expected to be complex because the degree of differences between parts/functions within a system is expected to be high as well as these parts of the system must be integrated by formal and informal connectivity. For example, the formal connectivity in a sustainable HRM structure can be established by completing a job analysis to identify the sustainable characteristics for employee competencies for a position and using those sustainable employee competencies characteristics (e.g. social consciousness) in the employee recruitment and selection processes. Furthermore, differentiation in sustainable organisational structure indicates if sustainable HRM specialists become part of the CSR department within the corporate business structure or part of the HRM as a functional department. Hence, it is important to understand the complexity of organisational structure by identifying the weak links due to organisational structure differentiation in an organisation and attempts to integrate the organisational structure using both formal and informal connectivity and consistency to promote a sustainable organisational structure.

The process characteristic of sustainability-based organisational design has to be self-reflexive or self-regulated based on the feedback obtained on sustainable development performance so as to alter the organisational strategies, goals and objectives without any external institutional pressures such as government and interest groups (Mariappanadar, 2014b). Finally, the boundary characteristic of organisation design of a sustainable HRM system is highly sensitive to external business environment, including changes to sustainable development indicators (e.g. GRI for sustainability indicators). Direct environment sensitivity is about the extent to which a HRM system scans and responds to external pressures, such as changes in governmental regulations, UN Global Compact initiatives and GRI for sustainability guidelines.

4.6 Sustainable HRM strategies

HRM strategies have two fundamental priorities for businesses (Boxall, 1998). The first priority is for an organisation to secure and manage the kind of HR that is necessary for organisational performance. The second priority is about how to develop HR for an organisation to achieve competitive advantage. Furthermore, HRM strategies are developed based on the organisational values of top level managers (Schuler, 1989). That is, the organisational values of achieving financial benefits for shareholders through improved organisational performance will facilitate organisations to develop strategic HRM strategies. Similarly, it is important to highlight the organisational values that facilitate development of sustainable HRM strategies. The dominant organisational values that are appropriate for the functional, capability and results oriented sustainable HRM are discussed next.

4.6.1 Functional sustainable HRM strategy

The functional HRM strategy is about the HRM process that is related to the functions of the HRM department that deals with specific issues relating to training, compensation functions and so on, to increase performance and pro-ductivity so that new and better HRM functions are developed to tackle similar issues in the future (Gubman, 2004). Hence, the functional sustainable HRM strat-egy is about developing specialist sustainable HR professionals within an HRM department or an organisation with knowledge about the values of sustainable HRM strategies as well as the characteristics of sustainable HRM practices for shaping sustainable HRM functions (i.e. recruitment, selection, performance appraisal, etc.). The sustainable HRM specialist will in turn facilitate line manag-ers in achieving the synthesis effects of HRM strategies using sustainable HRM functions. Hence, the functional sustainable HRM strategy specialist will be involved, along with other line managers, in designing HRM practices with sus-tainable HRM values to facilitate corporations to improve economic/financial, human/social and natural environmental outcomes of corporate sustainability.

4.6.2 Capability oriented sustainable HRM strategy

The capability oriented sustainable HRM strategy focuses on attracting employee competencies and developing a strong organisational culture, which are based on organisational values such as social consciousness, altru-istic motivation, care for stakeholders and the awareness of obscured harm of work on employees. The capability oriented sustainable HRM strategies with these organisational values will create unique value propositions for organisations to improve competitive advantage. Hence, the capability ori-ented sustainable HRM strategy highlights the sustainable competencies that are required to attract, train and motivate employees and develop sustainable organisational culture to achieve corporate sustainability outcomes.

4.6.3 Results oriented sustainable HRM strategy

The results oriented sustainable HRM strategy has become more important in the field of HRM because sustainable development is the focus of many corpora-tions in the twenty-first century. The measures for the economic/financial and natural environmental impacts of an organisation in achieving organisational performance are well developed in the literature (e.g. ISO14001 is a measure used by organisations to reduce the negative environmental impacts of their business operations). However, currently, the human/social performance measure for sus-tainable development is based on just satisfying legal obligations (i.e. employment standards). For example, the Labour Practices and Decent Work indicators – LA7 of the GRI for sustainability disclosure report (2014) – includes measures on occupational disease rate, injury rate and number of fatalities which are the measures provided by organisations to employment regulatory bodies as legal obligations for employment standards. Hence, the results oriented sustainable

HRM strategies facilitate the values and the characteristics of sustainable HRM practices to be incorporated into the current HRM functions beyond the legal obligations so that the positive impacts of those sustainable HRM practices on the human/social aspect of sustainable development can be voluntary.

For example, ethics of care for stakeholders, utilitarian instrumentalism and developmental humanism are the important organisational values of results oriented sustainable HRM strategies that can be incorporated into HRM functions (i.e. employee recruitment, selection, performance appraisal, etc.) to achieve the synthesis effects of sustainable HRM practices. Furthermore, humanistic organisational value for the workplace facilitates the synthesis effects of results oriented sustainable HRM practices for reducing negative impacts on the stakeholders (i.e. employees, natural environment, etc.) while improving organisational performance which highlights a balanced measure for the economic/finanical, human/social and natural environmental aspects outcomes of corporate sustainability. Hence, the reduction in the negative impacts imposed on the stakeholders can be objectively measured and explicitly reported or disclosed to stakeholders to highlight the achievement of the integrated economic/financial, human/social and natural environmental corporate sustainability outcomes.

4.7 Characteristics of sustainable HRM practices

The characteristics of HRM practices are those that shape and elicit behaviours and attitudes of employees towards work and organisations (Martell & Carroll, 1995). Hence, the characteristics of sustainable HRM practices have the potential to shape HRM practices to achieve the synthesis effects of HRM practices for achieving the integrated corporate sustainability outcomes. The characteristics of sustainable HRM practices are an employee's perceived organisational motives that facilitate an employee's behaviour and attitudes to improve organisational performance along with organisational interventions to reduce the simultaneous negative impacts on the stakeholders (i.e. employees, families, society's sustainable environmental management expectations, etc.). The characteristics of sustainable HRM practices can be understood based on the three sets of attributes of HRM practices. These attributes facilitate employees' perceptions of the organisational motives underlying the HRM practices they experience so that employees exhibit desired work characteristics, such as attitudes and behaviours, to ultimately improve organisational performance (Nishii et al., 2008).

The three sets of attributes of HRM practices are related to the three aspects of the synthesis effects of sustainable HRM practices according to the definition provided earlier in this chapter. Those included HRM attributes are instrumental in improving organisational performance, the HRM attributes of the low simultaneous harm of work on employees and other stakeholders while improving organisational performance, and finally reduce the negative impacts on the ecological system. Employee behavioural and attitudinal characteristics that are discussed in each of the attributes of sustainable HRM practices will provide insight into how each of these characteristics can facilitate HRM functions (i.e. recruitment, selection, employee motivation, etc.) to achieve the synthesis effects of HRM practices (see Figure 4.1). Furthermore, in each of the attributes of sustainable HRM practices an attempt is also made to highlight how the characteristics of sustainable HRM practices extend the characteristics of strategic HRM practices.

4.7.1 HRM attributes that are instrumental in improving organisational performance

4.7.1.1 Characteristics of employee competencies for sustainable HRM practices

Table 4.2 shows that strategic HRM practices facilitate an employee's KSA and these are characteristics of employee performance which positively impact on organisational performance (Huselid, 1995; Delery & Shaw, 2001). The characteristics of strategic HRM practices were extended with the characteristics of sustainable HRM practices (see Table 4.2) that are relevant for employee selection, performance appraisal and employee training, which enhance employee competencies (KSA) using a high level of social consciousness. Social consciousness highlights the importance of increasing organisational performance by achieving equilibrium with market requirements and the human/social needs of the stakeholders (Pandey & Gupta, 2008). For example, HRM practices regarding employee selection must be able to identify prospective employees with values of compassion and dispassion for the stakeholders (ie. employees, society's sustainable environmental management expectations, etc.) in employment testing. Subsequently, the new employees must be trained to use compassion and dispassion while using their competencies (KSA) for achieving the mutual interests of market requirements for organisations as well as the human/social and natural environmental needs of the stakeholders.

4.7.1.2 Characteristics of employee motivation for sustainable HRM practices

The strategic HRM practices (see Table 4.2) use employee-centred intrinsic and extrinsic motivators as characteristics to shape employee motivation (Arthur, 1994). Furthermore, organisations entice employees to contribute more effort for high performance by using different HRM practices that facilitate rewards and recognitions (Rynes et al., 2004). However, Michaelson (2005) highlighted the unethical aspect of HRM practices that use process-based employee motivation to entice employees with rewards and recognitions forever stretching high performance expectations, as they ultimately have negative impacts on employee well-being. Hence, the characteristics for sustainable HRM practices must extend to facilitating employee-centred intrinsic and extrinsic motivators with altruism (see Table 4.2). Altruistic motivators (Dovidio et al., 1990) increase the welfare of employees along with stakeholders (i.e. spouse/partner, children, caring for parents, disability, supply chain and society's sustainable environmental management expectations). Hence, individual and altruistic motivations are the essential employee motivation characteristics that sustainable HRM practices must have to facilitate the synthesis effects of HRM practices.

4.7.1.3 Characteristics of employee empowerment for sustainable HRM practices

HPWPs as part of strategic HRM (see Table 4.2) are intended to increase employee empowerment with the purpose of improving organisational performance and productivity (Shih et al., 2013). Psychological empowerment facilitated by sustainable HRM practices will enhance employees' decision-making opportunities and perceived competence for not only achieving valued organisational goals but also by extending it to the stakeholders to become sustainability champions. A sustainability champion is an advocate for the sustainable development of an organisation characterised by the use of both individualistic and pro-social value orientation in their empowered decision-making role which achieves benefits for the organisation and the stakeholders. That is, a sustainability champion's empowered decision making facilitated by HRM practices is guided by alignment (co-operation) or maximisation of organisational and employee outcomes with that of others (i.e. stakeholders) and equality (i.e. minimisation of absolute differences between organisational, employee and other stakeholder outcomes). Hence, the sustainability champion's empowered decision-making capabilities facilitated by sustainable HRM practices will improve the alignment between organisational and human/social, environmental performances to satisfy stakeholders' expectations (see Table 4.2).

4.7.2 HRM attributes of negative side effects of work

4.7.2.1 Characteristics of low health and social harm of work for sustainable HRM practices

The unintended side effects of health harm and social harm of work caused by HRM practices (e.g. HPWPs) were included as the characteristics of HRM practices based on the critical HRM perspective of HPWPs (Godard, 2001;

Burchielli et al., 2008) and the harm of work perspective from sustainable HRM literature (Mariappanadar, 2012a; De Prins et al., 2014). The harm or negative effects of work practices in sustainable HRM highlight the 'reduced' or 'loss of' personal, social and work-related health well-being outcomes that are caused by work restrictions imposed by HPWPs. These obscured or reduced well-being outcomes caused by HPWPs lead to 'welfare loss' for employees and stakeholders (e.g. employees' family and supply chain HR) based on the negative externality or social costs of harm of HPWPs (Mariappanadar, 2013; Mishra et al., 2014). That is, the negative externality or the social costs for the harm of work imposed by HPWPs on the stakeholders cannot be avoided by organisations attempting to maximise profits while operating in a free market. However, organisations have the 'ethics of care' for stakeholders from the holistic corporate sustainability perspective (Mariappanadar, 2012a; Ehnert et al., 2015) to reduce or lower the social costs of the health and the social harm of work imposed on the stakeholders. Hence, the characteristics of low health and social harm of work as criteria are used for sustainable HRM practices. The health harm of work is about an employee's perception of the restrictions imposed by work practices on achieving positive health, the increased risks of negative psychological health and the increased side effects of work (Mariappanadar, 2016). The social harm of work refers to the perceived severity of work restrictions imposed on family activities and the prevalence of effects of social harm of work, which reduce social well-being outcomes for employees (Mariappanadar, 2015; Mariappanadar & Ehnert, 2018).

The health and the social harm of work caused by HRM practices (e.g. HPWPs) not only produce a welfare loss for employees and their families due to the restrictions imposed by work in achieving improved well-being outcomes, but the harm of work also has negative impacts on organisational productivity/performance. For example, studies found that the negative impacts of work lead to work-related illnesses which subsequently have work-related health consequences such as lost productivity due to absenteeism (Godet-Cayre et al., 2006) and presenteeism (Dewa et al., 2004). Hence, the characteristics of sustainable HRM practices highlight that practices for performance management, employee retention and lay-offs must be implemented to produce the lowest level of health and social harm of work for improved welfare gains for employees and their families as well as improved productivity gains for an organisation to achieve the synthesis effects of HRM practices.

4.7.2.2 Characteristics of a sustainable corporate assistance programme

The characteristics of a sustainable corporate assistance programme are to identify organisational sources which will achieve reduction in the harm of work and work stress using organisational change management and wellness programmes. The sustainable corporate assistance programme was developed based on the employee assistance programme (EAP) principles. The sustainable corporate assistance programme extends the principles of EAP by including assistance in changing the organisational-level work restrictions imposed on employees as sources of harm of work along with the assistance provided in coping with the high harm of work at an individual employee level. That is, a corporate assistance programme as an intervention is centred around both organisational and individual employee levels instead of EAP which primarily focuses on interventions to help individual employees to cope with the harm of work. For example, an evaluation study of EAP performance (Berridge et al., 1997) found that 73 per cent of the employees reported that the counselling provided by EAP enabled them to cope with the problem of stress caused by work practices but that the problem (i.e. work practices) at the organisational level remained unresolved or unchanged. Hence, the sustainable corporate assistance programme highlights the importance of achieving workplace wellness along with worker wellness (Csiernik, 1995) based on interventions that take into consideration the organisation–individual interface. Furthermore, the sustainable corporate assistance programme will help organisations to recast their organisational identity based on the evidence of duty of care for employees and the stakeholders (i.e. employees' family, supply chain, etc.) and humanitarian organisational initiatives.

4.7.2.3 Characteristics of regeneration of HR base for sustainable HRM practices

HRM practices that facilitate the regeneration of an HR base for future supply to organisations are considered as characteristics for sustainable HRM practices, which highlight the HRM–labour market relationship (Ehnert, 2009). That is, some HRM practices, such as HPWPs and extreme work conditions (Granter et al., 2015), will deplete the future supply of skilled HR for a company and an industry due to the harm of work imposed on current employees by market forces (i.e. hyper-competition). For example, Scales (2006) has indicated that skills shortages experienced in the resources sector are because employers pay high wages when commodity prices are high and then cut employee numbers 'to the bone' when commodity prices drop, forcing highly skilled workers to move to other industry sectors permanently. Hence, this market-based HRM practice depletes the future supply of skilled human resources for the resources industry. Ehnert (2009) indicates that similar HRM practices and the strategies of companies in an industry are influenced by isomorphic institutional pressures such as the similarities in HRM practices while increasing workload or retrenching employees in an industry. Hence, the sustainable HRM practices of an organisation must demonstrate a high level of consideration for the regeneration of the pool of human resources for future supply to industries by achieving a low level of harm of HRM practices. This will benefit an organisation as well as an industry by providing access to a highly skilled workforce in the future to improve organisational performance.

4.7.3 Characteristics of sustainable HRM for environmental management

The environmental management literature indicates that economic activities by organisations are the main source for environmental degradation from the anthropocentrism perspective, and hence organisations have ethical and moral responsibilities to address the natural environmental issues (refer to Chapter 5 for more details). Jackson and Seo (2010) chose to integrate environmental sustainability characteristics to strategic HRM (see Table 4.2) instead of considering reshaping the field of HRM. However, Purser and colleagues (1995) indicated that organisational science focusing on natural environmental management should defamiliarise the dominant anthropocentrism and reframe it with ecocentric-based environmental management approaches to become a pro-environmental oriented organisation.

For example, a study on EMS among international hotels in the Red Sea resort found that ecocentric organisational values such as natural environmental altruism explained the differences in environmental practices when external institutional (i.e. regulatory) pressures were absent (Dief & Leeds, 2012). Hence, the characteristics of sustainable HRM to manage environment effectively include utilisation and conservation of environmental resources, environment orientation (i.e. care and concerns for environment) and ecocentric (i.e. environmental altruism). Including these characteristics for reframing various functions of sustainable HRM practices (i.e. employee selection, etc.) will engage employees in EMS to preserve the health of the ecosystem, and subsequently enhance an organisation's reputation on environmental management as part of corporate sustainability.

4.8 Paradoxes or tensions between using strategic and sustainable HRM practices

This chapter has highlighted that there is compatibility between an organisation's economic oriented approach using strategic HRM practices and the synthesis effects-based sustainable HRM practices. However, an organisation's

Organizational values for strategic HRM practices	Tension experienced in sustainable HRM decision making	Organizational values for sustainable HRM practices
Economic rationality		Economic rationality with social legitimacy
Person and organization oriented system		Organization, employees and stakehoders oriented system
Developmental orientation of system processes		Self-reflective orientation of system processes
Benefits to organization and employees		Organization with social consciousness
Organizational citizenship		Sustainability champion
Harm imposed on employees and stakeholders		Achieving workplace wellness along with worker wellness
Low consideration for future supply of HR		High consideration for future supply of HR

Figure 4.2   Possible paradoxes created due to different organisational values between strategic and sustainable HRM practices in organisation decision making

deliberate use of sustainable HRM practices based on humanistic organisational value in a dynamic competitive business environment will be contingent on multiple resources that are made available to, or constrained to use by, managers. Hence, it is important to indicate the possible tensions in using sustainable organisational values in HRM practices compared to the values that facilitate strategic HRM practices. For example, an organisation operating in Australia, one of the high-wage countries, in a hyper-competitive global market, uses technology and high work intensification as factors to promote efficiency. These HPWPs from the strategic HRM perspective will also improve organisational performance but will also have negative impacts on employees and their family well-being.

In this example, the organisation may be aware of the negative impacts of HPWPs on employees and other stakeholders but the paradox or tension created in an organisation's decision to consider sustainable organisational value-based HRM practices over efficiency-based strategic HRM practices may have limited impact on the organisation's decision to use sustainable HRM practices. However, the information provided in this chapter about the sustainable organisational values creates the tension in organisational decision making so that the tension can lead to changes in management values from just an efficiency oriented approach to organisational performance with stakeholders' well-being along with long-range economic rationality. Figure 4.2 shows the possible paradoxes between organisational values in organisations' decisions to use strategic and/or sustainable HRM practices to achieve corporate sustainability. It will be useful to refer to Chapter 3 in this book for more details to develop coping strategies to overcome the decision-making tensions shown in Figure 4.2.

4.9 Conclusion

The aim of this chapter was to provide an overview of various organisational values that shape an integrated sustainable HRM system that includes the characteristics of sustainable business strategies, sustainable organisational design, sustainable HRM strategies and practices to gain a new insight into sustainable people management issues in business organisations. In this chapter, the key basic assumptions in prior research and practice on HRM and performance as well as strategic HRM were challenged initially. Subsequently, the values of sustainable HRM were proposed to develop an integrated sustainable HRM system that goes beyond the traditional HRM focus on financial performance to develop a HRM system to achieve the synthesis effects of HRM practices. The synthesis effects of sustainable HRM practices highlight that organisations attempting to improve financial performance also have corporate social responsibilities to reduce the simultaneous negative impacts imposed on the stakeholders (i.e. employees, society's sustainable environmental management expectations, etc.) and also facilitate future HR regeneration. An integrated sustainable HRM system with sustainable organisational values enables the field of HRM to progress in a new direction to achieve economic/financial, human/social and natural environmental outcomes of corporate sustainability.

References

Alvesson, M. (1982). The limits and shortcomings of humanistic organization theory. *Acta Sociologica, 25*(2), 117–31.

Arthur, J. B. (1994). Effects of human resource systems on manufacturing performance and turnover. *Academy of Management Journal, 37*(3), 670–87.

Arthur, J. B. & Boyles, T. (2007). Validating the human resource system structure: A levels-based strategic HRM approach. *Human Resource Management Review, 17*(1), 77–92.

Berridge, J., Cooper, C. & Highley-Marchington, C. (1997). *Employee Assistance Programmes and Workplace Counselling*. Chichester: John Wiley & Sons.

Boxall, P. (1998). Achieving competitive advantage through human resource strategy: Towards a theory of industry dynamics. *Human Resource Management Review, 8*(3), 265–88.

Burchielli, R., Bartram, T. & Thanacoody, R. (2008). Work-family balance or greedy organizations? *Relations Industrielles/Industrial Relations, 63*(1), 108–33.

Chiva, R. (2014). The common welfare human resource management system: A new proposal based on high consciousness. *Personnel Review, 43*(6), 937–56.

Colakoglu, S., Lepak, D. P. & Hong, Y. (2006). Measuring HRM effectiveness: Considering multiple stakeholders in a global context. *Human Resource Management Review, 16*(2), 209–18.

Csiernik, R. (1995). Wellness, work and employee assistance programming. *Employee Assistance Quarterly, 11*(2), 1–13.

De Prins, P., Beirendonck, L. V., De Vos, A. & Jesse, S.egers, J. (2014). Sustainable HRM: Bridging theory and practice through the 'Respect Openness Continuity (ROC) model'. *Management Revue, 25*(4), 263–84.

Delery, J. E. & Shaw, J. D. (2001). The strategic management of people in work organizations: Review, synthesis, and extension. In Ferris, G. R. (ed.), *Research in Personnel and Human Resources Management*(Vol. 20, pp. 165–97). Stamford: JAI Press.

Dewa, C., Lesage, A., Goering, P. & Caveen, M. (2004). Nature and prevalence of mental illness in the workplace. *Healthcare Papers, 5*(2), 12–25.

Dief, M. E. & Font, X. (2012). Determinants of environmental management in the Red Sea Hotels: Personal and organizational values and contextual variables. *Journal of Hospitality & Tourism Research, 36*(1), 115–37.

Dovidio, J. F., Allen, J. L. & Schroeder, D. A. (1990). Specificity of empathy-induced helping: Evidence for altruistic motivation. *Journal of Personality and Social Psychology, 59*(2), 249–60.

Ehnert, I. (2009). *Sustainable Human Resource Management: A Conceptual and Exploratory Analysis from a Paradox Perspective*. London: Springer.

Ehnert, I., Parsa, S., Roper, I., Wagner, M. & Müller-Camen, M. (2015). Reporting on sustainability and HRM: A comparative study of sustainability reporting practices by the world's largest companies. *International Journal of Human Resource Management, 27*(1), 88–108.

Global Reporting Initiatives (GRI) for Sustainability (2014). Reporting Guidelines https://www.globalreporting.org/standards/g4/Pages/default.aspx Accessed on 22 September 2015.

Godard, J. (2001). High performance and the transformation of work? The implications of alternative work practices for the experience and outcomes of work. *Industrial and Labor Relations Review, 54*, 776–805.

Godet-Cayre, V., Pelletier-Fleury, N., Le Vaillant, M., Dinet, J., Massuel, M. & Leger, D. (2006). Insomnia and absenteeism at work. Who pays the cost?. *Sleep-New York then Westchester-, 29*(2), 179–84.

Granter, E., McCann, L. & Boyle, M. (2015). Extreme work/normal work: Intensification, storytelling and hypermediation in the (re) construction of 'the New Normal'. *Organization, 22*(4), 443–56.

Greenwood, M. R. (2002). Ethics and HRM: A review and conceptual analysis. *Journal of Business Ethics, 36*(3), 261–78.

Gubman, E. (2004). HR strategy and planning: From birth to business results. *People and Strategy, 27*(1), 13–23.

Huselid, M. A. (1995). The impact of human resource management practices on turnover, productivity, and corporate financial performance. *Academy of Management Journal, 38*(3), 635–72.

Husted, B. W. & de Jesus Salazar, J. (2006). Taking Friedman seriously: Maximizing profits and social performance. *Journal of Management Studies, 43*(1), 75–91.

Jackson, S. E. & Seo, J. (2010). The greening of strategic HRM scholarship. *Organization Management Journal, 7*(4), 278–90.

Jamali, D. R., El Dirani, A. M. & Harwood, I. A. (2015). Exploring human resource management roles in corporate social responsibility: The CSR-HRM co-creation model. *Business Ethics: A European Review, 24*(2), 125–43.

Kira, M. & Lifvergren, S. (2014). Sowing seeds for sustainability in work systems. In: I. Ehnert, W. Harry & K. J. Zink (eds) *Sustainability and Human Resource Management*. Berlin, Heidelberg: Springer. (57–81)

Lengnick-Hall, M. L., Lengnick-Hall, C. A., Andrade, L. S. & Drake, B. (2009). Strategic human resource management: The evolution of the field. *Human Resource Management Review, 19*, 64–85.

McWilliams, A. & Siegel, D. (2001). Corporate social responsibility: A theory of the firm perspective. *Academy of Management Review, 26*(1), 117–27.

Mariappanadar, S. (2003). Sustainable human resource management: The sustainable and unsustainable dilemmas of downsizing. *International Journal of Social Economics, 30*(8), 906–23.

Mariappanadar, S. (2012a). Harm of efficiency oriented HRM practices on stakeholders: An ethical issue for sustainability. *Society and Business Review, 7*(2), 168–84.

Mariappanadar, S. (2012b). The harm indicators of negative externality of efficiency focused organizational practices. *International Journal of Social Economics, 39*(3), 209–20.

Mariappanadar, S. (2013). A conceptual framework for cost measures of harm of HRM practices. *Asia-Pacific Journal of Business Administration, 5*(2), 15–39.

Mariappanadar, S. (2014a). Stakeholder harm index: A framework to review work intensification from the critical HRM perspective. *Human Resource Management Review, 24*(4), 313–29.

Mariappanadar, S. (2014b). Sustainable HRM: A counter to minimize the externality of downsizing. In: I. Ehnert, W. Harr & K. J. Zink (eds), *Sustainability and Human Resource* Management (pp. 181–203). Berlin, Heidelberg: Springer.

Mariappanadar, S. (2015). The social harm of work: A critical aspect of work intensification on work-family balance. Paper presented at the 2nd International Sustainable HRM Workshop, Kaiserslautern, Germany, 3–5 June.

Mariappanadar, S. (2016). Health harm of work from the sustainable HRM perspective: Scale development and validation. *International Journal of Manpower, 37*(6), 924–44.

Mariappanadar, S. & Ehnert, A (2018). The dark side of overwork: An empirical evidence of social harm of work from a sustainable HRM perspective. *International Studies of Management and Organization, 47*, 372–87.

Mariappanadar, S. & Kramar, R. (2014). Sustainable HRM: The synthesis effect of high performance work systems on organisational performance and employee harm. *Asia-Pacific Journal of Business Administration, 6*(3), 206–24.

Martell, K. & Carroll, S. J. (1995). How strategic is HRM?. *Human Resource Management, 34*(2), 253–67.

Michaelson, C. (2005). Meaningful motivation for work motivation theory. *Academy of Management Review, 30*(2), 235–38.

Mishra, R. K., Sarkar, S. & Kiranmai, J. (2014). Green HRM: Innovative approach in Indian public enterprises. *World Review of Science, Technology and Sustainable Development, 11*(1), 26–42.

Nishii, L., Lepak, D. P. & Schneider B. (2008). Employee attributions of the "why" of HR practices: Their effects on employee attitudes and behaviors, and customer satisfaction. *Personnel Psychology, 61*(3), 503–45.

Pandey, A. & Gupta, R. K. (2008). A perspective of collective consciousness of business organizations. *Journal of Business Ethics, 80*(4), 889–98.

Porter, M. E. & Kramer, M. R. (2002). The competitive advantage of corporate philanthropy. *Harvard Business Review, 80*(12), 56–68.

Preuss, L., Haunschild, A. & Matten, D. (2009). The rise of CSR: Implications for HRM and employee representation. *The International Journal of Human Resource Management, 20*(4), 953–73.

Purser, R. E., Park, C., & Montuori, A. (1995). Limits to anthropocentrism: Toward an ecocentric organization paradigm?. *Academy of Management Review, 20*(4), 1053–89.

Rodríguez, J. M. & Ventura, J. (2003). Human resource management systems and organizational performance: An analysis of the Spanish manufacturing industry. *International Journal of Human Resource Management, 14*(7), 1206–26.

Rowan, J. R. (2000). The moral foundation of employee rights. *Journal of Business Ethics, 24*(4), 355–61.

Rynes, S. L., Gerhart, B. & Minette, K. A. (2004). The importance of pay in employee motivation: Discrepancies between what people say and what they do. *Human Resource Management, 43*(4), 381–94.

Scales, M. (2006). Two steps forward, one back. *Canadian Mining Journal, 127*(6), 5–5.

Schuler, R. S. (1989). Strategic human resource management and industrial relations. *Human Relations, 42*(2), 157–84.

Shih, H., Chiang, Y. & Hsu, C. (2013). High performance work system and HCN performance. *Journal of Business Research, 66*(4), 540–46.

UN Global Compact (2014). *Overview of the UN Global Compact.* http://nbis.org/nbisresources/sustainable_development_equity/un_global_compact.pdf. Accessed on 22 September 2015.

Vandenberghe, C. & Peiró, J. M. (1999). Organizational and individual values: Their main and combined effects on work attitudes and perceptions. *European Journal of Work and Organizational Psychology, 8*(4), 569–81.

Van Lange, P. A. (1999). The pursuit of joint outcomes and equality in outcomes: An integrative model of social value orientation. *Journal of Personality and Social Psychology, 77*(2), 337–49.

Vogel, D. J. (2005). Is there a market for virtue? The business case for corporate social responsibility. *California Management Review, 47*(4), 19–45.

Von Glinow, M. A., Driver, M. J., Brousseau, K. & Prince, J. B. (1983). The design of a career oriented human resource system. *Academy of Management Review, 8*(1), 23–32.

5

Sustainable HRM theories: Simultaneous benefits for organisations and stakeholders

Sugumar Mariappanadar

5.1 Introduction

Many HRM practices have evolved over a period of time from the humanistic perspective to exercise increasing control over workers' lives and it has negative effects on stakeholders (e.g. employees, their family and society's sustainable environmental management expectations) beyond organisations. Human resources should be managed sustainably so that, for example, employees can continue to make positive contributions to their families and the community while they are actively employed in an organisation. In the HRM literature it is common to find that most HRM practices, in particular some of the HPWPs, are driven by organisations' internally referenced efficiency focused approach (Mariappanadar, 2003). HPWPs aim to assure greater flexibility and motivation of employees, to increase the participation of employees in decision making, and to take advantage of their problem-solving and communication skills. These HPWPs are shaped by strategic and economic aspirations of organisations to achieve competitive advantage through employees (Pfeffer, 1998). However, the critical HRM perspective (e.g. Legge, 1995; Ramsay et al., 2000) suggests that the economic aspirations of organisations using HPWPs may also have negative impacts on well-being issues relating to stakeholders. Hence, in this chapter the negative impacts of HRM practices in particular HPWPs on stakeholders are explored to explain one of the aspects of sustainable HRM.

It is useful to understand the definition of 'stakeholder' and the types of stakeholder that are relevant for sustainable HRM because the stakeholder aspect is an important component of sustainable HRM. There are many definitions of 'stakeholder' in the literature but the one most commonly used indicates that a stakeholder is: 'any individual or group who can affect or is affected by actions, decisions, policies, practices or goals of an organization' (Freeman 1984, p. 25). Clarkson (1995) classified stakeholders as primary and secondary. The primary stakeholders are typically the shareholders and investors, employees, customers, suppliers, the governments and communities that provide infrastructures and markets, and together they facilitate the organisation's survival. The secondary stakeholder groups are those who influence or affect, or are influenced or affected by, the organisation, but they are not engaged in transactions with the organisation and are not essential for its survival. Using a stakeholder aspect as a component of sustainable HRM would foster a moral relationship between organisations and employees instead of a purely instrumental approach to HRM (Greenwood & De Cieri 2007). Furthermore, a stakeholder-oriented HRM system is crucial for understanding intended and unintended impacts, and their effects on stakeholder satisfaction.

Guerci and Shani (2013) included employees and community in the classification of 'dependent' and 'discretionary' stakeholder groups respectively. They found in their study that employees as a dependent stakeholder group is moderately salient for HRM. That is, employees tend to have legitimate and urgent expectations from the organisation but have limited power to influence the employer. Hence, for their needs to be satisfied, employees as a stakeholder group must rely on the advocacy of other powerful stakeholders (e.g. employment relations, socially responsible investment practices) or on the benevolence and voluntarism (CSR initiatives) of the firm's management. Furthermore, communities as discretionary stakeholders lack both power and urgent claims; there is absolutely no pressure on managers to enter into an active relationship with communities. However, managers may choose to do so only if their organisations have strong CSR policies and practices. Therefore, in this chapter on the negative externality of HRM practices and harm of work theories are explained to highlight the unsustainable negative impacts which can be identified early to reverse the negative impacts to prevent future irreversible health and social/family impacts on employees and their families. Early identification of harm of work for reversible health and social benefits for stakeholders (e.g. employees, their families etc.) reflects the benevolence of a firm's management or holistic CSR initiatives (Van Marrewijk, 2003) to benefit the society as a whole in which organisations are considered as a part of the society.

To understand sustainable HRM, initially the perspectives of simultaneous effects on organisational performance and employee well-being are explained in this chapter. Secondly, the negative externality of HRM practices as a theory of sustainable HRM is explained to understand the negative effects of HRM practices on the stakeholders (i.e. employees, their families and society). Thirdly, the theory of harm of work is explained using a framework of harm indicators for work. Finally, the synthesis effects of HRM theory explain the ethical role of organisations to minimise the negative impacts imposed on the stakeholders (i.e. employees and society's sustainable environmental management expectations) while maximising organisational performance.

5.2 Perspectives of simultaneous effects of HRM practices

The simultaneous effects of HRM indicated in the framework of sustainable HRM theories (Figure 5.1) highlight that strategic HRM practices, such as HPWPs, work intensification, overwork etc., used to enhance organisational performances also have positive or sustainable and negative or unsustainable impacts on employee well-being. There are three different perspectives of simultaneous effects of HRM; they are the mutual benefits perspective, the critical HRM perspective and the synthesis effects perspective. The mutual benefits perspective believes that high employee job satisfaction among employees is evidence of benefits to an organisation through higher financial performance, better labour productivity, increased quality and diminished absenteeism (Appelbaum et al., 2000; Guest 1997; Wood et al., 2012).

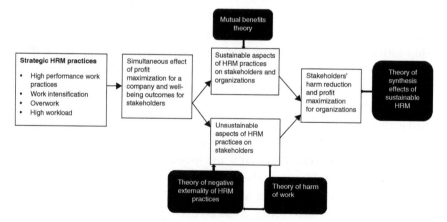

Figure 5.1 A framework of sustainable HRM theories from the harm of work and the synthesis effects perspectives

The critical HRM perspective (e.g. Legge, 1995; Ramsay et al., 2000) establishes that employers benefit most in terms of organisational performance from HPWPs, and that HPWPs are not beneficial or could even be harmful to employees in terms of their well-being. Furthermore, Van de Voorde and colleagues (2012) believe that HR practices that benefit employees' well-being might not be the ones that maximise organisational performance. Hence, organisations may need to make a trade-off in terms of which of the two outcomes to prioritise. That is, improved organisational performance is achieved at the cost of a reduced well-being outcome for employees.

The sustainable HRM focus extends beyond the mutual benefits and critical HRM perspectives, suggesting HRM practices should be designed to further organisational consideration of stakeholders' well-being outcomes while still achieving financial outcomes for organisations. That is, a third perspective, the 'synthesis effects' perspective regarding the simultaneous effects of HRM, has emerged in the sustainable HRM literature (refer to Figure 5.1). The synthesis effects perspective of HRM (Mariappanadar, 2014a) is where organisations must achieve financial outcomes using HRM while reducing the simultaneous harm of work imposed on the stakeholders (employees, their families and society's sustainable environmental management expectations). This third perspective adds value to the two earlier perspectives by suggesting that HRM practices are most likely to impose harm of work on employees (in terms of reducing personal, social and health well-being) while maximising organisational performances but attempts must be made at an institutional level to minimise this harm of work on employees. Hence, an institutional level intervention is required to minimise such harm of work created by HRM practices, and that is the focus of sustainable HRM. In this chapter the theory of negative externality of HRM and the harm of work theory (Figure 5.1) are discussed to gain insight into the reversible and irreversible harmful aspects of HRM practices on the stakeholders. Sustainability is explained in the field of health based on reversibility and irreversibility of biological systems for human performance (Toman, 2012). That is, health irreversibility indicates that the biological system has lost its capacity to return to normal level or original level of operation to enable normal human performances. However, reversibility is about recovery of employees' physical and mental states through normal rest and non–work-related experiences. The theory of synthesis effects of sustainable HRM (Figure 5.1) is used to indicate the importance for organisations to take steps to minimise the harm of work on stakeholders so as to naturally reverse negative health and social impacts on employees and their families while maximising organisational efficiency.

5.3 Theory of negative externality of HRM

Externality is an effect (intended or unintended) that, while it does not monetarily affect a company that causes the effect while producing goods and services, does harm the living standards of society as a whole. A standard definition of externality is, 'as being present when the actions of one agent directly affect the business environment of another agent, that is, the effect is not transmitted through prices' (Papandreou 1994, p. 5). The rationale for discussing externality is because organisations that use certain management practices, such as HPWPs, to internalise all their actions with respect to maximising employee productivity disregard the negative impacts it has on the well-being of the stakeholders (i.e. employees, their families and the community). Furthermore, there are social costs of negative impacts of those organisational practices imposed on or transferred by organisations to the stakeholders (employees, their families and the community) to pay for managing those negative impacts of work (Mariappanadar 2014a).

In this chapter externality is used as a market failure, which is 'any situation where some Paretian costs and benefits remain external to decentralized cost-revenue calculations in terms of prices' (Bator, 1958, p. 362). That is, a company has not been able to perceive or weigh up certain negative consequences of HPWPs on the stakeholders. The responsibility of the company is confined to its accountability to its shareholders and does not extend the boundaries beyond the shareholders to include the externality of such HPWPs on the stakeholders.

Positive and negative are the two types of externality. Positive externality is something that benefits society but the organisation as a producer of goods cannot maximise profit for shareholders. The negative externality is something that costs the organisation nothing for their practices, but it is costly for the stakeholders to manage negative impacts of those practices. Therefore, the theory of negative externality of HRM practices highlights an organisation's failure to assimilate the cost of negative impacts of HRM practices instead transferred to the stakeholders to manage the negative impacts (Mariappanadar, 2012b). The theory of negative externality is relevant for sustainable HRM because the theory helps to understand the social costs imposed on the stakeholders to manage negative impacts of certain HPWPs. Organisations can subsequently use this understanding of negative externality of HRM practices to reduce or minimise such negative impacts to improve well-being while increasing organisational performances. The opposite effect of externality is internalisation, that is, an organisation expands its boundary to include relevant stakeholders as part of the organisation to accommodate the social costs as part of the organisation's cost structure.

For example, one way of internalising the social costs of health issues of employees is by paying the 'private' health insurance premium of employees and their families where a country (e.g. Australia, Canada, the UK etc.) has a universal health care system run by the government. The 'private' health insurance premium provides the next higher level of health care cover for employees and their families which is over and above the universal health care system but it will reduce the use of stakeholders' tax monies for work-related health issues. However, by paying private health insurance premiums by organisations as an approach to internalise the negative impacts of work on stakeholders does not legitimise an organisation to continue to impose the harm of work on the stakeholders because the unsustainable organisational actions may lead to irreversible negative impacts on the stakeholders.

5.3.1 Attributes of negative externality of HRM practices

The attributes of negative externality facilitate the understanding of negative impacts of HRM practices on the stakeholders. The attributes of negative externality that are discussed here are based on the framework of negative externality of HRM practices proposed by Mariappanadar (2012b; 2014b). The attributes of negative externality of HRM practices are: (1) level of negative externality; (2) manifestation of negative externality; (3) impact of negative externality; and (4) avoidability of negative externality of HRM practices.

5.3.1.1 The attributes of level of negative externality

The level of negative externality of HRM practices is about employees' evaluation of high or low levels as dimensions of negative impacts on the stakeholders. For example, an employee, who appraises work intensification as having a low level of negative impacts on himself/herself before undertaking work activities, will show interest in being involved in those work activities with less anxiety and a greater sense of challenge and feeling of control in the situation (Gilbarco et al, 2010). Therefore, when employees, for example, perceive that work intensification through HPWPs has a low level of negative impacts then there is no conceivable psychological, social and health aspects of negative impacts on the stakeholders. However, the high level negative impact of work indicates the risk of irreversible work-related psychological and physical illnesses. For example, there is evidence in the literature that a high level of work intensity increases the chance of irreversible work-related illnesses among those working in managerial or professional roles (Burchell & Fagan,

2004). Deery and Jago (2008) also reported high work stress and strain caused irreversible psychosomatic disorders among the labour-intensive, low-paid service industry sectors such as the hospitality and tourism industries.

5.3.1.2 The attributes of manifestation of negative externality

There are two dimensions of manifestation attributes of negative externality of work – instantaneous and time-lagged – and they are based on the time perspective. The dimension of instantaneous negative externality of work refers to manifestation of negative impacts of certain HRM practices that impact on stakeholders within a short time frame (e.g. six months) after the introduction of those HRM practices. For example, the instantaneous manifestation attribute of negative externality of work not only has an immediate effect on the mood, arousal and behaviour of employees from the psychological aspect of negative impacts, but it can also have effects on relationships with family members, which is the social aspect of negative impacts. Furthermore, the instantaneous attribute of negative externality decreases the quality of interaction with the family members due to negative mood swings from acute work stress (Hoge, 2008). The long-term time frame of one to two years immediately after the introduction of particular HRM practices is used to understand the time lagged manifestation of negative impacts on the stakeholders. For example, employee depression and work-related psychosomatic disorders may be the time lagged manifestation of the negative externality of HRM practices. However, there is no clear evidence available in the literature to suggest that certain HRM practices may cause time lagged manifestation of harm of work, such as depression and psychosomatic disorders in employees.

5.3.1.3 The attributes of impact of negative externality

The impact attribute of negative externality of HRM practices includes temporary and enduring effects as two dimensions. The temporary dimension of the impact attribute of negative externality highlights minimal severity or reversibility of impact of HRM practices on the stakeholders which may result in no permanent or irreversible negative impacts. For example, employees with temporary work stress experience tend to use sick leave as a stress coping strategy to recuperate. Furthermore, it was also found in the literature that due to excessive demands at work, employees tend to increase presenteeism (Aronsson & Gustafsson, 2005) than avail sick leave. When an organisation is not supportive of distressed employees availing themselves of sick leave to recuperate, then it can result in increased severe or irreversible psychosomatic complaints, a higher rate of presenteeism and an increase in lost productive time (Stewart et al., 2003).

In contrast, the enduring dimension of the impact attribute of negative externality has a permanent or irreversible impact that causes greater discomfort, damage or distress to employees, their families and the community. For example, employees who experienced high work demands took their frustrations out on their spouse and children, and were also preoccupied with work issues. The price of this preoccupation or psychological attachment to work and work-related issues led to subsequent family-related issues such as loss of intimacy, companionship and shared recreational time in the family (Piotrkowski, 1979). These family issues may lead to marital separation and divorce, subsequently leaving an irreversible or permanent scar on employees', their spouses' and children's lives.

5.3.1.4 The attributes of avoidablity of negative externality

An avoidability attribute of negative externality explores negative impacts of HRM practices on the stakeholders due to avoidable or unavoidable internal or external environmental conditions (Mariappanadar, 2014b). For example, in situation-1, a corporate company (X) diversifies using a business strategy of either a takeover or merger strategy with a company (Y) identified as a 'cash cow'. Subsequently, company-X retrenches employees from company-Y to cut costs for further diversification of company-X. Employees in company-Y may feel that company-X is retrenching employees due to self-interest of the new owner-company and hence it is perceived that the situation could be 'avoidable' for company-X. Therefore, if an organisation implements certain HRM practices (e.g. retrenchment) due to an avoidable business environmental context then the impacts caused by such a strategy can be perceived as negative by the stakeholders. Furthermore, employees may perceive that it is unacceptable for them to cope with the negative impacts of an avoidable negative externality which the company has imposed on employees due to the new owner-company's self-interest. Hence, the organisation needs to take corrective actions to minimise the negative impacts imposed on the stakeholders to boost their holistic CSR reputation.

In another situation, if a company (Z) is under-performing due to a prolonged economic recession and decides to retrench employees in the company, then the employees and community may perceive this HRM strategy of employee retrenchment is because of an 'unavoidable' context and hence employees tend to tolerate the negative impacts. That is, the unavoidable dimension of avoidability attribute triggers a 'wait and see' approach among employees due to learned helplessness (Waters, 2007). Therefore, both the avoidable and the unavoidable dimensions of the avoidability attribute of negative externality of HRM practices have negative impacts on the stakeholders. However, the avoidable dimension will have perceived significant negative impacts on the stakeholders rather than the unavoidable dimension. This is because the stakeholders tolerate negative impacts caused by the unavoidable external context using learned helplessness as a coping mechanism but not the avoidable context.

5.3.2 The attributes of negative externality and sustainable HRM

The negative externality of HRM cannot be avoided in a free market environment but attempts should be made to contain or reduce the negative impacts caused by HRM practices on employees and the community. The attributes of negative externality of HRM practices are used to understand the different negative impacts on the stakeholders. For example, Mariappanadar (2012a) reviewed the negative externality of work intensification on the stakeholders (employees, their families and the community) using the attributes of negative externality of HRM practices. In this review, it was found that work intensification at surface level seems to be an efficient practice for the company, however, if the social costs of negative externality of work intensification imposed by organisations on the stakeholders were also taken into consideration while calculating the efficiency of an organisation then it will be more likely to reflect inefficiency. The social costs are the costs incurred by the stakeholders as third parties to an organisation to resolve the health and the social harm of work imposed by work intensification (more details about the social costs of harm of work are provided in Chapter 9). Furthermore, the analysis of negative externality of work intensification indicates to practitioners, researchers and labour advocacy groups the pseudo-efficiency of work intensification as a HPWP on the basis of externality. That is, the social cost of negative externality was not transmitted or internalised by organisations in the calculation of efficiency of work intensification. Furthermore, the analysis of negative externality of HRM practices on the stakeholders using the attributes of negative externality of HRM will facilitate HRM professionals to provide due considerations to sustainable HRM while calculating the efficiency and effectiveness of HPWPs.

Therefore, assessing the likelihood that the negative externality of HRM will in future be internalised and sustained to a much greater extent than in the past by organisations is important because recently politicians, socially conscious ethicists, economists and environmentalists have emerged as powerful advocacy groups to develop global institutions such as the WCED, GRI, UN Global Compact etc., to counter unsustainable development (e.g. negative externality of work on stakeholders and continuous environmental degradation). Hence, the negative externality of HRM practices theory plays an important role in shaping sustainable HRM as a discipline and profession to urge organisations to minimise the negative impacts on the stakeholders by internalising the costs of negative externality of HRM practices

5.4 The theory of harm of work

It is important to understand the negative impacts or harm indicators of the attributes of the negative externality have on the stakeholders (e.g. employees, their family members and the community) so as to evaluate and manage the harm of work (Mariappanadar, 2012b). Hence, the harm indicators of negative externality are used to identify the presence or manifestation of harm of work and can be used to raise awareness of managers and researchers of the negative consequence (harm) of work on the stakeholders (e.g. employees, their families and the community). Also, the harm indicators can trigger socially responsible organisations to develop sustainable HRM practices for early identification of negative impacts on the stakeholders which could be reversed through a natural non–work-related recovery processes. Before we explore the link between the different attributes of negative externality of HRM and harm (harm indicators) it is important to understand the theory of harm of work from the sustainable HRM perspective.

The theory of harm of work is about *those high performance work practices used by organisations to extract maximum skills, abilities and motivation of employees but which also 'restricts' employees from achieving positive work-related health and social well-being outcomes* (Mariappanadar, 2014a). The negative impacts of work are understood in the literature as work stress and strain, job demand-resources, work recovery experiences, work–family balance, work–family conflicts, and so on. However, the harm of work practices emphasises the restrictions imposed by work on employees' psychological, social and health well-being outcomes. Hence, the harm of work as a concept provides an opportunity to understand the negative effects of work from the leading indicators perspective to the other concepts discussed earlier from the literature so as to promote sustainability based on reversibility of negative effects on employees through natural work recovery processes.

The harm of work is understood based on the harm indicators caused by the restrictions of work imposed on the psychological aspect, the social or family aspect of employees' lives and employee work-related health harm or health harm of work. The theoretical background and the characteristics of harm indicators that are grouped into the three clusters to represent the psychological, social/family and health manifestation of harm of work are discussed next.

5.4.1.1 Psychological aspect of harm of work

The psychological aspect of harm of work highlights an employee's reduced future personal outcomes of paid work by the psychological harm indicators of work that are caused by the attributes of negative externality of HRM practices. For example, work-related problems with concentration, reduced clear thinking and decision making caused by work intensification, a bundle of HRM practices, are some of the psychological harm indicators of work. These psychological indicators of harm may affect an employee's work performance and that leads to reduced positive personal outcomes for employees such as opportunities for career development and progressions, and performance-based rewards in the organisation. The reduced personal outcomes for an employee, such as reduced future rewards and career growth are the disadvantages which that employee has to encounter due to longitudinal relative deprivation caused by the psychological aspect of harm of HRM practices.

The longitudinal relative deprivation of employees' career growth opportunities is defined as: '"supervisors" disadvantage some employees over a long period of time by depriving opportunities for challenging job experiences because of the supervisor's bias to disregard the psychological harm of HRM practices and attribute employees' limited personal capabilities to cope with the harm of HRM practices as a reason for deprived opportunities' (Mariappanadar, 2013). For example, a supervisor may perceive that those employees under his/her supervision who exhibit the psychological aspect of harm, such as lack of concentration, subsequent to the introduction of work intensification practices, have limited personal capabilities to cope with work intensification. Hence, the supervisor may deprive those employees of the opportunities for improving their future personal outcomes due to the supervisor's biased evaluation of limited personal capability to cope with work intensification as a cause for reduced employee performances.

The critics of longitudinal relative deprivation of employees' career growth opportunities may argue this is the disadvantage caused by the harm of the psychological aspect of HRM practices as an organisational level reason or it is due to the employee's *'inability to cope'* with the harm of work practices introduced by the organisation. Furthermore, it is common among managers in this context to attribute an employee's reduced performance due to work intensification (in the example discussed earlier) to his/her personal characteristics in coping with cognitive work stress of work intensification and play down the role of organisational level cause (see Lamontagne et al., 2007). Hence, the harm of organisational practices go unnoticed. However, Mariappanadar (2013) argues that the affected employee is disadvantaged in career growth by his/her manager through no fault of his/her individual capabilities to cope with cognitive work stress but it is an outcome of longitudinal relative deprivation triggered by the harm of HRM practices, which is an organisational factor. Hence, it is clear that the indicators of psychological aspect of harm of work do restrict and reduce positive personal outcomes for employees and it is logical to consider it as one of the organisational level aspects of harm of work.

5.4.1.2 Social harm of work

The social or family harm of work is about the perceived severity of work restrictions imposed on family activities and the prevalence of effects of social harm of work, which reduce social well-being outcomes for employees. For example, when workloads or work commitments restrict employees from spending quality time with their family members and friends, they will reduce their social well-being outcomes for employees and their families. The social harm of work highlights the unsustainable effect of work on employees' work–family adjustment. The social harm of work is understood based on three dimensions: the work restrictions on the family domain, negative impact of social harm and reduced role facilitations (Mariappanadar, 2015).

The work restriction on the family domain is about the perceived severity of restrictions, imposed by work commitments on employees, on engaging in the family domain activities. The negative impact of the social harm dimension explains the perceived evidence of negative consequences of work–family spillover effect on employees due to work commitments, which highlights an effect of the social harm of work on employees. The scarcity hypothesis indicates that energy put towards efforts in one role (i.e. work) will deplete the available energy and, hence, energy is unavailable for the other roles, such as family (Hammer et al., 2005). Furthermore, Frone (2000) revealed that employees who experienced high work–family conflict (negative spillover) were more likely to have affective disorders than those who were not experiencing this conflict.

The reduced role facilitations dimension of social harm is about the perceived reduced role facilitations to other aspects of family life of an employee due to increased work commitments. For example, Hammer et al. (2005) reported that increases in work–family positive spillover effects are related to several favourable psychological and physical well-being outcomes for employees.

5.4.1.3 Employee health harm of work

The health harm of work is defined as an employee's perception of restrictions for positive health and work-related leading indicators for negative health of work (Mariappanadar, 2016). The health harm of work can be explained by two different theoretical pathways: the physiological recovery mechanism and the unhealthy lifestyle factors. The physiological recovery mechanism and unhealthy lifestyle factors (van der Hulst, 2003) are not mutually exclusive and they may operate simultaneously. The physiological recovery mechanism proposes that insufficient recovery disturbs physiological processes (blood pressure, hormone excretion, sympathetic nervous system activity) and leads to physical health complaints (Rissler, 1977). The unhealthy lifestyle factors such as smoking and caffeine and alcohol consumption, unhealthy diet and lack of exercise cause physiological changes (e.g. high blood pressure, high cholesterol) and increased risk of cardiovascular disease and adverse health in general.

The health harm of work highlights two aspects, that is the restrictions imposed by work for improving positive health as well as work-related leading indicators for negative health. For example, regarding work restrictions for positive health, when work intensification restricts employees from being involved in socially and physically reinvigorating activities, subsequently that may lead to negative health consequences in future, which reduce positive well-being outcomes for employees. Regarding the second aspect of the health harm definition, the leading indicators can provide effective early warnings, by enabling risks or risk increases to be detected and mitigated, before negative health consequences occur. The leading indicators of occupational health performance can be defined as measures of the positive steps that organisations take to prevent an occupational health incident from occurring (Lingard et al., 2007). Furthermore, Weinstein (1984) grouped five categories of health risk factors (leading indicators), such as actions, heredity, physical/physiological, environmental and psychological, and found each of the five risk factor categories to be the strongest predictors of perceived risk for at least one of the twelve common health problems. Hence, the health harm of work provides an understanding of the restrictions of work on employees from performing other non-job or lifestyle activities so as to improve positive health as well as identifying work-related reversible or leading indicators for negative irreversible work-related health consequences.

5.4.2 The theory of harm of work and sustainable HRM

HRM professionals and business managers can use the theory of work harm and the three types of harm indicators of work to understand if an organisation has gone too far with 'increased' expectations of employee efficiency due to HPWPs. An early identification of harm of HPWPs is essential so that organisations can be proactive and introduce sustainable HRM strategies to reverse the impact of work practices on the health and social/family aspects of employees. Failing which, over a period of time, if not managed effectively, will lead to irreversible work-related health and social/family impacts on employees and their families.

5.5 The costs framework for harm of HRM practices

The costs framework (Figure 5.2) for harm of HRM practices (Mariappanadar, 2013) proposes three components to valuate the cost of harm of HRM, and they are the cost measures for the harm of work, identification and allocation of the cost of harm of work, and valuation of cost of harm of work. In this section the framework is used to appraise the costs of harm of HRM practices. The component of cost measures for the harm of work highlights the measure for the costs of harm of work using the welfare 'loss' to the stakeholders (e.g. employees, their family and the community) due to the harm of work. Welfare loss is a situation where marginal social benefit is not equal to marginal social cost and society does not achieve maximum utility (Khanna 2000). Welfare loss in the HRM context is about an employee being restricted by the harmful aspects of HRM practices for maximising the utility function of paid work for improving an individual's psychological, social and health well-being outcomes. The reason for using welfare loss in HRM because the definition of harm of work (Mariappanadar, 2012b) is about the harm it causes on employees and their family members, which impairs their effective utility function of paid and unpaid work. Hence, the harm of work theory provides the theoretical basis for the costs measures component of the framework.

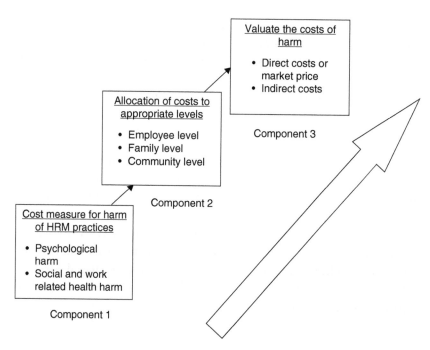

Figure 5.2 The costs framework for harm of HRM practices
Source: Adapted from Mariappanadar (2013).

The identification and allocation of cost of harm component of the framework (Figure 5.2) relates to badging the cost of harm of HRM practices to organisational, individual or/and societal level. This component of the framework is based on the negative externality of HRM practices theory which helps allocation of costs to appropriate stakeholders affected by the harm of work. The valuation of costs component of the framework explains the market prices or direct costs and indirect costs paid by the stakeholders to manage the harm of work imposed on them.

5.5.1 Cost measures component of the framework

The cost measures component of the framework highlights the welfare loss caused by the psychological, social and work related health harm indicators of HRM practices (Mariappanadar 2012b). Some of the harm indicators of psychological aspect of harm are burnout, problems with concentration, reduced clear thinking and decision making which are caused by work intensification (i.e. a bundle of HRM practices). These psychological indicators of harm may affect employee's work performance and that leads to reduced personal outcomes (welfare loss) such as reduced opportunities for career development and progressions, and reduced performance based rewards in the organisation. The reduced personal outcomes for an employee (e.g. reduced future rewards, career growth, etc.) are the costs which employees have to incur due to the psychological aspect of harm of HRM practices.

The cost measure for the social aspect of harm of work is developed based on the relationship between the social aspect of harm indicators of HRM practices and reduced positive social outcomes for employees and their family members as a set of criteria for welfare loss. For example, a decrease in quality of interaction with family members as a harm indicator of the social aspect of harm of HRM practices is due to the spillover effect of work-family conflict. Therefore, any social harm indicators such as work related divorce, separation or child neglect are included in the cost measure for the social aspect of harm of work. Finally, the cost measure for the work related health harm of work is based on the restrictions imposed by work for improving positive health (e.g. reduced socially and physically reinvigorating activities) as well as work-related risk or leading indicators for negative health.

5.5.2 Allocation of costs of harm to stakeholders

The allocation of costs of harm of work to the stakeholders is based on the theory of negative externality of HRM practices. The negative externality of HRM practices theory relates to the costs incurred by the stakeholders or third parties, such as employees, their family members (individual level) and the community (society level), to manage the harm imposed on them by work practices. Hence, the cost measure for the psychological aspect of harm of HRM practices is attributed to the individual employee or/and their family level. The cost measure for the social indicators of harm of work such as work related divorce and so on is also attributed to the individual level because the affected employees and their family members as the stakeholders incur the costs for managing the social harm of work. Furthermore, the cost measure for the work related health harm is attributed to the society or the community/government level. The work-related health costs are attributed to the society level because in countries with a universal health care system the government pays for the health care costs of the residents.

5.5.3 Valuation of costs of harm of HRM practices

The direct and indirect costs are used for the valuation of costs for managing the harm of work imposed by organisations on the stakeholders (employees, their families and the community) (Mariappanadar, 2013). The direct costs (Smith and Brown, 2000) for work-related health harm among countries with a universal health care system is about actual or proxy health system costs (operating costs for the organisation/hospital). For example, the direct health system costs for the treatment of work related psychosomatic problems in UK are an equivalent amount of approximately of US$3,070 for the community (Shaw & Creed, 1991). However, the individual-based costs and the external and intangible costs including lost earnings are relevant for the psychological and social cost measures of harm. That is, direct costs for an individual employee and his/her partner for a divorce caused by the spillover and crossover effect of social harm of work are approximately $30,000 in the USA (Schramm, 2006). Apart from this, it is important to take into account the intangible costs of retraining and redeployment, plus the value of lost earnings for employees when return to work after work related illnesses.

The indirect costs are those costs associated with welfare loss due to reduced ability to function as a 'normal' healthy person both on the job and during one's leisure time (Smith and Brown, 2000). For example, an employee on an annual salary of $70,000 who has been efficient and effective in achieving a set of performance standards before the introduction of increased workload in his/her current position will be used to illustrate this point. This employee's supervisor decides to increase the workload to his/her current position because it is commonly assumed in practice by supervisors that the best performing employees are capable of effectively handling the increased workload due to the employees' intrinsic motivation as well as for improved internal referenced efficiency (i.e. profits) for the organisations. On introduction of increased workload for this employee, he/she may start exhibiting any of the psychological harm indicators of HRM practices, such as lack of concentration and problems of clear thinking and decision making, and his/her work performance starts suffering. There is evidence in the literature to suggest that employees' work performance starts suffering after the introduction of increased workload (Cameron, 1998).

The supervisor for this employee subsequently may get frustrated or disappointed with the employee and develop performance evaluation bias towards the employee. Hence, the supervisor may relatively deprive or disadvantage the employee's involvement in any future challenging projects due to the performance evaluation bias towards the employee. This might cost the employee future career promotion leading to lost earnings from the position higher than his/her current position as well as welfare loss of using that additional income in leisure activities to improve his/her well-being. Assuming that the annual salary of $85,000 for the promoted position is higher than the current one on an annual salary of $70,000 then the employee has lost annually $15,000 in earnings as well as the welfare loss due to the lost additional income (Mariappanadar, 2013).

Another example for indirect costs of harm of work is an employee may seriously consider changing his/her career due to burnout, one of the psychological aspects of harm, caused by work intensification in the current job. Mirvis and Hall (1995) indicated that employees are confronted with the tension associated with 'hanging on' to versus 'letting go' of their current job with less opportunity to progress due to burnout. Mirvis and Hall also suggested that people who restart their career in a new occupation will have lower overall lifetime earnings than they would accrue in the traditional single career path. Furthermore, in a career change choice early retired executive earn on average less than 85 per cent of their former salary. These direct and indirect approaches of valuation of costs to employees and their family members (individual level) and communities (societal level) indicate social costs due to the harm of work.

In summary, the costs framework for harm of HRM practices suggests a sophisticated method to valuate the costs of harm for the stakeholders or third parties to an organisation to manage the psychological, social and work related health aspects of harm imposed on them by work. The cost measures component of the framework is based on the harm of work theory. Furthermore, the negative externality of HRM practices theory provides the theoretical basis for the allocation of costs component of the framework. Finally, the direct and indirect costs are used to valuate the costs incurred by the stakeholders for managing the harm of work imposed on them. Therefore, the negative externality of HRM practices theory and the harm of work theory together have contributed to the development of the costs component framework for harm of HRM practices to help valuate the costs of harm of work. The purpose of valuating harm of work is to highlight an organisation's 'care' or 'lack of care' for stakeholders. An awareness of the level of care for stakeholders based on the costs of harm of work imposed by organisations on stakeholders can subsequently encourage managers to introduce sustainable HRM strategies to enhance both profit maximisation for the organisation and also reduce the harm on the stakeholders. Hence, the cost framework for the harm of work is a useful technique for tangibly measuring the harm of work imposed on the stakeholders.

5.6 The theory of synthesis effects of HRM practices

Till now in this chapter an attempt has been made to explain different theories to understand the negative effects or harm of work imposed on the stakeholders (i.e. employees, and society's sustainable environmental management expectations) by HPWPs. Although the different theories of harm of work provide the basis to understand the harm of work, one of the main tenets of sustainable HRM is to reduce the harm of work while improving organisational performance. Hence, the theory of synthesis effects of HRM practices attempts to explain sustainable HRM practices from a holistic perspective to that of the theories of harm of work. The theory of synthesis effects of sustainable HRM practices is about improving organisational performances through HRM practices as well as attempting to 'reduce' the harm of those HRM practices on employees as well as the negative impacts on the natural environment. The synthesis effects of sustainable HRM practices are about improving organisational performance while simultaneously reducing the negative impacts on the stakeholders highlights that these three polarities are not mutually exclusive but they are mutually reinforcing.

5.6.1 Empirical evidence of the synthesis effects of HPWS

There are theoretical developments on the paradoxes and tensions between organisational performance and employee well-being in the field of sustainable HRM (Mariappanadar, 2003; Ehnert, 2009) but very little has been done to establish empirical evidence of the synthesis effects of high performance work systems (HPWS) such as flexi-time, home-based work, teleworking and a compressed working week. The study conducted by Mariappanadar and Kramar (2014) established empirical evidence of the simultaneous positive effects and the synthesis effects of HPWS on organisational performance and harm of work among employees working in companies in the East Asian Pacific region. For the first time, this study in the sustainable HRM literature examined empirically both the synthesis and the simultaneous effects of HPWS on organisational performance and harm of work among employees in five East Asian Pacific countries.

The study used CRANET data from Australia, Japan, New Zealand, the Philippines and Taiwan. The study found a different type of simultaneous effects to those of the positive effect of HRM practices on organisational performance and the negative effect on employee well-being as indicated by Legge (1995) and Ramsay et al. (2000) in the critical HRM perspective. That is, in Mariappanadar and Kramar's (2014) study they found that HPWS practices have negative effects on organisational performance and also increase harm of work among employees. However, this impact was not uniform for all HPWS practices. Teleworking and a compressed working week both increased employee harm and reduced organisational profitability, however, other practices such as flexi-time and home-based work did not have these effects. This suggests that some HR practices in a bundle could work together to improve organisational performance and reduce employee harm but the synthetic effects are not consistent for other HR practices in a bundle.

The study also revealed that the synthesis effects varied for different HPWS practices when they were studied with employee benefits and trade union presence in a company. Employee benefits had a positive direct impact to improve profitability and also reduce the harm of teleworking and home-based work. Furthermore, trade union influence, along with a bundle of flexi-time work and employee benefits, influenced the synthesis effects of HPWS to improve organisational performance as well as reduce the harm of work among employees.

This study revealed that different employment practices have varying effects on organisational and employee outcomes. In addition the contextual and organisational factors could influence the simultaneous and synthesis effects of these HRM practices. The study also suggests that practitioners need to consider the impact of HPWS on both organisational performance and the harm of work on employees which is rarely considered currently. This study was the first study to empirically examine the synthesis effects of HPWS on organisational performance and the harm of work among employees in the sustainable HRM literature. The empirical findings suggest that the simultaneous effect of HPWS on organisational performance and the harm of work among employees working in countries in the East Asian Pacific region has facilitated strategic HRM researchers and practitioners to appreciate the role of HPWS in causing work-related harm on employees. Furthermore, the findings from the study have created a new insight for managers and HRM professionals to appreciate that the synthesis effects of HRM practices from the sustainable perspective of improving organisational performance while simultaneously reducing the harm of work on stakeholders is possible. That is, an attempt to understand the harm of HPWPs is not 'anti-HRM' or a negative view but it can be considered as a 'positive' HRM intervention so as to develop strategies to minimise such harm of HPWPs.

5.7 Conclusion

The perspective of mutual benefits or simultaneous positive effects of HRM practices on organisational performance and employees is the important perspective that shaped strategic HR practices, such as HPWPs, overwork, work intensification etc. However, the critical strategic HRM advocates highlighted the negative effects or harm of work on employees more than the benefits they receive while improving organisational performance. Hence, in the chapter, the theory of negative externality of HRM was proposed initially to understand the organisation's failure to assimilate the cost of negative impacts of HRM practices instead transferred to the stakeholders (employees, their family members and society) to manage the negative impacts. Four attributes of negative externality of HRM were explained to understand the different aspects of negative impacts of HRM practices, in particular, strategic HR practices, imposed on the stakeholders.

Secondly, this chapter explained the theory of harm of work which is based on the negative externality of HRM practices. The theory of harm of work is about those high performance work practices used by organisations to extract maximum skills, abilities and motivation of employees but which also restricts employees from achieving positive work-related health and social well-being outcomes. The theory of harm of work extends the attributes of negative externality of HRM by identifying the harm indicators of work within the psychological, the social/family and the health aspects of harm of work caused by work restrictions imposed on employees to improve well-being outcomes. Hence, the harm of work reflects the reversible aspect of sustainability so that the organisation can introduce institutional intervention to prevent irreversible negative health and social impacts on employees and their families.

Finally, the theory of synthesis effects of sustainable HRM practices is about improving organisational performances through HRM practices while attempting to reduce the harm of work on employees as well as the negative impacts on the natural environment. The synthesis effects theory extends the theory of negative externality of HRM practices and the theory of harm of work by highlighting that sustainable HRM is not just based on the critical HRM perspective. However, by including 'improving organisational performance' as part of the definition of the synthesis effects of sustainable HR practices it incorporates one of the main tenets of strategic HRM to the understanding of sustainable HRM. That is, the three polarities of improving organisational performance while reducing the simultaneous harm of work imposed on the stakeholders (i.e. employees and society's sustainable environmental management expectations) are not mutually exclusive but they are mutually reinforcing for sustainable development. These three polarities of corporate sustainability are not mutually reinforcing because the negative externality of HRM on employees and environment cannot be avoided in a free market. However, attempts should be made to engage HR to contain or reduce the negative impacts on employees and the ecosystem. Hence, the various theories of harm of work for sustainable HRM discussed in the chapter highlight the evolution of concepts within the harm of work perspective of sustainable HRM to understand the unsustainable impacts of work on the stakeholders. However, the theory of synthesis effects of sustainable HRM practices encompasses both improved organisational performance for shareholders while reducing the simultaneous negative impacts on the stakeholders (i.e. employees and society's sustainable environmental management expectations) so as to achieve holistic corporate sustainability.

References

Appelbaum, E., Bailey, T., Berg, P. & Kalleberg, A. (2000). *Manufacturing Advantage: Why High Performance Work Systems Pay Off*. New York: Cornell University Press.

Aronsson, G. & Gustafsson, K. (2005). Sickness presenteeism: Prevalence, attendance-pressure factors, and an outline of model for research, *Journal of Occupational and Environmental Medicine*, 47(9), 958–66.

Bator, F. M. (1958). The anatomy of market failure, *Quarterly Journal of Economics*, 72, 351–79.

Burchell, B. & Fagan, C. (2004). Gender and the intensification of work: Evidence from the European working conditions surveys, *Eastern Economic Journal*, 30(4), 627–42.

Cameron, A. (1998). The elasticity of endurance: Work intensification and workplace flexibility in the Queensland public hospital system, *New Zealand Journal of Industrial Relations*, 23, 133–51.

Clarkson, M. E. (1995). A stakeholder framework for analyzing and evaluating corporate social performance, *Academy of Management Review*, 20(1), 92–117.

Deery, M. & Jago, L. (2008). A framework for work–life balance practices: Addressing the needs of the tourism industry, *Tourism and Hospitality Research*, 9(2), 97–108.

Ehnert, I. (2009). *Sustainable Human Resource Management: A Conceptual and Exploratory Analysis from a Paradox Perspective*. London: Springer.

Freeman, R. E. (1984). *Strategic Management: A Stakeholder Approach*. Boston, MA: Pitman.

Frone, M. R. (2000). Work–family conflict and employee psychiatric disorders: The national comorbidity survey, *Journal of Applied Psychology*, 85(6), 888–95.

Gilbarco, O., Ben-Zur, H., & Gadi Lubing, G. (2010). Coping, mastery, stress appraisals, mental preparation, and unit cohesion predicting distress and performance: A longitudinal study of soldiers undertaking evacuation tasks. *Anxiety, Stress and Coping*, 23(5), 547–62.

Greenwood, M. & De Cieri, H. (2007), 'Stakeholder theory and the ethics of HRM', In: A. H. Pinnington, R. Macklin, & T. Campbell (eds) *Human Resource Management: Ethics and Employment* (pp. 119–36). Oxford: Oxford University Press.

Guerci, M. & Shani, A. B. (2013). Moving toward stakeholder-based HRM: A perspective of Italian HR managers, *The International Journal of Human Resource Management*, 24(6), 1130–50.

Guest, D. (1997). Human resource management and performance: A review and research agenda, *International Journal of Human Resource Management, 8*, 263–76.

Hammer, L. B., Cullen, J. C., Neal, M. B., Sinclair, R. R. & Shafiro, M. V. (2005). The longitudinal effects of work-family conflict and positive spillover on depressive symptoms among dual-earner couples, *Journal of Occupational Health Psychology, 10*(2), 138–58.

Hoge, T. (2008). When work strain transcends psychological boundaries: An inquiry into the relationship between time pressure, irritation, work-family conflict and psychosomatic complaints, *Stress and Health, 25*(1), 41–51.

Khanna, N. (2000). Measuring environmental quality: An index of pollution. *Ecological Economics, 35*, 191–202.

Lamontagne, A. D., Keegel, T., Louie, A. M., Ostry, A. & Landsbegis, P. A. (2007). A systematic review of the job-stress intervention evaluation literature 1990-2005, *International Journal of Occupational and Environmental Health, 13*(1), 268–80.

Legge, K. (1995). *Human Resource Management: Rhetorics and Realities.* Basingstoke: Macmillan.

Lingard, H., Brown, K., Bradley, L., Bailey, C. & Townsend, K. (2007). Improving employees work-life balance in the construction industry: Project alliance case study, *Journal of Construction Engineering Management, 133*, 807–15.

Mariappanadar, S. (2003). Sustainable human resource management: The sustainable and unsustainable dilemmas of downsizing, *International Journal of Social Economics, 30*(8), 906–23.

Mariappanadar, S. (2012a). Harm of efficiency oriented HRM practices on stakeholders: An ethical issue for sustainability, *Society and Business Review, 7*(2), 168–84.

Mariappanadar, S. (2012b). The harm indicators of negative externality of efficiency focused organizational practices, *International Journal of Social Economics, 39*(3), 209–20.

Mariappanadar, S. (2013). A conceptual framework for cost measures of harm of HRM practices, *Asia-Pacific Journal of Business Administration, 5*(2), 15–39.

Mariappanadar, S. (2014a). Stakeholder harm index: A framework to review work intensification from the critical HRM perspective, *Human Resource Management Review, 24*(4), 313–29.

Mariappanadar, S. (2014b). Sustainable HRM: A counter to minimize the externality of downsizing. In: I. Ehnert, W. Harr & K. J. Zink (eds), *Sustainability and Human Resource Management* (pp. 181–203). Berlin, Heidelberg: Springer.

Mariappanadar, S. (2015). The social harm of work: A critical aspect of work intensification on work-family balance. Paper presented at the 2nd International Sustainable HRM Workshop, Kaiserslautern, Germany, 3–5 June.

Mariappanadar, S. (2016). Health Harm of work from the sustainable HRM perspective: Scale development and validation, *International Journal of Manpower, 37*(6), 924–44.

Mariappanadar, S. & Aust, I. (2018). The dark side of overwork: An empirical evidence of social harm of work from a sustainable HRM perspective. *International Studies of Management and Organization, 47*, 372–87.

Mariappanadar, S. & Kramar, R. (2014). Sustainable HRM: The synthesis effect of high performance work systems on organisational performance and employee harm. *Asia-Pacific Journal of Business Administration*, 6(3), 206–24.

Mirvis, P. H. & Hall, D. T. (1996). Psychological success and the boundaryless career. In: M. B. Arthur & D. M. Rousseau (eds) *The Boundaryless Career: A New Employment Principle for a New Organizational Era* (pp. 237–55). New York: Oxford University Press.

Papandreou, A. A. (1994). *Externality and Institutions*. Oxford: Clarendon Press.

Pfeffer, J. (1998). The real keys to high performance, *Leader to Leader*, 8, 23–29.

Piotrkowski, C. S. (1979). *Work and the Family System*. New York: Macmillan.

Ramsay, H., Scholarios, D. & Harley, B. (2000). Employees and high performance work systems: Testing inside the black box, *British Journal of Industrial Relations*, 38, 501–31.

Rissler, A. (1977). Stress reactions at work and after work during a period of quantitative overload, *Ergonomics*, 20, 13–16.

Schramm, D. G. (2006). Individual and social costs of divorce in Utah. *Journal of Family and Economic Issues*, 27, 133–51.

Shaw, J. & Creed, F. (1991). The cost of somatization. *Journal of Psychosomatic Research*, 35, 307–12.

Smith, A. F. & Brown, C. G. (2000). Understanding cost effectiveness: A detailed review. *British Journal of Ophthalmology*, 84, 794–98.

Stewart, W. F., Ricci, J. A., Chee, E., Morganstein, D. & Lipton, R. (2003). Lost productive time and cost due to common pain conditions in the US workforce., *Journal of American Medical* Association, 290, 2443–54.

Toman, M. (2012). 'Green growth': An exploratory review. Policy Research Working Paper No. 6067, The World Bank. https://openknowledge.worldbank.org/bitstream/handle/10986/9354/WPS6067.pdf?sequence=1 Accessed on 9 October 2018.

Van de Voorde, K., Paauwe, J. & Van Veldhoven, M. (2012). Employee wellbeing and the HRM : Organizational performance relationship: A review of quantitative studies, *International Journal of Management Reviews*, 14, 391–407.

Van der Hulst, M. (2003). Long work hours and health, *Scandinavian Journal of Work, Environment & Health*, 29, 171–88.

Van Marrewijk, M. (2003). Concepts and definitions of CSR and corporate sustainability: Between agency and communion, *Journal of Business Ethics*, 44, 95–105.

Waters, L. (2007). Experiential differences between voluntary and involuntary job redundancy on depression, job search activity, affective employee outcomes and re-employment quality, *Journal of Occupational and Organizational Psychology*, 80, 279–99.

Weinstein, N. D. (1984). Why it won't happen to me: Perceptions of risk factors and susceptibility, *Health Psychology*, 3(5), 431–57.

Wood, S., Veldhoven, M., Croon, M. & Menezes, L. (2012). Enriched job design, high involvement management and organizational performance: The mediating roles of job satisfaction and well-being, *Human Relations*, 65(4), 419–46.

6

Sustainable HRM for environmental management: Green HRM

Sugumar Mariappanadar

6.1 Introduction

Industrialisation has lifted millions of people out of poverty and provided a better quality of life in the developed and developing economies. However, rapid industrial growth has led to the degradation of the natural environment which threatens the quality of life of future generations. Organisations have taken proactive and reactive approaches to the environmental sustainability disruption caused by external pressures such as depleting natural resources, pro-environmental expectations of key stakeholders and global organisations (i.e. GRI, etc.) which reduce profit margins. Organisations, irrespective of using proactive or reactive approaches to environmental management, tend to include environmental sustainability as a part of corporate sustainability business strategy. Sustainable HRM strategy aligns with corporate business strategy to implement environmental sustainability using transformational and traditional HRM functions (Mariappanadar, 2003; Ehnert, 2009; Carrig, 1997).

Strategic HRM continues to dominate the field of HRM since the 1980s to use HR from the resource-based perspective to enhance more benefits for organisations than stakeholders. However, the recent environmental sustainability disruption imposed by external pressures requires the dominant strategic HRM to be incorporated or modified with pro-environmental organisational values to facilitate natural environmental sustainability as a part of corporate sustainability business strategy. Hence, in the HRM literature, the alignment of HRM with environmental sustainability is explained as a subset of sustainable HRM using different approaches such as greening of strategic HRM (Jackson & Seo, 2010; Dubois & Dubois, 2012), 'green' HRM (Renwick et al., 2013; Wagner, 2013; Renwick et al., 2016) and greening of functional and competitive HRM for environmental management systems (Fernández et al., 2003; Jabbour & Santos, 2008; Jabbour et al., 2010; Daily & Huang, 2001).

The aim of this chapter is to enhance HR professionals' understanding of the role of greening of HRM as a subset of sustainable HRM to engage both non-environmental and specialised environmental HR to implement environmental management to achieve economic and environmental aspects of corporate sustainability. In this chapter in particular HRM refers to HR practices to engage both non-environmental and specialised environmental employees because it is generally perceived in management that the role of specialised environmental employees (i.e. environmental engineers) is critical for environmental management. To achieve the aim of this chapter, two background sections are initially included separately to provide improved understanding of the literature on EMS and the role of HRM in EMS. This enhanced understanding of these two strands of literature will facilitate HR and management professionals to appreciate how the proposed new framework on the synthesis of green HRM extends the existing literature on green HRM to achieve simultaneously pro-organisational (economic) and pro-environmental outcomes of corporate sustainability.

In the background section for EMS, an institutional leadership perspective for corporate boards is discussed initially to highlight the role of governance to facilitate greening of HRM practices to enhance natural environmental sustainability. Subsequently, EMS is explained from the anthropocentrism and ecocentric perspectives. In the background section for the role of HRM in EMS, firstly, greening of HRM functions for implementing EMS from the anthropocentrism perspective to improve environmental performance is discussed. Finally, to extend the current green HRM literature a new framework of synthesis of green HRM with anthropocentric (pro-organisational) and ecocentric (pro-environmental) perspectives of HRM for environmental sustainability is explored to achieve economic/financial and environmental outcomes of corporate sustainability.

6.2 Background of environmental management system

In the greening of organisation literature there is very strong evidence to suggest that institutional responses to natural environmental sustainability expectations from key stakeholders are based on isomorphic pressures that originate within organisational fields (Hoffman, 2001). However, there is limited evidence in the literature from the institutional perspective that organisations attempt to take actions to uncouple from isomorphic pressures for environmental sustainability from other peer organisations, instead engaging in just ceremonial behaviour of following institutionalised rules of environmental management. Hence, a new institutional environmental sustainability leadership (IESL) perspective for corporate environmental governance is proposed for greening of HRM which is based on the idiosyncratic perspective (Kostova et al., 2008).

The neo-institutional theory (Kostova et al., 2008) indicated that an organisation's strategic choice of uncoupling from isomorphic pressures for environmental management is by acting substantially different or idiosyncratic from other peer organisations while responding to the institutional pressures. This is because organisations have complex internal and external business environments with possible inconsistencies and conflict among the interests, values, practices and routines used in the various management functions of an organisation including HRM function (Hoffman & Ventresca, 2002). Hence, there is merit for organisations to respond to the complex external environmental pressures by behaving idiosyncratically to other peer organisations by engaging employees with the use of HRM functions to gain legitimacy for their environmental management practices and gain leadership status in environmental sustainability. For example, Jackson and Seo (2010) and Jabbour et al. (2010) have indicated that HR as an intangible resource is the key to environmental sustainability.

The board of directors as a part of the governance function of an organisation is linked to its institutional context. Boards facilitate and control organisational actions by setting goals and limits, including involving HRM (both environmental specialist and non-environmental specialist employees) in environmental sustainability issues, within which managers and employees act (Mizruchi, 1983). Furthermore, the corporate board provides leadership for transformative system design for HRM in response to external pressures to institute change in organisational processes for facilitating employee engagement in achieving natural environmental sustainability (Dubios & Dubios, 2012). After establishing the Sarbanes-Oxley Act, boards and board directors are held personally liable for failing to adhere to environmental regulations. Hence, boards' involvement in environmental sustainability is relevant because environmental management practices require significant capital investments to gain legitimacy for environmental sustainability by achieving IESL through employee engagement for other organisations to follow.

Agency theory (Jensen & Meckling, 1976) is the perspective commonly used in the majority of research on corporate boards. This research tradition typically highlights formal incentives and control mechanisms, with a focus on how boards of directors may protect shareholder interests from opportunistic and self-serving managers through bonding or monitoring activities, particularly in situations where contracts are incomplete. However, a behavioural theory of boards and corporate governance (Van Ees et al., 2009) explains that the role of boards is to deal with conflicting expectations of key stakeholders and also emphasise board members' contributions in dealing with the complexity and associated uncertainty related to strategic decisions and the search for existing or new knowledge to solve organisational problems. Hence, behavioural theory of corporate governance highlights the role of boards in addressing natural environmental sustainability issues from the CSR perspective by engaging employees with the use of sustainable HRM (i.e. green HRM).

IESL is defined from the behavioural theory of corporate governance perspective as *boards provide leadership for a transformative sustainable HRM system to facilitate alignment between traditional HRM functions (employee selection, training, etc.) and natural environmental sustainability to gain social legitimacy.* This definition adds value to the institutional theory of corporate governance by highlighting the involvement of boards in setting up discretionary sustainable HRM strategies for proactive HRM functions to facilitate natural environmental sustainability. Engaging employees with pro-environmental discretional activities by using HRM practices will enhance natural environmental sustainability and publishing them well, organisations can build additional local support for environmental management practices and hence this can be a strategy for social construction for firm-specific legitimacy. Hence, achieving IESL by using sustainable HRM to engage employees with pro-environmental values provides corporate governance and managers with a new perspective to improve environmental sustainability to gain social legitimacy.

In the environmental sustainability literature there is evidence for organisations' idiosyncratic actions for natural environmental management which is based on the concept of positive environmental deviance (Walls & Hoffman, 2013). In this study, based on a behavioural governance approach, it was found that organisations positively deviate in their natural environmental practices when the boards have directors experienced in environmental management. However, organisations conform to isomorphic pressures while implementing natural environmental practices when an organisation is central in its institutional network. That is, the institutional networks create a shared social environment and as the organisation is centrally located in the network it experiences stronger pressure to conform to the social norms. It is evident from the reported study that positive deviance is based on the latitude of deviance from the regulatory norms practised by peer organisations. However, the discretionary strategic choice of an organisation based on the IESL perspective indicates the central role of HR and managerial interpretations in developing creative solutions and practices, irrespective of the existing regulatory norms, to facilitate natural environmental sustainability. Hence, the IESL perspective provides a theoretical basis for corporate governance to facilitate the alignment between greening of HRM as a part of sustainable HRM and natural environmental sustainability.

6.2.2 Environmental management system for sustainability

EMS is a tool used worldwide by any type of organisation to enhance an organisation's capabilities to continuously improve environmental performance. There are many definitions for environmental management (see Jabbour et al., 2010). In this chapter, environmental management includes commitment and policy, planning, implementation, measurement and evaluation, and review and improvement of environmental performance (Hersey, 1998). This environmental management definition evolved from Edwards Deming's quality cycle of 'plan-do-check-act'. EMS is an effective tool when an organisation creates environmental strategies and policies based on the issues encountered and communicated by the top management to the operational personnel.

In explaining the definition of EMS, planning includes organising resources, interacting with key stakeholders and setting up objectives, targets and innovative programmes for environmental management to prevent industrial pollution. Implementation includes identifying environmental specialist and non-environmental personnel with appropriate competence, employee training and awareness, and compensation, and publishes environmental reports to enhance communication between the organisation and key stakeholders. Measurement and evaluation in EMS is about objectively measuring the impact of business practices on natural environmental performance and monitoring the changes in environmental performances over a period of time. Also, based on the objective measurement of environmental performance it is important for organisations to evaluate compliance to regulatory and voluntary environmental standards set in consultation with key stakeholders. Finally, based on internal and external audit reports top management has to review the environmental performance to facilitate continuous improvement in environmental performance.

There are three reasons for organisations to develop EMS (Banerjee, 2001). Based on resource-based theory it was revealed that proactive adoption of EMS improved financial returns for organisations, subsequently, providing competitive advantages through cost reductions, new market potential and enhanced organisational reputation (Miles & Covin, 2000). Legitimacy from the institutional and stakeholder theories highlights the value orientation for implementing EMS is to benefit key stakeholders. That is, in response to the environmental regulatory pressures organisations broadly accept environmental norms and values in society so as to gain legitimacy in the eyes of key stakeholders to operate their businesses. Finally, organisational altruism facilitates organisations to reduce environmental negative impacts on the society because it is 'the right thing to do' for future generations (Bansal & Roth, 2000).

Morrow and Rondinelli (2002) have indicated that organisational motivations for adopting EMS, which includes improving energy efficiency, reduce the costs of fines and penalties for natural environmental standard violations, to satisfy customer pressure and to respond to corporate stakeholders' human/social and natural environmental expectations. Also, EMS can assist organisations to simplify and integrate their environmental protection programmes with their business strategy into a coherent framework to reduce environmental incidents and liabilities as well as financial performance. A study interviewed executives of manufacturing companies in the USA about what motivated them to adopt EMS to prevent pollution (Florida & Davidson, 2001). The study found that commitment to environmental improvement and the opportunity to attain corporate goals are the two most important motivations along with others for organisations that are early adopters of EMS for pollution prevention practices.

It was revealed in the literature that there are many benefits for organisations to implement EMS. For example, IBM reported that their worldwide EMS facilitated the corporation to validate the abilities of all of its facilities (i.e. manufacturing and design) to consistently and effectively meet the requirements for the corporate EMS and also to improve continuously (Morrow & Rondinelli, 2002). It was also found that EMS provides environmental and economic benefits for organisations (see Radonjic & Tominc, 2007). However, there are other studies that reveal EMS does not considerably improve environmental performance (e.g. Dahlstrom et al., 2003). Iraldo and colleagues (2009) indicated that EMS improved environmental performance depending on the degree of maturity in an organisation's implementation of EMS. Furthermore, EMS is used to prevent pollution and gain competitive advantage by improving an organisation's environmental reputation for key stakeholders. Hence, environmental management is the bridge for achieving the natural environmental and economic/financial aspects of corporate sustainability.

6.2.2.1 Perspectives of environmental management

Environmental management can be understood from two perspectives: anthropocentric and ecocentric perspectives. Anthropocentrism is about 'the belief that there is a clear and morally relevant dividing line between humankind and the rest of the nature, that humankind is the only principal source of value or meaning in the world' (Eckersley, 1992, p. 51). Anthropocentrism is a socially constructed moral hierarchy of the human–nature dualism by human beings which assumes that humans are 'above' or apart from other, more 'lowly' creatures (Purser et al., 1995). This social construction processes influence in shaping human conceptualisation and relationships with nature. That is, it is perceived by humans that nature is an assemblage of things that will follow mathematical laws, and science and technology helps humans to use the scientific information about nature for human advantage. Hence, according to anthropocentrism, human beings use scientific knowledge and technology as part of EMS to dominate their natural environment. EMS based on the anthropocentrism agenda provides legitimacy for an organisation to optimise and exploit the natural environment for the organisation's competitive advantage to achieve economic/financial gains.

The ecocentric perspective is radically different from the anthropocentrism perspective for environmental management. Ecocentrists are concerned about the human dominance in exploiting nature. Hence, the proponents of the ecocentric paradigm use ethical responsibility to effect change of human values, ethics, attitudes and lifestyles to appreciate equality of the intrinsic value of humans and non-humans as components of the ecosystem (Imran et al., 2014). Ecocentric values aim to preserve wilderness areas, protect the integrity of biotic communities, and the most relevant value for this chapter is to restore ecosystems to a healthy state of equilibrium (Purser et al., 1995).

Nature is the nucleus of total quality environmental management (TQEM) which is based on the ecocentric management perspective (Shrivastava, 1995). The processes of TQEM include how different organisational elements, such as missions, inputs, throughputs and outputs, are designed to preserve and improve the health of the ecosystem. For example, TQEM espouses long-term, global and environmental issues in addition to financial gains as parts of an organisation's mission. The ecocentric focus of TQEM is different from the anthropocentrism-based common EMS because TQEM facilitates designing organisational practices to preserve the health of the ecosystem whereas the other anthropocentric EMS focuses on maximising organisational benefits and in that process aims to limit the impact on the environment. Furthermore, TQEM goes beyond the involvement of HRM functions to facilitate employee engagement in EMS to include marketing for responsible consumption of goods, accounting on environmental costs, finance for long-term sustainable growth and organisational structure.

6.2.3 ISO14001 and European Union Eco-Management and Audit Scheme (EMAS)

Before discussing HRM practices' alignment to EMS, ISO14001 and EMAS are discussed to highlight how these two tools provide guidelines to organisations for implementing EMS. In the environmental management literature that implementation of EMS is based on the guidelines provided either by the European Union Eco-Management and Audit Scheme (EMAS) or International Standards Organization (ISO) 14001. In tracing the history of external certification for EMS, British Standard 7750 was introduced in the 1990s and it was followed by EMAS in 1993 and the ISO14000 series in 1996. It is important to understand the similarities and differences between EMAS and ISO14001 to understand the varied impacts these two systems have on organisations' natural environmental performance.

EMAS and ISO14001 are the two main international references for organisations aspiring to implement EMS and obtain certification for their environmental management processes. EMAS certification is issued by the National EMAS Competent Body and the public control authorities, while ISO14001 is issued by private bodies, but the private certifiers are verified by each country's environmental regulators (e.g. British Standards Institute, American National Standards Institute). ISO14001 has had international validity since its first issuing but EMAS only extended its scope to non-European countries in 2010. EMAS regulations impose more stringent requirements on external communications to key stakeholders than ISO14001. That is, EMAS requires organisations to complete yearly updates of a public document called the 'Environment Statement' which includes key performance indicators of important natural environmental aspects, environmental objectives and other relevant information on their EMS. The provided Environmental Statement will be audited and validated by the accredited verifier during the certification audit. However, such a transparency is not a requirement in ISO14001.

EMAS requires organisations to address additional issues on an initial environmental review report to ascertain the standard from where continuous improvements have started. Also, information on competence, training and awareness are additional requirements of the employees' involvement compared to ISO14001, which is relevant for developing HRM practices to address this important issue for effective implementation of EMS. Open dialogue with key stakeholders on natural environmental information and objectives and targets are additional issues addressed by EMAS to demonstrate that an organisation is pursuing continuous improvement principles. Considering the similarities and differences between these two international certifications for EMS, EMAS is found to be superior to achieve economic/ financial and natural environmental outcomes in organisations if they are in a mature stage of implementation of EMS (Iraldo et al., 2009). However, the adoption of ISO14001 improves natural environmental performance in the short term rather than in the long term because ISO14001 mainly determines improvements in the initial implementation phase of EMS (Testa et al., 2014).

Although EMS with EMAS or ISO14001 certification varies in the impacts on environmental performance, certification is an indicator of organisations' environmental responsibility which provides competitive advantage for companies in the USA and Europe. Furthermore, EMS certification requires strong employee participation, environmental training programmes for employees and improving awareness of employees on the negative impacts of their jobs on the environment (e.g. waste created) will improve an organisation's environmental performance (Morrow & Rondinelli, 2002). Hence, HRM plays an important role in enhancing employee participation and engagement in the implementation of EMS which is discussed next.

6.3 The role of HRM in environmental management system

Governments have introduced various environmental regulations to protect further degradation of the natural environment by industrialisation. In response to governments' environmental regulations organisations developed EMS to adhere to regulations to achieve pollution prevention. To improve natural environmental performance by using EMS an organisation has to engage in both non-environmental and specialised environmental employees (Dasgupta et al., 2000). All core HRM functions and processes should be aligned to environmental sustainability to achieve the natural environmental aspect of corporate sustainability business strategy (Cohen et al., 2010). Furthermore, many studies have highlighted the importance of HR, as non-environmental specialised, to be involved in EMS to improve an organisation's natural environmental performance (see Daily & Huang, 2001; Fernández et al., 2003; Jabbour et al., 2010; Jackson & Seo, 2010; Renwick et al., 2013). The environmental performance of the organisation is understood based on the level of pollution emissions released by a firm (Iraldo et al., 2009). Daily and Huang (2001) proposed the EMS-HR factor model to explain the alignment of HR factors, such as top management support, employee empowerment, teamwork and rewards, with the processes of implementing EMS in an organisation.

6.4 Green HRM

6.4.1 Greening of strategic HRM for environmental sustainability

Environmental sustainability is about preserving and maintaining the natural environmental life-support system (including atmosphere, water and soil) without which neither industrial production for economic benefits nor humanity could exist (Goodland, 1995). For example, if a healthy ozone layer shield depletes due to industrial pollution then ultraviolet B (UVB) radiation from the sun penetrates the ozone layer shield to cause consequential damage to humans (e.g. skin cancer, etc.) and crops (e.g. cotton production, etc.). Continuous depletion or damage by human activities to the irreplaceable and unsubstitutable environmental life-support system would be incompatible with sustainability. Jackson and Seo (2010) attempted to explain greening of strategic HRM to achieve environmental sustainability. They believed that strategic HRM's emphasis on using HR to achieve improved organisational performance can be similarly used to improve environmental sustainability. Thus, greening of strategic HRM can be achieved by improving the processes of an HRM system for environmental sustainability. That is, an HRM system plays an important role in satisfying the expectations of multiple stakeholders, such as customers, alliance partners, media and other stakeholders, to adopt ecofriendly practices.

It has been indicated that natural environmental sustainability is an important legitimacy for multinational corporations, and hence convergence of sustainability practices across subsidiaries facilitates an HRM system to encourage movement of talents to promote environmental sustainability (see Chapter 2 for more details of isomorphic and idiosyncratic pressures for convergence in MNCs' practices). Furthermore, greening of strategic HRM facilitates an HRM system to promote change in management capabilities (e.g. organisational learning) and create alignment with environmental sustainability. Finally, it will create an effective HRM system to enable employees' behaviours to achieve strategic targets for environmental sustainability (e.g. energy efficiency, waste reduction, etc.).

Dubois and Dubois (2012) have identified transformative and traditional levels of HRM for greening strategic HRM for environmental sustainability in the framework to enhance organisational leadership in environmental sustainability. This framework extends Jackson and Seo's approach in greening strategic HRM for environmental sustainability by including a transformative HRM system design in addition to the traditional functional level HRM. The framework recognises that insufficient natural resources for future productive economic activities of organisations, increasing expectations by regulators, investors, employees and customers, and radical transparency of organisational activities are the organisational contexts for greening strategic HRM (see Chapter 2 and Chapter 12 for more details on institutional contexts for sustainable HRM). The transformative system design of HRM highlights corporate board leadership in formulating HRM strategy and shaping organisational culture and work systems which are to be used in response to organisational contexts to institute change in organisational processes for facilitating HR to achieve environmental sustainability.

Traditional HRM is used in the framework to formalise the greening initiatives by the transformational HRM system design. That is, using job design, recruitment and selection, training and development, performance management and other HRM practices to achieve horizontal and vertical alignments of various management functions and levels to implement environmental sustainability. The framework indicates that significant progress in environmental sustainability could be achieved using green HRM as a part of sustainable HRM to align all other management functions (e.g. production, marketing, etc.) as a whole system to improve environmental sustainability. Furthermore, various HRM actions are suggested based on the framework to embed environmental sustainability in an organisation, which is useful for HRM and other professionals to incorporate in their practices. For example, leadership development for senior management as a transformational HRM should focus on developing leadership competencies in environmental sustainability to facilitate strategic planning and implementation.

Renwick and colleagues (2013) have indicated that the field of HRM is one of the minimally engaged areas of specialisation to improve environmental sustainability. Jabbour and colleagues (2010) reviewed the literature on the alignment between HRM functions and environmental management in companies. In the review it was revealed that a job description with environmental issues facilitated employees' commitment to environmental performance along with other job tasks in a position. Selecting employees who are sensitive to environmental issues contributed more effectively to a company's environmental management initiatives. Employee training on knowledge about a company's environmental policy is important for environmental management. Performance management based on employees' environmental performance prevents undesirable attitudes and reinforces exemplary behaviour towards environmental management. Finally, financial and non-financial rewards for employees as a function of HRM reinforce employees with a distinct potential to contribute to environmental management.

In a quantitative study (Jabbour et al., 2010) it was found that an environmental management focused job description, recruitment, training, performance appraisal and reward system facilitate alignment of these HRM functions to enhance internal (i.e. employees' involvement) and external (i.e. supply chain management) integrations of environmental management. Subsequent to the quantitative study, using a qualitative case study, Jabbour and colleges (2010) revealed that increase of productivity of inputs, reduction of environmental fines and access to environmental markets are the most common reasons for adopting ISO14001 in their respective companies.

6.4.2 Institutional level AMO framework for green HRM

Green HRM is defined as the HRM aspects of environmental management (Renwick et al., 2013). In a review of green HRM using the AMO theory (Appelbaum et al., 2000), Renwick and colleagues revealed that organisations gain the ability to incorporate green HRM by attracting high-quality employees to achieve the environmental goals of organisations, job descriptions and employee specifications which should emphasise the environmental aspects of the job. Subsequently, during job interviews it is important to evaluate job applicants' environmental knowledge, values and beliefs. Organisations should motivate employees by training them on important green HRM intervention to improve employee awareness of the environmental impact on their organisational activities. Adequate environmental knowledge among employees enhances a strong disposition to take environmental actions to manage organisation-related environmental issues. Performance management, pay and rewards systems are the useful HRM functions in motivating employees to improve environmental performance. Finally, it was also revealed in the review that wider involvement of non-environmental management specialist employees in environmental management is crucial for the successful implementation of ISO14001 to reduce pollution.

6.4.3 Employee level green behaviours

Organisational practices toward environmental management also shape individual employee values and beliefs (Dief & Font, 2012). Hence, in this section the individual employee level green behaviours are discussed so as to facilitate a comprehensive individual and organisational level understanding of environmental management. The new environmental paradigm (NEP) scale (Dunlap et al., 2000) is used to measure environmental attitudes, beliefs, values and world view of the general public as well as employees. It is a popular measure of environmental concern; a high score on NEP is treated as reflecting an employee's pro-environmental orientation. Dief and Font (2012) used the NEP scale in their study on determinants of environmental management in the hotel industry. They found that in an organisation operating in a context of a lack of regulatory framework the strong endorsement of the NEP of managers is irrelevant in implementing EMS. That is, employee level high pro-environmental orientation is not a strong predictor when there is a lack of an institutional level regulatory framework to guide the implementation of EMS. This finding suggests that irrespective of individual employee attitudes and values toward the environment, an institutional level action is the key determinant for improved environmental performance where there is a lack of environmental regulatory context.

Wagner (2013) established the link between an employee's perceived benefits (job satisfaction and employee retention) caused by an organisation's environmental sustainability activities and the implementation of EMS. This is an important study to highlight that an employee's perceived benefits of implementing EMS precedes the commonly discussed economic benefits of EMS to organisations in the green HRM literature (e.g. Renwick et al., 2013; Jabbour et al., 2010). The study also found that employee job satisfaction caused by an organisation's environmental sustainability activities is a stronger predictor of EMS implementation than the benefits of employee retention and past profitability. The study findings revealed that sustainability should be the core strategic and functional level of HRM to facilitate implementation of EMS.

An environmental sustainability specialist indicated that employees with pro-environmental values are more likely to enact green behaviours to enhance environmental performance. An individual employee's environmental sustainability knowledge is more important than awareness of environmental issues related to an organisation for pro-environmental behaviour. Furthermore, green organisational citizenship behaviour highlights an individual employee's green behaviour, such as initiative, altruism and compliance for achieving relevant environmental performance targets set by an organisation (Wiernik, Ones & Dilchert, 2013). Kim and colleagues (2017) proposed voluntary workplace green behaviour (VWGB) as an extension of green organisational citizenship behaviour. VWGB is about an employee's discretionary actions at work (e.g. using personal cups instead of disposable cups, recycling reusable things in the workplace, etc.) that contribute to environmental sustainability but are not part of formal environmental management policies or systems. VWGB is a pro-environmental or citizenship behaviour which benefits organisations by conserving resources for cost reduction as well as preserving the natural environment for organisational sustainability.

A study was conducted to explore the individual differences, leader behaviour and co-worker advocacy as determinants of VWGB among employees (Kim et al., 2017). The study found that conscientiousness and moral reflectiveness as factors for individual differences were linked to VWGB among individual group members and leaders. It was also found that leaders' green behaviour shaped the green behaviour of individual subordinates. Furthermore, work group peers as social influencers only strengthened the relationship between leaders' and subordinates' green behaviour but the group peers had to directly impact on employees' green behaviour. This study finding highlights the role of individual differences of employees along with their social context to determine employees' VWGB.

Positive employee environmental behaviour may lead to positive environmental behaviour in the employee's personal life too. This positive facilitation or spillover of environmental behaviour to a person's life domain is explained by green work–life balance (Muster & Schrader, 2011). Balancing employee ecofriendly behaviour in both work and life domains will enrich environmentally friendly experiences in both domains. That is, environment friendly work practices support employees to purchase and consume products that are produced with an environmental sustainability focus. The establishment of a green work–life balance is beyond the scope of traditional HRM and is an ambitious task for green HRM. Including a green work–life balance as part of individual employee level green HRM improves employee motivation, commitment and work satisfaction (Wagner, 2013), however, it has the potential for risk for organisations. For example, the risk of organisations' involvement in employees' private life choices could also be construed as exploiting employees' privacy and employees may react negatively.

6.5 A framework of synthesis of green HRM for environmental sustainability

The framework for greening strategic HRM by Dubois and Dubois (2012), which was discussed earlier in the background section on HRM role in EMS, fails to highlight the tension/paradox between strategic HRM that focuses on benefiting organisations and simultaneous long-term negative impacts on environmental sustainability. It is important to make HRM professionals aware of this paradox/tension between economic/financial and natural environmental outcomes to bring it the tension to the notice of other management professionals to achieve corporate sustainability business strategy. Furthermore, the various HRM practices suggested based on the framework for greening strategic HRM to embed environment sustainability facilitate 'mimicking' of actions by HR professionals. However, actions taken without anchoring those practices with appropriate pro-environmental organisational values (the core for environmental attitudes and behaviours) have limited use in managing the paradox/tension between economic and environmental outcomes of corporate sustainability. Hence, a new framework of synthesis of green HRM for environmental sustainability is proposed in this chapter which attempts to extend the anthropocentric environmental management with ecocentric green HRM practices to preserve the equilibrium of the ecosystem as well as utilise the natural resources for economic activities. The framework of synthesis of green HRM (Figure 6.1) indicates that there are two sets of environmental organisational values and characteristics which are synthesised in EMS to preserve the health of the ecosystem for environmental sustainability. The synthesis of green HRM *is to engage employees using HRM to achieve eco-effectiveness and eco-efficiency to synthesise the nature-business case for environmental sustainability to benefit the society.*

6.5.1 Anthropocentric green HRM

The anthropocentric pro-organisational values shape HRM practices to engage employees in eco-efficiency for reducing the ecological footprint for their business activities. The anthropocentrism paradigm supports the belief that humankind is the principle source of value or meaning in the world (Eckersley, 1992). Anthropocentrism is reinforced by the business case for implementing EMS for improving environmental performance through eco-efficiency to further economic sustainability (i.e. ensure liquidity while providing above average return to shareholders) of an organisation (Salzmann et al., 2005).

For example, the motive-based theory of stakeholder–firm interaction indicates that an organisation will be motivated to consider pro-environmental

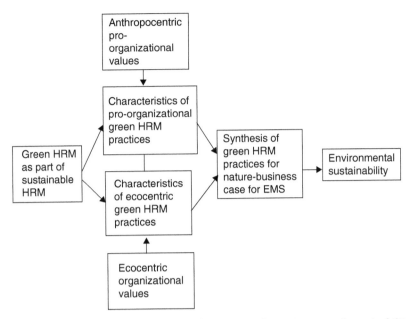

Figure 6.1 The framework of synthesis of green HRM for environmental sustainability

organisational behaviour only when the reciprocal resource exchange in organisation–stakeholder interactions is instrumental for an organisation's success in the financial market (Hahn, 2015; Salzmann et al., 2005). That is, employees as consumers of products/services of their company may choose to boycott the product and/or may influence other consumers through social media to do the same because of the company's lack of, or inadequate, pro-environmental organisational behaviour. Thus, employees and the society, as key stakeholders, control resources (i.e. sales revenue for the company) in the reciprocal organisation–stakeholder relationship which will have an instrumental negative impact on an organisation's financial performance.

The organisational values based on an anthropocentric perspective include firstly technological knowledge-derived value of utilitarian functionalism which subscribes to using technology innovation in EMS to promote an organisation's economic interests (Aktouf, 1992). Furthermore, the human–nature dualism leads to a common dilemma and from the anthropocentric perspective an individual makes rational calculations of the trade-offs between the costs of preservation and the benefits of economic development. Secondly, the egocentric orientation in the anthropocentric perspective highlights ethical egoism and self-interest as dominant value orientations for egocentric actors. Egocentric actors (organisations or individuals) are more likely to pursue economically advantageous action when encountering a paradox between environmental preservation and economic development (Purser et al., 1995).

The anthropocentric organisational values toward environmental sustainability shape the characteristics of HRM practices. The characteristics of HRM practices are about the underlying organisational motives to shape employee behaviour and attitudes at work to achieve organisational goals (Arthur, 1994; Nishii et al., 2008). In the greening of HRM literature, for example, Daily and Huang (2001) discussed the alignment of various HRM functions with EMS but not the characteristics of HRM practices. However, environmental management-focused HRM practices (Jabbour et al., 2010), leadership competencies in environmental sustainability (Dubois & Dubois, 2012) and a system-based greening of HRM are some of the characteristics of anthropocentric green HRM. Furthermore, employee awareness of environmental issues, high quality employees with environmental management competencies and motivating employees to improve environmental performance are the other key characteristics indicated by the review of green HRM (Renwick et al., 2016).

It is evident that the organisational values and the characteristics of green HRM based on the anthropocentric perspective focus on achieving eco-efficiency by engaging employees in EMS to pursue economic advantages for an organisation compared to preserving the health of the ecosystem. This organisational perception based on human–nature dualism is the most important concern for the UN Conference on Environment and Development in environmental degradation. Hence, it is important to reframe this currently dominant legitimised organisational perception which will lead organisations to use HRM for anthropocentric EMS and continue environmental degradation which has inherent risks for society. An ecocentric approach to green HRM is proposed in the next section as an extension to the anthropocentric EMS to preserve the equilibrium of the ecosystem.

6.5.2 Ecocentric green HRM

The environmental management literature indicates that economic activities by organisations are the main source of environmental degradation from the anthropocentrism perspective, and hence organisations have ethical and moral responsibilities to address the environmental issues (see Renwick et al., 2013). Purser et al. (1995) indicated that organisational science focusing on environmental management should defamiliarise the dominant anthropocentrism and reframe with ecocentric-based environmental management approaches to become pro-environmental oriented organisations. For example, a study on EMS among international hotels in the Red Sea resort found that ecocentric organisational values such as environmental altruism explained the differences in environmental practices when external institutional (i.e. regulatory) pressures were absent (Dief & Font, 2012). Hence, in this section characteristics based on ecological values, environment orientation and ecocentric organisational values are proposed for the ecocentric green HRM for EMS to reframe the anthropocentric green HRM practices to preserve the equilibrium of the ecosystem.

The ecocentric perspective highlights that organisations have moral obligations to maintain, preserve and/or restore the health of the ecosystem (i.e. a circular exchange of materials between living and non-living parts of a natural unit) in environmental management. Ecocentric green HRM is based on the ecocentric paradigm for management which was explained by Shrivastava (1995) using two concepts: industrial ecosystems and ecocentric management. The industrial ecosystems concept parallels the natural ecosystems, which is a network of independent organisms and their environment where resources are exchanged for each other to survive. Similarly, the industrial ecosystem highlights organisational populations' ecological interdependence and ecological performance of organisational populations.

Pro-environmental (ecocentric) management focuses on organisational elements (e.g. goals, values, management and HRM functions, etc.) that have an impact on nature. The pro-environmental management concept is relevant to propose new set organisational values and characteristics for the ecocentric green HRM framework which attempts to facilitate EMS to focus on the 'reversibility' of the functional performance of the ecosystem to achieve environmental sustainability. The ecocentric green HRM is to support organisations to use employees as a resource to go beyond the 'business' case and support the 'nature' case for environmental sustainability by focusing on eco-effectiveness (Dyllick & Hockerts, 2002). Eco-effectiveness is the processes designed for the environment to be healthy and renewable to achieve ecological sustainability. That is, eco-effectiveness is not about relative improvements in technology and business processes for environmental sustainability (i.e. eco-efficiency) but it is about overcoming the environmental sustainability issues of irreversibility.

Manson (2007) indicated that the concept of irreversibility is poorly defined in the environmental management literature, and hence Verbruggen (2013) provided a definition for reversibility to be used in ecology science. Reversibility is about the ecosystem's ability to maintain and restore the functional performance of the system. The difference between eco-effectiveness and eco-efficiency for green HRM is, the earlier attempts to engage employees by using the ecocentric green HRM to ensure that the EMS used in an organisation considers reversibility as the focus to preserve the health of the ecosystem. The latter eco-efficiency-based EMS aims to reduce environmental degradation using the anthropocentric green HRM but in the long term the environment will lose its inherent abilities for reversibility. Hence, including the ecocentric green HRM for eco-effectiveness along with the anthropocentric green HRM for eco-efficiency as a holistic EMS will enhance environmental sustainability by preserving the health of the ecosystem while utilising the natural resources prudently for economic activities.

6.5.2.1 Ecocentric organisational values for green HRM

Ecocentric (Purser et al., 1995) organisational values highlight that organisations have moral obligations to maintain, preserve and/or restore the health of the ecosystem in environmental management approaches. These are the pro-environmental organisational values that are proposed to shape the characteristics of green HRM practices so as to have comprehensive stakeholder engagement processes for environmental management. The ecocentric value is based on ecocentric environmental ethics which highlights that organisations have an ethical responsibility to sustain and preserve the health of ecosystems (Purser et al., 1995). That is, ecocentric ethics attempt to widen the boundary of an organisation to include natural ecosystems.

Furthermore, ecological values and environmental orientation are important organisational values for the ecocentric green HRM to facilitate restoring or reversing the health of the ecosystem. Ecological values (Wiseman & Bogner, 2003) of an organisation reflect conservation and protection of the environment (i.e. preservation approach) and also the utilisation of natural resources for economic activities. Environmental orientation (Banerjee, 2001), as an organisational value, reflects managerial (agents for organisations) perceptions towards respect, care and concern for the natural environment, and the organisation's responsiveness to external stakeholders (i.e. for our children and society). These organisational values will facilitate development of the characteristics of ecocentric green HRM practices to align HRM functions with EMS for reducing the ecological footprint and preserving the health of the ecosystem.

6.5.2.2 Characteristics of ecocentric green HRM for preserving the health of the ecosystem

In the ecocentric green HRM functions of employee selection and training it is important to conduct employment testing and train employees for environmental competencies on maintaining and preserving the health of the ecosystem which are relevant for the industry. For example, in the manufacturing industry, it is useful to conduct employment testing and training on environmental altruism for emission reduction and waste management in preserving the health of the ecosystem. Organisations can encourage employees to engage in the search for innovative solutions based on environmental altruism to environmental problems relating to those organisations (Fernández et al., 2003). The characteristics of performance management and the rewards system of ecocentric green HRM based on ecocentric values can help align employees' work behaviour and attitudes for environmental improvements while implementing corporate sustainability.

6.5.3 Synthesis of green HRM of environmental sustainability

The competing anthropocentrism and ecocentric perspectives provide rich understanding of the current state and the future aspired state of HRM involvement in environmental management to achieve environmental and economic aspects of corporate sustainability. There is no single perspective that can provide guaranteed solutions or guidance to shape green HRM for EMS to resolve the current and future environmental issues. Hence, in this section an attempt is made to explain how green HRM as a part of sustainable HRM practices could be synthesised with both pro-organisational (i.e. anthropocentric) and pro-environmental (i.e. ecocentric) perspectives of green HRM for implementing EMS to improve economic and environmental performances of organisations. The synthesis effect of green HRM is based on one of the sustainable HRM definitions (Mariappanadar, 2014) which is about *those HRM systems or bundles that enhance both profit maximisation for the organisation and also improve environmental performance to benefit the society.* Furthermore, these two polarities of an organisation's financial performance and environmental performance are not mutually exclusive but are rather, mutually reinforcing for achieving corporate sustainability.

The proposed synthesis effect of pro-organisational and pro-environmental perspectives shapes an internally consistent bundle of green HRM practices to improve environmental sustainability based on the configurational perspective. The configurational perspective envisages an internally consistent bundle of HRM practices to facilitate achieving an organisation's diverse pro-organisational and pro-environmental (i.e. restoring ecosystem) goals (Dyer and Reeves, 1995; Bae & Lawler, 2000). Hence, it is possible that the contradictory economic and environmental outcomes of corporate sustainability can be achieved by implementing a synthesised set of bundles of green HRM practices. Furthermore, the HR architecture (Posthuma et al., 2013) will facilitate a system or a bundle of internally consistent green HRM practices as part of sustainable HRM for achieving economic/financial and environmental outcomes of corporate sustainability.

Anthropocentric-based pro-organisational and ecocentric values-focused pro-environmental characteristics of HRM practices will facilitate employee participation and engagement to synthesise green HRM for achieving the diverse economic and environmental outcomes of corporate sustainability. For example, employee training and development should be used to gain knowledge and capabilities in synthesising pro-organisational and pro-environmental-focused HRM functions and processes to achieve contradictory but complementary economic/financial and natural environmental outcomes of corporate sustainability. In the paradox perspective, a synthesis or fusion is bound to happen when extreme characteristics of a paradox exist simultaneously and have bidirectional relationships between the extreme characteristics (Clegg et al., 2002).

For example, a review of environmental management literature revealed sound economic rationale for the business case for management environmental issues at an organisational level. Subsequently, there is evidence in the literature of a reverse relationship between financial performance and organisations implementing EMS. That is, organisations with adequate financial resources and in the mature stage of the industry life cycle are more likely to implement EMS compared to organisations who are in the early stages of the industry life cycle and have limited financial resources (Salzmann et al., 2005). It is useful to understand the reciprocal or reverse relationship between organisational financial performance and implementation of EMS for environmental sustainability. However, there is merit in the future to explore the synthesis of pro-organisational and ecocentric green HRM for implementing EMS to enhance environmental sustainability to achieve simultaneous economic/financial and environmental outcomes of corporate sustainability.

In capturing the varied impacts of the characteristics of green HRM practices on economic/financial and natural environmental outcomes of corporate sustainability based on the synthesis effects perspective of sustainable HRM is considered complex. However, Edwards (1995) devised an organisational research technique to fully capture the effects of multiple independent variables, such as the anthropocentric and the ecocentric green HRM practices for EMS, on the congruence or synthesis effects between multiple dependent variables (i.e. economic/financial and environmental performance). Hence, future research can attempt to test the synthesis effects of green HRM on corporate sustainability outcomes using Edwards' research technique.

6.6 Conclusion

The purpose of this chapter is to enhance HRM professionals' understanding of EMS to align HRM functions for environmental sustainability to achieve corporate sustainability. Green HRM as a part of sustainable HRM facilitates employee participation and engagement in the implementation of EMS to improve environmental performance. EMS is a tool, such as ISO14001 and EMAS, which is used by organisations to build their capabilities to continuously improve environmental performance (i.e. the level of pollution emissions released by a firm). A new IESL perspective was proposed to enhance the governance role of corporate boards to align green HRM to EMS for environmental sustainability. The IESL perspective is based on the idiosyncratic institutional theory which highlights the role of corporate boards and board of directors in using transformational HRM to provide leadership for all employees in various organisational levels to align traditional HRM functions with EMS for environmental sustainability.

Greening of HRM functions was discussed to provide HRM professionals with insights into the processes that can be used to align HRM functions with EMS, which are based on pro-organisational-focused (anthropocentric perspective) environmental management. Pro-organisational-focused EMS provides legitimacy for an organisation to use scientific knowledge and technology to optimise and exploit the environment for the organisation's competitive advantage to achieve economic gains. Furthermore, employee pro-environmental orientation, job satisfaction based on an organisation's environmental sustainability activities, VWGB and green work–life balance are the employee level green behaviours discussed in this chapter for environmental sustainability.

To extend the green HRM literature, which is currently dominated by pro-organisational (anthropocentric) values-based EMS for environmental performance, an attempt is made in this chapter to develop ecocentric green HRM for environmental sustainability. Green HRM based on the ecocentric perspective is radically different from the pro-organisational-focused environmental management. Ecocentric green HRM facilitates designing HRM practices for employee engagement to preserve and restore the health of the ecosystem. However, the pro-organisational oriented green HRM highlights the role of HRM in EMS to maximise organisational benefits while attempting to limit the negative impact on the environment. Hence, the framework of synthesis of green HRM for environmental sustainability was proposed to equip HRM and management professionals to effectively manage the paradox/tension between anthropocentric-based pro-organisational and ecocentric values-focused pro-environmental characteristics green HRM approaches for EMS. The new synthesis of the green HRM framework, as a part of sustainable HRM, will facilitate employee engagement for preserving and restoring the health of the ecosystem while utilising natural resources for economic benefits of organisations to achieve corporate sustainability.

References

Aktouf, O. (1992). Management and theories of organizations in the 1990s: Toward a critical radical humanism?. *Academy of Management Review, 17*(3), 407–31.

Appelbaum, E., Bailey, T., Berg, P. & Kalleberg, A. (2000). *Manufacturing Advantage: Why High Performance Work Systems Pay Off.* New York: Cornell University Press.

Arthur, J. B. (1994). Effects of human resource systems on manufacturing performance and turnover. *Academy of Management Journal, 37*(3), 670–87.

Bae, J. & Lawler, J. J. (2000). Organizational and HRM strategies in Korea: Impact on firm performance in an emerging economy. *Academy of Management Journal, 43*(3), 502–17.

Banerjee, S. B. (2001). Managerial perceptions of corporate environmentalism: Interpretations from industry and strategic implications for organizations. *Journal of Management Studies, 38*(4), 489–513.

Bansal, P. & Roth, K. (2000). Why companies go green: A model of ecological responsiveness. *Academy of Management Journal, 43*(4), 717–36.

Carrig, K. (1997). Reshaping human resources for the next century – Lessons from a high flying airline. *Human Resource Management, 36*(2), 277–89.

Clegg, S. R., da Cunha, J. V., & e Cunha, M. P. (2002). Management paradoxes: A relational view. *Human Relations, 55*(5), 483–503.

Cohen, E., Taylor, S. & Muller-Camen, M. (2010). HR's role in corporate social responsibility and sustainability. *Society for Human Resource Management (SHRM) Report, SHRM, Virginia,* Available at: www.shrm.org/about/foundation/products/Pages/SustainabilityEPG.aspx. Accessed 1 September 2017.

Dahlström, K., Howes, C., Leinster, P. & Skea, J. (2003). Environmental management systems and company performance: Assessing the case for extending risk-based regulation. *Environmental Policy and Governance, 13*(4), 187–203.

Daily, B. F. & Huang, S. C. (2001). Achieving sustainability through attention to human resource factors in environmental management. *International Journal of Operations & Production Management, 21*(12), 1539–52.

Dasgupta, S., Hettige, H. & Wheeler, D. (2000). What improves environmental compliance? Evidence from Mexican industry. *Journal of Environmental Economics and Management, 39*(1), 39–66.

Dief, M. E. & Font, X. (2012). Determinants of environmental management in the red sea hotels: Personal and organizational values and contextual variables. *Journal of Hospitality & Tourism Research, 36*(1), 115–37.

DuBois, C. L. & Dubois, D. A. (2012). Strategic HRM as social design for environmental sustainability in organization. *Human Resource Management, 51*(6), 799–826.

Dunlap, R. E., Van Liere, K. D., Mertig, A. G., & Jones, R. E. (2000). New trends in measuring environmental attitudes. Measuring endorsement of the new ecological paradigm: A revised NEP scale. *Journal of Social Issues, 56*(3), 425–42.

Dyer, L. & Reeves, T. (1995) Human resource strategies and firm performance: What do we know and where do we need to go? *International Journal of Human Resource Management, 6*(3), 656–70.

Dyllick, T. & Hockerts, K. (2002). Beyond the business case for corporate sustainability. *Business Strategy and the Environment, 11*(2), 130–41.

Eckersley, R. (1992). *Environmentalism and Political Theory*. Albany: State University of New York Press.

Edwards, J. R. (1995). Alternatives to difference scores as dependent variables in the study of congruence in organizational research. *Organizational Behavior and Human Decision Processes, 64*(3), 307–24.

Ehnert, I. (2009). *Sustainable Human Resource Management: A Conceptual and Exploratory Analysis from Paradox Perspective*. London: Springer.

Fernández, E., Junquera, B. & Ordiz, M. (2003). Organizational culture and human resources in the environmental issue: A review of the literature. *International Journal of Human Resource Management, 14*(4), 634–56.

Florida, R. & Davison, D. (2001). Gaining from green management: environmental management systems inside and outside the factory. *California Management Review, 43*(3), 64–84.

Goodland, R. (1995). The concept of environmental sustainability. *Annual Review of Ecology and Systematics, 26*(1), 1–24.

Hahn, T. (2015). Reciprocal stakeholder behavior: A motive-based approach to the implementation of normative stakeholder demands. *Business & Society, 54*(1), 9–51.

Hersey, K. (1998). A close look at ISO 14000. *American Society of Safety Engineers, 43*(7), 26–29.

Hoffman, A. J. (2001). Linking organizational and field-level analyses: The diffusion of corporate environmental practice. *Organization & Environment, 14*(2), 133–56.

Hoffman, A. J., & Ventresca, M. J. (2002). *Organizations, Policy and the Natural Environment: Institutional and Strategic Perspectives*. Stanford: Stanford University Press.

Imran, S., Alam, K. & Beaumont, N. (2014). Reinterpreting the definition of sustainable development for a more ecocentric reorientation. *Sustainable Development, 22*(2), 134–44.

Iraldo, F., Testa, F., & Frey, M. (2009). Is an environmental management system able to influence environmental and competitive performance? The case of the eco-management and audit scheme (EMAS) in the European Union. *Journal of Cleaner Production, 17*(16), 1444–52.

Jabbour, C. J. C., Santos, F. C. A. & Nagano, M. S. (2010). Contributions of HRM throughout the stages of environmental management: Methodological triangulation applied to companies in Brazil. *The International Journal of Human Resource Management, 21*(7), 1049–89.

Jabbour, C. J. C. & Santos, F. C. A. (2008). The central role of human resource management in the search for sustainable organizations. *The International Journal of Human Resource Management, 19*(12), 2133–54.

Jackson, S. E. & Seo, J. (2010). The greening of strategic HRM scholarship. *Organization Management Journal, 7*(4), 278–90.

Jensen, M. C. & Meckling, W. H. (1976). Theory of the firm: Managerial behavior, agency costs, and ownership structure. *Journal of Financial Economics, 2*, 305–60.

Kim, A., Kim, Y., Han, K., Jackson, S. E. & Ployhart, R. E. (2017). Multilevel influences on voluntary workplace green behavior: Individual differences, leader behavior, and coworker advocacy. *Journal of Management, 43*(5), 1335–58.

Kostova, T., Roth, K. & Dacin, M. T. (2008). Institutional theory in the study of multinational corporations: A critique and new directions. *Academy of Management Review, 33*(4), 994–1006.

Manson, N. A. (2007). The concept of irreversibility: Its use in the sustainable development and precautionary principle literatures. *The Electronic Journal of Sustainable Development, 1*(1), 3.

Mariappanadar, S. (2003). Sustainable human resource management: The sustainable and unsustainable dilemmas of downsizing. *International Journal of Social Economics, 30*(8), 906–23.

Mariappanadar, S. (2014). Stakeholder harm index: A framework to review work intensification from the critical HRM perspective. *Human Resource Management Review, 24*(4), 313–29.

Miles, M. P. & Covin, J. G. (2000). Environmental marketing: A source of reputational, competitive, and financial advantage. *Journal of Business Ethics, 23*(3), 299–311.

Mizruchi, M. S. (1983). Who controls whom? An examination of the relation between management and boards of directors in large American corporations. *Academy of Management Review, 8*(3), 426–35.

Morrow, D. & Rondinelli, D. (2002). Adopting corporate environmental management systems: Motivations and results of ISO 14001 and EMAS certification. *European Management Journal, 20*(2), 159–71.

Muster, V. & Schrader, U. (2011). Green work-life balance: A new perspective for green HRM. *German Journal of Human Resource Management, 25*(2), 140–56.

Nishii, L., Lepak, D. P. & Schneider, B. (2008). Employee attributions of the "why" of HR practices: Their effects on employee attitudes and behaviors, and customer satisfaction. *Personnel Psychology, 61*(3), 503–45.

Posthuma, R. A., Campion, M. C., Masimova, M. & Campion, M. A. (2013). A high performance work practices taxonomy: Integrating the literature and directing future research. *Journal of Management, 39*(5), 1184–220.

Purser, R. E., Park, C., & Montuori, A. (1995). Limits to anthropocentrism: Toward an ecocentric organization paradigm?. *Academy of Management Review, 20*(4), 1053–89.

Radonjič, G. & Tominc, P. (2007). The role of environmental management system on introduction of new technologies in the metal and chemical/paper/plastics industries. *Journal of Cleaner Production, 15*(15), 1482–93.

Renwick, D. W., Jabbour, C. J., Muller-Camen, M., Redman, T. & Wilkinson, A. (2016). Contemporary developments in Green (environmental) HRM scholarship.

Renwick, D. W., Redman, T., & Maguire, S. (2013). Green human resource management: A review and research agenda. *International Journal of Management Reviews, 15*(1), 1–14.

Salzmann, O., Ionescu-Somers, A. & Steger, U. (2005). The business case for corporate sustainability: Literature review and research options. *European Management Journal, 23*(1), 27–36.

Shrivastava, P. (1995). Ecocentric management for a risk society. *Academy of Management Review, 20*(1), 118–37.

Testa, F., Rizzi, F., Daddi, T., Gusmerotti, N. M., Frey, M. & Iraldo, F. (2014). EMAS and ISO 14001: The differences in effectively improving environmental performance. *Journal of Cleaner Production, 68*, 165–73.

Van Ees, H., Gabrielsson, J. & Huse, M. (2009). Toward a behavioral theory of boards and corporate governance. *Corporate Governance: An International Review, 17*(3), 307–19.

Verbruggen, A. (2013). Revocability and reversibility in societal decision-making. *Ecological Economics, 85*, 20–27.

Wagner, M. (2013). 'Green' human resource benefits: Do they matter as determinants of environmental management system implementation? *Journal of Business Ethics, 114*(3), 443–56.

Walls, J. L. & Hoffman, A. J. (2013). Exceptional boards: Environmental experience and positive deviance from institutional norms. *Journal of Organizational Behavior, 34*(2), 253–71.

M. Wiernik, B., S. Ones, D., & Dilchert, S. (2013). Age and environmental sustainability: A meta-analysis. *Journal of Managerial Psychology, 28*(7/8), 826–56.

Wiseman, M., & Bogner, F. X. (2003). A higher-order model of ecological values and its relationship to personality. *Personality and Individual differences, 34*(5), 783–94.

part IV

Sustainable HRM: Implementation, Measurement and Reporting

7

Implementing sustainable HRM practices

Sugumar Mariappanadar

7.1 Introduction

The aim of this chapter is to further develop the vision of how sustainable HRM practices can be implemented in business organisations. The aim of the chapter is achieved by firstly exploring three different theoretical frameworks. A framework of typologies of sustainable HRM is proposed for implementing sustainable HRM in organisations to achieve corporate sustainability. Subsequently, the framework for the classification of sustainable HRM (Gollan and Xu, 2014) and the framework for the resource regeneration strategy for sustainable HRM (Dorenbosch, 2014) are also explored. Secondly, the challenges of entrenched strategic HRM practices as organisational barriers and industry barriers to implementing sustainable HRM are discussed. Thirdly, institutional change initiatives are explained to overcome the entrenched strategic HRM organisational values as barriers for implementing sustainable HRM. Finally, the paradoxes in implementing strategic HRM and sustainable HRM to achieve the synthesis effects of HRM practices are explained.

7.2 A framework of typologies of sustainable HRM

The characteristics of sustainable HR practices as discussed in Chapter 4, include employee competencies with social consciousness to align the mutual interest of employees, the organisation and stakeholders, altruistic motivation and being a sustainability champion. Furthermore, creating awareness of, identifying and reducing the harm of work while improving organisational performance, as well as HR regeneration, are also identified as the characteristics of sustainable HRM. It is important to understand if these characteristics of sustainable HRM practices are 'best practices' or whether the effectiveness of these characteristics in achieving the synthesis effects of HRM practices for corporate sustainability are based on the configurational effects of job contexts. Hence, initially the perspectives of job contexts are explained and this is followed by an explanation of the typologies of sustainable HRM practices that seek to overcome the negative configurational effects of job contexts so as to engage employees to achieve corporate sustainability business strategy.

7.2.1 A configurational model of job contexts

In the management literature there are three different perspectives on contexts that are used as explanations for the effects of the characteristics of HRM practices concerning organisational performance, namely the universalistic, contingency and configurational perspectives (see Colbert, 2004). The universalistic, or 'best practice', perspective indicates that some characteristics of HRM practices are always better than others in facilitating organisational performance, and that all organisations should adopt these in practice, irrespective of the contexts in which organisations operate. The contingency perspective emphasises the effects of contingent variables (e.g. industry size, industry types, etc.) on organisational performance. The configurational perspective asserts that patterns of multiple interdependent HRM variables, such as the characteristics of HRM practices and context variables, are related to organisational performance. Hence, typologies of sustainable HRM practices are developed based on the configurational perspective.

In the configurational model, job contexts are those working conditions that are imposed by organisations on job roles during the different career life stages to facilitate or constrain employee behaviours (Lent & Brown, 2008) in achieving the financial performance of the organisation, the employee quality of life aspect of human/social and natural environmental outcomes of corporate sustainability business strategy. Furthermore, the characteristics of HRM practices are used to engage employees in different job roles to improve their performances so as to implement business strategies. Hence, in implementing sustainable HRM practices to facilitate employees' job performances and achieve corporate sustainability business aims it is important to align the characteristics of sustainable HRM to job contexts.

The three-dimensional configurational model of job contexts for sustainable HRM practices (Figure 7.1) includes work intensification, mutual benefits and the career life cycle as dimensions. These dimensions of job contexts are chosen for sustainable HRM practices because these work conditions improve organisational performances but are most likely misaligned with achieving corporate sustainability outcomes. Thus, the negative configurational effects of these dimensions reveal the misalignment between these dimensions of job contexts in achieving the diverse but interrelated corporate sustainability outcomes. For example, when young, employees enjoy work intensification in their jobs and are more career- and benefits-focused than driven by the stakeholder care position in their working life (Halrynjo, 2009). There are other employees who are well established in their career and they expect that the job contexts provide opportunities to reveal an organisation's care position for stakeholders while enhancing financial performance. However, the job contexts imposed by organisational practices based on the business case perspective (i.e. financial performance) will constrain employees in their job to care for stakeholders, and create misalignment between the job contexts for achieving the human/social outcome of corporate sustainability. Hence, each of the quadrants in the model highlights the alignment and/or misalignment of job contexts based on configurational effects for the *organisation–stakeholder care position.*

The organisation–stakeholder care position as a configurational effect is based on organisations' CSR for the ethics of care for stakeholders (Mariappanadar, 2012) and the holistic corporate sustainability (Van Marrewijk, 2003). In sustainable HRM the organisation–stakeholder care position *reflects organisation and stakeholder relationships which are understood according to the positive and negative configurational effects of interdependent job contexts so as to minimise the harm of work and improve stakeholder well-being while enhancing the financial aspect of corporate sustainability outcomes.*

The configuration effect of job contexts enhances our understanding that implementation of sustainable HRM practices are not universal or best practices but rather based on the positive and negative configurational effects of the three dimensions of job contexts that reveal the organisation–stakeholder care position in each of the quadrants (Figure 7.1). Thus, the configurational effects of the three dimensions of job contexts will enable HR professionals and managers to understand the alignment and misalignment in the organisation–stakeholders care position in each of quadrants of the model. Furthermore, in interpreting the configurational effects of job contexts on the organisation–stakeholders care position in each of the quadrants in the model, the effect does not relate to 'a job' but 'various jobs' across industry

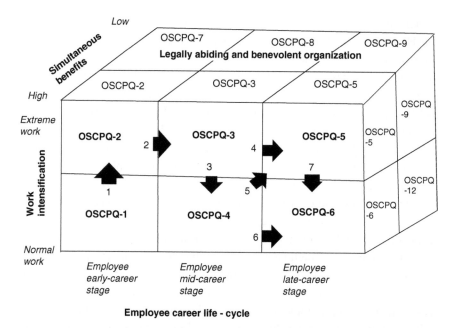

Figure 7.1 A configurational model of job contexts for the typologies of sustainable HRM

sectors where similar job contexts exist. Subsequently, the misalignment in the organisation–stakeholder care position in a quadrant will facilitate the implementation of the appropriate sustainable HRM typology to HRM functions to achieve the corporate sustainability outcome.

7.2.1.1 Structure of the configurational model of job contexts

The structure of the model presents the three dimensions of work intensification, mutual benefits and the career life cycle. Furthermore, each of the dimensions of the job contexts are explained with two elements in the configuration model.

Work intensification as a dimension and its elements. In the configurational model work intensification is identified as a job context for sustainable HRM because it is one of the most important changes to have taken place in work arrangements since the 1990s as a result of strategic HRM practices. Work intensification is a form of high performance work practice (HPWP), which intensifies employees' workloads. According to Boselie and colleagues (2006), work intensification is a common job context in most jobs today and this work practice is operationalised by HRM systems to manage employee activities such as increased workloads and involuntary overtime work and so on, for improving organisational activities. Work intensification includes both the extensive effort of work or overwork, that is, long hours, and the intensity of work or workload.

In the model (Figure 7.1) work intensification as a job context for sustainable HRM practices is depicted with two elements, extreme work and normal work. Granter et al. (2015) indicated that work intensification is a form of 'extreme work' and it has become 'the new work' paradigm of the twenty-first century. In the new work paradigm extreme work is not stigmatised as 'dirty' because work can also be challenging as well as provide a strong occupational identity for prestigious, highly paid professionals. Hence, extreme work has become a common and socially acceptable practice in job roles imposed by organisations, and hence professionals are now expected to develop resilience to cope with or even embrace this new work paradigm. However, normal work, as the opposite element to extreme work, indicates the acceptable or normal wear and tear on an employee's body and mind that is inflicted by workplace stress, injury and exhaustion in jobs. Normal wear and tear on an employee's body and mind is explained in medical sustainability as 'reversible' (Dyllick & Hockerts, 2002), and is relevant for sustainable HRM. That is, in the job context of sustainable HRM, an employee's body and mind must be able to recover and reverse back to 'normality' after sufficient rest or lean work time after a long work day. The reversibility of body and mind to normality for the sustainable HRM perspective does not include 'pseudo normality' which is attempted by some employees through the regular use of alcohol or illegal drugs.

Simultaneous benefits dimension and its elements. In the strategic HRM literature simultaneous benefits, as a job context, are imposed by organisations to highlight mutual benefits of HPWPs for an organisation and its employees. Many studies have indicated that HPWPs (a type of strategic HRM practice), which are developed according to mutual benefits theory, have positive impacts on organisational performance as well as on employees. For example, HPWPs improve employee job satisfaction because of improved working conditions such as an increase in work flexibility (Giannikisa & Nikandrou, 2013), empowerment (Shih et al., 2013) and family benefits (see Combs et al., 2006). However, the critical HRM literature (see Godard, 2001; Mariappanadar, 2014b) contradicts the mutual benefits claims of HPWPs and indicates that HPWPs benefit organisations more than employees and have negative simultaneous effects, imposing harm of work, on employees.

The high and low simultaneous benefits are the two elements of the simultaneous benefits context which are depicted in the model. The element of high simultaneous benefits in the model (Figure 7.1) indicates mutual benefits, which is about the perceived financial benefits for organisations as well as the benefits for employees through work flexibility and job satisfaction. The low simultaneous benefits element highlights that employees perceive that the benefits they receive due to HPWPs are not equitable to that of the benefits to the organisation. This happens because employees perceive that there is an alleged breach in the psychological contract with the organisation, which reduces their intrinsic job benefits such as reduced job satisfaction and organisational commitment, and enhances the employee's intention to leave the organisation (Giannikisa & Nikandrou, 201). For example, an organisation may have achieved increased benefits due to the casualisation of a job which simultaneously affords low benefits for employees such as decreased job satisfaction (Wooden & Warren, 2004) and organisational commitment (De Kuyper et al., 2008). Therefore, in the low simultaneous benefits element there is the employee's perceived disparity in the equitability of mutual benefits between an organisation and its employees. Furthermore, the low simultaneous benefits may be imposed by an organisation or employees may choose to have low simultaneous benefits because of factors relating to their career life-cycle stages.

Employee-career life-cycle dimension and its elements. An employee's career is about his/her relationship to an employing organisation. This relationship is considered as a job context in the model because it can also be described as career opportunities provided by organisations to foster psychological conditions to enhance willingness to perform better to achieve an individual employee's aspirations to progress up the organisation's hierarchy for greater intrinsic and extrinsic benefits (Rosenbaum, 1979; Lam et al., 2012). Apart from this career opportunity by organisations, an individual employee's career is also influenced by the employee's attitudes and behaviours in response to factors such as increasing life span, changing family structures (e.g. dual-career couples, single working parents, employees with care responsibilities including child care and for elder family members) and individuals seeking to fulfil personal learning, development and growth (Hall, 2004).

In the model (Figure 7.1) the three career stages are explained based on employee early, mid- and late career stages (Lam et al., 2012), and are used as elements of the career life cycle in the model. In the proposed configuration model the early career stage indicates the time period during which individual employees enter the labour market and explore varied career opportunities as well as form attitudes and behaviour toward career. The mid-career stage highlights the advancement and maintenance of one's work-related image, some level of achievement, and the enhancement and affirmation of the work-related self-concept. The late career stage reflects the period when individual employees have reached the peak of their career achievements and are inclined to take on leadership roles in an organisation. There are others who are preparing to lower work engagement for transition to retirement and are exploring ways of engaging with society.

7.2.1.2 Processes of the configurational model of job contexts

The process aspect of the model is theoretically explained according to the positive and negative configurational effects of the dimensions of job contexts for

Table 7.1 List of typologies of sustainable HRM practices

1. Career ready for sustainability typology

2. Sustainability awareness typology

3. Sustainability excellence typology

4. Corporate sustainability assistance typology

5. Sustainability culture typology

6. Sustainability veteran typology

7. Legally abiding and benevolent organisation typology

the organisation's stakeholder care position in each of the quadrants as depicted in Figure 7.1. It is important to first explain the harm of work as an important negative configurational effect of job contexts so as to subsequently implement characteristics of sustainable HRM practices into HRM functions to reduce the harm of work imposed on stakeholders (i.e. employees and their families) and achieve the human/social aspect of the corporate sustainability outcome.

The harm of work is defined as those strategic HPWPs used by organisations to extract maximum skills, abilities and motivation from employees but which also 'restrict' employees from achieving positive work-related health and social well-being outcomes (Kramar, 2014; Mariappanadar, 2012). A review of the negative effects of strategic HRM practices (i.e. work intensification) revealed three types of harm of work on employees, their family members and society: psychological; health-related; and social (see Mariappanadar, 2014a). An empirical study found support for the health harm of work as a construct which was different from that of the job stressors-based construct such as the work recovery experiences (Mariappanadar, 2016). Hence, understanding the negative configurational effects of job contexts from the harm of work perspective (see Chapter 5 for details) will facilitate developing and implementing the characteristics of typologies of sustainable HRM practices to HRM functions so as to reduce the health harm and the social/family of work imposed on the stakeholders (i.e. employees and their families).

The process aspects of the positive and the negative configurational effects of job contexts for the organisation–stakeholder care position are described with an example for each of the quadrants of the model along with the typologies of sustainable HRM practices in the next section. This is done because, in particular, the negative configurational effects of job contexts for the organisation–stakeholder care position are used as the basis for developing appropriate characteristics for different typologies of sustainable HRM practices. The typologies of sustainable HRM can be embedded to HRM functions to overcome the negative configurational effects of the harm of work imposed on the stakeholders in each of the quadrants of the model.

Finally, the direction of arrows depicted in the model (Figure 7.1) highlights the process of the configurational model. The arrows show the normative transition of employees from a job with similar job contexts of one OSCPQ to another in the model depending on an employee's experienced positive and negative configurational effects of job contexts in the current quadrant and the career opportunities provided by the organisation. For example, by working through multiple jobs in the precarious employment category, an employee may develop work-ready skills, attitudes and behaviours (i.e. positive configurational effect) in jobs with job contexts of OSCPQ-1 to transition (see Arrow-1) to OSCPQ-2. The transition of employees from a OSCPQ to another depending on the experienced configurational effects of job contexts explains the need for customising the typology of characteristics of sustainable HRM practices while implementing appropriate characteristics to HRM functions to achieve corporate sustainability.

7.2.2 Typologies of sustainable HRM practices

The typologies of sustainable HRM practices are proposed based on the set of characteristics for sustainable HRM practices discussed in Chapter 4. The proposed typologies of sustainable HRM practices (see Table 7.1) facilitate in achieving corporate sustainability through the synthesis effects of minimising the harm of work caused by the negative configurational effects of job contexts on employees while maximising benefits for organisations and individual employees in each of the quadrants in the configurational model. For example, employees in jobs with job contexts of the OSCPQ-2 of the model may disregard the harm of work while operating in the 'extreme work' condition to achieve high simultaneous benefits for an organisation and themselves compared to employees in the OSCPQ-4 who may choose to have low simultaneous benefits to avoid the high-level harm of work. The configurational effects of job contexts on an organisation and its employees are different between employees discussed in the example. Hence, typologies for sustainable HRM practices will also have to vary for employees in jobs of OSCPQ-2 and OSCPQ-4 so as to achieve the synthesis effects of HRM practices to facilitate corporate sustainability. In this section, initially the profile of employees and configurational effects of job contexts in each of the OSCPQs are discussed. Subsequently, the characteristics of HRM practices are theoretically explained for each of the OSCPQs to overcome the negative configurational effects of job contexts using typologies of sustainable HRM practices. This is done to indicate that when typologies of sustainable HRM are implemented or embedded to HRM functions in an organisation, depending on the configurational effects of job contexts then those characteristics can be layered to the dominant strategic HRM practices so as to lead to institutional change. It is important to note that in this section hereafter when a typology of sustainable HRM practices is suggested for implementation to HRM functions (e.g. recruitment and selection, etc.) to achieve corporate sustainability for a OSCPQ, the quadrant not only represents the job contexts but also highlights the relevance to various jobs across industry sectors with similar configurational effects of job contexts in those jobs.

7.2.2.1 Career ready for sustainability typology for OSCPQ-1

The structure of 'career ready for sustainability' typology for jobs in the OSCPQ-1 includes the normal work condition and low simultaneous benefits as the job contexts for employees who are in the early career life-cycle stage. The general profile of employees belonging to the OSCPQ-1 is young, most likely having completed school or university studies, exploring various jobs to choose a future career for themselves and generally employed in precarious employment (Cohen, 1991). The configurational effects in the OSCPQ-1 are that the organisation gains more in simultaneous benefits than employees in precarious jobs (Quinlan et al., 2001). Furthermore, the harm of work (negative configurational effects) on employees caused by precarious employment category is also low. The harm of work on employees is low in the OSCPQ-1 because employees are exposed to normal job contexts which provide adequate time for quicker physical and psychological recovery after work (Sonntag et al., 2010).

The characteristic of the career ready for sustainability typology for the OSCPQ-1 should be able to redress the low simultaneous benefits (i.e. imbalance created in mutual benefits) of precarious employment for employees by providing pre-employment training. This characteristic will allow employees to advance to a future continuous or permanent employment position to achieve mutual benefits. There is evidence in the literature that pre- and post-employment training by organisations to address skill deficits as they arise in the workplace, such as sustainability competencies (KSA) is beneficial (see Perkins & Scutella, 2008). This typology of sustainable HRM practices for the OSCPQ-1 should include characteristics while implementing HRM functions such as identifying potential prospective employees for the organisation and providing pre- and post-employment training to develop sustainability competencies (KSA) to align with the mutual interests of employees, the organisation and job contexts to facilitate an employee to become career-ready for a future full-time position.

The transition of employees from the OSCPQ-1 to jobs in the OSCPQ-2 is indicated by Arrow-1 in Figure 7.1. This is based on the assumption that employees have obtained the required employability competencies either based on pre- and post-employment training and work-ready experiences during the precarious employment stage with an organisation. Alternatively, jobs with the contexts of OSCPQ-2 also indicate that employees may join an organisation in an entry level full-time job after gaining employability skills from an external educational or vocational institution and/or work-related experiences from other similar organisations.

7.2.2.2 Sustainability awareness typology for OSCPQ-2

The dominant job contexts in the OSCPQ-2 are the extreme work condition and high simultaneous benefits for organisations as well as to employees in the early career life-cycle stage. There are two negative configurational effects in the OSCPQ-2 based on the current dominant strategic HRM practices literature. Firstly, individual employee motivation improves simultaneous benefits for organisations and employees but fails to consider the benefit of care for the stakeholders to achieve holistic corporate sustainability (Van Marrewijk, 2003). Secondly, the configurational effect of job contexts in the OSCPQ-2 highlights highly obscured harm of work imposed on employees.

The characteristics of HRM practices for the sustainability awareness typology that are appropriate for jobs with the contexts of OSCPQ-2 highlight that employee selection and training must facilitate employees' competencies to use social consciousness to align with mutual interest of employees, organisations and the job contexts and create awareness of altruistic motivation and about being a sustainability champion. Also, training must create awareness among employees in early career jobs about the obscured harm of work which may have long-term detrimental impacts on health and family life. Creating awareness of the obscured unintended harm of work on employees as characteristics of sustainable HRM practices will also benefit organisations as well as employees because it will reduce the costs associated with employee absenteeism and presenteeism to achieve improved productivity gains. In the normal course of career progression, employees are likely to transition from jobs with the contexts of OSCPQ-2 to OSCPQ-3, which is indicated by Arrow-2, and the characteristics of sustainability excellence typology of sustainable HRM practices for OSCPQ-3 are discussed in the next section.

7.2.2.3 Sustainability excellence typology for OSCPQ-3

The high simultaneous benefits for employees and organisations and the extreme work condition in the employee mid-career stage are the important job contexts that interact in jobs of the OSCPQ-3. The positive configurational effect of the job contexts in the OSCPQ-3 is high positive mutual benefits for employees as well for the organisation. The negative configurational effects of these job contexts are high levels of job involvement which increase the likelihood of an individual experiencing a work–life imbalance among mid-career stage employees (Darcy et al., 2012). However, there is empirical evidence that employees who want to achieve a high work-related self-concept and are involved in extreme work or work intensification are more likely to encounter increased health harm of work (Mariappanadar, 2016) and the social/family of work (Mariappanadar & Aust, 2018).

The characteristics of sustainability excellence typology of sustainable HRM practices for jobs in the OSCPQ-3 are to enhance the quality of instrumental outcomes for organisations and employees. As well, improving the quality of work–life balance with a reduced social and health harm of work should be considered while implementing HRM functions. For example, the characteristics for sustainability excellence typology indicate that employee selection, training and performance evaluation must promote social consciousness for the mutual interests of employees, organisations and stakeholders and strengthen altruistic motivation. HRM strategies and practices should be initiated to measure and identify the health harm and the social/family harm of work as leading indicators for occupational health and work–family balance so as to introduce organisational-level interventions to reduce the harm of work on the stakeholders (i.e. employees, their families and the society).

It is indicated in the OSCPQ-3 (Figure 7.1) that there are two pathways (Arrow-3 and Arrow-4) where employees may transition to other jobs due to the positive and negative configurational effects of job contexts in the OSCPQ-3. Employees transition to either a job with the job contexts of OSCPQ-5 or OSCPQ-4, depending on how well employees cope with the paradox of high job involvement in a job with the configurational effects of job contexts in the OSCPQ-3 using the characteristics for the sustainability excellence typology. Hence, the proposed characteristics for the corporate sustainability assistance typology for jobs in the OSCPQ-4 and the sustainability culture typology for jobs in the OSCPQ-5 are different.

7.2.2.4 Corporate sustainability assistance typology for OSCPQ-4

The profile of employees in jobs with the contexts of the OSCPQ-4 is of those who accept that the harm of HRM practices as inevitable in the extreme work condition. In this scenario, employees from jobs with job contexts of the extreme work and the high simultaneous benefits (i.e. OSCPQ-3) may voluntarily choose to transition (see Arrow-4) to jobs with the 'normal' work and the low simultaneous benefits as the job contexts (i.e. OSCPQ-4). For example, long working hours were consistently associated with poor work–life outcomes (Pocock et al., 2007). Furthermore, it is common among some employees who are exposed to high work intensification to move to a job with a normal work condition to improve work–life outcomes or/and avoid work-related illnesses (Eller et al., 2009). Hence, employees voluntarily transition to jobs with the contexts of OSCPQ-4 to improve employees' work–life balance and reduce the health harm and the social/family of work which are the dominant configurational effects of the normal work and low simultaneous benefits of the jobs contexts on this quadrant. For example, Greenhaus et al. (2001) have indicated that work–family conflicts increase employees' intentions to withdraw from a career job that contradicts their life values.

Kirk and Brown (2003) have indicated that high levels of perceived managerial support such as corporate assistance programmes for organisational-level interventions and organisational change management for workplace wellness will increase the likelihood of an individual experiencing work–life balance and employee well-being. Hence, organisations have a CSR to implement organisational-level interventions to achieve workplace wellness along with employee wellness so as to facilitate future HR regeneration (Ehnert, 2009) or HR conservation (Mariappanadar, 2003) to enhance continuous supply of skilled HR for corporate sustainability. For example, when the state government in Victoria, a state in Australia, privatised public hospitals many experienced nurses permanently quit the nursing profession due to the work intensification that was caused by privatisation, which then created a shortage of skilled nurses in the state (Mariappanadar, 2003). Hence, the characteristics of corporate sustainability assistance typology facilitates HRM practices to achieve the reduction in harm of work on employees through organisational-level work change interventions to achieve workplace wellness along with employee wellness to enhance simultaneous benefits for an organisation and its employees. In addition, this typology will facilitate regeneration of the future supply of skilled HR practitioners.

If the corporate sustainability assistance is effective through appropriate organisational-level change interventions in reducing the harm of work for employees and improving work–life balance among employees belonging to jobs with the contexts of OSCPQ-4, then they might transition (see Arrow-5) to a job with the contexts of OSCPQ-5. Alternatively, if the intervention of corporate sustainability assistance typology has not achieved the desired effects of facilitating employees to transition to jobs with the contexts of OSCPQ-5 then they might choose to transition (see Arrow-6) to jobs with the contexts of OSCPQ-6 or choose to start a new career.

7.2.2.5 Sustainability culture typology for OSCPQ-5

The senior-level managers who transitioned from jobs with job contexts of the OSCPQ-3 to the OSCPQ-5 should become ambassadors or role models for corporate sustainability development by promoting sustainability culture within the organisation. The structure of the OSCPQ-5 includes the extreme work condition and the high simultaneous benefits for an organisation and its employees as the job contexts in the late career stage. The key configurational effects of jobs in the contexts of OSCPQ-5 are high mutual benefits for an organisation and its employees based on a performance-oriented culture, and the high harm of work on employees.

To translate a high performance-oriented culture to a sustainable culture the following characteristics are proposed for the sustainability culture typology of sustainable HRM practices for jobs in the OSCPQ-5. The characteristics of sustainability culture typology include considering employees with proven sustainability and excellence credentials for sustainability leadership roles. They should be trained and coached further to use their leadership position to shape and support HRM policies and practices to develop, or change, organisational culture to reinforce the sustainable HRM characteristics that are highlighted in the career ready for sustainability, sustainability awareness, sustainability excellence, and corporate sustainability assistance typologies so as to facilitate organisations to achieve the synthesis effects of HRM practices for corporate sustainability. Organisations also must introduce HRM practices to measure and identify the health harm and the social/family harm of work as part of an employee wellness programme to reduce the harm of work on the stakeholders (i.e. employees and their families).

7.2.2.6 Sustainability veteran typology for OSCPQ-6

The job contexts of jobs in the OSCPQ-6 reflect that employees are in a pre-retirement stage with the normal work condition or in a phased retirement plan and low simultaneous benefits. The configurational effects of job contexts in the OSCPQ-6 highlight psychologically disengaged employees and they explore opportunities for early exit or bridge employment. Bridge employment is a process used to characterize the transition of older employees from full-time employment to full-time retirement (Mariappanadar, 2013).

Considering psychological disengagement of employees from the organisation as a configurational effect of the job contexts of jobs in the OSCPQ-6, the characteristics of sustainability veteran typology include mentoring of early career employees on the sustainable HRM practices. This characteristic will facilitate veteran or older employees to improve their psychological engagement with the organisation as well as create a smoother passing of the sustainability baton to younger employees (Liebowitz, 2010). The mentoring role by the veteran employees will also benefit the organisation in succession planning for the organisation's corporate sustainability initiatives as well as being self-enhancing for the veteran employees. The characteristics of HRM practices for the sustainability veteran typology also include those practices that facilitate mentoring and succession planning for corporate sustainability for the benefit of an organisation. Finally, organisational assistance for retirement career counselling must be included to identify post-retirement occupations and leisure activities to enhance post-retirement satisfaction and overall life satisfaction for employees operating in jobs within the contexts of OSCPQ-6.

7.2.2.7 Legally abiding and benevolent organisation typology for OSCPQ-7 to OSCPQ-12

This block of quadrants includes six OSCPQs (OSCPQ-7 to OSCPQ-12). These quadrants highlight the job contexts for jobs in which employees are highly vulnerable of being exploited by some organisations for their own benefits (i.e. greed). This characterization of organisations does not relate to all organisations because many commercial organisations are law-abiding and ethical. Employees in this block of quadrants are vulnerable to economic exploitation and occupational injury because they are international student-workers, recent immigrants or undocumented employees with very limited local kin support networkds, a lack of cultural knowledge and in many cases inadequate non-wage income support (Nyland et al., 2009).

The dominant job contexts in jobs of OSCPQ-7 to OSCPQ-12 include forced long working hours (extreme work), fear of repercussions and low simultaneous benefits for employees (i.e. they receive below minimum wages). The negative configurational effects of these dominant job contexts on employees in these jobs of OSCPQs are economic exploitation and increased occupational injury. For example, an Australian company, which has more than 615 convenience stores that sell fuel, coffee, snacks and other products across Australia, generates an annual sale of approximately Aus $3.6 billion. The company is licensed to operate franchise stores from a US company. The media (Australian Broadcasting Corporation (ABC) and the Fairfax group) reported the serious exploitation of employees (predominantly international student-workers, recent immigrants, etc.) with the company paying half the prescribed minimum wages and doctoring payroll records to show a reduced number of hours worked when actually employees worked double the recorded time. The Australian Government Senate Committee conducted an inquiry and found that the exploitation of employees was rampant in many of the company-owned stores as well as in their franchisees in spite of the company making huge profits for a long period of time (ABC, 2015).

This is evidence of an organisation which gains high benefits while employees encounter simultaneous low benefits and the negative configurational effects of job contexts that include economic exploitation, increased occupational injuries and the harm of work on employees such as depression and an increased risk of suicide (ABC, 2015). Although there are only a few such organisations that operate in this way, it is important to uncover and discuss these business practices because if these organisations do not change their organisational values, strategies and practices by themselves or through oversight by the regulatory bodies, then the exploitative practices will be adopted by other businesses in the industry, a scenario which will ultimately have unacceptable ramifications for employees, competitors, communities and the government.

Apart from the legal and punitive perspectives for curtailing exploitative practices within organisations, the perspective of benevolence from justice and trust highlights the characteristics of HRM practices that can change the exploitative practices of organisations on those jobs. For example, Mayer and colleagues (1995) have highlighted that benevolence (doing/being good) and integrity (adherence to a set of acceptable principles) are the two important attributes of an organisation (a trustee) to show distributive justice even when employees (the truster) are in a 'willingness to be vulnerable' in the economic exchange relationship of these jobs. Hence, to overcome the negative configurational effects of job contexts in jobs of these OSCPQs, organisations must develop or modify their existing HRM practices with the characteristics of a legally abiding and benevolent organisation typology. This typology will enhance collective self-concepts, of being benevolent, abiding by the employment law, and being ethical and fair in resource allocation (procedural justice), that match with employees' inputs (distributive justice) for these jobs.

7.3 Embedding characteristics of sustainable HRM typologies to HRM functions

The typology-specific characteristics of sustainable HRM practices can facilitate HRM professionals to customise those characteristics to different HRM functions (i.e. recruitment, selection, training and development, performance appraisal, rewards, workplace wellness, etc.), depending on the misaligned or negative configurational effects of job contexts, so as to achieve corporate sustainability outcomes. For example, the characteristics of sustainability awareness typology which include encouraging pro-social value orientation in empowered decision making and also identifying the negative aspects of obscured harm of work on employees are relevant to employee selection, training, performance appraisal and retention for jobs with negative configurational effects of job contexts in the OSCPQ-1 for achieving corporate sustainability. When employees transition to jobs with negative configurational effects of job contexts in the OSCPQ-2, the characteristics of the sustainability awareness typology are strengthened and operationalised by HRM practices to achieve the synthesising effects of corporate sustainability during performance evaluation, training, reward and retaining of employees. When experiencing difficulty in coping with the negative configurational effects of job contexts in the jobs of OSCPQ-3, employees then transition to jobs with job contexts in the OSCPQ-4. It is suggested that organisations provide organisational-level interventions such as workplace wellness assistance as a HRM function, which is part of the corporate sustainability assistance typology, to facilitate employees to overcome the harm of work and return to the high performance job context of the OSCPQ-5 to achieve high simultaneous benefits for the organisation and its employee.

In summary, it is important to note that there are a set of core characteristics of sustainable HRM practices, such as creating awareness of sustainability, altruistic motivation, and pro-social-oriented decision making, that are relevant to and should be embedded within recruitment, selection, training and development, performance-based rewards, performance appraisal, and career advancement to enhance corporate sustainability outcomes. However, reduction in the health and the social/family of work on employees and their families, workplace wellness, veteran mentoring of early career employees are the unique characteristics of sustainable HRM practices. These unique characteristics are relevant to and should be incorporated into performance appraisal and career promotion as HRM functions, depending on the misalignment or negative configurational effects of job contexts in jobs encountered by employees, to achieve corporate sustainability. Hence, it is evident that the sets of core and unique characteristics of typologies of sustainable HRM practices can be embedded within different HRM functions to different jobs depending on the negative configurational effects of job contexts in each of the OSCPQs to achieve corporate sustainability outcomes.

7.4 A scheme of classification of sustainable HRM for corporate sustainability

Gollan and Xu (2014) have developed a scheme of classification (i.e. typology) of sustainable HRM that is based on the interaction of classifications of sustainable HRM including the level of organisational commitment to sustainability and the function of HR involvement (see Figure 7.2). This scheme of classification is based on interaction at the organisational level (i.e. the organisation's commitment to sustainability) and HRM practices and so is different from the framework of typologies for sustainable HRM, as the latter deals with the configuration of HRM practices as appropriate to different job contexts. The organisational commitment classification

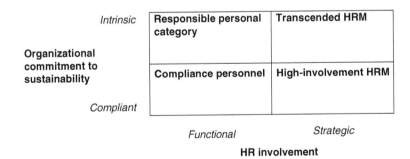

Figure 7.2   A scheme of classification of sustainable HRM (after Gollan & Xu's (2014) framework)

includes two dimensions, the intrinsic and the compliance-based commitment, and the HRM involvement classification includes functional and strategic dimensions. Hence, under this classification scheme of sustainable HRM there are four categories of sustainable HRM based on the interaction between the two classifications. These are responsible personnel, compliance personnel, transcended HRM and high-involvement HRM.

The compliance personnel category features a functional focus in HRM on organisational sustainable strategy based on compliance. That is, organisations in this category provide welfare to society and staff within the limits of regulations and conform to the socially driven business norms. The HRM functional role is implemented with very limited participation in an organisation's strategic planning. The high-involvement HRM category highlights HR is involved in an organisation's strategic planning, whereas the organisation's initiatives towards sustainability are simply compliance-oriented.

The responsible personnel category emphasises a high level of organisational commitment to sustainability and is driven by the intrinsic value of the organisational cultures, which facilitate the organisation to be environmentally and socially responsible. However, the HRM functional role in this category of organisations is one of very limited participation in strategic planning, which is rather directed by top management. Finally, the category of transcended HRM the sustainability development initiatives of an organisation is driven by intrinsic commitment and it is embedded in the organisation's culture and strategy. Furthermore, HRM is involved in the strategic planning for sustainability. Such organisations take a holistic corporate sustainable approach where sustainable development is fully integrated and embedded in every aspect of an organisation as part of the societal approach to corporate sustainability (Van Marrewijk, 2003). The societal approach of corporate sustainability suggests that organisations are responsible to society as a whole, of which they are an integral part.

7.5 Resource regeneration strategy for sustainable work performance

7.5.1 Employee vitality: A quality standard for sustainable HRM

HR regeneration is one of the key characteristics of sustainable HRM along with reducing harm of work. Human energy resources recovery or recuperation is important for regeneration of human resource. For example, when an employee is fully recovered the next day or during lean periods in a working day this will improve organisational performance. Binnewies et al. (2009) found in their study that employees showed higher work performance on days when they were well rested in the morning compared to those days when they had recovered poorly. In the contemporary high work performance literature there is evidence that high work performance drains employee energy resources and provides limited opportunity to recover and regenerate energy resources (e.g. Meijman & Mulder, 1998). However, Docherty et al. (2002) proposed that regeneration of human energy compared to draining of energy during work was as one of the main differences between sustainable work and intensive work. Hence, Dorenbosch (2014) proposed a four-category framework of sustainable work performance for regeneration of human energy resources using employee vitality and proactivity. Employee vitality is defined in many ways but in the sustainable work performance framework (Figure 7.3) it is explained as both mental and physical energy of employees (Dorenbosch, 2014). Furthermore, proactivity is 'self-initiated and future-oriented action that aims to change and improve the situation or oneself' (Parker et al., 2006, p. 636).

Institutional theory provides explanation for both individual and organisational actions (Dacin et al., 2002). The typologies of characteristics of sustainable HRM and the classification of sustainable HRM for corporate sustainability (Gollan & Xu, 2014) emphasise actions at the organisational level, whereas the sustainable work performance framework (Dorenbosch, 2014) is related to employee-level actions. Although, the sustainable work performance framework is about employee-level actions for high performance, it focuses on organisational-level allocation of resources for employee recovery and revitalisation for high work performance.

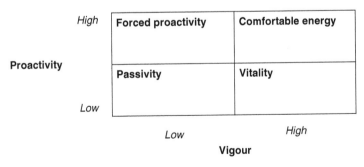

Figure 7.3 Sustainable work performance framework (after Dorenbosch, 2014)

In the framework it is indicated that employee vitality is a sustainable work performance concept and employees with vitality can manage work performance resource constraints (i.e. time, energy and competence constraints) effectively to achieve organisational performance as well as improved health. Furthermore, the framework was developed based on the interplay between vigour and proactivity. That is, employees with high proactivity will find innovative ways to complete some of the work tasks more effectively so as to save energy and have vigour (i.e. time and energy) for performing other work tasks to achieve high performance. It is presumed in the framework that employee vitality has a reciprocal relationship between vigour and proactivity. Hence, with the background information discussed here let us explore the sustainable work performance framework.

The four-category framework of sustainable work performance was developed based on the interplay between proactivity and vigour. The four categories of the framework are vitality, passivity, forced proactivity and comfortable energy. Each of the categories signifies different representations of the employee's resource expenditure and its consequent risks to their high work performance in the future. High vitality employees have high energy levels which they are prepared to proactively allocate towards job improvements self-development and who are also resilient to various constraints (i.e. time, energy and competence constraints) for achieving high performance. However, passivity is about lower vigour and in such cases engagement in proactive behaviour at work is rare. The forced proactivity category concerns cases where employees experience a decline in vigour which forces them to increase their efforts in reinvigorating by making proactive changes within the job context or oneself. In this struggle for resources (i.e. time, energy and competence) an employee might lose extra resources to a point where the employee gives up and slips into the category of passivity. Finally, the comfortable energy category refers to those employees with high vigour but who expend their efforts in proactive behaviours at work to a lower extent. In the next section the sustainable HRM strategy is discussed; this seeks to strike a balance between work performance and resource regeneration.

7.5.2 Sustainable HRM strategy to facilitate resource regeneration

Empirical evidence from a study by Dorenbosch (2014) revealed that the group of employees with high vitality tends to invest more time in high work performance without draining their energy levels. Furthermore, the study found employees with a combination of high vigour and high proactivity contributed to improve on their efforts for high performance without draining their energy resources. Hence, it is important for organisations to develop strategies to monitor employee proactivity and vigour as an indication of the level of employee vitality in a work unit to understand the sustainability risks for regeneration of human energy. Identifying sustainability risks will facilitate HR managers and line managers to acquire knowledge on the job-specific resource constraints (i.e. time, energy and competence constraints) to work performance over time. For example, the mental and physical energies of employees can be drained and depleted by high and heavy work demands when employees have limited control over the depletion of their energy. Hence, organisations should provide training to employees on improving employees' work styles to increase employee vitality and sustain it.

Employee work style is about a response to work demands in a certain job contexts and is a learned behaviour (Bongers et al., 2006). A study by Van Scheppingen and colleagues (2014) found that an employee work style based on autonomous regulations of organisations (intrinsic motivation) improved employee vitality at work as well as reduced presenteeism. That is, organisational interventions to improve employee vitality should offer choice, personal mastery, fun and positive interpersonal behaviour so as to facilitate resource regeneration of energy for employees to achieve sustainable high performance. Furthermore, improved employee vitality as an important characteristic of sustainable HRM will reduce presenteeism to improve organisational performance. Hence, employee vitality will be able to synthesise work performance and resource regeneration to achieve sustainable work performance. However, the configuration of typologies of sustainable HRM characteristics from the organisational-level perspective challenges the ever-growing organisational expectations to increase employee vitality because over a period of time employee vitality might reach the irreversible non-sustainable level.

7.6 Overcoming barriers to implementing sustainable HRM practices

Barriers obstruct management actions to implement the characteristics of sustainable HRM practices to HRM functions. Industry barriers and organisational barriers are formidable barriers to implementing or embedding sustainable HRM practices into HRM functions in an organisation and are discussed in this section. As well, an attempt is made in this section to explain how to overcome these barriers so as to improve the legitimacy of sustainable HRM practices.

7.6.1 Industry barriers

Industry barriers are about the special and unique features of the business activity with which a company operates. Competitive pressure is an industry barrier that is more relevant to implementing sustainable HRM in an organisation. For example, take the same organisation (an Australian chain of convenience stores) that was discussed earlier in the section on legally abiding and benevolent organisation typology and its illegal practice of exploiting employees with overwork and underpay. Other competitors in the fuel retailing industry are more likely to follow this Australian chain's practice of underpaying their employees due to isomorphic institutional pressure to avoid competitive disadvantage in an attempt to achieve cost leadership. For example, a Fairfax Media (2016) investigation, after revealing the illegal HR practices of the Australian chain, also revealed that another multinational oil company in Australia in its fuel retail outlets underpaid employees. Hence, the fuel retailing industry's operations in Australia have become an industry barrier (i.e. avoid competitive disadvantage) to adopting sustainable HRM practices in their HRM functions due to hypercompetitive pressures.

7.6.1.1 Strategic choice to overcome industry barriers

An institutional freedom perspective for sustainable HRM highlights that organisations shape their own institutional contexts and become an organisational leader in developing and promoting sustainable HRM practices. That is, an organisation, instead of conforming to isomorphic pressures from other peer organisations or simply engaging in the ceremonial behaviour of following institutionalized rules of HRM practices, can rather become a leader in the industry. Organisations using the institutional freedom perspective for sustainable HRM practices and policies as strategic choices don't consider that the legitimacy for sustainable HRM practices is based on isomorphism pressure from the institutional contexts because legitimacy is more of a social construct. For example, organisations in the fuel retailing industry in Australia may engage in socially responsible behaviour by developing sustainable HRM practices that are not practised by other competitors.

By engaging in this discretional activity on developing sustainable HRM and communicating them effectively to the society, organisations can build additional local support for sustainable HRM practices and this can be a strategy for social construction for firm specific legitimacy. Hence, it is possible for organisations in a hyper-competition market to develop a strategic choice that conforms to stakeholders' CSR demands and develop sustainable HRM practices instead of succumbing to the isomorphic pressures of an industry.

7.6.2 Organisational barriers

Entrenched strategic HRM practice is an organisational barrier to implementing sustainable HRM practices. Entrenchment from the institutional theory perspective highlights the presence of a practice within an organisation which is unlikely to be abandoned even under external pressure (Zeitz et al., 1999). An entrenched practice such as strategic HRM highlights the involvement of strategic (i.e. business strategies) and operational (i.e. HRM functions) aspects of an organisation, managers' deeply held values (i.e. a focus on the bottom line) and the commitment of considerable resources. Hence, the entrenched organisational-level practices and managers' values about strategic HRM are the organisational barriers to implementing the emerging sustainable HRM practices. An attempt is made next to explain the initial functional and social perceptions that are organisational barriers to implementing sustainable HRM, and then the institutional change initiatives to overcome these barriers.

7.6.2.1 Strategies to overcome organisational barriers

Dacin et al. (2002) have highlighted that the functional organisational barrier for transforming management practices is due to the perceived utility value associated with those practices. For example, the perceived utility value of strategic HRM is to provide mutual benefits to organisations through increased productivity and both tangible and intangible benefits to employees for contributing to increased productivity. This taken-for-granted utility value of strategic HRM practices as legitimate institutional practices has been established in the HRM literature but these practices also simultaneously impose negative impacts or harm of work on stakeholders (i.e. employees, their families and the society) rather than just the benefits for employees. Hence, the perceived reduced utility value of increased organisational performance for the stakeholders must be highlighted to practitioners, researchers, advocacy groups and the government so as to initiate the need for transforming strategic HRM practices with the characteristics of sustainable HRM. The institutional change initiative, such as expanding the performance-focused institutional boundary of strategic HRM practices by including stakeholders' well-being as part of sustainable HRM, will enhance the utility value for organisations as well as stakeholders. Hence, this institutional initiative will overcome the functional barriers to implementing sustainable HRM.

Existing legitimate institutional practices that are used to engage human resources to benefit shareholders act as the social organisational barrier for the transformation of strategic HRM practices into sustainable HRM practices. However, the shift in the interests and expectations of communities, advocacy groups, and governments on socially responsible organisational behaviour towards key stakeholders, such as employees, their families, have triggered organisations to take necessary actions to overcome the social organisational barrier. . For example, communities and advocacy groups are beginning to indicate to large corporations and governments that strategic HRM practices – the existing legitimate institutional HRM practice – have started to negatively affect employees' and their families' health and work–life balance. Hence, there are social pressures for organisations to transform their existing strategic HRM practices into sustainable HRM practices to achieve the human/social outcome of corporate sustainability.

Greenwood et al. (2002) have indicated in their institutional change model that the prevailing dominant norms or practices (i.e. strategic HRM practices) go through a critical stage of layering with new theorisation, diffusion (i.e. increasing objectification) and re-institutionalisation or legitimation of new practices (i.e. sustainable HRM practices). Layering institutions is a concept that is about the partial renegotiation of some elements of a given set of institutions while leaving others in place (Thelen, 2003). That is, the sets of characteristics of sustainable HRM as a new institutional form can be added to the characteristics of strategic HRM instead of dismantling entrenched HRM practices. Parrado (2008) has indicated that layering is an ideal institutional change initiative to embed changes typical of new practices (i.e. sustainable HRM) into a particular institution's traditional approach (i.e. strategic HRM) and management. Hence, over a period of time the current dominant strategic HRM practices will be layered with the characteristics of sustainable HRM practices from different typologies which will overcome the social barrier and become legitimate institutional practices for corporate sustainability.

7.7 Paradoxes in implementing strategic and sustainable HRM practices

Sustainable HRM is a new organisational form which attempts to extend the boundary of entrenched strategic HRM practices in the field of HRM. A new organisational form in institution theory highlights wherein institutional entrepreneurs (i.e. researchers in a new field) actively define, justify, and push the theory and values underpinning a new form of organisation (Rao et al., 2000). When attempts are made to extend the boundary of entrenched strategic HRM practices to include typology-specific characteristics of sustainable HRM practices, these create tensions among practitioners and researchers in the field of HRM in deciding on one set of characteristics of HRM practices over another set. It is important to note that the tensions created by paradoxes are not bad but it depends on whether paradoxes facilitate institutional change in HRM practices or instead foster institutional inertia to continue with the entrenched practices such as strategic HRM. Ehnert (2014) has indicated synthesis as a cognitive mode of coping with the tensions of paradoxes in sustainable HRM. That is, integrating organisations' economic outcomes with stakeholders' human/social and society's sustainable environmental management expectations outcomes by engaging employees using HRM functions will lead to the synthesising of HRM practices (Mariappanadar, 2014b). The integration of dualities of a set of economic outcomes for organisations and a set of human/social and natural environmental outcomes for stakeholders is explained with an institutional change initiative to cope with the paradoxes.

7.7.1 Overcoming paradoxes of implementing sustainable HRM

Sustainable HRM is an institutional theory (Mariappanadar & Kramar, 2014) which provides the basis for why organisations should be interested in extending their actions to include human/social and environmental outcomes for stakeholders while attempting to improve organisational performance. Institutional change theory explains that the institutional change starts with 'deinstitutionalisation' so that this process will facilitate the emergence of new forms of practices in organisations (Davis et al., 1994). Institutionalists believe that an emerging new theory in a field will layer practices with new practices along with entrenched practices to benefit the society and/or natural environment. That is, the organisational boundary of strategic HRM practices is extended to layer stakeholders' outcomes so as to reduce the negative impacts imposed on employees and the natural environment and also facilitate HR regeneration while organisations also improve their performance.

Extending strategic HRM's organisational boundary and layering stakeholders' human/social and environmental expectations with it can facilitate the integration of dualities as a coping strategy for the synthesising effects of sustainable HRM to achieve corporate sustainability. Corporate sustainability is about the management approaches used by organisations in achieving the three pillars (i.e. economic/financial, human/social and natural environmental outcomes) of sustainable development (UN Global Compact, 2014).

7.8 Conclusion

In this chapter, three different frameworks were used as the theoretical basis for implementing sustainable HRM within organisations. Firstly, the framework of typologies of sustainable HRM highlight the sets of core and unique characteristics of sustainable HRM that can be embedded into different HRM functions for various jobs to achieve corporate sustainability outcomes. The typologies of sustainable HRM practices are implemented into HRM functions (i.e. employee selection, training, performance management, etc.) depending on the negative configurational effects of job contexts for the organisation–stakeholder care position in different quadrants of the proposed new model. Secondly, the scheme of classification of sustainable HRM indicates responsible personnel, compliance personnel, transcended HRM and high-involvement HRM as four categories. Each of the categories explains various levels of organisational involvement in developing and implementing strategies for corporate sustainability. Finally, the framework for the resource regeneration strategy of sustainable performance was used to explain that employees with high vigour and high proactivity will be able to synthesise work performance and human resource regeneration.

Competitive pressure was used as an industry barrier that obstructs management actions from embedding characteristics of sustainable HRM into HRM functions within an organisation. Furthermore, the institutional freedom perspective was presented as a strategic option for an organisation to overcome competitive pressure and gain legitimacy for sustainable HRM practices. Entrenched strategic HRM in organisations was explained as an organisational barrier to implementing more recent sustainable HRM practices. It was suggested that layering as an institutional change initiative will facilitate the transition of implementing the characteristics of sustainable HRM practices using different typologies with those of existing strategic

HRM practices so that the new organisational form, with the combination of characteristics, will become a legitimate institutional practice for corporate sustainability. Finally, the integration of dualities as a coping strategy was suggested to overcome the paradoxes that HR professionals will encounter in implementing recent sustainable HRM in the face of entrenched strategic HRM practices within the organisation. That is, the boundaries of strategic HRM could be expanded to accommodate the layering of the characteristics of sustainable HRM and this will synthesise the dualities of both strands of HRM practices to achieve corporate sustainability.

References

ABC (Australian Broadcasting Corporation) (2015). [7-Eleven] management vow to fully refund all exploited workers http://www.abc.net.au/news/2015-09-24/7-eleven-workers-paid-up-to-70k-for-visa-inquiry-told/6801194. Accessed on 16 May 2016.

Binnewies, C., Sonnentag, S. & Mojza, E. J. (2009). Daily performance at work: Feeling recovered in the morning as a predictor of day-level job performance. *Journal of Organizational Behavior, 30*(1), 67–93.

Bongers, P. M., Ijmker, S., Van Den Heuvel, S. & Blatter, B. M. (2006). Epidemiology of work related neck and upper limb problems: Psychosocial and personal risk factors (part I) and effective interventions from a bio behavioural perspective (part II). *Journal of Occupational Rehabilitation, 16*(3), 272–95.

Boselie, P., Dietz, G. & Boon, C. (2006). Commonalities and contradictions in HRM and performance research. *Human Resource Management Journal, 15*(3), 67–94.

Cohen, A. (1991). Career stage as a moderator of the relationships between organizational commitment and its outcomes: A meta-analysis. *Journal of Occupational Psychology, 64*(3), 253–68.

Colbert, B. A. (2004). The complex resource-based view: Implications for theory and practice in strategic human resource management. *Academy of Management Review, 29*, 341–58.

Combs, J., Liu, Y., Hall, A. & Ketchen, D. (2006). How much do high-performance work practices matter? A meta-analysis of their effects on organizational performance. *Personnel Psychology, 59*(3), 501–28.

Dacin, M., Goodstein, J. & Scott, W. (2002). Institutional theory and institutional change: Introduction to the special research forum. *The Academy of Management Journal, 45*(1), 43–56.

Darcy, C., McCarthy, A., Hill, J. & Grady, G. (2012). Work–life balance: One size fits all? An exploratory analysis of the differential effects of career stage. *European Management Journal, 30*(2), 111–20.

Davis, G. F., Diekmann, K. A. & Tinsley, C. H. (1994). The decline and fall of the conglomerate firm in the 1980s: The deinstitutionalization of an organizational form. *American Sociological Review, 59*(4), 547–70.

De Cuyper, N., De Jong, J., De Witte, H., Isaksson, K., Rigotti, T. & Schalk, R. (2008). Literature review of theory and research on the psychological impact of temporary employment: Towards a conceptual model. *International Journal of Management Reviews, 10*, 25–51.

Docherty, P., Forslin, J. & Shani, A. B. (2002). *Creating Sustainable Work Systems: Emerging Perspectives and Practice.* London: Routledge.

Dorenbosch, L. (2014). Stiking abalance between work effort and resource regeneration: Vitality as a sustainable performance concept. In: I. Ehnert, W. Harry, & K. J. Zink (eds) *Sustainability and Human Resource Management* (pp. 155–80). Berlin, Heidelberg: Springer.

Dyllick, T. & Hockerts, K. (2002). Beyond the business case for corporate sustainability. *Business Strategy and the Environment, 11*(2), 130–41.

Ehnert, I. (2009). *Sustainable Human Resource Management: A Conceptual and Exploratory Analysis from a Paradox Perspective.* London: Springer.

Ehnert, I. (2014). Paradox as a lens for theorizing sustainable HRM: Mapping and coping with paradoxes and tensions. In: I. Ehnert, W. Harry, & K. J. Zink (eds), *Sustainability and Human Resource Management* (pp. 247–71). Berlin, Heidelberg: Springer.

Eller, N. H., Netterstrøm, B., Gyntelberg, F., Kristensen, T. S., Nielsen, F., Steptoe, A. & Theorell, T. (2009). Work-related psychosocial factors and the development of ischemic heart disease: A systematic review. *Cardiology in Review, 17*, 83–97.

Fairfax Media (2016). Caltex warned its service station owners of regulator raids. http://www.smh.com.au/business/workplace-relations/caltex-warned-its-service-station-owners-of-regulator-raids-20161102-gsg8qn.html. Accessed on 23 November 2016.

Giannikisa, S. & Nikandrou, I. (201). The impact of corporate entrepreneurship and high performance work systems on employees' job attitudes: Empirical evidence from Greece during the economic downturn. *The International Journal of Human Resource Management, 24*, 1–23.

Godard, J. (2001). High performance and the transformation of work? The implications of alternative work practices for the experience and outcomes of work. *Industrial & Labor Relations Review, 54*(4), 776–805.

Gollan, P. J. & Xu, Y. (2014). Fostering corporate sustainability: Integrative and dynamic approaches to sustainable HRM. In: I. Ehnert, W. Harry & K. J. Zink (eds), *Sustainability and Human Resource Management.* (225–46). Berlin, Heidelberg: Springer.

Granter, E., McCann, L. & Boyle, M. (2015). Extreme work/normal work: Intensification, storytelling and hypermediation in the (re) construction of 'the New Normal'. *Organization, 22*, 443–56.

Greenhaus, J. H., Parasuraman, S. & Collins, K. M. (2001). Career involvement and family involvement as moderators of relationships between work–family conflict and withdrawal from a profession. *Journal of Occupational Health Psychology, 6*, 91–100.

Greenwood, R., Suddaby, R. & Hinings, C. R. (2002). Theorizing change: The role of professional associations in the transformation of institutionalized fields. *Academy of Management Journal, 45*(1), 58–80.

Hall, D. T. (2004). The protean career: A quarter-century journey. *Journal of Vocational Behavior, 65*(1), 1–13.

Halrynjo, S. (2009). Men's work–life conflict: Career, care and self-realization: Patterns of privileges and dilemmas. *Gender, Work & Organization, 16*(1), 98–125.

Kirk, A. & Brown, D. F. (2003). Employee assistance programs: A review of the management of stress and wellbeing through workplace counselling and consulting. *Australian Psychologist, 38*(2), 138–43.

Kramar, R. (2014). Beyond strategic human resource management: Is sustainable human resource management the next approach? *The International Journal of Human Resource Management, 25*(8), 1069–89.

Lam, S. S., Ng, T. W. & Feldman, D. C. (2012). The relationship between external job mobility and salary attainment across career stages. *Journal of Vocational Behavior, 80*(1), 129–36.

Lent, R. W. & Brown, S. D. (2008). Social cognitive career theory and subjective wellbeing in the context of work. *Journal of Career Assessment, 16*(1), 6–21.

Liebowitz, J. (2010). The role of HR in achieving a sustainability culture. *Journal of Sustainable Development, 3*, 50–57.

Mariappanadar, S. (2003). Sustainable human resource management: The sustainable and unsustainable dilemmas of downsizing. *International Journal of Social Economics, 30*, 906–23.

Mariappanadar, S. (2012). Harm of efficiency oriented HRM practices on stakeholders: An ethical issue for sustainability. *Society and Business Review, 7*, 168–84.

Mariappanadar, S. (2013). Do retirement anxieties determine bridge employment preference? A study among pre-retirees in the Australian construction industry. *Personnel Review, 42*, 176–204.

Mariappanadar, S. (2014a). Sustainable HRM: A counter to minimize the externality of downsizing. In: I. Ehnert, W. Harr & K. J. Zink (eds), *Sustainability and Human Resource Management* (pp. 181–203). Berlin, Heidelberg: Springer.

Mariappanadar, S. (2014b). Stakeholder harm index: A framework to review work intensification from the critical HRM perspective. *Human Resource Management Review, 24*(4), 313–29.

Mariappanadar, S. (2016). Health harm of work from the sustainable HRM perspective: Scale development and validation. *International Journal of Manpower, 37*(6), 924–44.

Mariappanadar, S. and Aust, I (2018). The Dark Side of Overwork: An Empirical Evidence of Social Harm of Work from a Sustainable HRM perspective, *International Studies of Management and Organization, 47*, 372–387.

Mariappanadar, S. & Kramar, R. (2014). Sustainable HRM: The synthesis effect of high performance work systems on organisational performance and employee harm. *Asia-Pacific Journal of Business Administration, 6*(3), 206–24.

Mayer, R. C., Davis, J. H. & Schoorman, F. D. (1995). An integrative model of organizational trust. *Academy of Management Review, 20*(3), 709–34.

Meijman, T. F. & Mulder, G. (1998). Psychological aspects of workload. In: P. J. D. Drenth, H. Thierry & C. J. De Wolff (eds) *Handbook of Work and Organizational Psychology* (Vol. 2) (pp. 3–33). Hove: Psychology Press.

Nyland, C., Forbes-Mewett, H., Marginson, S., Ramia, G., Sawir, E. & Smith, S. (2009). International student-workers in Australia: A new vulnerable workforce. *Journal of Education and Work, 22*, 1–14.

Parker, S. K., Williams, H. M. & Turner, N. (2006). Modeling the antecedents of proactive behavior at work. *Journal of Applied Psychology, 91*(3), 636–52.

Parrado, S. (2008). Failed policies but institutional innovation through 'layering' and 'diffusion' in Spanish central administration. *International Journal of Public Sector Management, 21*(2), 230–52.

Perkins, D. & Scutella, R. (2008). Improving employment retention and advancement of low-paid workers. *Australian Journal of Labour Economics, 11*, 97–144.

Pocock, B., Williams, P. & Skinner, N. (2007). *The Australian Work and Life Index (AWALI): Concepts, Methodology and Rationale.* Adelaide: Centre for Work and Life, Hawke Research Institute, University of South Australia.

Quinlan, M., Mayhew, C. & Bohle, P. (2001). The global expansion of precarious employment, work disorganization, and consequences for occupational health: A review of recent research. *International Journal of Health Services, 31*(2), 335–414.

Rao, H., Morrill, C. & Zald, M. N. (2000). Power plays: How social movements and collective action create new organizational forms. *Research in Organizational Behavior, 22*, 237–81.

Rosenbaum, J. E. (1979). Tournament mobility: Career patterns in a corporation. *Administrative Science Quarterly, 24*(2), 220–41.

Shih, H., Chiang, Y. & Hsu, C. (2013). High performance work system and HCN performance. *Journal of Business Research, 66*(4), 540–46.

Sonnentag, S., Kuttler, I. & Fritz, C. (2010). Job stressors, emotional exhaustion, and need for recovery: A multi-source study on the benefits of psychological detachment. *Journal of Vocational Behavior, 76*(3), 355–65.

Thelen, K. (2003). How institutions evolve: Insights from comparative historical analysis. In: Mahoney, J. & Rueschemeyer, D. (eds), *Comparative Historical Analysis in the Social Sciences.* Cambridge: Cambridge University Press, 208–40.

UN Global Compact (2014). Overview of the UN Global Compact. http://nbis.org/nbisresources/sustainable_development_equity/un_global_compact.pdf. Accessed on 22 September 2015.

Van Marrewijk, M. (2003). Concepts and definitions of CSR and corporate sustainability: Between agency and communion. *Journal of Business Ethics, 44*(2), 95–105.

Van Scheppingen, A. R., de Vroome, E. M., Ten Have, K. C., Zwetsloot, G. I., Bos, E. H. & van Mechelen, W. (2014). Motivations for health and their associations with lifestyle, work style, health, vitality, and employee productivity. *Journal of Occupational and Environmental Medicine*, *56*(5), 540–46.

Wooden, M. & Warren, D. (2004). Non-standard employment and job satisfaction: Evidence from the HILDA survey. *Journal of Industrial Relations*, *46*, 275–97.

Zeitz, G., Mittal, V. & McAulay, B. (1999). Distinguishing adoption and entrenchment of management practices: A framework for analysis. *Organization Studies*, *20*(5), 741–76.

8

Bridging sustainable HRM theory and practice: The Respect, Openness and Continuity model

Peggy De Prins

Inspired by the three 'Ps' ('people', 'planet', 'profit') of CSR, 'Respect', 'Openness' and 'Continuity' (ROC) are positioned as the three building blocks of sustainable HRM (De Prins et al., 2014). Although the attention to these blocks is not new in itself, our contribution lies in the critical reflection on and redirection of existing HRM practices, systems and themes towards the ROC model. In this chapter we focus on 'hands-on' management approaches for implementing sustainable HRM. The purpose is to explore some of the management challenges of sustainable HRM and the opportunities for the academic and practitioner community to work effectively together to address some of these challenges.

Based on an extensive literature, combined with focus groups and a pilot design and roll-out of a sustainable HRM learning and development programme, we've developed twelve practical approaches for sustainable HRM. Within each approach some examples of sustainable HRM (best) practices are given. The basic assumption behind the twelve approaches is that sustainable HRM is perceived as a social construction. The language used by theorists, researchers and practitioners to describe sustainable HRM is as a form of social action, creating understandings regarding what sustainable HRM is, as well as about the effects it is presumed to have on social life and the structuring of employment relationships (Keegan & Boselie, 2006). The aim of the ROC model is to build a sense giving (rather than a normative) framework for classifying and positioning (or repositioning) new initiatives and experiments, as well as existing practices and traditions within the domain of sustainable HRM.

8.1 The triple P translated: Introduction of the ROC model

Consistent with De Lange and Koppens (2007), we define sustainable HRM as a specific form of personnel management that is explicitly linked with the external business environment of the organization, which is focused on respect for the human workforce and in which the interests of the employer, the workers and societal interests are balanced with each other. Several definitions of sustainable HRM exist in the literature (see Ehnert & Harry, 2012; Kramar, 2014). The definition of De Lange and Koppens (2007) in which the triple P ('Planet, People and Profit') is 'translated' into 'Respect, Openness and Continuity' (ROC) (Figure 8.1) offers a good starting point in our opinion. In recent years the triple P vocabulary has gained popularity in light of its practicality from the perspective of managers and scholars. Just as the triple P rhetoric has contributed to CSR, the ROC model has the potential to support the implementation and mainstreaming of sustainable HRM practices.

According to De Lange and Koppens (2007), sustainable HRM differs from mainstream HRM because of the following characteristics:

1. A renewed focus on respect for the internal stakeholders in the organisation, the employees (Respect). HRM practices within the 'Respect' building block are typically appreciation of and engaging with employees.
2. External business environmental awareness and outside-in perspective on HRM (Openness), typically with connecting and inclusive HRM practices.
3. A long-term approach, in terms of both economic and societal sustainability terms and about individual employability (Continuity). HRM practices here are typically innovative and career-oriented.

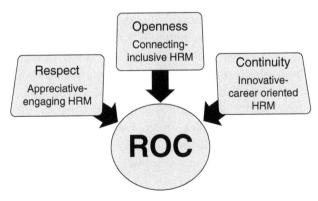

Figure 8.1 The Respect Openness Continuity (ROC) model of sustainable HRM

Based on a critical review of three mainstream theoretical perspectives on strategic HRM we discuss the building blocks of sustainable HRM in this sections (see also Table 8.1). According to Paauwe (2012), the field of HRM, by nature, reflects developments in society and trends in the academic disciplines (psychology, strategic management and so on) that contribute to the field. During the 1990s, strategic HRM emphasised the following three perspectives: (1) the link between HRM and financial performance; (2) the fit between HRM and strategy; and (3) HRM and the sustainable competitive advantage (the resource-based view). The narrative style of many HRM articles focuses on 'strategy' and the 'search for strategic added value through people'. The HRM literature of that time was dominated by 'what employers want' (Boselie, 2010). In contrast to this unilateral strategic perspective, today's discussions concerning sustainable HRM are more balanced, recognising the fact that 'what employers want' is not necessarily the same as 'what employees want' and 'what society/external stakeholders want' (see also the synthesis effects of sustainable HRM in Chapter 5).

Before presenting the model in more detail, we address its primary underlying assumptions. These assumptions are related to the theoretical roots and foundations of the ROC model, as well as to its implementation possibilities.

1. The ROC model is based on the assumption that sustainable HRM forms the next, complementary stage in the tradition of HRM thinking. It reframes and revises the mainstream principles of strategic HRM, which were dominant in HRM thinking beginning in the 1980s.
2. Sustainable HRM highlights the synthesis paradox (Clegg et al., 2002; Mariappanadar, 2013, 2014). In this 'both/and' approach, organisations can use strategic HRM practices to maximise their profits, in addition to reducing the harm of HRM practices on the stakeholders, given that these two polarities are not mutually exclusive but mutually reinforcing.
3. As mentioned, one basic assumption is that sustainable HRM can be classified as a social-constructivist concept (Keegan & Boselie, 2006). The idea of 'knowledge as substance' is replaced by the idea of 'knowledge as participation'. Knowledge is developed, spread and applied within active working relationships between the members of a practice/community. In the sections that follow, we adhere to this assumption, referring to the twelve approaches to implementing sustainable HRM. Instead of being normative or descriptive, this discussion is intended to stimulate the practical community to explore and apply the concept of sustainable HRM according to the various dimensions of the ROC model.

Table 8.1 Theoretical antecedents and overview of practical approaches to implementing sustainable HRM

	People Respect	Planet Openness	Profit Continuity
Basic concept	'Searching for the Human in HRM'	'HRM from the outside in'	'Long-term scope of HRM'
Theory Mainstream strategic HRM perspective revisited	Resourced-based view revisited	Strategic fit revisited	Long-term performance/long-term employment relationships revisited
Theoretical antecedents	Ethical and critical HR theory	Institutional and stakeholder theory	
Key questions	'How can we strengthen our employees (even more) as VIP-internal stakeholders?'	'How can we connect our HRM policy (even more) with our other stakeholders and the underlying values, standards and developments in society?'	'How do we make sure that our employees and our organizations are (even more) future-proof?'
Characteristics of HRM practices	Appreciative; engaging	Connecting; inclusive	Innovative; career-oriented
Practical approaches to implementing sustainable HRM	1. Integrate humanity and sustainability in mission and value statements 2. Combine a competency and talent-based approach to sustainable HRM 3. Mainstream decent and meaningful work 4. Act as a transformational leader for sustainable HRM	5. Combine HRM differentiation with a collective mindset 6. Invest in sustainable networks and social capital 7. Go for an inclusive approach to sustainable HRM 8. Be sensitive to diversity and environmental management	9. Optimise organisational structure and processes 10. Dare to co-create 11. Strive for sustainable careers 12. Encourage sustainable retention

191

8.2 First sustainable HRM block: Respect

The first building block of the ROC model stems from the ethical and critical tradition related to 'respect'. With respect, we refer to the search for the 'human' in HRM theory and practices. Respect calls for a smarter and more respectful attitude towards resources, and especially towards human resources.

8.2.1 Theoretical background

The relationship between ethics and HRM has been the subject of recent discussion. The turning point was the subsequently well-established proposal that ethics should be considered central to the HRM function (Rhodes & Harvey, 2012; Voegtlin & Greenwood, 2016). According to Guest and Woodrow (2012), HRM professionals should act as 'ethical stewards'. They might do this by aiming for a strong HRM system, forming alliances for the formulation and implementation of policy, seeking opportunities for promoting worker well-being and, more generally, seeking to make ethical choices whenever the opportunity arises (Guest & Woodrow, 2012). The latter is reflected in various contexts, including in the daily events within an organisation, in conflicts between line managers and their subordinates and in situations in which a worker is transferred to another team. From an ethical and humanity perspective, such daily issues are certainly not solely the responsibility of HRM. If HRM passes this responsibility purely to line management, however, then HRM is at risk of becoming locked in an ivory tower. The meaning of ethics and humanity for HRM is thus an important issue for the future (see also Chapter 4).

As also referred to in Chapter 4, the critical HRM literature contains many calls for bringing humanity back into HRM. According to Van Buren et al. (2011), the strategic HR business partnership role has made HR more organisation- than employee-focused, leading to a lack of concern for the employee welfare perspective. In a book, Bolton and Houlihan (2007) suggest that, even though people appear to be of central concern in HRM theory, HRM practice and the workplace experience, the rich, warm and unpredictable faces of humanity are all too clearly absent. By managing the employment relationship solely in economic terms, humanity is 'squeezed out' and the resource is therefore never seen in its full light. Scholars of CSR would refer to this as a tension between the logic of Profit and the logic of People. In the revision of the strategic HRM tradition, it implies the recognition and revaluation of the basic characteristics of the 'human' within the resource-based view.

As remarked by Lengnick-Hall and colleagues (2009): 'While strategic HRM research has drawn substantially from the resource-based view of the firm to emphasize the strategic and the resource factors in strategic HRM activities, at times it appears that the "human" element has been neglected' (Lengnick-Hall, Lengnick-Hall, Andrade & Drake, 2009, p. 70). The key question within this block is: 'How can we strengthen employees as key internal stakeholders?'

8.2.2 Practical approaches to implement 'Respect': Appreciative and engaging HRM

Bringing the 'human' component back into HRM means a renewed focus on respect for the internal stakeholders, the employees, by implementing an appreciative and engaging HRM. This means recognising the richness and complexity of the target focus, namely employees as human beings, and consequently the fact that this complexity cannot be reduced to economic indicators. In the next paragraphs, four approaches are suggested to bring this Respect ambition into practice.

8.2.2.1 Integrate humanity and sustainability in mission and values

The sustainable people management approach is assumed to flourish more in organisations with a balanced and stakeholder-oriented mission and value statement (see also Chapter 4). To generate enough engaging power, the mission and value statement must be inspiring not only for external clients but also, and mainly, for the internal employees. Growing only because that is what is needed to please the shareholders is not engaging for employees; they can't identify with it. Realising sustainable growth with multiple stakeholders (employees including) is more ambitious and gives a broader and more appreciative framework for the employee. The mission statement of Johnson & Johnson can be illustrating.

Credo Johnson & Johnson

We believe our first responsibility is to the **doctors, nurses and patients, to mothers and fathers and all others** who use our products and services. In meeting their needs everything we do must be of high quality. We must constantly strive to reduce our costs in order to maintain reasonable prices. Customers' orders must be serviced promptly and accurately. Our suppliers and distributors must have an opportunity to make a fair profit.

We are responsible to our **employees,** the men and women who work with us throughout the world. Everyone must be considered as an individual. We must respect their dignity and recognize their merit. They must have a sense of security in their jobs. Compensation must be fair and adequate, and working conditions clean, orderly and safe. We must be mindful of ways to help our employees fulfill their family responsibilities. Employees must feel free to make suggestions and complaints. There must be equal opportunity for employment, development and advancement for those qualified. We must provide competent management, and their actions must be just and ethical.

We are responsible to **the communities** in which we live and work and to the world community as well. We must be good citizens – support good works and charities and bear our fair share of taxes. We must encourage civic improvements and better health and education. We must maintain in good order the property we are privileged to use, protecting the environment and natural resources.

Our final responsibility is to our **stockholders.** Business must make a sound profit. We must experiment with new ideas. Research must be carried on, innovative programs developed and mistakes paid for. New equipment must be purchased, new facilities provided and new products launched. Reserves must be created to provide for adverse times. When we operate according to these principles, the stockholders should realize a fair return.[1]

8.2.2.2 Combine a competency and talent-based approach to sustainable HRM

Competency management proceeds from an organisation's mission, vision and strategy, which are ultimately rendered as a profile of desired competencies, and which become the focal point for various HRM applications. Observed human behaviour is compared against the desired profile. The greatest opportunity for development is sought in the weakest competencies of people, and this demands considerable additional effort from them. One consequence of this conclusion is that many practitioners and scholars have sought refuge in an entirely different approach. This could explain the increasing popularity of talent management (Michaels & Axelrod, 2001), which proceeds from people's strengths. Talent management builds on the

---

[1] https://www.jnj.com/about-jnj/jnj-credo

appreciation of the strong aspects of an individual. Underlying interests and 'talents' are identified, with the goal of drawing relevant connections between these interests and competencies and the roles and/or positions in one or more organisational contexts. The synthesis approach of sustainability (see also Chapter 5) enables the combining of these different perspectives. This approach concerns dialogue, and is characterised by mutual respect and by the search for and discussion of possibilities and opportunities for both individual and organisation. In this approach, the organisation's mission is matched to the individual's passion, as is the case with IKEA.

Growing with IKEA

We see every person as a talent with the curiosity to learn and the possibility to grow and develop. Co-workers are encouraged to try different roles, and many people change between functions and countries several times in their careers. This increases understanding and learning within the organisation, and benefits us all in our professional roles and as human beings. It's part of our culture to give co-workers big responsibilities. Learning in the business makes people grow – and when people grow, IKEA grows too.[2]

8.2.2.3 Mainstream decent and meaningful work

As we mentioned before, both critical and other HRM scholars have been providing arguments for bringing the 'human' back into the HRM rhetoric. For example, Gratton (2001) was one of the leading HRM scholars to call for re-humanisation within the HRM and human capital discourse. According to Gratton, people are fundamentally different from financial capital and technology. If people are placed at the centre of sustained competitive advantage (within a resource-based view), it becomes necessary to account for the fundamental characteristics of human capital. Understanding these basic differences induces an entirely new way of thinking and working in organisations. In contrast to financial or technological capital, people are seen as functioning in time, giving meaning and having a soul (Gratton, 2001). Therefore, a new focus on decent and meaningful work forms the heart of the 'Respect' pillar of our ROC model.

---

[2] https://www.ikea.com/ms/ko_KR/pdf/yearly_summary/ys_welcome_inside_2012.pdf

> **Get 1 hour back at Nokia**
>
> We are all striving to make our work meaningful, productive and engaging by focusing on what's important, minimizing routine tasks and reducing clutter. Nokia's Get 1h back movement can help us reach this goal: through time-saving techniques and 'work smarter' tips it aims to give every one of us at least one hour back every week – moving us closer to a working environment which will support our future success. Even small changes to our everyday way of working can make a huge difference. And when teams make these changes together, the impact can be even more powerful.[3]

From an engaging and motivational perspective, meaningful work is often understood as a consequence of work aligning with a person's intrinsic motivations. One of the most popular theories within the field of work motivation is self-determination theory (Deci & Ryan, 2010). According to this theory, intrinsic motivation is caused by a few fundamental needs that must be fulfilled. These needs are called ABC needs, namely autonomy, belongingness, competence. Within the ILO (2016) definition of decent work, we find about the same needs. Decent work involves opportunities for work that is productive and delivers a fair income, security in the workplace and social protection for families; has better prospects for personal development and social integration, with the freedom for people to express their concerns, and to organise and participate in the decisions that affect their lives; as well as offers equality of opportunity and treatment for all women and men. Both perspectives of mainstreaming decent and meaningful work are assumed to contribute to accelerating progress towards the achievement of rehumanisation goals within HRM.

8.2.2.4 Act as a transformational leader

Engaging and appreciative HRM is not only a matter of decent and meaningful work, but also of engaging leadership. An empirical research (Segers et al., 2010) shows that especially perceived transformational leadership styles result in high-quality leader–member exchange (LMX) relations, which increases directly, and also indirectly, individuals' engagement. The

---

[3] https://www.nokia.com/sites/default/files/nokia_people_and_planet_report_2016_respecting_3.pdf

opposite was observed for directive leadership, which was operationalised in terms of task-oriented behaviour, with a strong focus on targets, close supervision and control of subordinate actions. The results indicated that leaders who demonstrated a visionary leadership style together with an individualised consideration increased, both directly and indirectly, the vigour, dedication and absorption of their followers at work, and their global subjective feeling of happiness. Other researchers (e.g. Tims et al., 2011; Xu & Cooper, 2011) also have shown that there are multiple ways in which leadership behaviours are associated with employee engagement. For example, daily transformational leadership related positively to employees' daily engagement, and daily levels of optimism fully mediated this relationship (Tims et al., 2011).

Engagement drives performance at VOLVO

A highly engaged workforce makes all the difference for a company, as high engagement fuels both performance and innovation. The voice of the employees is captured yearly in the Volvo Group Attitude Survey (VGAS). 93% of all employees responded in the 2017 edition of the survey. For the second year in a row, there was an increase in the Employee Engagement Index, from 72% engaged employees in 2016 to 75% in 2017. The open and honest dialogue between employees and leaders across the organization has been a key driver behind the strengthened engagement. To maintain the upward trend, we will continue to focus on dialogue and increased collaboration.[4]

There is also a link between transformational leadership and wider sustainability thinking and implementation of CSR within the organisation. Groves and LaRocca (2011) found that only transformational leadership was associated with follower beliefs in the stakeholder view of CSR. According to Metcalf and Benn (2013), leadership for sustainability requires transformational leaders who can read and predict through complexity, think through complex problems, engage groups in dynamic adaptive organisational change and have the emotional intelligence to adaptively engage with their own emotions associated with complex problem solving. Leaders and leadership

---

[4] https://www.volvogroup.com/content/dam/volvo/volvo-group/markets/global/en-en/news/2018/mar/Annual-Report-2017-PDF-2018-03-13-02-00-55.pdf

is a key interpreter of how sustainability within the organisation 'links' to the wider systems in which the organisation sits, which brings us to the second building block of the ROC model: Openness.

8.3 Second sustainable HRM block: Openness

Openness brings the stakeholder perspective to HRM; it implies considering HRM from the 'outside in', recognising the occurrence of societal issues and trends such as diversity, the growing need for work–life balance, and an ageing workforce, which require an organisational response. In other words, it recognises the social embeddedness of the organisation and considers relevant institutional forces and stakeholder groups.

8.3.1 Theoretical background

Stakeholder theory represents a significant part of the debate in business ethics, and it shows many obvious connections to HRM (Greenwood & Freeman, 2011). The theory suggests that the organisation's purpose, principles and relationship to society should be a shared process, in which employees are at the centre, in addition to social partners, customers and social movements (for example, the green movement). Along the same lines, it can be argued that every organisation is like a mini-society, reflecting the same societal issues and trends. Dealing with diversity, work–life balance, ageing, scarcity, pollution and other issues should also be included on any HRM agenda. Secondly, institutional theory can account for the societal embeddedness of HRM practices. Paauwe and Boselie (2003, 2007) argue that, in addition to strategic (that is, vertical) fit and horizontal fit, organisational success through HRM depends on the organisation–environmental fit. They present a model of HRM based on the institutional mechanisms for organisational isomorphism developed by DiMaggio and Powell (1983).

For example, isomorphism results from formal and informal pressures on organisations exerted by other organisations on which they are dependent and by cultural expectations in the societies in which they function. In HRM, isomorphism includes the influence of social partners (for example, trade unions and works councils), labour legislation and governments (Paauwe & Boselie, 2003). From a broader perspective, isomorphism can also refer to a connection between the prevailing social norms and values and other processes (for example, participation of mothers, the elderly and immigrants in the labour market). The presence of these different isomorphic pressures on HRM, however, does not necessarily mean that organisations and their stake-holders see the institutional environment as restrictive. Organisations are able to create additional room by opting for specific HRM systems (Paauwe & Boselie, 2003; Boon, 2008). The key question within the second pillar of Openness is: 'How can we connect our HRM policy (even more) with our other stakeholders and the underlying values, standards and developments in society?'

8.3.2 Practical approaches to implement Openness: Connecting and inclusive HRM

Organisations will always have to be aligned with the society, not only in economic and technological terms, but also in societal terms. In the next set of practical approaches we will focus on two specific themes: individualisation on the one hand, social inequality on the other.

8.3.2.1 Combine HRM differentiation with a collective mindset

The individualisation process implies that the identity of people is less determined by the group(s) to which they belong. The identity is a personal identity, not a collective one. Traditional institutions such as the church and family lose their impact and are no longer the only sense makers. De-traditionalisation and de-institutionalisation are the norm. More and more people have the freedom to write their life history themselves. That does not mean that people now are all making very original choices; they tend more towards a situation or an identity of 'predictable uniqueness'. The urge of the individual 'to belong' is very basic. The prescribed social biography is replaced by an 'elective biography', a 'reflexive biography' or a 'do-it-yourself biography' (Beck, 1992).

Within HRM, increasing attention is being given to the individualisation of HRM practices. Whether focusing on talent management, work–life balance, diversity management or age-conscious HRM, the basic assumption is often that employees differ in terms of their needs, talents, interests, expectations, performance, knowledge and skills, and that organisations should consider these differences when implementing HRM practices. This phenomenon is called HRM differentiation and entails creating differences between employees in terms of their training opportunities, remuneration, flexibility, participation, autonomy and so on (Marescaux et al., 2012).

Sustainable HRM implies that customisation forms a core element of HRM, and it should not be regarded as exceptional treatment for some critical talent within the organisation. Individualisation offers opportunities for both organisations and employees, given the relative unpredictability of the context for either party – organisations due to the volatile socio-economic environment, and workers due to their life-stage situations. However, HR managers should take several things into consideration. For example, special care must be given towards the 'have nots', who may develop negative perceptions of favourability and subsequently lower affective organisational commitment. As research has shown (Krehbiel & Cropanzano, 2000; Marescaux et al., 2012), implementing and communicating a clear and procedurally just (e.g. consistent, free of bias) policy may be one way that procedural justice can counter negative reactions following unfavourable outcomes. Applied to career management this means, for instance, that the focus on individualisation is balanced with organisational needs. By keeping track of organisational evolutions and evolutions in the broader socio-economic environment, organisational needs for competencies and implications for careers can be formulated and communicated systematically towards employees, thereby contributing to a clear psychological contract (De Prins et al., 2015).

'Ikuboss' measures needed in a time of diversifying human resources (Toyota)

Toyota implements 'Ikuboss' measures to promote the development of workplace environments where diverse human resources including women, seniors, employees providing nursing care to family members, and others can work with enthusiasm. In order to develop supervisors who can understand and support sensitivities that value the careers of subordinates and perform management based on flexible attitudes and positions (i.e. Ikubosses), we implemented an Ikuboss Trial where 200 managers experienced working from home. As a result, more than 90% of the participants felt that working from home is significant and increases productivity. This also led to greater acceptance of use of the Working at Home Program. In addition, Ikuboss Declarations prepared by 500 managers were posted on the Sodatete Net intranet. Measures being taken in individual worksites and messages to subordinates were posted in succession, promoting a culture of mutual support for the activities of diverse members.[5]

---

[5] http://www.toyota-global.com/sustainability/report/archive/sr17/pdf/sdb17_058-073_en.pdf

8.3.2.2 Invest in sustainable networks

Sustainable HRM aims to customise, but also to connect. It supports networking and connections between people, teams, organisations and the ecological environment. The purpose of these relationships and connections can be very different. It can be about emotional and relational binding, about task-oriented co-operation, about the supply chain, about knowledge exchange or about searching for 'shared value'. The nature and intensity of the network will ultimately result in a certain amount of social or sustainability capital of both the organisation and its employees (Lengnick-Hall & Lengnick-Hall, 2006).

Patagonia's supply chain

Our Social/Environmental Responsibility (SER) team can veto a decision to work with a new factory (as can, as always, our Quality team). This practice is rare in the apparel business and keeps us out of factories that don't share our social and environmental values. We have also trained our Sourcing and Supply Planning teams in responsible purchasing practices to minimise negative impact on the factory workers and the environment that could result from our own business decisions. Our sourcing and quality staff work closely with our SER team and hold a joint weekly meeting to make supply chain decisions. We have three big projects in progress.

- We are working within the industry to help make the living-wage principle a concrete reality for garment workers. (…)
- We are intensifying our efforts to improve labour conditions in the supply chain beyond the cut-and-sew factories (the textile mills, dye houses, etc.).
- In a proactive effort to encourage and strengthen our factories' ability to manage fire safety, we joined and seed funded the Fair Labor Association's Fire Safety Initiative.[6]

An important role for sustainable HRM is to build social capital as an organisational competence. Innovation or new contacts not only come from top management. High-performing employees are often members of different interesting networks, which enables them to create value and gain

---

[6] http://eu.patagonia.com/gb/en/corporate-responsibility-history.html

more knowledge. Decision makers in firms should also be aware that HRM practices aimed at individuals often spill over to their social relationships. Consequently, even HRM interventions that affect a single individual can in time have far-ranging and systemic effects on a firm's social network and, in turn, on internal knowledge transfer (Kaše et al., 2009).

8.3.2.3 Aim for an inclusive approach

In addition to individualisation, social inequality is an important context factor in sustainable HRM. Despite the best of intentions, many HRM initiatives run the risk of creating a 'Matthew effect'. This term refers to the following biblical passage: 'for whoever has, will be given more, and they will have abundance. Whoever does not have, even what they have will be taken from them.' Applied to career practice, this could mean that employees who are already firmly established in their careers will tend to be proactive in discussing their own employability with their supervisors or HRM consultants, while those who feel more vulnerable or who are not as well equipped to assess their own employability are at risk of being overlooked and thus less employable (De Vos & Van der Heijden, 2017). The scholars therefore propose that, in many companies, career policy has more to do with talent management for a few rather than it does with developing a career policy for all employees. Those who fall outside this group and who adopt a passive attitude with regard to their careers are thus more likely to fall outside of the career policy as well. Although they do have a job, they do not have a career. If the job disappears, any career they might have had will also be in jeopardy.

Diversity & Inclusion (D&I) at Southwest airlines

Diversity & Inclusion (D&I) has always been important to the Heart of Southwest. We champion an inclusive Culture valuing the unique perspectives of all. Intensifying our focus on D&I over the last several years has significantly increased the diversity of our thinking and how we approach our business. We're proud that 82 percent of Employees who took our 2016 Employee survey reported that Southwest created an business environment where People of diverse backgrounds can succeed. Fostering an inclusive Culture that values the unique perspectives of all Employees is a clear and ongoing focus for Southwest.[7]

---

[7] http://southwestonereport.com/2016/stories/where-people-of-diverse-backgrounds-can-soar/

One apparent paradox in this regard is that, during the transition from a purely human-capital approach to a sustainable HRM approach, companies tend to adopt HRM policies that are somewhat less inclusive. If a company has traditionally devoted disproportionate attention to an exclusive focus on high-level talent, it will need to take corrective actions in order to make the transition to a more sustainable form of HRM possible. This implies that the other target groups (e.g. low-skilled employees) will temporarily receive more attention. The HRM policy and personnel practices that are intended to correct this imbalance focus primarily on a specific target group and make the system more inclusive. If the Matthew effect is not corrected and continues to operate, there is a risk that a two-speed HRM will emerge: a 'sustainable' and 'strategic' policy for the core employees and a 'light' or 'disposable' version for those on the periphery. This situation could thus be described as human capital theory in action (Lepak & Snell, 2002). Sustainable HRM will give attention to both the core and the periphery, and in the long term avoids focused attention only to a limited percentage of the workforce, for whatever reason this might be.

8.3.2.4 Be sensitive to diversity and environmental management

Within the classic HRM discourse, elite or standard employees often possess the following characteristics, in addition to being highly skilled: male, white, middle-aged, physically and mentally healthy, married, and fully and primarily available for work. As a result of this stereotype (among other factors), the labour reserve on the labour market currently consists primarily of 'disadvantaged groups', whose characteristics are diametrically opposed to those of the aforementioned typical, idealised standard employee: female, ethnic minority, low-skilled, young or 'vintage', interrupted career and so on. Given these divergent characteristics (the list of which could be endlessly supplemented), the development of an inclusive policy should be accompanied by the development of a diversity policy. Such a policy should go beyond exhibiting passive tolerance for diversity to be capable of actively supporting and promoting the increasing level of heterogeneity, while serving as a springboard for the sustainable creation of value (Gilbert et al., 1999).

Diversity is only one typical HRM practice within the Openness pillar of sustainable HRM. Another typical example of the outside-in perspective is known as 'green HRM' (Dubois & Dubois, 2012; Renwick et al., 2012). In the green HRM literature, terms such as 'green employees', 'green careers' and 'green jobs' are becoming increasingly common. Renwick et al. (2012) call for the integration of the literature on environmental management system (EMS) with research on HRM. One prominent theme in the EM literature is that effective outcomes cannot be achieved simply by making changes to production processes, products or raw materials. They also depend on changes in the corporate culture, in the sense that organisations have deeply embedded values that support long-term sustainability. An organisational culture that encourages EM is one that stimulates employees to make suggestions for activities that improve the natural environment, in addition to giving them the freedom to engage in such activities (see Chapter 6 on green HRM).

Environmental awareness activities in the home (Yamaha Group)

The Yamaha Group provides support and training to improve the environmental awareness of our employees and to promote eco activities that employees can perform as part of their daily routines. The Yamaha Group has worked with the Yamaha labor union to promote eco-conscious activities in daily life through projects and tools such as keeping track of eco-conscious household activities, 'Smart Life in My Home Commitments' that accomplish eco-conscious activities suitable to each employees' home, and the 'My Eco Commitment Coloring Page' for families with children.[9]

---

[8] https://cdn2.hubspot.net/hubfs/481927/local_sustainability_initiatives%202016.pdf
[9] https://www.yamaha.com/en/csr/download/latest/pdf/csr_report2017_web_05.pdf

8.4 Third sustainable HRM block: Continuity

A third building block within the ROC model is the long-term perspective from the viewpoints of both the organisational relationship and the employee relationship. Companies strive to create conditions under which they can survive over a relatively long time, and sustainable HRM can contribute to this process.

8.4.1 Theoretical background

With the publications of Arthur (1994), Huselid (1995) and MacDuffie (1995), a decade of discussions on the added value of HRM started. In a balanced approach, exclusively high scores on either financial individual or social performance are considered as undesirable for the long-term survival of an organisation. The latter approach combines the insights from an economic perspective with those from an institutional perspective in order to create a balanced and sustainable position for the organisation (Paauwe et al., 2013). As such, sustainable HRM differs substantially from the mainstream HRM.

The Continuity dimension can also be seen as an individual challenge within the employment relationship. The essence of the employment relationship is the supply of labour by the employee in return for a wage. The idea within exchange relationships is that these elements persist only if the exchange is in balance. Organisations can opt for HRM policies focused on mutual investments within a long-term perspective (Rousseau, 2005). Implications for the employer include investments in training or other forms of competence or career development initiatives. Implications for the employee include loyalty or the opportunity to develop skills that can be carried into the future (Tsui et al., 1997). In contrast, the exchanges in short-term labour relationships are limited to the provision of labour for a wage, without any guarantee of job security. The relational dimension is clearly missing in this context (Montes & Irving, 2008).

Within the literature on human capital (Lepak & Snell, 2002), these types of employment relationships are related to the strategic orientation and strategic importance of human capital. Current research shows that organisations whose workforces are characterised by low value and low uniqueness tend to be less concerned with the intra-organisational mobility of their employees and to offer fewer career management practices, while holding individual employees less accountable for managing their own careers (De Vos & Dries, 2013). Scholars have interpreted these findings as implying that such organisations tend to adopt a laissez-faire approach to career management, assigning organisational priority to neither career management nor continuity.

In contrast, this reality has been subjected to strong criticism within the literature on labour relations and stakeholder management. Questions concerning the treatment of low-wage, dependent workers are among the most central in ethical analyses of contemporary employment relationships (Van Buren & Greenwood, 2013). The ways in which organisations treat this group of stakeholders, who lack power and meaningful ways of changing the terms of exchange with their employers, should be a central focus of work in business ethics and stakeholder analysis. Given that stakeholders co-create value, one role of managers should be to create deals in which all of the firm's stakeholders – including low-wage workers – can ultimately win.

8.4.2 Practical approaches to implement Continuity: Innovative and career-oriented HRM

Continuity encompasses a long-term perspective for organisations as well as for their employees. An innovative as well as a career-oriented HRM can support this continuity ambition of sustainable HRM.

8.4.2.1 Optimise organisational structure and processes

Many companies are conscious of the relevant developments taking place within their general and industry environments, and they are capable of translating them into a vision of the future – but that is not the end of the story. Whether external business environmental awareness leads to continuity depends on whether the company is able to translate this vision into a suitable organisation of tasks. The organisation of tasks should promote the behaviour that is needed in order to realise the vision of the future. A rich tradition has sprung up around this basic assumption with regard to redesign and socially innovative visions on tasks and the organisation of labour. The current discourse on policy management and sustainability has eagerly adopted such terms as 'innovative labor organisation', 'social innovation', 'the new way of working' and 'smarter organisation' (e.g. McGill & Slocum, 1994; Pol & Ville, 2009).

One feature that these concepts have in common is that they are often positioned as opposites of the Taylorist model of labour organisation. Taylorist principles separate the need for control from the capacity for control. This

Self-managing teams at Buurtzorg

Buurtzorg is a pioneering healthcare organisation established 10 years ago with a nurse-led model of holistic care that has revolutionised community care in the Netherlands.

Client satisfaction rates are the highest of any healthcare organisation. Staff commitment and contentedness is reflected in Buurtzorg's title of Best Employer (4 out of the last 5 years). And impressive financial savings have been made. 'Essentially, the program empowers nurses (rather than nursing assistants or cleaners) to deliver all the care that patient's need. And while this has meant higher costs per hour, the results have been fewer hours in total. Indeed, by changing the model of care, Buurtzorg has accomplished a 50 percent reduction in hours of care, improved quality of care and raised work satisfaction for employees.' Self-managing teams have professional freedom with responsibility. A team of 12 work in a neighbourhood, taking care of people needing support as well managing the team's work. A new team will find its own office in the neighbourhood, spend time introducing themselves to the local community and getting to know GPs and therapists and other professionals. The team decide how they organise the work, share responsibilities and make decisions, through word of mouth and referrals the team build-up a caseload.[10]

is compensated by wages that increase rapidly in response to productivity – until growth stagnates and the market demands not only greater productivity, but also greater quality, flexibility, innovation and sustainability. Experience has shown that an organisation based on the extensive division of labour cannot meet these demands, and this places their continuity and survival in jeopardy. It also gives rise to the call for innovative labour organisations, characterised by integral redesign or organisational structure. That is, less division of labour by shifting more towards teamwork, more self-direction and the expansion of tasks. Experts rightly add that the emergence of self-direction and innovative labour organisation requires adopted processes and conditions. Elements of organisational process include employee commitment and participation to the change, supporting leadership and supporting information systems.

---

[10] https://www.buurtzorg.com/about-us/

8.4.2.2 Dare to co-create

Co-creation is one way in which to realise a sustainable commitment to change. Co-creation involves giving people the responsibility and space that they need in order to share knowledge and accomplish things together. The intention is to cross knowledge from various perspectives and images of reality in order to discover concrete possibilities for improvement, to develop solutions, to contribute to a process of change and to arrive at a policy for which there is a base of support. The construction of new meanings allows the co-creation of a new reality, which can lead to a feasible situation (at least temporarily) or serve as a catalyst for taking shared action. The objective is to arrive at long-term solutions to complex problems (Prahalad & Ramaswamy, 2004; Lee, Olson & Trimi. 2012). The co-creation dialogue is not intended to 'get it right'. The ambition is to end up into a 'both-and' thinking rather than 'either-or'. Differences in opinion may be used for renewal and innovation, rather than for conflict.

Culture and strategy sessions at AES

Each year, our senior leaders both at the global and SBU level travel to various business locations to discuss our corporate strategy and the results of our most recent AES-wide culture survey. The goal of these sessions is to focus on the direction we are taking as a company, share our plans to support our strategy and discuss how we will strengthen our culture to work together successfully.[11]

The co-creation process is also primarily self-directed or, at the most, facilitated. For leaders, it thus involves taking a step back – foregoing the urge to take centre stage in order to place others in the spotlight. This is the paradox of leadership in a process of co-creation: in substantive terms, not allowing the management perspective to take precedence over other perspectives and constantly assigning responsibility and trust to the entire group with regard to the process, particularly when doing so is difficult (Ferdig, 2007). Co-creative leaders recognise that the experience of change itself, and the dissonance it creates, fuels new thinking, discoveries, and innovations that can revitalise the health of organisations (and by extension the health of communities and

---

[11] https://s2.q4cdn.com/825052743/files/doc_downloads/sustanaibility/2015/2015_AESSustainabilityReport.pdf

the earth). Paradox, contradictory and differing viewpoints are recognised as natural characteristics of healthy systems (Ferdig, 2007).

The long-term ambition of the co-creation process fits with the continuity dimension of the ROC model. Also, the social-constructivist roots of the co-creation process fit within complexity and sustainability thinking. Not only the nature of organisational change, but also the nature of broader sustainability challenges seems to be such that a routine problem-solving approach falls short. Instead, such transitions require a more systemic and reflexive way of thinking and acting, bearing in mind that our world is one of continuous change and uncertainty (Wals & Schwarzin, 2012).

8.4.2.3 Strive for sustainable careers

As proposed by Newman (2011), sustainable careers have three features. First, they must include opportunities for renewal – times when employees pause briefly to reinvigorate themselves. Second, they must be flexible and adaptable. Half of what we think we know now will be obsolete in a few years. Individuals and firms need to be continuous and flexible learners, ready to travel new roads as conditions dictate. Finally, sustainable careers must include opportunities for integration across life spheres and experiences that lead to wholeness, completeness and meaning. A job with high challenges, work pressure or stress today might hence have important consequences for an individual's work ability in the long run but is often not considered from that perspective. Sustainable career management balances a focus on today's needs with anticipation of future consequences by creating so-called 'smart jobs' which stimulate not merely performance but also learning, growth and employability (Hall & Las Heras, 2010). In doing so, it does not limit its attention to strategic workforce planning exercises for critical target groups, but complements this with a wider perspective on evolutions that can be expected among, or will have an impact on, the total workforce both within and beyond the organisation.

Using fully fledged career development systems at Toshiba

Toshiba supports the career development of each employee in an effort to maximize his/her current and future job performance. The Career Design System, for example, provides each employee with an annual opportunity to discuss and share their views on long-term career development plans as well as on mid-term goals for skill acquisition,

---

improvement, and the way to utilize such skills with their superiors. Performance Management System gives each employee a semi-annual opportunity to review and discuss with their superiors their job performance over the past six months as well as their job objectives for the next six months. We also have career development systems that encourage employees to plan their careers autonomously. For example, our Internal Job Posting System allows each employee to apply for personnel transfer in order to fill a vacant post announced by a division, and the Internal FA System enables each employee to apply for personnel transfer to a division of their choice.[12]

8.4.2.4 Encourage sustainable retention

As is the case for other topics relating to sustainable HRM, the essence of sustainable retention is to arrive at a precarious balance. If too few employees leave the organisation, calcification will occur in both the staff and the organisation. No young employees are added, resulting in a process of ageing and de-juvenation. The organisation becomes rigid and loses strength. On the other hand, excessive, undesirable turnover creates a risk of losing substantial knowledge, experience and networks. The 'learning organisation' thus becomes a hollow concept, and process stability is placed in jeopardy. The literature on the labour market refers to employee turnover that exceeds a basic level of turnover that is customary in the sector of which the organisation is a part (Ilmakunnas & Maliranta, 2005).

One way to realise sustainable retention is to enter into and renew the psychological contract, which refers to the mutual expectations of the employer and the employee about their employment relationship (Rousseau, 2005). Agreements concerning effort, availability, performance level, talent utilisation and other aspects in exchange for such aspects as the pace of career opportunities, work quality, engagement and retention are 'specified' within the psychological contract. The many changes taking place in organisations in recent years have drawn increasing attention to breaches in the psychological contract and the ways in which stakeholders react to such breaches. If such breaches are perceived as unjustified, they can be detrimental to both motivation and retention. Studies have demonstrated that employees usually have difficulty letting go of matters that have been perceived as promises (e.g.

---

[12] http://www.toshiba.co.jp/csr/en/report/files/pdf4_3_3.pdf

Robinson & Morrison, 2000; Zhao et al., 2007). Keeping the psychological contract open to discussion will continue to play a crucial role – whether within the framework of developmental and career reviews or within the framework of creating a personal development plan.

Dealing with structural changes at Henkel

Preserving jobs and dealing responsibly with necessary structural changes are important to us. To secure the company's competitiveness, we continually adapt our structures to market conditions. If jobs are affected by this, we enter a solutions-oriented dialog with the employee representatives before actions are taken. In doing so, we follow all applicable codetermination legislation and apply the required procedures for each action. We aim to reach agreements with socially compatible arrangements for the employees. To date, we have been able to manage the necessary restructuring measures while reconciling interests. The actions involved range from early retirement through to support with professional reskilling and refocus.[13]

8.5 Summary and conclusions

Inspired by the three 'Ps' ('People', 'Planet', 'Profit') of CSR, we have positioned 'Respect', 'Openness' and 'Continuity' as the three building blocks of sustainable HRM. In this chapter, we illustrate the three dimensions by summarising several theoretical and applied concepts and dynamics. Many of the elements addressed in previous literature are not necessarily new. New elements include the critical reflection and redirection of existing HRM practices, systems and themes towards the ROC model. Sustainable HRM is therefore a more complementary perspective. Its aim is not to replace the strategic HRM perspective, but to extend the unilateral organisation benefit-focused perspective of business management. This perspective brings HRM into a next stage of maturity. To accomplish this, it draws on inspiration derived from the CSR approach, from ethical and critical HRM and from stakeholder and institutional theory. Owing to the positioning of the concept of sustainable

---

[13] https://www.henkel.com/blob/739776/3e48b2a4f265f0a1518f3f150cc7afbc/data/2016-sustainability-report.pdf

HRM as a social-constructivist concept, the ROC model challenges HRM practitioners to implement sustainable HRM in co-creation with the academic community. The ROC model aims to bridge theory and practice. It provides a framework and new vocabulary for classifying and positioning (or repositioning) new initiatives and experiments, as well as existing practices and traditions within the domain of sustainable HRM.

References

Arthur, J. B. (1994). Effects of human resource systems on manufacturing performance and turnover. *Academy of Management Journal, 37*, 670–87.

Beck, U. (1992). *Risk Society: Towards a New Modernity* (Vol. 17). Los Angeles & London: Sage.

Bolton, S. & Houlihan, M. (2007). *Searching for the Human in Human Resource Management.* London: Palgrave Macmillan.

Boon, C. (2008). HRM and Fit: Survival of the Fittest. Erasmus University Rotterdam: ERIM PhD Series Research in Management 129.

Boselie, P. (2010). *Strategic Human Resource Management A Balanced Approach.* London: McGraw-Hill.

Clegg, R. S., Vieira Da Cunha, J. & Pina E Cunha, M. (2002). 'Management paradoxes: A relation view'. *Human Relations, 55*, 483–503.

De Lange, W. & Koppens, J. (2007). De duurzame arbeidsorganisatie. Amsterdam: WEKA uitgeverij.

De Prins, P., De Vos, A., Van Beirendonck, L. & Segers, J. (2015). Sustainable HRM for sustainable careers: Introducing the 'Respect Openness Continuity (ROC)'-model. In: A. De Vos & B. Van der Heijden (eds) *Handbook of Research on Sustainable Careers* (pp. 319–34). Cheltenham: Edward Elgar Publishing.

De Prins, P., Van Beirendonck, L., De Vos, A. & Segers, J. (2014). Sustainable HRM: Bridging theory and practice through the 'Respect Openness Continuity (ROC)'-model. *Management Revue, 25*(4), 263–84.

De Vos, A. & Dries, N. (2013). Applying a talent management lens to career management: The role of human capital composition and continuity. *The International Journal of Human Resource Management, 24*, 1816–31.

De Vos, A. & Van der Heijden, B. I. M. (2017). Current thinking on contemporary careers: The key roles of sustainable HRM and sustainability of careers. *Current Opinion on Environmental Sustainability, 28*, 41–50.

Deci, E. L. & Ryan, R. M. (2010). *Self-Determination.* Hoboken, NJ: John Wiley & Sons.

DiMaggio, P. J. & Powell, W. (1983). The iron cage revisited' institutional isomorphism and collective rationality in organizational fields. *American Sociological Review, 48*, 147–60.

Dubois, C. L. Z. & Dubois, D. A. (2012). Strategic HRM as social design for environmental sustainability in organization. *Human Resource Management, 51*, 799–826.

Ehnert, I. & Harry, W. (2012). Recent developments and future prospects on sustainable human resource management: Introduction to the special issue. *Management Revue, 23*, 221–38.

Ferdig, M. A. (2007). Sustainability leadership: Co-creating a sustainable future. *Journal of Change Management, 7*(1), 25–35.

Gilbert, J. A., Stead, B. A. & Ivancevich, J. M. (1999). Diversity management: A new organizational paradigm. *Journal of Business Ethics, 21*(1), 61–76.

Gratton, L. (2001). *Living Strategy: Putting People at the Heart of Corporate Purpose.* London: Prentice Hall.

Greenwood, M. & Freeman, R. E. (2011). Ethics and HRM: The contribution of stakeholder theory. *Bussines and Professional Ethics Journal, 30*, 269–92.

Groves, K. S. & LaRocca, M. A. (2011). An empirical study of leader ethical values, transformational and transactional leadership, and follower attitudes toward corporate social responsibility. *Journal of Business Ethics, 103*(4), 511–28.

Guest, D. E. & Woodrow, C. (2012). Exploring the boundaries of human resources managers responsabilities. *Journal of Business Ethics, 111*, 109–19.

Hall, D. T. T. & Heras, M. L. (2010). Reintegrating job design and career theory: Creating not just good jobs but smart jobs. *Journal of Organizational Behavior, 31*(2–3), 448–62.

Huselid, M. A. (1995). The impact of human resource management practices on turnover, productivity and corporate financial performance. *Academy of Management Journal, 38*, 625–72.

Ilmakunnas, P. & Maliranta, M. (2005). Worker inflow, outflow, and churning. *Applied Economics, 37*(10), 1115–33.

ILO (International Labor Organization). (n.d.). Conventions and Recommendations. http://www.ilo.org/global/standards/introductionto-international-labour-standards/conventions-and-recommendations/lang–en/index.htm. Accessed on 17 July 2017.

Kaše, R., Paauwe, J. & Zupan, N. (2009). HR practices, interpersonal relations, and intrafirm knowledge transfer in knowledge-intensive firms: A social network perspective. *Human Resource Management, 48*(4), 615–39.

Keegan, A. & Boselie, P. (2006). The lack of impact of dissensus inspired analysis on developments in the field of human resource management. *Journal of Management Studies, 43*, 1491–511.

Kramar, R. (2014). Beyond strategic human resource management: Is sustainable human resource management the next approach?. *The International Journal of Human Resource Management, 25*, 1069–89.

Krehbiel, P. J. & Cropanzano, R. (2000). Procedural justice, outcome favorability and emotion. *Social Justice Research, 13*(4), 339–60.

Lee, S. M., Olson, D. L. & Trimi, S. (2012). Co-innovation: Convergenomics, collaboration, and co-creation for organizational values. *Management Decision, 50*(5), 817–31.

Lengnick-Hall, M. L. & Lengnick-Hall, C. A. (2006). International human resource management and social network/social capital theory. In: G. K. Stahl & I. Björkman (eds) *Handbook of Research in International Human Resource Management* (pp. 475-487). Cheltenham: Edward Elgar.

Lengnick-Hall, M. L., Lengnick-Hall, C. A., Andrade, L. & Drake, B. (2009). Strategic human resource management: The evolution of the field. *Human Resource Management Review, 19*, 64-85.

Lepak, D. P. & Snell, S. A. (2002). Examining the human resource architecture: The relationships among human capital, employment, and human resource configurations. *Journal of Management, 28*, 517-43.

MacDuffie, J. P. (1995). Human resource bundles and manufacturing performance: Organizational logic and flexible production systems in the world auto industry. *Industrial and Labor Relations Review, 48*, 197-221.

McGill, M. E. & Slocum, J. W. (1994). *The Smarter Organization: How to Build a Business that Learns and Adapts to Marketplace Needs.* Hoboken, NJ: John Wiley & Sons.

Marescaux, E., De Winne, S. & Sels, L. (2012). HR practices and HRM outcomes: The role of basic need satisfaction. *Personnel Review, 42*(1), 4-27.

Mariappanadar, S. (2013). A conceptual framework for cost measures of harm of HRM practices. *Asia-Pacific Journal of Business Administration, 5*(2), 15-39.

Mariappanadar, S. (2014). Stakeholder harm index: A framework to review work intensification from the critical HRM perspective. *Human Resource Management Review, 24*(4), 313-29.

Metcalf, L. & Benn, S. (2013). Leadership for sustainability: An evolution of leadership ability. *Journal of Business Ethics, 112*(3), 369-84.

Michaels, H.-J. Axelrod (2001). *The War for Talent.* Boston, MA: Harvard Business School Press.

Montes, S. D. & Irving, P. G. (2008). Disentangling the effects of promised and delivered inducements: Relational and transactional contract elements and mediating role of trust. *American Journal of Applied Psychology, 93*, 1367-81.

Newman, K. L. (2011). Sustainable careers: Lifecycle engagement in work. *Organizational Dynamics, 40*, 136-43.

Paauwe, J. (2012). HRM als leer- en ontwikkelingstraject. *Tijdschrift voor HRM, 15*, 11-12.

Paauwe, J., Boon, C. T., Boselie, P. & Den Hartog, D. N. (2013). Reconceptualizing fit in strategic human resource management: 'Lost in translation'?. In J. Paauwe, D. E. Guest & P. M. Wright (eds) *HRM and Performance: Achievements and Challenges.* Chichester: John Wiley & Sons, 61-77.

Paauwe, J. & Boselie, P. (2003). Challenging 'strategic HRM' and the relevance of the institutional setting. *Human Resource Management Journal, 13*, 56-70.

Paauwe, J. & Boselie, P. (2007). HRM and societal embeddedness. In P. Boxall, J. Purcell & P. M. Wright (eds) *The Oxford Handbook of Human Resource Management.* Oxford: Oxford University Press, 166-84.

Pol, E. & Ville, S. (2009). Social innovation: Buzz word or enduring term?. *The Journal of Socio-Economics*, *38*(6), 878–85.

Prahalad, C. K. & Ramaswamy, V. (2004). Co-creation experiences: The next practice in value creation. *Journal of Interactive Marketing*, *18*(3), 5–14.

Renwick, D. W. S., Redman, T. & Maguire, S. (2012). Green HRM: A review and research agenda. *International Journal of Management Reviews*, *15*, 1–14.

Rhodes, C. & Harvey, G. (2012). Agonism and the possibilities of ethics for HRM. *Journal of Bussiness Ethics*, *111*, 49–59.

Robinson, S. L. & Morrison, E. W. (2000). The development of psychological contract breach and violation: A longitudinal study. *Journal of organizational Behavior*, 525–46.

Rousseau, D. (2005). *I-Deals: Idiosyncratic Deals Employees Bargain for Themselves.* New York: M.E. Sharpe.

Segers, J., De Prins, P. & Brouwers, S. (2010). 12 Leadership and engagement: A brief review of the literature, a proposed model, and practical implications. *Management*, *34*, 143–69.

Tims, M., Bakker, A. B. & Xanthopoulou, D. (2011). Do transformational leaders enhance their followers' daily work engagement?. *The Leadership Quarterly*, *22*(1), 121–31.

Tsui, A. S., Pearce, J. L., Porter, L. W. & Tripoli, A. M. (1997). Alternative approaches to the employee-organization relationship: Does investment in employees pay off?. *Academy of Management Journal*, *40*, 1089–121.

Van Buren, H. J., Greenwood, M. & Sheehan, C. (2011). Strategic human resource management and the decline of employee focus. *Human Resource Management Review*, *21*, 209–19.

Van Buren, H. J. & Greenwood, M. (2013). Ethics and HRM education. *Journal of Academic Ethics*, *11*, 1–15.

Voegtlin, C. & Greenwood, M. (2016). Corporate social responsibility and human resource management: A systematic review and conceptual analysis. *Human Resource Management Review*, *26*(3), 181–97.

Wals, A. E. & Schwarzin, L. (2012). Fostering organizational sustainability through dialogic interaction. *The Learning Organization*, *19*(1), 11–27.

Xu, J. & Cooper Thomas, H. (2011). How can leaders achieve high employee engagement?. *Leadership & Organization Development Journal*, *32*(4), 399–416.

Zhao, H. A. O., Wayne, S. J., Glibkowski, B. C. & Bravo, J. (2007). The impact of psychological contract breach on work-related outcomes: A meta-analysis. *Personnel Psychology*, *60*(3), 647–80.

9

Measurements for sustainable HRM practices

Sugumar Mariappanadar

9.1 Introduction

Top-level managers in companies are keen to have evidence for the role of HRM functions in improving organisational performance so as to maximise profit for companies in a highly competitive market. Fuelled by this concern, early academic researchers have demonstrated the impact of individual HR functions (employee selection, training, performance appraisal, etc.) on organisational performance (see Borman, 1991; Terpstra & Rozell, 1993). Subsequently, Huselid (1995) used a bundle of HR practices and linked to organisational performance to convince top-level managers that HR practices have a strategic role in enhancing organisational performance. However, Rogers and Wright (1998) extended the role of strategic HRM from a micro-level (i.e. HR practices or function level) to a macro-level (i.e. stakeholders and temporal dynamics) perspective to understand organisational performance. It is evident from the growth of strategic HRM that there has been strong emphasis on developing various valid measures to operationalise HR functions and practices as well as organisational performance to prove the strategic value of HR in managing profit for companies.

The macro-level or multiple stakeholders-based understanding of organisational performance is closely aligned with corporate sustainability and sustainable development. Hence, sustainable HRM as a field evolved to emphasise the role of HRM in facilitating organisations to achieve corporate sustainability. Sustainable HRM is a field with varied objectives to take care of multiple stakeholders (e.g. employees their families, and society's sustainable environmental management expectations) and hence it is too complex for a single measurement technique or tool that can measure the diverse sustainable and unsustainable effects of HRM on stakeholders.

A framework is provided to understand the role of measurements in facilitating sustainable HRM practices so as to facilitate corporate sustainability (Figure 9.1). Corporate sustainability is about the management approaches used by organisations in achieving the three pillars (i.e. economic/financial, human/social and environmental outcomes) of sustainable development (UN Global Compact, 2014). It is shown in Figure 9.1 that organisations using strategic HR practices (organisational practices) to achieve economic sustainability or improve organisational performance simultaneously create sustainable and unsustainable impacts on stakeholders. For example, in the critical HRM literature there is evidence to indicate that strategic HRM in the process of enhancing organisational performance at the micro or individual level creates harm, side effects or unsustainable impacts on stakeholders such as employees (Boselie et al., 2006; Van de Voorde et al., 2012), their families (Mariappanadar, 2014) and the society's sustainable environmental management expectations (Jabbour et al., 2010).

In this chapter different techniques (indices and survey scales) to measure different aspects of the sustainable and unsustainable effects of HRM practices are explored. The measures of unsustainable impacts of organisational practices on stakeholders will trigger organisational-level interventions to

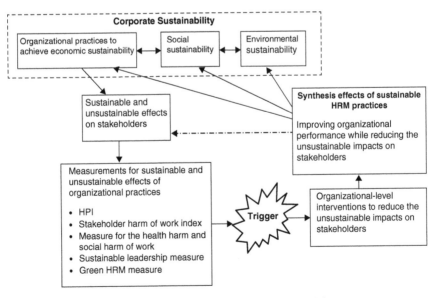

Figure 9.1 The role of measurements in facilitating sustainable HRM practices

reduce the unsustainable impacts in order to achieve the synthesis effects of sustainable HRM (Mariappanadar, 2014; Mariappanadar & Kramar, 2014). That is, organisations, while maximising organisational performance, must also reduce the simultaneous harm of work on the stakeholders (i.e. employees, their families) and negative environmental impacts to accomplish corporate sustainability. Hence, it is indicated in the framework (Figure 9.1) that the synthesis effects of sustainable HRM will facilitate corporate sustainability.

9.2 Measurements for sustainable HRM

It is important to be aware that sustainable HRM is a new and evolving discipline and theoretical domain and not a theoretical construct (i.e. an attribute of HRM) within the field of HRM. Hence, sustainable HRM as a theoretical domain provides opportunity to develop and measure aspects of sustainable HRM from different perspectives, which will enrich the field of sustainable HRM. However, research on measurements of sustainable and unsustainable effects of HRM are in the early stages of development. Therefore, the measures used for reporting sustainable and unsustainable effects of management practices of corporations were drawn from the field of occupational health and safety and human capital, and used in the field of sustainable HRM.

For example, different types of sustainability assessment methodologies, such as Global Reporting Initiatives (GRIs) for sustainability and sustainable Asset Management reporting for the Dow Jones Sustainability Index, use occupational health and safety as measures to highlight a corporation's initiatives so as to address the unsustainable impacts of management practices on stakeholders (employees and their families). This information is used as the background for each of the indices and measures discussed. Subsequently, how the measures could be used to design sustainable HRM practices is discussed under each of the measures. This approach will facilitate our understanding of how the measures for sustainable and unsustainable effects of various HRM functions, HRM practices and HPWPs could be used to develop and shape sustainable HRM.

As stated earlier in this chapter, sustainable HRM is a complex field that seeks to achieve diverse objectives, and a single measure is inappropriate and inadequate. However, in similar complex fields such as environmental science, there are indices available to capture the sustainable and/or unsustainable health effects of pollution based on multiple measures (e.g. computable general equilibrium, Nam et al., 2010; and damages from exposure to pollution,

Khanna, 2000). Hence, in this section two indices are discussed, one each for capturing sustainable and unsustainable effects of HRM to highlight the usefulness of indices in capturing the complexity of multiple measures. Initially, an index to capture the sustainable effects of HRM practices on stakeholders is explained, and this is followed by an index to capture the unsustainable effects of HRM practices on stakeholders.

9.2.1 Human potential index

Osranek and Zink (2014) translated a framework for the human potential index (HPI) which was published by the Federal Ministry of Labour and Social Affairs (Germany). The HPI includes twelve value drivers that are related to HRM practices. The HPI is borrowed from the field of human capital as a measure for sustainable HRM. Hence, these twelve value drivers are related to enhancing human capital for achieving corporate performances. It is believed that the human capital-based twelve HPI value drivers are linked to preserving and caring for stakeholders while organisations attempt to achieve economic goals, and hence are aligned with sustainable HRM. One of the tenets of sustainable HRM is to conserve and preserve human resources for future use and enhance long-term organisational performance. Hence, organisations use these twelve value drivers as a precondition to evaluate sustainable HRM practices for improving organisational performance.

The twelve HPI value drivers are compensation and benefits, change management, work–life balance, communication and information, leadership, personnel development, human resources planning and selection, employee retention, demographic developments, promoting health, HR strategy and HRM, and equal opportunities and diversity. For example, Landesbank Baden-Württemberg (LBBW) used these twelve HPI value drivers as sustainable HRM measures to achieve corporate performance, which includes benefits for stakeholders (shareholders, employees and communities), and reported these value drivers in the company's Annual Report (LBBW, 2015). The limitation of the HPI as a tool for sustainable HRM is that it does not have clearly defined processes to reveal the importance of each of the twelve value drivers in influencing corporate performance.

9.2.2 The stakeholder harm of work index

The stakeholder harm of work index is the first harm of work index published in the HRM literature to capture diverse unsustainable aspects of HPWPs on stakeholders (e.g. employees, their family and the community).

The stakeholder harm of work index is defined as 'a catalogue to capture the harmful (unsustainable) aspects of reduced psychological, social and work related health well-being outcomes for the stakeholders (employees, their families, and the community) and the aggregate social costs of welfare loss due to such harmful aspects caused by either a specific form of HPWP or a bundle of HPWPs' (Mariappanadar, 2014). HPWPs are shaped by organisations' strategic and economic aspirations to achieve competitive advantage through its employees (Pfeffer, 1998). The stakeholder harm of work index is developed based on the negative externality of HRM practices theory, the harm of work theory and the principles of the costs framework for the harm of HRM practices. In this section, first the principle of the costs framework for the harm of work is explained, which provides the theoretical basis for the stakeholder harm of work index. Subsequently, the structure and the usefulness of the stakeholder harm of work index are explained.

9.2.2.1 The costs framework for harm of work

The costs framework for harm of work (Mariappanadar, 2013) proposes three components to evaluate the cost of harm of HRM. They are the cost measures for the harm of work, identification and allocation of the cost of harm of work, and valuation of cost of harm of work. The component of cost measures for the harm of work highlights the measure for the costs of harm of work using the welfare 'loss' to the stakeholders (e.g. employees, their family and the community) due to the harm of work. Welfare loss is a situation whereby marginal social benefit is not equal to marginal social cost and society does not achieve maximum utility (Khanna, 2000). Welfare loss in the HRM context is about an employee being restricted by the unsustainable aspects of HRM practices for maximising the utility function of paid work for improving an individual's psychological, social and health well-being outcomes. The reason for using welfare loss in HRM is that it provides a definition of harm of work (Mariappanadar, 2012b) and emphasises the unsustainable impacts of work that is imposed on employees and their family members, which impairs or restricts employees' well-being outcomes. Subsequently, the reduced well-being outcomes diminish effective utility function or welfare and result in loss of paid and unpaid work. Hence, the harm of work theory (see Chapter 5) provides the theoretical basis for components of the costs measures framework for the harm of work.

The cost measures component of the framework highlights the welfare loss for the stakeholders (employees, their families and the society) caused by the psychological, social and work-related health harm indicators of HRM practices. Some of the harm indicators of the psychological aspect of harm of work for employees are burnout, problems with concentration, reduced clarity of thought and decision making which are caused by work intensification (i.e. a bundle of HRM practices). These psychological indicators of harm of work may affect an employee's work performance and thus lead to reduced personal outcomes (welfare loss) such as reduced opportunities for career development and progressions, and reduced performance-based rewards in the organisation. The reduced personal outcomes for an employee (e.g. reduced future rewards, career growth, etc.) are the costs which the employee has to incur due to the psychological aspect of harm of work imposed by HRM practices.

The cost measure for the social aspect of harm of work is developed based on the relationship between the social aspect of harm indicators of HRM practices and reduced positive social outcomes for employees and their family members as a set of criteria for welfare loss. For example, a decrease in quality of interaction with family members as a harm indicator of the social aspect of harm of HRM practices is due to the spillover effect of work–family conflict. Therefore, any social harm indicators such as work-related divorce, separation or child neglect are included in the cost measure for the social aspect of harm of work. Finally, the cost measure for the work-related health harm of work for employees is based on the restrictions imposed by work for improving positive health (e.g. reduced socially and physically reinvigorating activities) as well as the work-related risk or leading indicators for negative health inflicted by HRM practices.

9.2.2.1.1 Allocation of costs of harm of work to stakeholders

The identification and allocation of the cost of harm of work component of the framework relates to assigning the cost of harm of HRM practices at the organisational, individual and/or societal level. This component of the framework is based on the negative externality of HRM practices theory (see Chapter 5), which helps to allocate the costs to appropriate stakeholders affected by the harm of work. The negative externality of HRM practices theory relates to the costs incurred by stakeholders or third parties, such as employees, their family members (individual level) and the community (society level), to manage the harm of work imposed on them by work practices. Hence, the cost measure for the psychological aspect of harm of HRM practices is attributed to the individual employee and/or his/her family level. The cost measure for the social indicators of harm of work, such as work-related divorce and so on, is also attributed to the individual level because the affected employee and his/her family members, as the stakeholders, incur the costs of managing the social harm of work. Furthermore, the cost measure for the work-related health harm of work is attributed to the society or the community/government level. The work-related health costs are attributed to the society level because in countries with a universal health care system the government pays for the health care costs of the residents.

9.2.2.1.2 Valuation of costs of harm of HRM practices

The valuation of costs component of the framework explains the market prices or direct costs and indirect costs paid by the stakeholders (employees, their families and the community) to manage the harm of work imposed on them. The direct costs (Smith & Brown, 2000) for work-related harm of work on health among countries with a universal health care system is about actual or proxy health system costs (operating costs for the organisation/hospital). For example, the direct health system costs for the treatment of work-related psychosomatic problems in the UK are an equivalent amount of approximately of US$3,070 for the community (Shaw & Creed, 1991). However, the individual-based costs and the external and intangible costs, including lost earnings, are relevant for the psychological and social cost measures of harm of work. That is, direct costs for an individual employee and his/her partner for a divorce caused by the spillover and crossover effect of social harm of work are approximately US$30,000 in the USA (Schramm, 2006). Apart from this, it is important to take into account the intangible costs of retraining and redeployment, as well as the value of lost earnings for employees when returning to work after work-related illness.

The indirect costs are those costs associated with welfare loss due to the reduced ability to function as a 'normal' healthy person, both on the job and during one's leisure time (Smith & Brown, 2000). For example, an employee on an annual salary of $70,000, who has been efficient and effective in achieving a set of performance standards before the introduction of increased workload in his/her current position, will be discussed to illustrate this point. This employee's supervisor decides to increase the workload to his/her current position because it is commonly assumed in practice by supervisors that the best performing employees are capable of effectively handling an increased workload. The increase in workload by the supervisor is based on the assumption from the self-determination motivation theory (Deci & Ryan, 1985) that suggests that employees' best performance is based on intrinsic motivation which improves internal referenced efficiency (i.e. profits) for the organisation. On introduction of the increased workload, the employee may start to exhibit any of the psychological harm indicators of HRM practices, such as lack of concentration and problems with clarity of thought and decision making, and his/her work performance starts to suffer. There is evidence in the literature to suggest that employees' work performance begins to suffer after the introduction of an increased workload (Cameron, 1998).

The employee's supervisor subsequently may become frustrated or disappointed with the employee and develop performance evaluation bias towards the employee. Hence, the supervisor may relatively deprive or disadvantage the employee's involvement in any future challenging projects due to the performance evaluation bias towards them. This might cost the employee future career promotion leading to lost earnings from the position higher than his/her current position as well as welfare loss of using that additional income in leisure activities to improve his/her well-being. Assuming that the annual salary of $85,000 for the promoted position is higher than the current one on an annual salary of $70,000 then the employee has lost annually $15,000 in earnings as well as the welfare loss due to the lost additional income. These direct and indirect approaches of valuation of costs to employees and their family members (individual level) and communities (societal level) indicate social costs due to the harm of work.

9.2.2.2 *Structure of the stakeholder harm of work index with illustrations*

The labels of the stakeholder harm of work index structure (Table 9.1), columns (C1 to C4) and rows (R1 to R3) are based on the cost measures framework for harm of work (Mariappanadar, 2013) discussed earlier. In exploring the structure of the index, columns (C2 to C4) in the stakeholder harm of work index represent the cost measure domains for the psychological (C2), social (C3) and work-related health aspects of harm of work (C4). Each of the cost measure domains include harm indicators (C2a, C3a and C4a) and social costs or welfare loss caused by the harm indicators (C2b, C3b and C4b). For example, the type of harm indicators (C2a) such as work-related exhaustion and burnout highlight reduced future personal outcomes of paid work or welfare loss for employees and their family members and are aggregated into the cost measure for the psychological domain of harm of work (C2). Similarly, neglect of spouse/partner, children, elderly parents and divorce are the harm indicators of the spillover and crossover effects of work–family conflict experienced by employees and their family members (C3a) which are clustered into the cost measure for the social domain of harm of work practices (C3). Insomnia, depression and coronary heart disease are the harm indicators (C4a) clustered into the cost measure for the work-related health domain of harm of work (C4).

Table 9.1 The stakeholder harm of work index

Costs attributed to relevant stakeholder (C1)	Cost measures of harm of high-performance work practices (HPWPs)					
	The cost measure for the psychological aspect of harm of work (C2)		The cost measure for the social aspect of harm of work (C3)		The cost measure for the work-related health aspect of harm of work (C4)	
	Type of harm indicators (C2a)	Direct/indirect social costs (C2b)	Type of harm indicators (C3a)	Direct/indirect social costs (C3b)	Type of harm indicators (C4a)	Direct/indirect social costs (C4b)
Employees – R1	Work-related exhaustion and burnout	Employees change their career path due to burnout and hence earn 85 per cent less at the time of retirement compared with what they would have earned in their the former career	Preoccupation with work-related problems	Cost of loss of intimacy, companionship and shared recreational time in the family leading to marital dissatisfaction	Insomnia caused by high job demands	It costs $136 (€100) per employee for absenteeism associated with insomnia in addition to performance impairment (e.g. irritability, fatigue)
Employees' family members – R2	Restrictions in spouses' leisure activities due to depressed employees	The social costs for spouses' reduced leisure activities	Increased conflict between partners leading to divorce	Direct average costs of $ 30,000 for each spouse in the affected relationship	Negative work experiences of male partners are linked with greater alcohol abuse, anxiety, and medication use among their spouses	Social costs for the affected employees' family in managing the associated problems linked to employees' negative work experiences

Society/government) – R3	Alcohol abuse having detrimental effect on affected employees' work capabilities	Transitional unemployment and increased cost of welfare payments for the government	Increased conflict between partners leading to divorce	Direct and indirect costs to the government $30,821 per divorce	Work-related coronary heart disease (CHD) Crossover effect of employees' work harm of HPWPs on their spouses' mental health, i.e. depression	Annual per capita direct health care costs of $839 for individuals with CHD Annual per capita health and disability costs of $5,415 to society for caring for affected individuals with depression

Source: Adapted from Mariappanadar (2014).

To evaluate the social welfare costs of the harm of work imposed by HPWPs on stakeholders, it is important to theoretically link the harm indicators to welfare losses caused by reduced future personal, social and work-related health outcomes for the stakeholders. Therefore, the columns in Table 9.1 (C2b, C3b and C4c) are used to record the direct/indirect social costs of welfare loss caused by each of the harm indicators. These three processes will help managers and researchers to catalogue and reveal the types of harm of HPWPs along with the social costs or welfare loss for the stakeholders.

Rows R1 to R3 within column C1 help to capture the social costs of the harm of HPWPs for employees, their family members and the government/society as stakeholders. There are two reasons for assigning the social costs of harm of work to individual stakeholders instead of combining it for multiple stakeholders (e.g. employees and their family members, employee and work-related health, and employees' family members and health). Firstly, according to the negative externality of HRM practices discussed earlier in the chapter, the social costs of welfare loss of the harm of work caused by the independent, spillover and crossover effects of the harm of HPWPs are imposed on individual stakeholders (employees, their families and the community) to manage the harm of work. Hence, the calculated social costs of welfare loss for the stakeholders to manage the harm of HPWPs have to be assigned to each stakeholder according to the relevance of the harm of work imposed on the stakeholders and this is depicted in rows R1 to R3.

Row R1 is used to capture the spillover effect of the psychological, social and work-related health harm of HPWPs on employees as a stakeholder. R2 captures the crossover effect of the psychological, social and work-related health harm of HPWPs on employees' family members as a stakeholder. The primary objective of R3 is to capture the externality or social costs imposed on the society/government for the psychological, social and work-related health harm of HPWPs experienced by both employees and their family members. Although R1 to R3 of the stakeholder harm of work index captures externality or social costs of work-related harm for individual stakeholders, it has the ability to capture the social costs of harm of work imposed on multiple stakeholders simultaneously or over time by analysing the costs column wise.

9.2.2.3 Usefulness of the index for developing sustainable HRM practices

9.2.2.3.1 Aggregate social costs of harm of work

The index can be used to capture the multilayered social costs of harm of HPWPs for stakeholders due to the crossover effect of harm of work from the employee level to their family level and subsequently to the societal level.

For example, work-related insomnia imposes social costs on employees (costs relating to performance impairment), then crossover to family members (caring for employees affected by insomnia) and finally on society, which bears the costs for treating both the affected employees and their family members. Similarly, divorce caused by marriage dissatisfaction triggered by the high work demands of HPWPs costs the employee, their family and society. Therefore, the stakeholder harm of work index has the ability to capture and reveal to practitioners and researchers the harm of work and the associated costs of those unsustainable aspects of HPWPs on individuals as well as on multiple stakeholders.

It is revealed by the stakeholder harm of work index that there is a clear trend of direct and indirect social costs of HPWPs imposed on employees and their family members (individual level) and communities (societal level). Furthermore, if organisations attempt to internalise the social costs or pay for the costs of harm of work imposed on the stakeholders by HPWPs, which are used to maximise profit, then the profit margin achieved in this process may not indicate the 'true' profit but rather highlight the risk for a negative margin. Does this mean that organisations cannot have higher profit margins by caring for their stakeholders? Certainly it is possible for organisations to achieve higher profit margins even after caring for their stakeholders based on the synthesis effects of sustainable HRM (Mariappanadar, 2014). That is, an awareness of the level of ethics of care for stakeholders based on the stakeholder harm of work index can subsequently encourage managers to introduce sustainable HRM strategies to enhance the profit margin for the organisation by also reducing the harm of HPWPs on stakeholders. The ethics of care in the HRM context refers to the ethical choices organisations face when seeking to maximise profit as well as to reduce the harmful aspects of HRM practices on the stakeholders, such as employees, their families and communities, so as to maintain harmonious relations between the employer involved and the stakeholders (Mariappanadar, 2012a).

9.2.2.3.2 Stakeholder harm of work index for a self-regulating system

The stakeholder harm of work index can facilitate a self-regulating system whereby an organisation can manage harm of work practices to achieve sustainable HRM. The process of self-regulation for managerial effectiveness involves three subprocesses: standard setting, discrepancy detecting and discrepancy reducing for various stakeholders. Therefore, the stakeholder harm of work index can help managers identify and capture the harm of certain work practices so as to detect discrepancy in the ethics of care for the stakeholders so as to introduce HR policy and practice for change interventions to minimise the harm of work. Subsequently, by using the index it is possible to evaluate over a period of time the harm of work imposed on the stakeholders, determine the effectiveness of any intervention in minimising the harm of certain work practices that are imposed on the stakeholders, and achieve financial performance for the organisation (see dotted line in Figure 9.1).

The stakeholder harm of work index offers HR practitioners detailed knowledge of the industry in which companies are operating to identify the harm of HPWPs and set standards for management-based regulation and social self-regulation. This will arguably lead to more practicable standards for the negative consequences on stakeholders as well as allow more effective monitoring. There is also the potential for utilising peer firm pressure and for successfully internalising responsibility for compliance when social self-regulation is used. Because self-regulation contemplates ethical standards of conduct or CSR which extend beyond the letter of the law, it may significantly raise the standards of firms' behaviour within an industry. Alternatively, the government and labour advocacy groups can use the benchmark on harm of HPWPs based on the harm of HPWPs captured in the stakeholder harm of work index to encourage or reform industrial relations law to take punitive actions against non-compliant companies within that industry.

9.3 Measures for the harm of work

The stakeholder harm of work index is a useful tool to capture and catalogue the harm of work and also the aggregate social costs of the harm of HPWPs practices imposed on single and multiple stakeholders. Sustainable HRM accepts the simultaneous positive and negative impacts on organisation performance and employee well-being respectively, and hence emphasises the synthesis effects of HRM practices. That is, organisations can improve organisational performances through HRM practices as well as attempt to 'reduce' the harm of HRM practices on employee well-being because these two polarities are not mutually exclusive but are instead mutually reinforcing. Therefore, the synthesis effects of sustainable HRM add to the simultaneous effects perspective by measuring harm of work practices so that organisational- or institutional-level intervention can be planned to reduce the harm of work. Once, the harm of work imposed on employees and their families is objectively measured, then the organisation can develop sustainable HR strategies and systems (see Chapter 4) for sustainable HRM practices to reduce the harm of work so as to achieve corporate sustainability. Hence, the measure to identify the health harm of work and the social harm of work imposed on employees as stakeholders is important and discussed in this section.

In the organisational psychology and HRM literature (e.g. Lazarus, 2000; Boselie et al., 2006) there has been plenty of research carried out to understand the unsustainable aspects of work on employees and their families based on work stress and strain theories. However, the health harm of work was developed as a measure for sustainable HRM to be different from that of common work stress and strain measures. Hence, the differences between work stress and strain and the health harm of work are discussed next.

9.3.1 Difference between the health harm of work practices and work stress

It is important to explain the differences between the health harm of work and work stress based on the focus and process of the two concepts. The differences will highlight the importance for a separate tool to capture the health harm of work which can be used in the future sustainability assessment. First, exploring the focus of both concepts, more than three decades of research on work stress and strain have led to the belief that work stress and strain are the causes of work-related illnesses and therefore employees' reduced work performance. It is commonly believed in the field of HRM and organisational psychology that work stress provides a broad understanding of the harm or negative 'side effects' (Boselie et al., 2006) of work practices. Studies on work stressors (at the individual, group, organisational and extra-organisational levels), appraisal and coping strategies on health and social (family) outcomes are common in the occupational stress literature (see Lazarus, 2000; Penley et al., 2002; Selye 1976). The health harm of work practices is different from that of work stress and strain because the health harm of work is related to positive health or prevention-focused measures, whereas work stress is considered from an occupational illness perspective. Positive health and positive psychology are competence models of health and are an alternative to the dominant physical and psychological illnesses model. Moreover, positive health and positive psychology advocate a proactive approach to identifying lead indicators of work-related psychological disorders and chronic disease to enhance prospects of positive well-being (Seeman, 1989).

Secondly, concerning the difference in the process for achieving the focus of both concepts, according to the definition of the health harm of work, the focus is on how certain work practices 'refrain' employees from achieving positive health and well-being outcomes. Hence, the health harm of work is used as lead indicators of employees' positive health and well-being outcomes instead of using occupational stress which is predominately used as an agent that causes disorders or illnesses (see Sauter et al., 1990). For example, the high health harm of work as a measure can predict or act as leading indicators of the future reduced positive health and well-being outcomes for employees which lead to reduced employees' work performance. Work practices related leading indicators are defined in the occupational health and safety literature as early warning signs of potential failure in organisational practices so as to enable organisations to identify and correct deficiencies in organisational practices and employee behaviour before they trigger injuries, diseases and damages (Sinelnikov et al., 2015). On the other hand, the high work strain as a measure indicates that the damage to an employee's psychological and physical health outcomes which already has happened based on the non-specific responses to the work related stressors (see Selye, 1974), and hence work strain is not a leading indicator but a cause for occupational health and well-being outcomes.

For example, when an organisation introduces job outsourcing as a turnaround strategy for improving financial outcomes this may create job insecurity among existing employees, and hence employees may spend longer hours at work so as to avoid their position being made redundant. The long working hours may restrict employees in finding time to get involved in physical activities to improve positive physical or psychological health well-being outcomes. Therefore, the health harm of work is about preventative measures to improve positive well-being outcomes for employees before the non-specific responses of work-related stressors (Selye, 1974) lead to work-related ill health, and subsequently reduce employees' work performances. The focus and process-based explanations provided indicate the differences between the health harm of work and work stress and form the basis for the development of the health harm of work as a new measure, using the perspective of work restrictions on employees' positive health.

The harm of work as a nomenclature may sound 'negative' and contradict the positive health focus as the theoretical basis for the measure. However, the focus of harm of work is to identify leading indicators of occupational illnesses, which are negative, so as to prevent future occupational health issues for employees. Hence, the nomenclature of the 'harm' of work as a measure for sustainable HRM may sound 'negative' but it is used for the early identification of 'reversible' health issues or positive health to prevent future 'irreversible' occupational illnesses for employees. Sustainability is explained in the field of health based on reversibility and irreversibility of biological systems for human performance (Toman, 2006). That is, in health, irreversibility indicates that the biological system has lost its capacity to return to a normal level or its original level of operation to allow normal human performances. Therefore, the harm of work measures help organisations to identify the occupational health issues using leading indicators, which are observable behavioural indicators, for reversible biological system conditions so that people can enjoy normal work and non-work functioning. For example, lack of time for physical exercise due to work overload can be a leading indicator for future irreversible health conditions, such as high blood pressure or high cholesterol-based cardio vascular diseases (CVD). Hence, if an organisation takes steps to identify lack of time for physical exercise as a part of a harm of work then the organisation might have an opportunity to reverse employees' physical state through normal rest and lifestyle recovery experiences before they reach the irreversible stage of future CVD. The health harm of work scale is discussed next.

9.3.2 The health harm of work measure

The health harm of work was defined as an employee's perception of the restrictions on achieving positive health and work-related leading indicators for negative health outcomes. The health harm of work measure was designed and developed by Mariappanadar (2016) to identify the cognitive, behavioural and physical aspects of the health harm of work so as to promote sustainable HRM. The measure uses fourteen items (see Table 9.2) to reveal three dimensions of the health harm of work scale, which include the work restrictions for positive health, the risk factors for psychological health, and the side effects of work. The dimension of work restriction for positive health is about the restrictions imposed on an employee's non–job-related activities which improve their health. The dimension of risk factors for psychological health indicates the perceived effects of health harm of work on an employee's cognitive, behavioural and physical conditions that have the potential for the future onset of negative health issues.

Finally, the dimension of side effects of work emphasises the perceived unintended adverse side effects of work practices that are imposed on employees while an organisation is pursuing its intended business goals. The risk factors for the psychological health and the side effects of work as reflective dimensions of the health harm of work indicate the restrictions imposed by work on employees to achieve health and well-being outcomes. The discriminant validity of the scale development study (Mariappanadar, 2016) revealed that the dimensions of the health harm of work scale are different from that of the dimensions of the work recovery experience scale (Sonnentag & Fritz,

Table 9.2   Items for the health harm of work scale

Instruction: Please indicate how strongly you agree or disagree that your current paid work causes the following effects on you.

Measurement scale: Each item was measured using a 6-point Likert scale (1 – strongly disagree to 6 –strongly agree).

Scale items
1. I am often emotionally drained when I get home.
2. I am struggling to balance work and play.
3. I feel that I have increased my consumption of coffee.
4. I frequently have disturbances to normal sleep.
5. I have increased my consumption of alcohol to relax after a day's work.
6. My self-confidence is negatively affected.
7. It is difficult for me to find time to implement strategies to control my weight.
8. I am often irritable when I get home.
9. My emotional health is negatively affected.
10. I rarely find time to do regular physical exercise.
11. I feel so 'down in the dumps' that nothing can cheer me up.
12. I rarely take regular breaks from work.
13. I feel nervous of late.
14. I take too many sick leaves of late.

Scoring: Risk factors for psychological health – items 1, 6, 8, 9, 11 & 13; Restrictions for positive health – items 2, 7, 10, & 12; Side effects of work – items 3, 4, 5 & 14.

Score interpretation: High scores on the dimensions of the scale were indicative of high restrictions imposed by work on improving positive health, increased risk factors for psychological health and increased side effects of work.

Source: Mariappanadar (2016).

2007), which is based on the work stress and strain theories. Furthermore, the study on the health harm of work found that overwork, a type of work intensification, increased the manifestation of the three dimensions of health harm of work. Hence, knowledge construction based on empirical research evidence on the health harm of work is important to enrich our understanding of sustainable HRM.

9.3.3 Usefulness of the health harm measure

The health harm of work measure can be used by the proponents of the mutual benefits perspective, the critical HRM perspective and the synthesis effect perspective of sustainable HRM, for the first time, an objective measure for health harm of work. Practitioners may wonder why organisations should be interested in understanding the harm of work on employees' health when a national health system will provide health care for employees. In countries where there is no national health care system for their citizens, a few organisations provide health insurance for employees to provide health care. The compelling reason for practitioners to become aware of the health harm of work is to prevent or delay the onset of work-related illnesses because employee work-related illnesses lead to work-related health consequences such as lost productivity due to absenteeism and presenteeism. Hence, it is important for practitioners to understand that organisations have to be pro-active in measuring the health harm of work as a leading indicator of negative health outcomes for employees. This will facilitate organisations in reducing the health harm of work by using the sustainable HRM practices discussed in Chapter 4 to prevent or delay the onset of work-related illness manifestation, and subsequently the related productivity loss due to absenteeism and presenteeism.

The health harm of work measure is a valid work context-based sustainable HRM assessment tool to measure the positive and/or negative impacts of management practices on employees' occupational health. Corporations can objectively measure and disclose the health harm of work in the GRIs for sustainability along with other measures such as type of injury, occupational diseases, lost days, work-related fatalities and so on. The objective health harm of work measure can become materiality for reporting occupational health in GRIs. Materiality from non-financial information focuses on the scope or relevance of issues to be addressed for the benefit of a business and its stakeholders. Furthermore, a time frame for materiality highlights a corporation's commitment to meet the needs of the present without compromising the needs of future generations, with a long-term and forward-looking view. Developing the work context-based health harm of work measure as materiality for occupational health will facilitate organisations in identifying, analysing and documenting the health harm of work to be used as leading indicators of negative occupational health impact on employees. Hence, future research in the field of occupational health and safety performance should focus on testing the causal relationships between the dimensions of health harm of work and work-related illnesses. Therefore, the health harm of work measure can provide new opportunities for practice and research to consider using the measure as leading indicators for occupational health as well as for improving organisational performance by increasing productivity and reducing absenteeism and presenteeism (see Figure 9.1).

9.3.4 The social harm of work measure

Work–life balance from the role orientation perspective emphasises the extent to which an individual is equally engaged in and equally satisfied with both his/her work role and his/her family role (i.e. work–family facilitation). However, the phenomenological or process perspective for work–life balance highlights that jobs may promote work–family facilitation, but they may also lead to work–family conflict. Furthermore, there is a possible third option for understanding work–family balance. That is, the attempt to achieve positive balance in work–family roles or work–family facilitation based on resources gained to benefit family life may also 'restrict' or 'restrain' employees from performing their desired roles in the family domain and achieving family well-being. For example, work intensification by HPWPs will provide both financial and psychological resources for an employee to have a satisfying family life (work–family facilitation), but the same work intensification might restrict or restrain his/her availability for family activities to improve family well-being. Hence, the social harm of work addresses an important aspect of work–life balance for family well-being outcomes.

The social harm of work is about employees' perceived severity of restrictions imposed by work on family activities and the prevalence of negative effects of work–family restrictions on employees and their family, which reduce family well-being outcomes for employees. The social harm of work is measured using seventeen items (Table 9.3) to highlight the characteristics of social harm of work. The three dimensions of the social harm of work scale are the work restrictions on the family domain, the negative impacts of work–family restrictions and the reduced work–family role facilitations. The work restrictions on the family domain as a dimension are defined as employee's perceived severity of work restrictions on engaging in family activities. The reduced family role facilitation dimension of social harm of work is defined as the perceived reduced work role facilitation to other aspects of an employee's family life. Finally, the negative impacts of the work restriction dimension are about the perceived negative consequences of work to family restriction on employees. The study by Mariappanadar while validating the social harm of work scale found that the dimensions of social harm of work are different from that of the unidimensional work–family facilitation scale (Grzywacz & Butler, 2005b) and the multidimensional work–family conflict scale (Carlson et al., 2000).

9.3.5 Usefulness of the social harm measure

The social harm of work measure has made an important contribution to the employees' family aspect of the sustainable HRM literature (e.g. Mariappanadar & Aust, 2018) as well as to the work–family balance literature

Table 9.3 Items for the social harm of work scale

Instruction: Please indicate how strongly you agree or disagree that your current paid work causes the following effects on you.

Measurement scale: Each item was measured using a 6-point Likert scale (1 – strongly disagree to 6 – strongly agree).

Scale items
1. My spouse/partner often mentions that I don't care as much about him/her because of me being preoccupied with my work.
2. Increasingly, I have started to neglect my family and/or friends due to increased work commitments.
3. The amount of time my spouse/partner and I spend in shared recreational activities has reduced a lot because of increased work commitments.
4. My family/friends dislike the fact that I am often preoccupied with my work while I am at home.
5. Increase in negative marital interactions as a result of my work commitments.
6. Certain work practices introduced in my organisation have led to a decrease in my quality of interactions with family and/or friends.
7. I feel guilty for spending too much time at work and not enough time with my family and/or friends.
8. I get angry more often with my spouse/partner due to increased work pressures caused by certain management practices.
9. The day-to-day support and encouragement provided by my spouse/partner has reduced considerably because my work has alienated me from my family.
10. Certain work practices have started affecting my family life negatively.
11. A physical intimate relationship with my spouse/partner is very rare nowadays due to work strain.
12. I often feel that I want to be left alone after work rather than spend time with family and/or friends.
13. My work is one of the most important reasons for the breakdown in my relationship with my spouse/partner.
14. I rarely involve myself in voluntary community activities due to work commitments.
15. I rarely attend my children's school and sports activities due to my work commitments.
16. I seldom take time off from work to spend time with my children due to increased work commitments.
17. All other reasons (e.g. financial, etc.) being favourable, I seldom manage to go to the movies/restaurants with my family due to increased work commitments.

Scoring: Work–family restrictions – items 1 to 8); Negative impacts of work–family restrictions – items 9 to 13; Reduced work–family role facilitation – items 14 to 17.

Score interpretation: High scores on the dimensions of the scale were indicative of high work–family restrictions, increased negative impacts of work–family restrictions and reduced work–family role facilitation.

(e.g. Greehaus, Collins & Shaw 2003; Grzywacz & Butler, 2005b). Developing the social harm of work scale based on work restrictions on the family domain that reduce family well-being while employees attempt to achieve work–family balance can be a new antecedent for enriching the understanding of employee's quality of life. That is, the measure for social harm of work will help HR professionals to identify the social harm of work imposed on employees by certain strategic HRM practices which are deemed to enhance positive balance in work–family roles and work–family facilitation for employees. There is a compelling reason to measure the social harm of work as part of sustainable HRM because, if no attempt is made by HR practitioners and line managers to reduce the social harm of work, it will increase work–family imbalance. This will escalate absenteeism and presenteeism which subsequently will increase productivity losses for an organisation. Hence, sustainability HRM, which facilitates minimised social harm of work imposed by organisational practices on employees, will enhance corporate sustainability including the economic and social sustainability of organisations (see Figure 9.1).

9.4 Measure for sustainable leadership

Sustainable leadership or honeybee leadership is an institutional-level approach and does not focus on leaders' individual characteristics. Sustainable leadership (Avery & Bersteiner, 2011) is about those behaviours, organisational practices and systems that facilitate enduring value for all stakeholders (i.e. shareholders, employees, society's sustainable environmental management expectations, future generations and the community). Furthermore, honeybee leadership assumes that an organisation can be sustainable only when stakeholders' needs are taken into consideration as part of the business strategies and practices. Sustainability leadership is assessed using twenty-three criterion practices, which broadly include organisational domains such as organisational culture, systems and processes to create and sustain an organisation based on its core social values.

The twenty-three sustainable leadership criterion practices are CEO and top-team leadership, consensual and devolved decision making, ethics, challenging financial markets, strong systemic innovation, knowledge sharing, long-term perspective, promotion-from-within, strong organisational culture, strong people priority, high quality, high staff retention, highly skilled workforce, strong social responsibility, strong environmental responsibility, broad stakeholder focus, self-governing teams, considered uncertainty and change as process, cooperative union-management relations, trust, innovation, staff engagement and self-management.

A measure for sustainable leadership is included in this chapter because seventeen of the total twenty-three sustainable leadership criterion practices are relevant for developing and shaping sustainable HRM practices (Suriyankeitkaew & Avery, 2014). Those seventeen criterion practices are top management leadership, consensual and devolved decision making, ethics, knowledge sharing, long-term perspective, strong organisational culture, strong people priority, high staff retention, highly skilled workforce, strong social responsibility, strong environmental responsibility, broad stakeholder focus, self-governing teams, cooperative union-management relations, trust, staff engagement, and self-management. The twenty-three sustainable leadership criterion practices can be measured by using Avery and Beg-steiner's (2011) sustainable leadership questionnaire. This questionnaire has fifty-seven items that are measured using the Likert scale.

9.4.1 Usefulness sustainable leadership indicators to develop sustainable HRM practices

A study using sustainable leadership criterion practices found that amicable labour relations, staff retention, strong and shared vision and high staff engagement, which are related to sustainable HRM practices, positively predicted enhanced overall stakeholder satisfaction (Suriyankeitkaew & Avery, 2014). Furthermore, the study also found criterion practices including organisational culture (e.g. strong and shared vision), system (e.g. strategic and systemic innovations) and processes (e.g. quality) are related to overall stakeholder satisfaction. Hence, the measure for sustainability leadership provides better insight for practitioners and researchers to enhance stakeholder satisfaction which is an integral part of sustainable HRM.

9.5 Measure for green HRM practices

The natural environment is one of the three pillars of sustainable development, and hence environmental sustainability is an important issue for senior managers, government policy makers and stakeholders (consumers, shareholders and regulatory agencies). Renwick and his colleagues (2013), in a review of the green HRM research, revealed that different HRM practices are key factors for environmental performance (i.e. toxic emissions, the development of eco-friendly products, etc.). That is, hiring employees with specific environmental competencies, developing environmental competencies and skills, and evaluating employee performance based on green behaviours and rewarding those green behaviours are related to improved environmental performance of a corporation. Green HRM practices from the resource-based theory indicate that employees as a key resource are sensitive to environmental issues and have environmental competencies that will facilitate an organisation in achieving competitive advantage.

Guerci et al. (2016) have developed a green HRM measure based on studies conducted by Renwick et al. (2013) and Jabbour et al. (2010). Guerci and his colleagues developed a scale with three green HRM practices that will have a favourable impact on an organisation's environmental performance. The three green HRM practices are green hiring, green training and involvement, and green performance management and compensation. Green hiring was proposed as a dimension of green HRM measure because new employees hired with environmental competencies will be more sensitive to environmental issues and hence improve the organisation's environmental performance. This dimension included two indicators, which are 'employee selection based on natural environmental criteria' and 'employee attraction through environmental commitment'.

The green training and involvement dimension of the green HRM practices scale reflects that employees will have high engagement towards green behaviours when they are trained in green behaviours and provided with adequate support for active involvement in green behaviours. This dimension was measured using four indicators, namely 'environmental training for employees', 'environmental training for managers', 'job descriptions that include environmental responsibilities' and 'employee involvement in environmental issues'. The final dimension of the scale, green performance management and compensation practices, allows employees to align their behaviours with the environmental goals of the organisation. The indicators were 'environmental goals for managers', 'managers evaluation includes environmental performance', 'employees evaluation includes environmental performance', 'non-monetary incentives for environmental performance' and 'variable compensation based on environmental performance'.

9.5.1 Usefulness of the green HRM measure to develop sustainable HRM practices

The green HRM scale is a useful measure because there is evidence in the literature that green HRM practices improve an organisation's environmental performance (Guerci et al., 2016). That is, green HRM practices can be considered as a bundle HRM practices deploying a firm-specific resource (i.e.

human resources) to increase the firm's environmental performance on recycling of wastage, increased use of renewable energy and so on. Furthermore, the green HRM scale can help organisations identify and develop employees with environmental competencies so as to be prepared to handle any future stakeholder pressures on environmental issues so as to achieve environmental sustainability (see Figure 9. 1).

9.6 Conclusion

Over the past thirty years strategic HRM gained a strong foothold in the field of HRM because it provided metrics to objectively understand the role of HR functions and practices in enhancing organisational performance. Sustainable HRM has gained recognition in the field of HRM because it highlights organisational effort to promote social sustainability as a part of corporate sustainability. Hence, it is important to objectively measure the sustainable and unsustainable effects of HRM practices on an organisation and its relevant stakeholders for sustainable HRM, as a new field, to sustain and flourish over a long period of time. These objective measures for sustainable and unsustainable effects of HRM practices will facilitate HR practitioners and managers to develop a bundle of sustainable HRM practices to achieve the synthesis effects of HRM practices to reduce the unsustainable effects or harm of work imposed on employees as a stakeholder and which also improve organisational performance. Hence, in this chapter different measures for sustainable practices and the unsustainability or harm of work were explained.

There are two indices which were discussed in this chapter, one each for capturing sustainable and unsustainable impacts of HRM on stakeholders. The role of HRM in enhancing sustainable impacts on stakeholders was discussed using the human potential index (HPI). The HPI is based on human capital theories and highlights twelve HPI value drivers that facilitate organisational practices to improve care for stakeholders while improving organisational performance. The stakeholder harm of work index is a useful tool to capture and catalogue the personal, social and health harm of work (unsustainable effects) and also the aggregate social costs of the harm of HPWPs practices imposed on single and multiple stakeholders (i.e. employees, their families and society). It is apparent that the stakeholder harm of work index can be used by managers and HR professionals as a tool to facilitate a comprehensive understanding of diverse harm of work aspects and the associated social costs of the unsustainable aspects of HPWPs imposed on the stakeholders. The captured harm of work will facilitate HR professionals in understanding the level of care provided by an organisation to its stakeholders to achieve sustainable HRM. Furthermore, it is a useful tool to capture and monitor the harm of HPWPs on stakeholders over a period of time so as to self-regulate organisational practices to evaluate the reduction of harm of work on stakeholders after the introduction of planned organisational-level interventions. Furthermore, the stakeholder harm of work index can help organisations, labour advocacy groups, trade unions and public policy makers to measure and benchmark the harm of HPWPs so as to implement appropriate HR policy and practices change interventions as self-regulations for sustainable HRM.

The harm of work as a new concept in the field of sustainable HRM was developed to understand the unsustainable impacts of HRM practices on employees. Hence, the two types of harm of work, the health harm and the social harm, were objectively measured so that large organisations can use these types of harm of work as materiality for sustainable HRM initiatives. Occupational health and well-being are used as materiality in sustainability assessments and reporting. The health harm and the social harm of work are measured to act as leading indicators for occupational health and well-being and social well-being for employees respectively. In this context, the differences between the health harm of work and work stress and strain based on the focus and process of the two concepts were explained to indicate that the health harm of work is a different construct from that of work stress so as to prevent negative occupational health and well-being for employees. The health harm of work includes three dimensions which are the work restrictions for positive health, the risk factors for psychological health and the side effects of work. It was discussed in this chapter that work intensification increased the three dimensions of health harm of work and hence the measure is important for enriching our knowledge about sustainable HRM. Furthermore, large organisations can objectively measure and disclose the health harm of work in the GRI for sustainability and other sustainability reports (e.g. Sustainability Asset Management by RobecoSAM for the Dow Jones Sustainability Group Index) so that an independent third party can audit the materiality disclosed for sustainable HRM initiatives.

The social harm of work highlights the severity of work restrictions as perceived by employees that are imposed on family activities as a result of organisational practices which subsequently reduce family well-being outcomes for employees. The three dimensions of the social harm of work scale are the work restrictions on the family domain, the negative impacts of work–family restrictions and the reduced work–family role facilitations. These three dimensions of the social harm of work were found to be different from that of constructs such as work–family facilitation and work–family conflicts from the work–family balance literature. The social harm of work is a useful measure to reveal the unsustainable family impacts of organisational practices on employees, and the measure can trigger HR practitioners to introduce organisational-level interventions to reduce the social harm of work and promote sustainable HRM. It is important to understand the measure of health harm and the social harm of work because it can trigger the need for organisations to reduce the harm of work on employees which will lead to improved organisational performance by increasing productivity and reducing absenteeism and presenteeism.

Sustainable leadership or honeybee leadership is an institutional-level approach and is not based on leaders' individual characteristics, hence it is relevant to the field of sustainable HRM. The measure for sustainable leadership includes twenty-three criterion practices, of which seventeen are related to sustainable HRM practices because those practices enhanced stakeholder satisfaction. Hence, the measure for sustainability leadership provides better insight for practitioners and researchers to enhance stakeholder satisfaction which is an integral part of sustainable HRM. Finally, the roles of green HRM in improving large corporations' environmental performance were discussed. The three green HRM practices were green hiring, green training and involvement, and green performance management and compensation. It was discussed that green HRM practices as a bundle can facilitate an organisation in deploying a firm-specific HR strategies and practices to increase a firm's environmental performance on recycling of waste, an increased use of renewable energy and so on.

References

Avery, G. C. & Bergsteiner, H. (2011). *Sustainable Leadership: Honeybees and Locusts Approaches*, New York: Routledge.

Borman, W. C. (1991). Job behavior, performance, and effectiveness. In M. D. Dunnette & L. M. Hough (Eds.), *Handbook of industrial and organizational psychology* (pp. 271-326). Palo Alto, CA, US: Consulting Psychologists Press.

Boselie, P., Dietz, G. & Boon, C. (2006). Commonalities and contradictions in HRM and performance research. *Human Resource Management Journal*, 15(3), 67–94.

Cameron, A. (1998). The elasticity of endurance: Work intensification and workplace flexibility in the Queensland public hospital system. *New Zealand Journal of Industrial Relations, 23*(3),133–51.

Carlson, D. S., Kacmar, K. M. & Williams, L. J. (2000). Construction and initial validation of a multidimensional measure of work–Family conflict. *Journal of Vocational Behavior, 56*(2), 249–76.

Deci, E. L., & Ryan, R. M. (1985). *Intrinsic Motivation and Self-determination in Human Behavior.* New York: Plenum.

Greenhaus, J. H., Collins, K. M. & Shaw, J. D. (2003). The relation between work-family balance and quality of life. *Journal of Vocational Behavior, 63*(3), 510–31.

Grzywacz, J. G. & Butler, A. B. (2005b). The impact of job characteristics on work-to-family facilitation: Testing a theory and distinguishing a construct. *Journal of Occupational Health Psychology, 10*(2), 97.

Guerci, M., Longoni, A. & Luzzini, D. (2016). Translating stakeholder pressures into environmental performance–The mediating role of green HRM practices. *The International Journal of Human Resource Management, 27*(2),262–89.

Huselid, M. A. (1995). The impact of human resource management practices on turnover, productivity, and corporate financial performance. *Academy of Management Journal, 38*(3),635–72.

Jabbour, C. J. C., Santos, F. C. A. & Nagano, M. S. (2010). Contributions of HRM throughout the stages of environmental management: Methodological triangulation applied to companies in Brazil. *The International Journal of Human Resource Management, 21*(7),1049–89.

Khanna, N. (2000). Measuring environmental quality: An index of pollution. *Ecological Economics, 35,* 191–202.

Lazarus, R. S. (2000). Toward better research on stress and coping. *The American Psychologist, 55,* 665–73.

LBBW (Landesbank Baden-Württemberg) (2015). Annual Report L. B. B. W. Accessed on 15 September 2016. http://www.lbbw.de/media/investor_relations/pdf_investorrelations/2016/LBBW_Annual_Report_2015.pdf

Mariappanadar, S. (2012a). Harm of efficiency oriented HRM practices on stakeholders: An ethical issue for sustainability. *Society and Business Review, 7*(2),168–84.

Mariappanadar, S. (2012b). The harm indicators of negative externality of efficiency focused organizational practices. *International Journal of Social Economics, 39*(3),209–20.

Mariappanadar, S. (2013). A conceptual framework for cost measures of harm of HRM practices. *Asia-Pacific Journal of Business Administration, 5*(2),15–39.

Mariappanadar, S. (2014). Stakeholder harm index: A framework to review work intensification from the critical HRM perspective. *Human Resource Management Review, 24*(4),313–29.

Mariappanadar, S. (2016). Health harm of work from the sustainable HRM perspective: Scale development and validation. *International Journal of Manpower, 37*(6), 924–44.

Mariappanadar, S. & Aust, I. (2018). The dark side of overwork: An empirical evidence of social harm of work from a sustainable HRM perspective. *International Studies of Management and Organization, 47,* 372–87.

Mariappanadar, S. & Kramar, R. (2014). Sustainable HRM: The synthesis effect of high performance work systems on organisational performance and employee harm. *Asia-Pacific Journal of Business Administration, 6*(3),206–24.

Nam, K. M., Selin, N. E., Reilly, J. M. & Paltsev, S. (2010). Measuring welfare loss caused by air pollution in Europe: A CGE analysis. *Energy Policy, 38,* 5059–71.

Osranek, R. & Zink, K. J. (2014). Corporate human capital and social sustainability of human resources. In: I. Ehnert, W. Harry & K. J. Zink (eds) *Sustainability and Human Resource Management* (pp. 105–26). Berlin, Heidelberg: Springer.

Penley, J. A., Tomaka, J. & Wiebe, J. S. (2002). The association of coping to physical and psychological health outcomes: A meta-analytic review. *Journal of Behavioral Medicine, 25,* 551–603.

Pfeffer, J. (1998). The real keys to high performance. *Leader to Leader, 8,* 23–29.

Renwick, D. W., Redman, T. & Maguire, S. (2013). Green human resource management: A review and research agenda. *International Journal of Management Reviews, 15*(1), 1–14.

Rogers, E. W. & Wright, P. M. (1998). Measuring organizational performance in strategic human resource management: Problems, prospects and performance information markets. *Human Resource Management Review, 8*(3), 311–31.

Sauter, S., Murphy, L. & Hurrell, J. (1990). Prevention of work-related psychological disorders: A national strategy proposed by the national institute for occupational safety and health. *American Psychologist, 45,* 1146–58.

Schramm, D. G. (2006). Individual and social costs of divorce in Utah. *Journal of Family and Economic Issues, 27,* 133–51.

Seeman, J. (1989). Toward a model of positive health. *American Psychologist, 44,* 1099–109. 10.1037/0003-066X.44.8.1099

Selye, H. (1976). *The Stress of Life.* New York: McGraw-Hill.

Shaw, J. & Creed, F. (1991). The cost of somatisation. *Journal of Psychosomatic Research, 35*(2–3), 307–12.

Sinelnikov, S., Inouye, J. & Kerper, S. (2015). Using leading indicators to measure occupational health and safety performance. *Safety Science, 72,* 240–48.

Smith, A. F. & Brown, G. C. (2000). Understanding cost effectiveness: A detailed review. *British Journal of Ophthalmology, 84*(7), 794–98.

Sonnentag, S. & Fritz, C. (2007). The recovery experience questionnaire: Development and validation of a measure for assessing recuperation and unwinding from work. *Journal of Occupational Health Psychology, 12*(3), 204–21.

Suriyankietkaew, S. & Avery, G. C. (2014). Leadership practices influencing stakeholder satisfaction in Thai SMEs. *Asia-Pacific Journal of Business Administration, 6*(3), 247–61.

Terpstra, D. E. & Rozell, E. J. (1993). The relationship of staffing practices to organizational level measures of performance. *Personnel Psychology, 46,* 27–48.

Toman, M. A. (2006). The difficulty in defining sustainability. *The RFF Reader in Environmental and Resource Policy, 2.*

UN Global Compact (2014). *Overview of the UN Global Compact.* http://nbis.org/nbisresources/sustainable_development_equity/un_global_compact.pdf. Accessed on 22 September 2015.

Van de Voorde, K., Paauwe, J. & Van Veldhoven, M. (2012). Employee wellbeing and the HRM – Organizational performance relationship: A review of quantitative studies. *International Journal of Management Reviews, 14*(4), 391–407.

10

Sustainability reporting and sustainable HRM

Elaine Cohen, Iris Maurer, Sugumar Mariappanadar and Michael Müller-Camen

10.1 Introduction

The aim of this chapter is to link the internal measurement of sustainable HRM to external reporting and communication with stakeholders. Key international reporting guidelines – such as the Global Reporting Initiative (GRI) Standards and the UN Global Compact Communication on Progress (COP) – will be discussed and their link to sustainable HRM highlighted. Whereas these guidelines provide an incentive for organisations to report about sustainability-related practices, they do not prescribe performance standards or measure the achievement against them. However, three reporting tools that have emerged over the last decade – B-Corps, the Economy-of-the-Common-Good and the Future Fit standards – provide performance standards as well as transparency requirements and therefore offer a more challenging level of adherence.

The GRI Sustainability Reporting Standards (GRI, 2016) offer a globally relevant framework to support a standardised approach to reporting on an organisation's positive or negative impacts on the natural environment, society and the economy, in a way which is useful and credible to stakeholders (employees, shareholders, suppliers, civil society and local communities). The GRI, like many other sustainability reporting and disclosures, is a voluntary standard and companies are not required to externally audit their reports. The GRI builds on and references, among others, the UN Global Compact's 'Ten Principles', the OECD Guidelines for Multinational Enterprises and the UN Guiding Principles on Business and Human Rights. Almost all of the world's largest companies now disclose human/social and natural environmental information in standalone sustainability reports, integrated reports and/or on their company websites. This reporting helps organisations and their stakeholders to understand the abstract sustainability issues in more tangible and concrete terms, as well as providing a management tool to facilitate an organisation's activities and strategies to align with sustainability.

10.2 Sustainability reporting by corporations

Over the last three decades, most large organisations have publicly committed themselves to be responsible organisations. They claim that they no longer focus solely on serving shareholders, but also respond to the expectations of other stakeholders such as employees, customers, regulators, local communities and NGOs which include trade unions and human/social and environmental activist organisations. In addition to a focus on profits, corporations today propose the pursuit of a 'triple bottom line' in which they aim to improve their economic/financial, environmental and human/social impacts. The efforts and progress made towards achieving such an improvement in these corporate impacts are documented annually in CSR and/or sustainability reports which are published by 92 per cent of the largest 250 global corporations, 73 per cent of the largest 100 national companies in 45 countries (KPMG, 2015) and, increasingly by smaller companies as well.

Nevertheless, there has been a development over time. In the 1970s, there was an expansion of reporting practices from financial to non-financial issues, in most cases social subjects. Standalone social and/or community relations reports were published to disclose relevant information and provide evidence of progress. The focus of reporting in the 1980s remained social issues, but, a decade later, the emphasis shifted from human/social to environmental reporting due to significant comparative advantages of environmentally friendly products and the cost-benefits of environmental production efficiencies, and also because of increasing public awareness of negative environmental impacts such as global warming, water scarcity, polluted waterways and more. Consequently, the environmental report became a standard among large companies and, in some cases, replaced social reporting whereas, in other cases, was combined to create a CSR report that covered both social and environmental impacts. After the turn of the millennium, the norm became the CSR report, the sustainability report, the corporate (social) report or the corporate citizenship report (Fifka, 2013). These covered economic, environmental and social issues, as proposed by Elkington's 'triple bottom line' (Elkington, 1999).

In spite of increasing global efforts at standardisation in CSR reporting and metrics, significant national differences remain in the extent and content of CSR reporting. For example, research by Chen and Bouvain (2009) indicates that CSR reports by German companies and those by firms from the UK, the USA and Australia differ on some aspects such as workers' and social issues, and, in other aspects, such as environmental issues they were similar. Furthermore, a comparison among the fifty largest companies in the UK and in Finland suggests that the cultural and socio-economic environment has an influence on the extent of sustainability reporting. Here, governmental regulation can improve the extent of reporting (Fifka & Drabble, 2012).

10.3 The global reporting initiative framework

10.3.1 Stakeholder engagement and materiality related to HRM

An important driver of the quality of sustainability reports and thus for international standardisation of sustainability reporting is the GRI (Kolk & Perego, 2010), a non-profit multi-stakeholder organisation with an aim to increase business contribution through transparency. Considering the increasing pressures for sustainability reporting (e.g. Hahn & Kühnen, 2013), companies have responded by voluntarily reporting on various aspects of sustainability (KPMG, 2015) as a means of demonstrating greater transparency and, hence, their accountability to their stakeholders (Roberts, 2009). In the absence of regulatory requirements, in 2000, the GRI provided the first set of guidelines that provided a baseline for sustainability reporting, covering the core issues that multiple stakeholders could reasonably expect companies to disclose, while aiming to achieve comparability of disclosures by companies around the globe and challenging companies to report in a balanced way, including both positive and negative impacts and challenges. After the first iteration of the GRI framework (G1) in 2000, four subsequent updated frameworks were published: G2 (2002), G3 (2006), G3.1 (2011) and G4 (2013) (GRI, 2017b). The next step was to move from a widely adopted 'framework' to a set of formal 'standards' for sustainability reporting. Therefore, in October 2016, GRI launched the modular, interrelated GRI Standards to replace the G4 framework, advising companies to use the GRI Standards for sustainability reporting with effect from reports published after 1 July 2018 (GRI,

2017b). The main advantage of the standards is their increased credibility due to a new independent governance structure at GRI (making endorsement of GRI Standards more likely by regulatory bodies), and that, due to the modular structure, the standards can be modified or new standards added without the need to publish an entirely new framework. Today, the GRI is the leading framework for voluntary sustainability reporting and widely used by large multinational companies (KPMG, 2015; Ehnert et al., 2016).

The starting point for using the GRI Standards is the so-called 'Foundation' as part of the 'Universal Standards'. Here GRI provides Reporting Principles, which are crucial for organisations to achieve high quality in their sustainability reporting. The organisation is not required to disclose exactly how it applied the Reporting Principles but it must claim to have done so to meet the required GRI Standards when preparing its sustainability report. They consist, on the one hand, of the principles for defining report content and, on the other hand, of the principles for defining report quality. The former principles help organisations to decide on the content of their sustainability reports. These are as follows (GRI, 2016):

1. **Stakeholder Inclusiveness:** 'The reporting organization shall identify its stakeholders, and explain how it has responded to their reasonable expectations and interests' (GRI, 2016, p. 8).
2. **Sustainability Context:** 'The report shall present the reporting organization's performance in the wider context of sustainability' (GRI, 2016, p. 9).
3. **Materiality:** The report shall comprise either topics that 'reflect the reporting organization's significant economic/financial, environmental, and human/social impacts' (GRI, 2016, p. 10) or topics that 'substantively influence the assessments and decisions of stakeholders' (GRI, 2016, p. 10).
4. **Completeness:** 'The report shall include coverage of material topics and their Boundaries, sufficient to reflect significant economic, environmental, and social impacts, and to enable stakeholders to assess the reporting organization's performance in the reporting period' (GRI, 2016, p. 12).

Based on the Stakeholder Inclusiveness and the Materiality Principles, organisations shall prioritise topics for inclusion in the report. Thus, they are not expected to report on all performance indicators. However, organisations shall provide a list of the material topics which they have identified in the process of defining report content. Moreover, the reporting organisation shall explain for each material topic why the topic is material, the Boundary for the material topic and 'any specific limitation regarding the topic Boundary' (GRI, 2016).

Stakeholders can take appropriate actions only after a comprehensive and reasonable assessment of the organisation, and for this a certain quality of information must be provided. Therefore GRI defines six principles for reporting quality which organisations must take into account when they report about their economic/financial, environmental and human/social impacts using the standards. These principles are accuracy, balance, clarity, comparability, reliability and timeliness (GRI, 2016).

1. **Accuracy:** 'The reported information shall be sufficiently accurate and detailed for stakeholders to assess the reporting organization's performance' (GRI, 2016, p. 13).
2. **Balance:** 'The reported information shall reflect positive and negative aspects of the reporting organization's performance to enable a reasoned assessment of overall performance' (GRI, 2016, p. 13).
3. **Clarity:** 'The reporting organization shall make information available in a manner that is understandable and accessible to stakeholders using that information' (GRI, 2016, p. 14).
4. **Comparability:** 'The reporting organization shall select, compile, and report information consistently' (GRI, 2016, p. 14). Furthermore, 'the reported information shall be presented in a manner that enables stakeholders to analyze changes in the organization's performance over time, and that could support analysis relative to other organizations' (GRI, 2016, p. 14).
5. **Reliability:** 'The reporting organization shall gather, record, compile, analyze, and report information and processes used in the preparation of the report in a way that they can be subject to examination, and that establishes the quality and materiality of the information' (GRI, 2016, p. 15).
6. **Timeliness:** 'The reporting organization shall report on a regular schedule so that information is available in time for stakeholders to make informed decisions' (GRI, 2016, p. 16).

Besides the Reporting Principles, the Foundation also contains the basic process for sustainability reporting, and the two basic approaches for using the GRI Standards. Organisations can use the GRI Standards either as a comprehensive framework to prepare a sustainability report in accordance with the Standards or they can use selected Standards to report specific information (GRI, 2016).

10.3.2 HRM-related GRI disclosures and performance indicators

The Universal Standards comprise the 'General Disclosures' and the 'Management Approach'. Contextual information such as the organisational profile, strategy, ethics and integrity, governance, stakeholder engagement and reporting practices are required to be reported among the General

Disclosures. General Disclosures relating to the organisational profile and the stakeholder engagement each contain an HRM-related disclosure. Besides the Universal Standards, GRI provides 'Topic-specific Standards'. They contain, according to the 'triple bottom line', economic/financial, environmental and human/social performance indicators. The Economic Standards comprise thirteen performance indicators (GRI, 2016), of which six are relevant to HRM. In contrast, and not surprisingly, the Environmental Standards do not contain HRM-related indicators. The Social Standards include thirty-four performance indicators (GRI, 2016). Of these, twenty-one performance indicators are directly relevant to HRM. Considering the General Disclosures and all Topic-specific Standards, twenty-nine of the seventy-seven performance indicators, which is more than a third, are HRM-related (see Table 10.1). We will now discuss these in detail.

Table 10.1 GRI disclosures and performance indicators and HRM relevance

Disclosures and Performance Indicators Directly Relevant to HRM

General Disclosures

102–8 Information on employees and other workers

102–41 Collective bargaining agreements

Economic Standards

201–3 Defined benefit plan obligations and other retirement plans

202–1 Ratio of standard entry level wage by gender compared to local minimum wage

202–2 Proportion of senior management hired from the local community

205–2 Communication and training about anti-corruption policies and procedures

205–3 Confirmed incidents of corruption and actions taken

206–1 Legal actions for anti-competitive behaviour, anti-trust, and monopoly practices

Social Standards

401–1 New employee hires and employee turnover

401–2 Benefits provided to full-time employees that are not provided to temporary or part-time employees

401–3 Parental leave

402–1 Minimum notice periods regarding operational changes

403–1 Workers representation in formal joint management-worker health and safety committees

403–2 Types of injury and rates of injury, occupational diseases, lost days, and absenteeism, and number of work-related fatalities

403–3 Workers with high incidence or high risk of diseases related to their occupation

403–4 Health and safety topics covered in formal agreements with trade unions

404–1 Average hours of training per year per employee

404–2 Programmes for upgrading employee skills and transition assistance programmes

404–3 percentage of employees receiving regular performance and career development reviews

405–1 Diversity of governance bodies and employees

405–2 Ratio of basic salary and remuneration of woman to men

406–1 Incidents of discrimination and corrective actions taken

407–1 Operations and suppliers in which the right to freedom of association and collective bargaining may be at risk

408–1 Operations and suppliers at significant risk for incidents of child labour

409–1 Operations and suppliers at significant risk for incidents of forced or compulsory labour

410–1 Security personnel trained in human rights policies or procedures

412–1 Operations that have been subject to human rights reviews or impact assessment

412–2 Employee training on human rights policies or procedures

412–3 Significant investment agreements and contracts that include human rights clauses or that underwent human rights screening

* Detailed information about the disclosures and indicators can be accessed through the following source: GRI (2016).

The environmental indicators of GRI do not refer to HRM policies and practices. This is probably due to the focus on environmental impacts on resources and planetary effects, rather than the people processes required to deliver them. However, in recent years, green HRM literature has emerged (see, for example, Jackson et al., 2011) which suggests that people management can have important implications for the environmental record of firms. Increasingly, companies are referring to the establishment of 'Green Teams', 'Recycling Teams' and even extension of environmental initiatives by employees from the workplace to their communities or their own homes. The establishment of a culture of environmental stewardship and the involvement of employees in driving environmental efforts surely contribute to improving overall corporate environmental performance (Haddock-Miller, Sanyal & Müller-Camen, 2016). Yet this is not recognized within the GRI Standards.

10.3.2.1 General disclosures related to HRM

In order to provide stakeholders with information on employees and other workers, GRI requires the reporting organisation to disclose (1) the 'total number of employees by employment contract (permanent and temporary)' by gender and region; (2) the 'total number of employees by employment type (full-time and part-time)' by gender; (3) 'whether a significant portion of the organization's activities are performed by workers who are not employees', and 'if applicable, a description of the nature and scale of work performed by workers who are not employees'; (4) 'any significant variations in the numbers reported' in the first three disclosures; and (5) 'an explanation of how the data have been compiled, including any assumption made' (GRI, 2016, p. 10). The breakdown by gender allows insights into the gender representation across the organisation, and the optimal use of human resources and talent (GRI, 2016) (as well as the social impacts of inclusive hiring policies and practices). Furthermore, the reporting organisation shall report the 'percentage of total employees covered by collective bargaining agreements' (GRI, 2016, p. 30). It is important to note that GRI does not ask the percentage of employees who are trade union members. This is because GRI is concerned with who receives representation, and the social responsibility of organisations to enable this, rather than individual affiliations.

10.3.2.2 Economic indicators related to HRM

Economic indicators address the impacts of a business on its stakeholders, and on global, national and local economies. Sustainability, in the 'triple bottom line' context, assumes a fundamental robustness in terms of financial performance and an understanding of a company's economic effects on society. GRI Standards, therefore, require a reporting company to disclose the extent and nature of such economic impacts (if they are material to that organisation's impacts). The six economic indicators which are of direct relevance to HRM are: (1) 'defined benefit plan obligations and other retirement plans'; (2) 'ratio of standard entry level wage by gender compared to local minimum wage'; (3) 'proportion of senior management hired from local community'; (4) 'communication and training about anti-corruption policies and procedures'; (5) 'confirmed incidents of corruption and actions taken'; and (6) 'legal actions for anti-competitive behaviour, anti-trust, and monopoly practices' (GRI, 2016). These indicators reflect the direct impact of HRM policies on its stakeholders and local economies, well beyond the internal aspects of HRM. As an employer, a sustainable organisation will seek to compensate employees beyond minimum wage levels which are usually determined as providing the most basic needs of employees for subsistence with dignity (food, shelter and utilities, clothing, health care and education). The legal minimum wage (where it exists) in most countries is usually not sufficient to afford employees to live decently. For example, a calculation by the Living Wage Foundation in the UK places the minimum wage needed to live at £8.45–£9.75 whereas the national minimum wage standard is £7.05–£7.50 (LivingWage.org). Furthermore, wages above the minimum wage and retirement plans can be important for employees' long-term economic well-being (GRI, 2016). The following quote from an Indian oil and gas company illustrates the ratio of standard entry level wage to the local minimum wage:

> BPCL is compliant with the minimum wages prescribed in all the states it has presence. The ratio of entry level wages to minimum wages is 1.48, based on the minimum wages paid to unskilled contract laborers. We do not discriminate between any of our male and female employees, both permanent and contract. In many of our projects we pay more than the minimum wages in order to encourage and retain our workers. Our payment policy prescribes paying our contract employees 25% above the statutory requirement. (Bharat Petroleum, 2015, p. 51)

Interestingly, GRI requires companies to disclose compensation rates in comparison to minimum wages. However, as mentioned, the minimum wage is often an irrelevant measure from a social standpoint. A comparison to an independently calculated living wage could be more meaningful in terms of social impact – and several companies are now reporting their progress. The 2015–2016 Sustainability Report for the Esprit fashion company states:

> we joined the Action Transformation Collaboration (ACT) program in September 2015, which entails that Esprit, together with other ACT member brands, will address and work towards a fair living wage in the textile industry – a topic that we identified to be critical to ensure social compliance and sustainability in our supply chain in the long-term. (Esprit Holdings Limited, 2016, p. 9)

Similarly, local hiring is a way to show commitment to local communities while ensuring a local workforce (e.g. nationals of the countries of operation) that is familiar with local culture, customs and work processes. There is a significant positive economic impact in upskilling local employees, particularly in countries where expatriates are the norm or locals are disadvantaged. Local hiring also supports business continuity, reduces cost (expatriation comes with a major price tag) and builds local stakeholder relationships. A German multinational automotive manufacturing company states this in its sustainability report as follows:

> Volkswagen supports the recruitment and qualification of local personnel as a way of developing the local communities and regions in which we operate. This applies

for example at the new Audi México plant and at the new plant in Urumqi (China), where we plan to employ the groups that make up the region's population on a pro rata basis. (Volkswagen, 2015, p. 64)

10.3.2.3 Social performance indicators related to HRM

Social indicators are largely formulated using the ILO's legally binding Conventions and non-binding Recommendations. These set out basic principles and rights at work and thus are to a large extent HRM-related. Principles and rights at work which are considered as fundamental are freedom of association, the right to collective bargaining, the elimination of forced labour, the abolition of child labour, equal remuneration and non-discrimination concerning employment and occupation (ILO, n.d.). In addition to the ILO Conventions and Recommendations, the ILO's 'Tripartite Declaration of Principles concerning Multinational Enterprises and Social Policy', the OECD Guidelines for Multinational Enterprises, the UN Guiding Principles on Business and Human Rights, and UN Conventions and Declarations such as the 'Convention on the Elimination of All Forms of Discrimination against Woman' and the 'Universal Declaration of Human Rights' were often used as references to the reporting requirements in the Social Standards. The twenty-one performance indicators that are relevant to HRM and listed in Table 10.1 will now be examined in detail.

10.3.2.3.1 Reporting requirements: Employment

The reporting requirements with regard to employment comprise three performance indicators. First, companies shall report the total number and rate of new employee hires and of employee turnover by age group, gender and region. Second, the 'benefits provided to full-time employees that are not provided to temporary or part-time employees' shall be disclosed. Third, parental leave by gender shall be indicated (GRI, 2016). One important aspect of sustainability practice, which can be discerned from these GRI indicators, is gender equality. Companies that do not positively encourage the hiring of women may demonstrate gender imbalance in their overall employee or employee turnover figures, and perhaps even evidence of discrimination. Gender balance has been shown to support delivery of improved business results (Catalyst, 2011) as well as strengthen local economies. Indeed, gender ratio improvement (at executive, management and non-management levels) is seen as a critical success factor in the mining and extractives sector in several emerging economies. An example for the promotion of employment of women at different hierarchical levels is provided by the Japanese company JFE Steel:

> JFE Steel aims to have female workers account for 10% of new hires for non-clerical positions (FY2012: 19, FY2013: 22, FY2014: 24, FY2015: 48). The company also is striving to create a better working environment for woman by building additional facilities, such as shower rooms and lavatories. (JFE Group, 2015, p. 18)

Benefits provided to full-time employees such as life insurance, health care, disability and invalidity coverage, parental leave, retirement provision or stock ownership are an important aspect in ensuring a company's workforce has a basis for financial stability and does not become a burden on the local economy in times of sickness or other problems. The provision of benefits also contributes to employee retention (GRI, 2016). ExxonMobil, an American multinational oil and gas company, expresses this as follows:

> Our benefits programs are an integral part of a total remuneration package designed to support our long-term business objectives, as well as attract, retain and reward the most qualified employees. The goal is to be responsive to the needs of employees throughout their careers and into retirement. Ensuring access to affordable health care helps employees manage health care issues and reduce related financial concerns. Benefits coverage for spouses is based on legally recognized spousal relationships in each country where we operate. The funding levels of qualified pension plans comply with applicable laws or regulations. Defined benefit pension obligations are fully supported by the financial strength of ExxonMobil or the respective sponsoring affiliate. The company provides retirement benefits that support our long-term career orientation and business models. (ExxonMobil, 2015, p. 19)

10.3.2.3.2 Reporting requirement: Labor/management relations

In regard to labour/management relations, GRI Standards require organisations to report the 'minimum number of weeks' notice typically provided to employees and their representatives prior to the implementation of significant operational changes that could substantially affect them' (GRI, 2016, p. 6) and organisations with collective bargaining agreements shall also report 'whether the notice period and provisions for consultations and negotiation are specified in collective agreements' (GRI, 2016, p. 6) . Specific decisions should not be made without taking into account employee's perspective or the perspective of their representatives. Hence, prior consultation in form of a dialogue is important (GRI, 2016). Continental, a multinational

German automotive manufacturing company, discloses this indicator in the following way:

> The Executive Board reports to the Supervisory Board on matters regarding (upcoming) operational changes in the corporation, informing the employee representatives at the same time. Continental ensures that employees are informed about major operational changes early on. [...] These representatives likewise inform Continental about changes at an early stage. We comply with all legal regulations relating to notice periods as well as those governed separately by collective bargaining agreements. (Continental, 2015, p. 25)

By offering employees extended advanced notice of operational changes, a business demonstrates respect and concern for the well-being of employees in situations where workplace changes may lead to job losses, job changes or transfers – and, importantly, supports a positive transition in the local economy by affording employees time to seek alternative employment and therefore avoiding the need to claim unemployment benefits from the state.

10.3.2.3.3 Reporting requirements: Occupational health and safety

Occupational health and safety is one of the most basic forms of corporate responsibility (although often covered by legal requirements in most countries) and is often managed by professional, often certified, Safety Managers, whose presence in the business is required by law in most countries. The Safety Manager will typically address aspects of the physical working environment, industrial hygiene, safety training and risk assessments related to occupational disease. However, in addition, safety management (e.g. hours spent in training, hours and days lost due to accidents, etc.) has a potentially significant impact on business continuity and employment costs (including insurance premiums), so organisations have an interest in the creation of a zero-accident workplace. Similarly, good safety performance reduces the health care costs of local economies. GRI Standards provide four performance indicators in this area: First, the organisations shall report the 'level at which each formal joint management-worker health and safety committee typically operates', and the percentage of workers 'that are represented by formal joint management-worker health and safety committees' (GRI, 2016, p. 7). Second, the 'types of injury and rates of injury, occupational diseases, lost days, and absenteeism, and number of work-related fatalities' with a breakdown by region and gender shall be disclosed for all employees (GRI, 2016). Third, information whether there are workers 'involved in occupational activities who have a high incidence or high risk of specific diseases'

(GRI, 2016, p. 10) shall be indicated. Fourth, 'health and safety topics covered in formal agreements with trade unions' shall be stated (GRI, 2016).

In regard to the health and safety committees in place, many companies indicate that they have such committees, but they do not provide the percentage or they state that the percentage is not currently available. This can be illustrated by the following quote from Wells Fargo, an American bank:

> Many of our locations have safety committees. In addition, it is the responsibility of all managers and supervisors to continually review their operations and working conditions, and where required, provide adequate protection, instruction, information, training and supervision. (Wells Fargo, 2016 p. 81)

10.3.2.3.4 Reporting requirements: Training and education

In a sustainable business, investment is made in the development of employee skills and competencies resulting in both business benefits (more capable employees) and a contribution to society (more employable employees). To provide insights into an organisation's efforts in employees' personal development and career advancement, it shall disclose (1) the average training hours per year per employee by gender and by employee category (e.g. by level and/or by function); (2) employee training programmes that aim to improve skills, and transition assistance programmes that support employees reaching retirement age or terminated employees (GRI, 2016); and (3) the 'percentage of total employees by gender and by employee category who received a regular performance and career development review' (GRI, 2016, p. 9).

Instead of training being defined primarily as necessary to meet business objectives, training and personal development are seen as adding value to individuals which becomes an equally important driver for training and development and may influence the content of such programmes. In cases of downsizing, for example, employees released by a company should have amassed an arsenal of skills and competencies during their tenure, which makes them more employable by other companies. This fulfils an obligation to employees as stakeholders in their company, but also makes a significant societal contribution, lessening the burden of high unemployment costs.

10.3.2.3.5 Reporting requirements: Diversity and equal opportunity

Diversity, equal opportunity and health and safety aspects of sustainable organisations have implications for the way companies manage diversity on governing bodies, manifest non-discrimination through equal opportunity and identify specific health risks for employees and address them. There-fore, organisations shall report the percentage of individuals within governance bodies and per employee category by gender, age group and other relevant diversity categories such as minority groups. In addition, the 'ratio of the basic salary and remuneration of woman to men for each employee category, by significant locations of operations' (GRI, 2016, p. 7) shall be disclosed.

Recent research based on GRI 3.0 suggests that, of all core labour performance standards, the ratio of basic salary for women to men is the least reported. Only 50 per cent of Forbes 250 companies that have adopted the GRI guidelines claim that they report on this indicator. Furthermore, of those that do, very few organisations provide the salary data required by GRI (Parsa et al., 2018). Instead, claims such as the following by the German Chemical Company Evonik Industries are common:

> The remuneration of many members of our workforce includes bonus payments that are dependent on the company's business performance or the personal performance of the employee. Remuneration is therefore based on objective criteria such as responsibility, the required knowledge and skills, and performance; personal characteristics such as gender, age, etc. do not have any impact. (Evonik Industries, 2016, p. 58)

10.3.2.3.6 Reporting requirements related to human rights

It is interesting that the concept of human rights extends right throughout an organisation's value chain, whereby organisations assume responsibility for contracting with suppliers for the provision of goods and services in a way which encourages or requires suppliers to adhere to similar human rights standards. This shared responsibility in the value chain has been widely exposed for many years through stories of human rights abuses in apparel industry supply chains in the mid-1990s and in more recent years in electronics industries (sweatshops). It is now widely understood that practices which force unreasonably low pricing in vendor organisations can lead to continued human rights abuses and that global organisations bear part of the responsibility to address such issues (Akorsu & Cooke, 2011). Such practices include the use of child labour, unpaid and/or excessive overtime hours, lack of reasonable hygiene facilities and safety measures or restriction of freedoms such as confiscation of passports or prevention of employee association and collective bargaining. Additional abuses may also include violence such as beatings, rape or other forms of unreasonable physical abuse. Sustainable HRM should take a proactive role in ensuring that all employees involved in supply chain activities are aware of the implications for potentially explosive human rights issues. In 2012, Cohen, Taylor and Muller-Camen suggested that the HRM function should become responsible for social issues outside the organisational boundaries. Meanwhile, other authors have made similar demands (Muller-Camen & Elsik, 2015; Schuler and Jackson, 2014). In this way, HRM influence could extend to creating systems which inherently encompass organisational values based on respect for human rights throughout all operations that the company is engaged in and not limited to operations directly under the company's control.

Most of the HRM issues discussed above are covered by the GRI Social Standards. More specifically, the GRI human rights performance indicators are as follows: (1) 'incidents of discrimination and corrective actions taken'; (2) 'operations and suppliers in which the right to freedom of association and collective bargaining may be at risk'; (3) 'operations and suppliers at significant risk for incidents of child labour'; (4) 'operations and suppliers at significant risk for incidents of forced or compulsory labour'; (5) 'security personnel trained in human rights policies or procedures'; and (6) human rights assessment. The human rights assessment comprises 'operations that have been subject to human rights reviews or impact assessments', 'employee training on human rights policies or procedures', and 'significant investment agreements and contracts that include human rights clauses or that underwent human rights screening' (GRI, 2016). Many companies indicate that they manage their human resources in compliance with the respective law and or with their internal policies. An example regarding the observance of child labour is the mining company Coal India:

> We respect and promote fundamental human rights. We understand the potential adverse impacts on human rights and responsible to mitigate or eliminate them. We neither employ nor encourage child labour in any of our operations. We abide by The Mines Act, 1952, which prohibits the employment of children below 18 years of age in a mine. Providing a clause to prevent deployment of child labour in all our NITs are under approval of the competent authority. We follow proper checks and audits as per the Act, to ensure no child is employed in the mines through medical examinations for age proof. (Coal India, 2015, p. 44)

However, the GRI framework does not include all aspects of sustainable HRM. Among the three more significant aspects of sustainable HRM which are not covered in the GRI framework are employee volunteering programmes, sustainable employer branding and green HRM (Cohen et al., 2012).

10.3.3 Limitations of the existing social and environment performance indicators of GRI

There are four limitations regarding the disclosures and performance indicators of GRI that are related to sustainable HRM. Firstly, the performance standards relating to occupational health and safety (i.e. Social Standards 403–1 to 403–4 – refer to Table 10.1) fall short of delivering a full picture of the impacts on employees of an unsafe workplace and the ways in which a company protects workers. Hence, reporting on the health and safety outcomes for employees based on the six principles for reporting quality (referred to in Section 10.3.1 in this chapter) is currently outcome-oriented and not process- or improvement-oriented. Recently (2017), GRI initiated a public consultation process on the new draft GRI Standard 403 to include leading indicators for occupational health in greater alignment with recent developments in occupational health and safety management and reporting practices. The new focus will be greater context in the form of management approach disclosures relating to management systems, hazards and risks, hierarchy of controls, worker participation, consultation, information and training, and indicators that reflect more closely the impact on workers rather than on organisational productivity. In addition, for the first time, it is proposed that GRI Standard 403 include a new disclosure on worker access to voluntary programmes to address major non–work-related health risks, for example smoking, physical inactivity, unhealthy diets – indicating a new perspective on the proactive role of organisations to help employees manage their health, rather than simply protecting them in a safe work environment. This revised approach to improve quality of reporting on occupational health and safety highlights the attempt GRI has taken to overcome the limitations of occupational health reporting indicated earlier in this chapter.

Secondly, as indicated in Chapter 6 employee engagement using green HRM for environmental sustainability is key to achieving environmental outcomes of corporate sustainability. Furthermore, it is indicated in Chapter 6 that the International Standards Organization (ISO) 14001 and European Union Eco-Management and Audit Scheme (EMAS) can be used as tools for implementing environmental management systems (EMS) and include some alignment of green HRM to EMS to enhance natural environmental sustainability. However, GRI environmental performance indicators do not include HRM-related indicators and hence this can be seen as another limitation of the GRI Standards.

Thirdly, a further limitation of GRI reporting is how it determines materiality. Companies are asked to define material topics as the basis of reporting, and prioritise these topics in terms of the size and scale of their impacts on society and the natural environment, and in terms of the interests of stakeholders. In practice, GRI does not prescribe a robust methodology for determining material topics, and this tends to subordinate HRM-related issues to other economic/financial and natural environmental issues which can be more easily defined and quantified. In general, companies engage with external stakeholders and receive inputs that relate to materiality of issues relating to products, markets, economies, natural environment and so on, and the only stakeholder voice for employees tends to be internal, and this is often undervalued. So a limitation of GRI Standards is the almost inevitable subordination of employee issues to other sustainability performance aspects.

Fourthly, the GRI reporting structure promotes reporting performance indicators within the economic/financial, human/social and environment categories separately from each other and hence facilitates reporting of a shopping list of issues which favours a top-down three-pillar approach to identifying non-integrated issues across the organisation (Fonseca, McAllister & Fitzpatrick, 2014). This is a limitation according to the latest BellagioSTAMP (2009) Principles for assessment and measurement for sustainable development. The original Bellagio Principles were developed by a team of experts in 1997 and included ten principles to provide guidance for the measurement of human/social, economic/financial and environmental outcomes and promote best practices. Subsequently, in 2009, a similar expert group process, using the original principles developed the Bellagio Sustainability Assessment and Measurement Principles (Bellagio STAMP). However, the latest STAMP includes only eight principles (Pintér et al., 2012): (1) guiding vision; (2) essential considerations; (3) adequate scope; (4) framework and indicators; (5) transparency; (6) effective communications; (7) broad participation; and (8) continuity and capacity. Principle (2), on essential considerations, highlights that the assessment of progress towards sustainable development will consider:

- The underlying human/social, economic/financial and environmental system as a whole and the interactions among its components, including issues related to governance
- Dynamics and interactions between current trends and drivers of change
- Risks, uncertainties, and activities that can have an impact across boundaries
- Implications for decision making, including trade-offs and synergies.

Hence, according to Principle (2) of STAMP, measurement and reporting of sustainable development outcomes in silo fashion using the GRI reporting process is a limitation because it should not be based on a list of issues but rather an integrative reporting approach which captures the spillover and crossover effects of management approaches while delivering corporate sustainability outcomes from a holistic perspective.

10.4 From reporting standards to the assessment of sustainability performance

The GRI basically provides standards for sustainability reporting. Although these standards implicitly state what organisations should and should not do, the GRI does not attempt to measure or assess how sustainable or responsible an organisation is, or provide a framework for evaluating the sustainability performance of a company, either independently or compared to other firms. In other words, GRI Standards do not provide assessment tools or a corporate sustainability assessment. In addition to GRI, other voluntary corporate sustainability initiatives such as the UN Global Compact exist. The UN Global Compact provides guidelines for sustainability actions, and therefore it is also not a tool to assess the corporate sustainability. Even if the UN Global Compact is not an assessment tool regarding corporate sustainability, scholars who have adopted the governance perspective view the UN Global Compact as an expression of a new global public domain. This new public domain creates several opportunities and constraints that affect the exercise of global governance (Rasche et al., 2013). Frameworks which provide an assessment of corporate performance include emerging frameworks such as 'B-Corp' and the 'Economy of the Common Good' which will be examined in more depth subsequently (Section 10.4.2 and 10.4.3). In addition, another form of assessment has emerged, the Future Fit Framework that sets a minimum threshold for responsible business practice, rather than a graded assessment on a scale. While the minimum threshold concept may seem inadequate as it is just that – minimum – and does not encourage companies to strive to achieve higher performance, the Future Fit Framework has a bold approach where minimum thresholds are actually absolute achievement of zero negative impacts, even though the scope of the framework is rather limited (Future Fit Foundation, n.d.). More details are provided later in this chapter (Section 10.4.4).

10.4.1 UN Global Compact

The UN Global Compact is the world's largest initiative in the corporate sustainability area, with more than 12,000 corporate and non-business participants. Furthermore, corporate and non-business participants are based in over 160 countries, thus the initiative has a wide geographic reach. The Global Compact is a policy initiative created by the United Nations in 1999, which asks organisations to adhere to ten universal principles which underpin responsible business practices. The principles cover human rights (principles 1–2), labor standards (principles 3–6), environmental stewardship (principles 7–9) and anti-corruption (principle 10), and are derived from the Universal Declaration of Human Rights, the ILO's Declaration on Fundamental Principles and Rights at Work, the Rio Declaration on Environment and Development(and the United Nations Convention Against Corruption (UN Global Compact, 2014). With regard to human rights, 'businesses should support and respect the protection of internationally proclaimed human rights; and make sure that they are not complicit in human rights abuses' (UN Global Compact, 2014, p. 11). The labor standards focus on social issues within and beyond the organisational boundaries. More specifically it is suggested that 'businesses should uphold the freedom of association and the effective recognition of the right to collective bargaining; the elimination of all forms of forced and compulsory labor; the effective abolition of child labor; and the elimination of discrimination in respect of employment and occupation' (UN Global Compact, 2014, p. 11).

In committing to uphold these principles, organisations also commit to report annually on their progress in doing so. The COP report (see Section 10.1) is a public disclosure to organisational stakeholders which shows the progress made in the implementation of the ten principles into strategies and operations. The COP must contain three issues: (1) 'a statement by the chief executive expressing continued support for the Global Compact'; (2) 'a description of practical actions that the company has taken or plans to undertake to implement the Global Compact principles'; and (3) 'a measurement of outcomes regarding the degree to which targets/performance indicators were met, or other qualitative or quantitative measurements of results' (UN Global Compact, 2014, p. 40). If organisations fail to report or do not meet the criteria over time, they can be excluded from the initiative (UN Global Compact, 2014). Using these principles as an umbrella framework of a corporate sustainability policy, HRM can develop a set of policies and processes that align with the principles and ensure they are manifested in the practices of the organisation. For example, HRM can provide – based on the corporate or HRM strategy – training to raise employee awareness regarding human rights as well as environmental issues and anti-corruption. However, Rasche and Waddock (2014) suggest improving the quality, transparency and comprehensiveness of COP reporting. This must take place together with the enlargement of the participant base. They argue that 'systematic changes in social and environmental problems areas are only possible if more participants engage more deeply with the initiative, realigning their strategies and business models to ensure adherence to the principles' (Rasche & Waddock, 2014, p. 215). Besides this, the complete voluntariness of the initiative can be misleading due to institutional pressures which induce companies to become a signatory (Rasche et al., 2013).

10.4.2 B-Corp

Unlike the UN Global Compact, there is a private organisation behind the B (Benefit)-Corp Movement. The B-Corps certification is awarded by a non-profit called B-Lab, founded by individuals looking to establish 'business as a force for good'. The idea is that B-Corps meet the highest standards of verified, overall human/social and environmental performance, public transparency, and legal accountability and align their missions with those of society. The focus is less on increasing profits and more on responsible and socially beneficial operations. Companies who have attained B-Corps certification include well-known organisations such as Ben & Jerry's, Patagonia and Seventh Generation. In some US states, B-Corps are even legally recognised. The B-Corps organisation has defined about 150 criteria for organisations that want to use 'business as a force for good' (Honeyman, 2014). Those organisations that fulfil about half of them can attain to B-Corp certification. Table 10.2 presents a summary of HRM practices suggested as 'good' practices by the movement. Many of these are practices not common in for-profit organisations listed on the stock market (though many are becoming increasingly prevalent). Nevertheless, the B-Corp movement is growing and has expanded from the USA to other countries.

10.4.3 Economy of the Common Good

The Economy of the Common Good is a movement that originated in German-speaking countries and which has also gained a strong foothold in Spain (Felber, 2015). It is somewhat more radical than the B-Corp movement as it explicitly specifies certain business practices such as hostile takeovers and the non-acceptance of trade unions as negative criteria. The core element for its assessment of sustainable business practices is the Common Good Matrix. For different stakeholders (such as employees, suppliers, customers)

Table 10.2 HRM-related indicators of B-corp and economy of the common good

	B-Corp	Economy of Common Good
Pay and benefits	Pay a living wage (56ff); Determine average pay ratios and cap this at some level (58–59); Offer retirement plan (59); Egalitarian benefits (94–95); 'Evaluate employees and management of their performance with regard to the company's social and environmental targets. Consider tying social and environmental performance to bonuses or other rewards' (123)	Just income distribution, paying at least a living wage, limiting the pay gap. 'Excessive income inequality within a business' is negative criteria
Working hours	'Give employees part-time, flextime, or telecommuting options, as appropriate' (69)	'Reduction of overtime, eliminating unpaid overtime, reduction of total work hours, contribution to the reduction of unemployment'
Employee volunteering	'Offer incentives for employees to organize service days and/ or volunteer activities, and set a goal to increase the percentage of employees who participate. Communicate your efforts through a written community service policy' (81)	Not mentioned
Health and well-being	'Expand your company's health and wellness programs' (65); 'Create an employee committee to monitor and advise on occupational health and safety' (70)	Corporations should offer 'occupational safety and work-place health promotion including work–life balance/ flexible working hours'
Green HRM	'Provide employees with incentives to use alternative commuting options to get to work' (103)	'Promotion of environmentally friendly behavior of employees'
Equality and diversity	'Expand the diversity of your board of directors, management team, and suppliers so that they represent a range of cultures, religious beliefs, ethnicities, sexual orientations, physical abilities, and genders' (80)	Foster 'equal opportunity and diversity'

Table 10.2 (Continued)

	B-Corp	Economy of Common Good
Employment creation	'Create job opportunities for chronically underemployed populations, such as at-risk youth, homeless individuals, or individuals who were formally incarcerated' (76) 'Target and hire more than 10 % of total workers from chronically underemployed populations (e.g. low-income or formerly incarcerated people and/or extensively train and invest in these workers.'	'Ensure just distribution of work volume among all persons who are able to work. Enterprises make mutual efforts to ensure that all human beings are given a fair proportion of the gainful work available, with no one having too little or too much. To this end they successfully eliminate overtime and then even build up "undertime," promoting *further* reduction of the legal core working hours in this way.' 'Job cuts or moving jobs overseas despite having made a profit' is negative criteria
Corporate democracy	Not included	'Our ideal is to obtain the highest possible degree of employee co-determination regarding all crucial decisions (at least in the work area) and legitimization of executives through elections by employees. An essential prerequisite for any form of democracy is comprehensive transparency within the company, which allows employees to make sound decisions for the company in the pursuit of achieving common goals.'
Human rights (HRM issues in supply chain)	'Publicly disclose the social and environmental performance of your suppliers' (90) 'Focus on alleviating poverty through your supply chain by sourcing through fair wage-certified suppliers; provide technical assistance and/or capacity building to small-scale suppliers or use contracts to guarantee future purchases and payments to suppliers' (138)	

Source: Honeyman (2014).

and values (such as human dignity, ecological sustainability and social justice) it defines policy goals. For example, ecological sustainability with regard to employees implies that organisations should promote the environmentally friendly behaviour of employees (8). Table 10.2 compares HRM policy areas and practices suggested by the B-Corp and the Economy of the Common Good movement.

10.4.4 Future Fit Framework

Similar to the B-Corp movement, the Future Fit Framework was created by a non-profit foundation set up but individuals looking to make business an engine that can help everyone on the planet flourish. Rather than establishing goal areas and rating or assessing corporate performance, the Future Fit Framework establishes absolute performance objectives – or thresholds – for companies to achieve in order to be 'future fit' These include four broad areas: Respecting nature (environmental impacts), Thinks Circular (managing waste), Fosters Wellbeing (of customers and employees) and Strengthens Society (through ethics, payment of taxes and other responsible business practices). Examples of threshold targets include energy is from renewable sources, products emit no greenhouse gases, and operational waste is eliminated. Of the twenty-three performance thresholds included in the framework, five directly relate to employees and HRM:

1. Employee health is safeguarded
2. Employees are paid at least a living wage
3. Employees are subject to fair employment terms
4. Employees are not subject to discrimination
5. Employee concerns are actively solicited, impartially judged and transparently addressed.

These objectives are largely covered by other frameworks, but, arguably, remain minimal in their scope and do not address aspects of employee relations that go significantly beyond compliance, such as opportunity for growth and development; positive contribution to employee well-being beyond health and safety; gender pay ratios; addressing labour rights including collective bargaining; and positively promoting diversity and inclusion rather than ensuring absence of discrimination. There appears to be strong backing for the Future Fit Framework from influential professionals in the sustainability field, and it can be considered a useful tool for focused strategy and disclosure, including important HRM standards.

10.5 Current sustainable HRM theories to enrich performance indicators of GRI

Harm of work to health as a sustainable HRM theory is used to explain the leading indicator for occupational health (see Chapter 9 for more details). Sinelnikov et al. (2015) maintained that leading indicators for occupational health performance must be able to predict health outcomes and should be capable of changing those outcomes using HRM interventions. That is, the health harm of work (refer to Chapter 9 for more details) as a measure could be used to proactively prevent or delay the onset of certain work-related occupational health issues. Thus, the assessment and voluntary disclosure of the health harm of work among employees will improve the quality of reporting based on accuracy, clarity, comparability and reliability. Hence, in alignment with the proposed changes to GRI 403 for including leading indicators for occupational health as part of management approaches, the health harm, a new construct derived from the sustainable HRM perspective, can be a useful assessment tool to proactively manage the leading indicators for employee occupational health issues.

Green HRM from the sustainable HRM perspective addresses the limitation of not including aspects of HRM practices in the environmental performance indicators of GRI Standards. In HRM literature, the alignment of HRM with environmental sustainability is explained as a subset of sustainable HRM using different approaches such as greening of strategic HRM, 'green' HRM, and greening of functional and competitive HRM for environmental management systems (refer to Chapter 7). Furthermore, an environment management system such as EMAS or ISO 14001 requires strong employee participation, environmental training programmes for employees and improved awareness among employees of the negative impacts of their jobs on the environment (e.g. waste created) in order to improve an organisation's environmental performance (Morrow & Rondinelli, 2002). Hence, sustainable HRM with the help of green HRM plays an important role in enhancing employee participation and engagement in the implementation of an environmental management system. This could be recommended for inclusion in any revision of GRI environmental performance indicators to improve to overall understanding of an organisation's environmental culture and practice.

Sustainable HRM is built on the 'synthesis paradox' perspective of HRM (see Chapter 1) to explore the tension in achieving diverse economic, social and environmental outcomes of sustainability rather than organisations reporting these outcomes as silos either by suppressing or ignoring the tension. That is, organisations must achieve financial outcomes with minimal negative impacts or harm of work imposed on stakeholders (employees, their families, the environment and communities). A study by Mariappanadar and Kramar (2014) has provided empirical evidence that the synthesis effect of sustainable HRM practices has a moderating effect of improving organisation profitability as well as reducing the harm of work imposed on employees (refer to Chapter 5 for more details). Hence, the synthesis effects of sustainable HRM provide theoretical as well as empirical evidence to overcome the limitation of reporting on sustainability outcomes through an integrated approach to understand the complexity of simultaneous effects of management approaches used in achieving diverse corporate sustainability outcomes.

10.6 Conclusion

This chapter has given an overview of selected tools used by businesses for a systematic and transparent reporting of HRM issues in sustainability reports. GRI is the most widely used framework. HRM topics play an important role in the implementation of GRI reporting for an organisation. This becomes even more prevalent if one considers social issues in the supply chain as part of the remit of the HRM function. Although academic research (see Ehnert et al., 2016) has suggested that GRI could be the basis for the measurement of sustainable HRM practices, GRI as well as the UN Global Compact are primarily reporting (rather than performance) frameworks. Chapter 10 has introduced different measurement systems of sustainable (and unsustainable) HRM developed by academics and NGOs. B-Lab and the Economy of the Common Good provide metrics for the assessment of sustainable and unsustainable business practices with a strong focus on HRM as opposed to providing tools for the writing of sustainability reports. We also have discussed possible limitations for sustainability reporting using GRI and also indicated how sustainable HRM theories could help practitioners overcome the limitations of GRI.

References

Akorsu, A. D. & Cooke, F. L. (2011). Labour standards application among Chinese and Indian firms in Ghana: Typical or atypical. *International Journal of Human Resource Management, 22*(13), 2730–48.

Bharat Petroleum (2015). *Sustainable Development Report 2014–15*. https://www.bharatpetroleum.com/sustainability/sustainability-reports.aspx. Accessed on 31 July 2017.

Catalyst (2011). *The bottom line: Corporate performance and women's representation on boards (2004–2008).* http://www.catalyst.org/publication/479/the-bottom-line-corporate-performance-and-womens-representation-on-boards-20042008. Accessed on 31 July 2017.

Chen, S. & Bouvain, P. (2009). Is corporate responsibility converging? A comparison of corporate responsibility reporting in the USA, UK, Australia, and Germany. *Journal of Business Ethics, 87*(1), 299–317.

Coal India (2015). *Sustainability Report 2014–15.* https://www.coalindia.in/DesktopModules/DocumentList/documents/Sustainability_Report_2014-15_of_CIL_Verified_and_Assured_12102015.pdf. Accessed on 3 August 2017.

Cohen, E., Taylor, S. & Muller-Camen, M. (2012). *HRM's Role in Corporate Social and Environmental Sustainability.* SHRM Foundation's Effective Practice Guidelines Series, Alexandria.

Continental (2015). *GRI Report 2014.* https://www.continental-corporation.com/resource/blob/62994/9f4e7a222430ddbdc5a59879d51b9e33/gri-report-2014-en-data.pdf. Accessed on 3 August 2017.

Ehnert, I., Parsa, S., Roper, I., Wagner, M. & Muller-Camen, M. (2016). Reporting on sustainability and HRM: A comparative study of sustainability reporting practices by the world's largest companies. *International Journal of Human Resource Management, 27*(1), 88–108.

Elkington, J. (1999). *Cannibals with Forks. The Triple Bottom Line of 21st Century Business.* Oxford: Capstone.

Esprit Holdings Limited (2016). *Sustainability Report.* http://www.esprit.com/press/sustainabilityreport/GRI201516.pdf. Accessed on 5 September 2017.

ExxonMobil (2015). *Corporate Citizenship Report 2014.* http://cdn.exxonmobil.com/~/media/global/files/corporate-citizenship-report/2014_ccr_full_digital_approved.pdf. Accessed on 25 April 2017.

Felber, C. (2015). *Change Everything: Creating an Economy for the Common Good.* Zed Books, London.

Fifka, M. S. (2013). Corporate responsibility reporting and its determinants in comparative perspective–A review of the empirical literature and a meta-analysis. *Business Strategy and the Environment, 22*(1), 1–35.

Fifka, M. S. & Drabble, M. (2012). Focus and standardization of sustainability reporting–A comparative study of the United Kingdom and Finland. *Business Strategy and the Environment, 21*(7), 455–74.

Fonseca, A., McAllister, M. L. & Fitzpatrick, P. (2014). Sustainability reporting among mining corporations: A constructive critique of the GRI approach. *Journal of Cleaner Production, 84,* 70–83.

Future Fit Foundation (n.d.). *About Us.* http://futurefitbusiness.org/about-us/. Accessed on 5 September 2017.

GRI (2016). GRI Standards Download Centre. https://www.globalreporting.org/standards/gri-standards-download-center/?g=e2060443-4dc2-48b0-8434-ac04a4da934e. Accessed on 10 November 2017.

GRI (Global Reporting Initiative) (2017a). *G4 Sustainability Reporting Guidelines.* https://www.globalreporting.org/information/g4/Pages/default.aspx. Accessed on 25 April 2017.

GRI (Global Reporting Initiative) (2017b). *GRI's History.* https://www.globalreporting. org/information/about-gri/gri-history/Pages/GRI's%20history.aspx. Accessed on 25 April 2017.

Haddock-Millar, J., Sanyal, C. & Müller-Camen, M. (2016). Green human resource management: A comparative study of a US MNC. *International Journal of Human Resource Management, 27*(2), 192–211.

Hahn, R. & Kühnen, M. (2013). Determinants of sustainability reporting: A review of results, trends, theory, and opportunities in an expanding field of research. *Journal of Cleaner Production, 59,* 5–21.

Honeyman, R. (2014). *The B Corp Handbook: How to Use Business as a Force for Good.* Oakland, CA: Berrett-Koehler Publishers. https://www.globalreporting. org/standards/gri-standards-download-center/?g=e2060443-4dc2-48b0-8434-ac0 4a4da934e. Accessed on 9 June 2017.

ILO (International Labor Organization). (n.d.). *Conventions and Recommendations.* http://www.ilo.org/global/standards/introduction-to-international-labour-st andards/conventions-and-recommendations/lang–en/index.htm. Accessed on 17 July 2017.

Industries, E. (2016). Sustainability Report 2015. http://corporate.evonik.de/_layouts/ Websites/Internet/DownloadCenterFileHandler.ashx?fileid=2884. Accessed on 3 August, 2017.

Jackson, S. E., Renwick, D. W., Jabbour, C. J. & Muller-Camen, M. (2011). State-of-the-art and future directions for green human resource management: Introduction to the special issue. *German Journal of Human Resource Management, 25*(2), 99–116.

JFE Group (2015). *CSR Report 2015.* http://www.jfe-holdings.co.jp/en/environment/ csr_report/csr2015e.pdf. Accessed on 31 July 2017.

Kolk, A. & Perego, P. (2010). Determinants of the adoption of sustainability assurance statements: An international investigation. *Business Strategy and the Environment, 19*(3), 182–98.

KPMG (2015). *The KPMG Survey of Corporate Reporting 2015.* https://assets.kpmg. com/content/dam/kpmg/pdf/2016/02/kpmg-international-survey-of-corporate-responsibility-reporting-2015.pdf. Accessed on 31 July 2017.

Mariappanadar, S. (forthcoming). Work-related leading indicators of occupational health outcomes.

Mariappanadar, S. & Kramar, R. (2014). The synthesis effect of high performance work systems on organisational performance and employee harm. *Asia-Pacific Journal of Business Administration, 6*(3), 206–24.

Morrow, D. & Rondinelli, D. (2002). Adopting corporate environmental management systems: Motivations and results of ISO 14001 and EMAS certification. *European Management Journal, 20*(2), 159–71.

Muller-Camen, M. & Camen, J. (2018). Sonnentor and the economy of the common good. In E. O'Higgins & L. Zsolnai (eds) *Progressive Business Models: Creating Sustainable and Pro-social enterprise* (pp. 123–42). Cham: Palgrave Macmillan.

Muller-Camen, M. & Elsik, W. (2015). IHRM's role in managing ethics and CSR globally. In: D. G. Collings, G. T. Wood, & P. M. Caligiuri (eds) *The Routledge Companion to International Human Resource Management* (pp. 552–61). London: Routledge.

Parsa, S., Roper, I., Muller-Camen, M. & Szegitvari, E. (2018). Have labour and human rights disclosures enhanced corporate accountability? *Accounting Forum, 42,* 47–64.

Pintér, L., Hardi, P., Martinuzzi, A. & Hall, J. (2012). Bellagio STAMP: Principles for sustainability assessment and measurement. *Ecological Indicators, 17,* 20–28.

Rasche, A., Waddock, S. & McIntosh, M. (2013). The United Nations Global Compact: Retrospect and prospect. *Business & Society, 52*(1), 6–30.

Rasche, A. & Waddock, S. (2014). Global sustainability governance and the UN Global Compact: A rejoinder to critics. *Journal of Business Ethics, 122*(2), 209–16.

Roberts, J. (2009). No one is perfect: The limits of transparency and an ethic for 'intelligent' accountability. *Accounting, Organizations and Society, 34*(8), 957–70.

Schuler, R. & Jackson, S. E. (2014). Human resource management and organizational effectiveness: Yesterday and today. *Journal of Organizational Effectiveness: People and Performance, 1*(1), 35–55.

Sinelnikov, S., Inouye, J. & Kerper, S. (2015). Using leading indicators to measure occupational health and safety performance. *Safety Science, 72,* 240–48.

UN Global Compact (2014). *Guide to Corporate Sustainability.* https://www.unglobalcompact.org/docs/publications/UN_Global_Compact_Guide_to_Corporate_Sustainability.pdf. Accessed on 17 August 2017.

Volkswagen (2015). *Sustainability Report 2014.* http://sustainabilityreport2014.volkswagenag.com/sites/default/files/pdf/en/Volkswagen_SustainabilityReport_2014.pdf. Accessed on 3 August 2017.

Wells Fargo (2016). *Corporate Social Responsibility Report 2015.* https://www08.wellsfargomedia.com/assets/pdf/about/corporate-responsibility/2015-social-responsibility-report.pdf. Accessed on 3 August 2017.

part V

Developing the Future of Sustainable HRM

Sustainable HRM roles and competencies

Sugumar Mariappanadar and Robin Kramar

11.1 Introduction

Sustainable HRM seeks to develop and implement policies designed to achieve objectives in three pillars of sustainable development or the triple bottom line approach which include economic/financial, human/social and environmental aspects. It challenges the strategic HRM paradigm which has dominated the rhetoric of HRM since the 1990s. The strategic HRM paradigm emphasises the use of HR for the achievement of economic (e.g. financial) outcomes for organisations. During the last couple of decades the roles of HR professionals required to further strategic HRM and achieve economic objectives have been well developed and have changed in response to the emerging economic and technological contexts. However, during this period, there has also been an increasing awareness of the negative impacts of work organisations on individuals, families, communities, the natural environment and the economy while organisations pursue their business strategies with the primary focus to improve financial performances.

Table 4.2 presented the characteristics of sustainable HRM practices from the institutional or organisational level. Hence, in this chapter, Figure 11.1 is provided to explain how the organisational-level characteristics of sustainable HRM practices influence and shape the sustainable HR roles from the employee 'self'-perspective to achieve sustainable HRM performance outcomes of a work-related position in an organization. That is, the characteristics of sustainable HRM practices set the organisational behaviour and employees' attitudes and expectations towards work in different job positions. The roles for a position provide a platform for employees to perform sustainable positional expectations using their competencies to achieve sustainable HRM performance outcomes. The sustainable HRM performance outcomes include improved organisational performances and pro-social organisational behaviour towards the key stakeholders (i.e. employees, their families, supply chain HRM practices, society's sustainable environmental management expectations). Each of these sustainable HRM performance outcomes are explained in this chapter while explaining different sustainable HR roles. Hence, in this chapter, first, the generic roles and competencies for HR are discussed. Secondly, strategic HR roles and competencies are discussed to highlight the background for sustainable HR roles and competencies in the context of disruption caused by socially responsible or pro-social expectations by organisations' key stakeholders (see Chapter 4 for more details on pro-social characteristics of sustainable HRM practices). Pro-social organisational behaviour is about positive social acts implemented by organisations in their business activities to produce and maintain the well-being and integrity of key stakeholders (Hahn, 2015). Finally, the sustainable HR roles and competencies are provided.

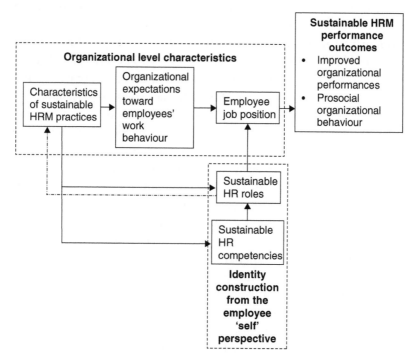

Figure 11.1   Link between sustainable HRM characteristics and sustainable
HR roles for sustainable HRM performance outcomes

11.2 Introduction to HR roles and HR competencies

11.2.1 HR roles

HR roles are defined as positional roles from two different perspectives in the literature. The constructionist perspective defines positional roles as having a crucial function in the established institutionalised practice for achieving organisational goals (Berger & Luckmann, 1966). However, from the open systems perspective a positional role is one whereby there is a continuous process of sending, receiving and responding to behavioural and attitudinal expectations that are used to evaluate the work-related activities of any person occupying a given organisational position (Katz & Kahn, 1966; Simpson & Carroll, 2008). It is evident from these two perspectives that positional HR roles (Legge, 1978; Storey, 1992; Ulrich, 1998; Ulrich et al., 2008) are defined in the literature as a relatively stable structure of the social interactions in a work-related position.

For example, Legge (1978) indicated four roles for personnel managers (in the 1980s HRM was referred to as personnel management) based on the contingencies of the times and to exploit possible power bases in an organisation to gain credibility for their role as personnel managers. The roles include problem solvers; conformist innovators who adjust existing processes to achieve organisational success; and deviant innovators, who try to change the existing processes by gaining acceptance for a different set of evaluation criteria for organisational success.

11.2.2 HR competencies

It is important to understand general management competencies before exploring the management function to specific HR competencies. In the literature, management competencies are explained as observable performance, the standard of outcome of a person's performance and the underlying attributes of a person's performance (Hoffmann, 1999). The underlying attributes for an individual employee's performance proposed by Boyatzis (1982) are the most common explanation used in the literature because they focus on the required individual inputs to produce competent performance in a job or positional roles. Furthermore, management competency is explained from the process of becoming a competent employee for a desired performance contingent on a given social context (Antonacopoulou & FitzGerald, 1996). Hence, the latter definition of management competency highlights how individual employees realise their personal capabilities by using meta-abilities or higher-order enabling competencies that drive other skills and abilities for higher job performance (Buckley & Monks, 2004).

In the HRM literature, HR competencies are explained using the underlying meta-abilities and attributes of an employee for achieving improved performance in HR roles while interacting with social job/position contexts. For example, forty-seven HR competencies were identified for HR professionals to effectively perform in their roles, and there structured into four categories based on empirical research. These are the classical industrial relations (IR) category, with five competencies; the traditional HR category, with seventeen competencies; the *new* HR with nineteen competencies; and finally; the personal HR competencies with six competencies (Johnson & King, 2003).

11.3 Strategic HR roles and competencies

For more than two decades the discussion on the role of HRM professionals has taken place within a framework provided by strategic management. HR professionals have been encouraged to take roles which develop and implement a value-enhancing HR strategy for firms and to participate in business strategic decision-making processes. For example, this requires HR roles associated with persuading the top management to pay attention to some critical HR issues, provide valuable information and insights on HR-related business issues, and work closely with line managers to solve staff problems (Schuler, 1990; Wei & Lau, 2005). They also help develop specific human capital and generate tacit organisational knowledge. In brief, the strategic HR roles and competencies can improve organisational effectiveness (Long & Ismail, 2011), and the emphasis has been on achieving financial and business outcomes. Hence, in this section strategic HR roles and competencies are explained as a background to the development of sustainable HR roles and competencies.

11.3.1 Strategic HR roles

Initially, in the strategic HR literature, Storey (1992) proposed four HR roles whereby he tried to capture the changing role of HR professionals due to intense role ambiguity caused by reduced security in managerial and functional roles in organisations. In this context, Storey introduced the role of 'advisor' and 'change makers' at the strategic level to enhance organisational performance. Furthermore, the role of 'regulators' indicates the interventionist role of HR professionals, and the role of 'handmaidens' provides specific services as requested by the line managers (i.e. managers performing core functions of a business).

Ulrich (1998) initially prescribed four HR roles for capturing the future new roles of HR. The 'strategic partner' role focuses on using HR to successfully implement business strategies and achieve customer expectations. The 'change agent' role is about delivering organisational culture change and transformation. 'Employee champions' facilitate developing employee commitment and competencies, and the 'administrative expert' focuses on continuous improvements to organisational efficiency by revising HRM processes and functions. Subsequently, Ulrich et al. (2008) proposed five HR roles that are different from the earlier four roles, which include the HR role in service centres, corporate HR, embedded HR, and centres of expertise and operational executors. These roles would enable HR professionals to become partners in the strategic management process through their expert knowledge, and become one part CEO and one part functional expert (Tebbel, 1999).

During the twenty years since Ulrich first identified the HR professionals' roles in 1998, the context of organisations has changed enormously. Competition has increased for businesses in the developed economies because of the market pressures created by developing economies (e.g. China, India, Brazil, etc.). Furthermore, uncertainty about the future has become extremely evident, with substantial stock market fluctuations and the global financial crisis (GFC). Hence, the reliance on strategic HR roles consistent with a strategic HRM approach was strengthened, with increasing emphasis on delivering financial results to a business to cope with uncertainties in the hyper-competitive global business context. Research found that the activities and functions of HR needed to operate like a business and it was necessary to define particular, specific outcomes that HR could deliver to a business (Ulrich et al., 2012).

11.3.2 Strategic HR competencies

The different sets of HR competencies were discussed in the literature to highlight that HR competencies evolved over a period of time, depending on the business contexts in which organisations operate. For instance, according to Wei and Lau (2005), strategic HR competency refers to the ability of HR to develop and implement an effective HRM system that is instrumental in achieving a firm's strategic goals. Furthermore, HR activities have proven to have positive impacts on business performance (i.e. financial performance) by approximately 10 per cent. Furthermore, the strategic contribution of HR to business performance accounts for 43 per cent (Brockbank et al., 1999). Hence, HR competencies gained recognition in the field of strategic HR to contribute to an organisation's competitive advantage beyond management competencies.

Strategic HR competency is about the underlying attributes of HR professionals that are important for enduring organisational performance and to make HR most effective. HR competencies are explained and understood in varied ways in the literature. For example, Ulrich et al. (1995) defined HR competencies as those competencies demonstrated by HR professionals when they add value to their business. They proposed three HR competency domains for performing the strategic HR role so as to add value to organisational performance. The three HR competency domains are 'knowledge of the business', which is not the ability to do all the business functions but rather the ability to understand them; 'delivery of HRM practices', which is about going beyond knowledge and being able to provide HRM practices to organisational members; and 'management of change processes', which concerns the knowledge, skills and abilities to deliver change management.

A study found five core strategic HR competencies: knowledge of business, strategic contribution, personal creditability, HR delivery and measurement. These competencies varied among different levels in HR practice, such as HR directors, HR managers, HR generalists, HR specialists and vice-presidents of HR (Ramlall, 2006). Furthermore, strategic HR competencies include HR professional ability, business-related ability and interpersonal ability (Dutton & Ashford, 1993; Wei & Lau, 2005). These abilities enable HR practitioners to perform their work duties and to communicate and coordinate with both top management and other line or core business functions (Long & Ismail, 2011; Schuler, 1990).

11.4 Sustainable HR roles and competencies

In the earlier section on strategic HR roles and competencies, it has been discussed that strategic HR roles and the aligned strategic HR competencies focus on achieving financial outcomes to gain strategic importance in achieving business strategies. Currently, there are growing socially responsible or pro-social organisational behaviour expectations among stakeholders and it has become an important disruptor for organisations. However, strategic HR roles and competencies provide very limited capabilities for HR professionals to facilitate organisations in coping with the disruption caused by stakeholders' expectations. Hence, sustainable HR roles and competencies that provide broader roles and competencies for HR professionals than the strategic HR roles to align with stakeholders' expectations to enhance competitive advantage of organisations are discussed in this section. Initially the need for sustainable HR roles is explained. Subsequently, sustainable HR roles and sustainable HR competencies are discussed to facilitate HR professionals to enable organisations to achieve sustainable HRM performance outcomes for corporate sustainability as competitive advantage. Corporate sustainability is about the management approaches used by organisations to integrate and achieve the three pillars (i.e. economic/financial, human/social and environmental outcomes) of sustainable development based on important stakeholders' expectations (UN Global Compact, 2014).

11.4.1 Need for sustainable HR roles

The need for sustainable HR roles is explained using two reasons which include the disruption in business strategy caused by pro-social organisational behaviour expectations by stakeholders, and the limitation of position-based strategic HR roles to handle the disruption. Firstly, stakeholders' expectations of organisations to behave socially responsible are explained by the stakeholders relationship management theory. That is, stakeholder relations management focuses on easing stakeholder pressure such as stakeholders' pro-social organisational behaviour expectations while improving organisational performance by strengthening the voluntary side of corporate sustainability (Steurer et al., 2005). Hence, the growing stakeholder pressure for pro-social organisational behaviour expectations has led Ulrich and Dulebohn (2015) to indicate the importance of considering internal and external stakeholders as contexts while transforming strategic HR roles. However, the strategic HR roles currently available in the literature are inadequate for HR professionals to facilitate organisations to voluntarily handle the stakeholder pressure which has caused disruption to organisations' performance-focused business strategies. Hence, this has led to the need for developing sustainable HR roles that can enrich HR professionals in effectively managing the stakeholder relationship to achieve corporate sustainability.

Secondly, the roles proposed by Legge (1978), Storey (1992) and Ulrich (1998, 2008, 2015) are considered as 'position'-based roles for HRM functions. That is, the role theory used in these three typologies of roles is characterised by the assumption that the acquisition of role is a formal, sequential and staged processes of socialisation into an occupation or job position (Simpson & Carroll, 2008). Positional roles are defined as a relatively stable structure of the social interactions in a work-related position (e.g. Berger & Luckmann, 1966; Katz

& Kahn, 1966; Simpson & Carroll, 2008). However, it is evident from the literature (e.g. Caldwell, 2003; Buckley & Monks, 2004) that, in practice, positional roles overlap, conflict and create competing demands (tensions and paradox) to satisfy the pro-social organisational behaviour expectations of stakeholders by HR professionals in a job position. Hence, sustainable HR roles are developed with identity constructions to overcome the limitation of positional roles in handling the dynamic nature of the current job structure. That is, sustainable HR role identities highlight the conduct of an employee at the expected organisational level (i.e. positional roles) and identity construction that happens from the 'employee self-perspective' while the employee is performing the expected organisational-level conduct in multiple positional roles.

11.4.2 Sustainable HR roles

HR roles must be aligned to the business strategy to facilitate organisations to achieve competitive advantage. For example, an organisation develops business strategies to achieve corporate sustainability and the HR roles must be aligned to those business strategies. Hence, *sustainable HR roles are about HR professionals managing the opportunities and constrains of corporate sustainability using stakeholder relations management (including employees, consumers and natural environment) to achieve sustainable HRM performance outcomes.* HR professionals need to use both positional roles and identity construction in sustainable HR roles so as to effectively manage stakeholder relations to achieve sustainable HRM performance outcomes for corporate sustainability. It is important to understand the link between positional roles and identity construction so as to grapple with the understanding of sustainable HR roles.

In the literature, roles are also explained using identity construction which adds value to the understanding of the position-based roles. That is, the term identity construction refers to persons who have multiple identities in a social group of a social network of relationships in positions they occupy and play roles that lead to peoples' happiness (Stryker & Burke, 2000). The identity construction perspective recognises a positional role as an inherently incomplete and emergent intermediary allowing individuals not only to perform, but also to improvise and play with the multiplicity of roles that they encounter in their social and intersubjective experiences (Simpson & Carroll, 2008). A role identity construction is a dynamic, relational process in which knowledge (i.e. new information) is constructed in social relations and that new information on positional roles acts as an intermediary to negotiate and broker, and to legitimise actions in work domains. Hence, it is indicated that identity construction mediates the meaning-making processes of HR professionals in positional roles, in which job expectations are fragmented. Furthermore, identity construction facilitates handling multiplicity, fluidity and competing demands of expectations of a position.

Positional roles act as boundary objects for a job position or capture the dedicated roles for sustainable HR and subsequently identity construction facilitates the translation and interpretation of meanings between or overlapping domains of those positional roles. Thus, sustainable HR roles are explained with identity construction to recognise that HR professionals appreciate the dynamic and exploratory potentials of multiple unfolding identities within the prescribed positional roles while managing stakeholder relations management for achieving sustainable HRM performance outcomes.

11.5 Types of sustainable HR roles

Three different sustainable HR roles are proposed which include the dedicated sustainable HR positional roles, which identify construction for integrated sustainable HR roles, and which identify construction for the synthesising of sustainable HR roles. The dedicated sustainable HR roles highlight that each of the roles within this positional role have a set of boundaries to perform the institutionalised activities to achieve sustainable HRM performance outcomes. However, the other two roles are based on identity construction which is effective in handling the role tension created in achieving diverse sustainable HRM performance outcomes. Hence, the proposed three sustainable HR roles will facilitate HR professionals to exhibit behaviour and attitudes towards corporate sustainability while exploring potential multiple roles unfolding in a dynamic job roles context.

11.5.1 Dedicated sustainable HR positional roles

The dedicated sustainable HR roles for achieving corporate sustainability strategy include three broad positional roles which are developed based on the roles proposed by Ulrich et al. (2008) . They are the strategic sustainable HR roles, operational sustainable HR roles and the standardised HR service.

11.5.1.1 Strategic sustainable HR role

McWilliams and Siegel (2001) indicated that an organisation's CSR actions include progressive work practices and hence sustainable HRM practices, as progressive work practices are treated as CSR actions. Hence, in this chapter the strategic sustainable HR role is explained as one of the CSR actions/initiatives of an organisation. Improvements in the market value of a company are not just based on financial performance, but CSR initiatives such as sustainable HRM practices are also equally important. *The strategic sustainable HR role is about HR professionals engaging in the business strategy for corporate sustainability by including sustainable HR as a CSR action to create value or benefits for the organisation as well as for key stakeholders.* Thus, HR professionals performing the strategic sustainable role cater to the CEO and/or senior management to facilitate alignment of HR to business strategies for corporate sustainability. The strategic sustainable HR role includes two dedicated roles: stakeholder custodian role and the sustainable business partner role, both of which are based on stakeholder theory. The stakeholder theory explains stakeholder relation management by using corporate and stakeholder perspectives (Steurer, 2006). That is, the stakeholder custodian role highlights the power and legitimacy of stakeholders in accomplishing their claim for an organisation's pro-social actions towards stakeholders while improving organisational performance. Furthermore, the role of sustainable business partner is based on the corporate perspective of stakeholder theory which explains the instrumental aspect of key stakeholder relation management and achievement of traditional corporate objectives.

A theoretical perspective of CSR from the industrial organisation or strategic aspects is also helpful in understanding the stakeholder custodian and sustainability business partner roles. CSR from the industrial organisation perspective is referred to as 'the private provision of public goods' (McWilliams & Siegel, 2011). That is, the motivation of organisations to serve society at the cost of profits is considered as CSR, whereas if the motivation of an organisation is towards the bottom line then the action is 'privately' responsible. However, critics of organisations' motivation for private and social benefits believe that it is not easy to ascertain the genuine motivation of an organisation.

Baron (2001) suggested that instead of arguing about the 'true' motives of an organisation for using CSR initiatives, the practical approach to this issue is to capture the creation of value or benefits to both organisations and stakeholders. Value creation of sustainable HRM practices is used as an indicator for the benefits of such CSR initiatives to both organisations and the key stakeholders. For example, an organisation might introduce a liberal HR practice such as maternity and paternal leave for its employees, and the organisation's motivation may be to attract and retain employees who are strategically important human capital to improve the bottom line of the organisation. However, irrespective of the organisation's bottom line-driven motivation such practices also benefit employees who are parents who can use this type of leave to satisfy their paternal role which also means in the future those children can contribute to society as good citizens.

The value creation or benefits of sustainable HRM as a CSR initiative for an organisation is explained using the resource based theory. Resource based theory explains how managers can identify those resources that provide sustained competitive advantage for an organisation (Barney, 1991). There is evidence in the literature that when human capital is aligned to an organisation's strategic positioning then it leads to improved organisational performance (e.g. Batt, 2000). Sustainable HRM knowledge and expertise will be important human capital for HR professionals to use in their role as a stakeholder custodian and as a sustainability business partner. Hence, in this section the focus is on the practical approach to understanding the value or benefits created by sustainable HRM as a CSR initiative to stakeholders and to an organisation using the stakeholder custodian role and the sustainability business partner role respectively. Understanding these two strategic sustainable HR roles is important for HR professionals so they can engage with the CEO and/or senior management to highlight the value creation of sustainable HRM as an aspect of CSR to achieve sustainable HRM performance outcomes for corporate sustainability. We start the discussion in this section with the stakeholder custodian role first and follow it with an explanation of the sustainability business partner role because of strategy formulation processes. That is, firstly, the key stakeholders' value or benefit expectation needs to be analysed along with other important strategic inputs (e.g. the external business environment) so as to use that information while formulating a corporate sustainability business strategy.

11.5.1.1.1 Stakeholder custodian role

In the corporate sustainability business strategy formulation HR professionals can use the stakeholder custodian role to engage with other business strategy formulation teams within an organisation to conduct a demand analysis for perceived benefits of sustainable HRM practices as a CSR initiative by stakeholders including customers. That is, customers as a stakeholder perceive sustainable HRM practices as a CSR initiative along with the bundle of other product/service attributes while making a purchase decision about a product/service. Hence, the demand analysis of sustainable HRM as a CSR initiative by the stakeholder custodian role will be beneficial for HR professionals to use in the business strategy formulation. For example,

BMW in their Global Reporting Initiatives (GRI, 2017) for sustainability have reported a materiality analysis of important aspects of sustainability which include fuel efficiency and CO_2 emissions (environmental outcome), occupational health and safety (social), and economic impacts on society as sustainable HRM demands by stakeholders in formulating their business strategy.

The demand for understanding the need for sustainable HRM can be through a participatory approach. The participatory approach is used to assess the demand for sustainable HRM as a pro-social initiative by an organisation through a survey or interview. For example, BMW used multiple focused groups as a participatory approach in their materiality analysis to gain insight into stakeholders' perception of the importance of sustainable HRM practices as part of an organisation's business strategies. Furthermore, the approach includes the annual employee survey which includes information on the sustainable and unsustainable (i.e. health and social harm of work) impacts of work on employees, their families and society as stakeholders. More information on the measurement of sustainable and unsustainable impacts on stakeholders is provided in Chapter 9.

HR professionals using the stakeholder custodian role subsequent to evaluating stakeholders' demand for sustainable HRM practices from organisations through participatory and/or expert-based approaches must evaluate the cost of satisfying this demand. However, this might sound useful in theory but evaluating the value creation by the pro-social characteristics of sustainable HRM practices might be a challenge. However, Williams and Siegel (2011) have indicated that it is possible to evaluate the value addition to organisations based on their CSR initiatives such as sustainable HRM practices through the reputation gained.

The reputation gained by an organisation from the implementation of sustainable HRM practices can also be used as a labour market screening strategy (App et al., 2012) to attract highly motivated and productive employees to gain competitive advantage. Also, the reputation of sustainable HRM can pre-empt government regulatory intervention which will provide cost savings for organisations in implementing new systems to adhere to regulations (Baron, 2001). Hence, *the stakeholder custodian role is about HR professionals understanding the demand for sustainable HRM practices from an organisation by key stakeholders to benefit stakeholders and improve reputation for the organisation.* The reputation gained by organisation will provide competitive advantage for organisations and this is discussed next in the discussion on the sustainability business partner role and how this strategic input can be used in business strategies.

11.5.1.1.2 Sustainability business partner

Once it is established that customers demand sustainable HR as one of the attributes that are valued in a purchase decision about a product/service then it becomes the sustainability business partner's role to engage with senior management to include this valued attribute in the business strategy. Hence, *the sustainability business partner's role is about HR professionals using the demand for sustainable HRM by key stakeholders to engage in business strategy development so as to improve the organisation's reputation and create value or benefits to the organisation.* That is, the enhanced reputation for implementing sustainable HRM practices can be a strategic resource for an organisation to improve profits by increasing revenue through premium pricing or consumer loyalty. Hence, in the dedicated sustainability business partner role, HR professionals must engage with senior management to highlight the demand for pro-social characteristics of sustainable HRM practices by stakeholders (including customers) and use this strategic input for formulating a business strategy that offers differentiation for the organisation to achieve and sustain competitive advantage.

For example, in their empirical study Siegel and Vitaliano (2007) established that consumers considered the reputation of a company when they used experience goods (e.g. shampoo) for which they could not ascertain the quality of the product till they bought and used it on themselves. Hence, in a personal products industry in which experience goods are sold, businesses can set hedonic pricing (Rosen, 1974) or mark-ups in pricing due to the differentiation strategy driven by the reputation gained for pro-social characteristics of sustainable HRM practices. In the service industries HR constitutes a significant component of total cost. Hitchcock & Willard (2002) provided evidence that when an organisation gains a reputation in the market for its pro-social actions towards stakeholders by implementing sustainable HRM practices, it enhances the quality of recruitment, retention and productivity of employees which lowers labour costs and offsets the cost of extra resources required for implementing sustainable HRM strategies and practices. See Chapter 4 for the characteristics of sustainable HRM practices and Chapter 7 for implementing sustainable HRM practices for more details.

HR professionals using the sustainability business partner role can highlight to an organisation's senior management that sustainable HRM practices as a CSR action can attract ethical investors and lower the cost of financial capital (Baron & Diermeier, 2007). That is, lower financial capital could be attracted because an organisation engaging in CSR enhances its reputation among financial capital providers who are very sensitive to the risks associated with an organisations irresponsible such as that demonstrated by BP with the oil spill in the Gulf of Mexico. Furthermore, investors share an interest in an organisation's pro-social actions towards stakeholders such as promoting employee well-being, diversity on the company board and so on (Sharfman & Fernando, 2008).

Once HR professionals performing the sustainability business partner role engage in embedding key stakeholders' demands for pro-social organisational actions into the corporate sustainability business strategy they should also perform the audit role. That is, the sustainability business partner role should audit the organisation to establish the HR resources required and to identify problems that exist in achieving the corporate sustainability business strategy. The audit function of this role is important as it identifies the alignment or misalignment in the current organisational culture to that of the expected culture to satisfy the key stakeholders' pro-social organisational behaviour expectations.

In summary, it is evident that HR professionals adopting the strategic sustainable roles (i.e. the stakeholder custodian role and the sustainability business partner role) should be able to engage with the top management to include sustainable HRM as part of the business strategy to enhance the organisation's reputation for pro-social actions towards key stakeholders. The reputation gained by organisations from implementing sustainable HRM strategies and practices will create value for the organisation as well as for stakeholders. Furthermore, this role entails HR professionals auditing the existing organisational culture to assess the compatibility of implementing sustainable HRM strategies and practices to achieve the corporate sustainability business strategy. Any information found about the discrepancies between the expected and the existing organisational culture as part of the audit should be made available to those in operational sustainable HR roles, which is discussed in Section 11.2, so as to redress key stakeholders demands and improve the reputation of an organisation. Finally, it is commonly perceived that an organisation's pro-social actions towards stakeholders may increase the costs of operating a business, whereas major research findings were provided in this section to indicate that the reputation gained through pro-social actions such as implementing sustainable HRM practices will lower the cost of sourcing financial capital and labour, which will offset the cost of the additional resources required for the implementation of such practices.

11.5.1.2 Operational sustainable HR roles

Ulrich et al. (2008) indicated that line managers impose greater demands on HR professionals who are involved in the strategic agenda of an organisation with operational aspects of HRM functions such as conducting recruitment interviews, compensation reviews, managing disciplinary action and so on. Hence, the operational sustainable HR role is proposed as a dedicated role for both HR professionals and line managers. The purpose of operational sustainable HR role is to convert ideas from the strategic sustainable HR roles, which are tailored to an organisation's needs, to operational HRM practices of managing the organisation's workforce. That is, HR professionals adopting the operational sustainable HR role must be able to develop and implement operational plans for line managers that can be executed in a timely manner so as to blend sustainable HRM strategies with practices. The operational sustainable HR role further includes being a campaigner for sustainability systems and a patron of the sustainability culture. These two additional roles are proposed as part of the operational sustainable HR role because in the HR literature there is evidence that the organisational culture mediates the HRM systems to achieve business strategies (e.g. Lado & Wilson, 1994; Lau & Ngo, 2004).

11.5.1.2.1 HRM system of sustainability role

In the strategic HRM literature the HRM system is explained as a bundle of HRM practices used to achieve organisational goals (Bowen & Ostroff, 2004). However, role theorists explain the organisation as a system of roles that provides a set of attitudinal and behaviour expectations in an institutionalised social structure (i.e. position) to achieve organisational goals (e.g. Ashforth, 2000). It is important to understand the similarities and differences between an HRM system based on a bundle of HRM practices and an HRM system with a bundle of HR roles. Let us start with the definition of HRM practices, which concerns the characteristics of HRM practices that shape and elicit employees' behaviours and attitudes towards work and the organisation (Martell & Carroll, 1995). This means, for example, that recruitment as an HR practice has different characteristics from that of the performance management practice. Hence, in the strategic HRM literature system-based HRM practices indicate that a bundle of such complementary HRM practices (i.e. recruitment, performance management, etc.) are integrated as part of the HRM system to improve organisational performance. However, these interdependent HRM practices are enacted by roles in an institutionalised social structure or a job position to achieve sustainable HRM performance outcomes (see Figure 11.1). Hence, the focus of the HRM system of sustainability role is to design a bundle of internally consistent roles for implementing HRM functions and processes to achieve contradictory but complementary sustainable HRM performance outcomes for corporate sustainability strategy.

We have decided to use the functional roles and HRM processes in explaining the HRM system of sustainability roles based on Cascio's (2005) suggestion while proposing roles for the future evolution of HRM as a field. HR professionals, while using the HRM system of sustainability roles, are expected to perform basic transactional HRM functions for line managers to achieve sustainable HRM performance outcomes. The basic transactional HRM functions for this role include recruitment, staffing, training and development, performance management, compensation and benefits, and occupational health and safety. In adding value to these basic transactional HRM functions, Chapter 4 provides a detailed list of sustainability characteristics for these transactional HRM functions so that professionals enacting the HRM system as part of the sustainability role will be able to achieve sustainable HRM performance outcomes.

HRM processes from the role perspective are explained based on the HRM system process definition by Bowen and Ostroff (2004). That is, *the sustainable HRM process is about how the sustainable HRM system can be designed to create shared meaning about the characteristics of HRM practices to be enacted in the role to achieve sustainable HRM performance outcomes.* Chapter 4 provides more details about the sustainability characteristics of an HRM system to achieve business strategies which could be used as processes for the HRM system of the sustainability role.

Cascio (2005) indicated five common core processes that are used by large organisations in managing HR to achieve improved organisational performance. These five processes are included in the HRM system of sustainability to achieve sustainable HRM performance outcomes. The processes for the HRM system of sustainability role include, firstly, facilitating employees to have a *common understanding* of an organisation's mission, values and goals towards corporate sustainability. Secondly, promoting *clear expectations* between employees and their managers on sustainable HRM performance in performance management. Thirdly, monitoring organisational practices to ensure they are *compliant* with laws and regulations specific to a country as well as to key stakeholders' expectations. Fourthly, enhancing employees' *commitment* to their job as well as satisfying key stakeholders' expectations. Finally, developing organisational capability with appropriate knowledge, skills and abilities for employees to use individually and in a team to achieve sustainable HRM performance outcomes.

In summary, it is important to note that HR professionals in this operational sustainable role need to achieve *sustainable HRM* performance outcomes using transactional HRM functions and the common HRM processes which go beyond the *strategic* HR performance outcomes of achieving just the organisational performance. The HRM system and processes (Bowen & Ostroff, 2004) discussed in this role are linking mechanisms that result in a sustainability culture or a shared construction of the meaning of sustainability among employees to achieve sustainable HRM performance outcomes. Hence, in Section11.2 the patron role of sustainability culture is discussed to moderate the link between the HRM system of sustainability roles and achieving sustainable HRM performance outcomes for corporate sustainability.

11.5.1.2.2 Patron role of sustainability culture

The values of senior-level managers, such as the CEO, make a significant contribution to shaping the organisational culture towards sustainability. Organisational culture is about leaders creating, and sharing with members, the sustainability values, commitments and aspirations they intend to achieve in the business domain (Fernández et al., 2003). Hence, to implement the sustainable HRM performance outcomes which are shaped by the HRM system of sustainable HR roles by engaging with senior-level managers, it is important to develop an organisational culture that facilitates such implementation. That is, the organisational culture with respect to addressing key stakeholders' demands for sustainable HRM performance outcomes subsequently strengthens employees' pro-social actions towards stakeholders in their job roles. This link between organisational culture and HR action is strong because the characteristics of the organisational culture comprise learnt, shared and transmitted behaviour (Schein, 1990). Now that the importance of the organisational culture for sustainable HRM performance outcomes (i.e. pro-social actions towards stakeholders, etc.) has been explained, we turn next to the patron role of sustainability culture for the HR professional to indicate how this role can facilitate change in the organisational pro-social culture to implement the corporate sustainability business strategy.

In explaining the patron role of sustainability culture, we have used three of the six future HR player roles suggested by Ulrich and Beatty (2001), which include the HR builder role, the HR facilitator and HR as conscience. Firstly, HR professionals performing the patron role of sustainability culture should integrate the HRM system and processes that are aligned to the corporate sustainability business strategy as a builder of organisational culture. That is, HR professionals while using the patron role of sustainability culture should consider innovating HRM systems and processes for sustainable HRM performance outcomes (i.e. pro-social behaviours towards key stakeholders) and also encourage those practices to be shared across management functions develop a strong culture. Secondly, where misalignment between business strategies and sustainable HRM system and process exists then HR professionals as facilitators or change agents should use the role to propose a change agenda for the organisation's culture and to get resources for individual employees and teams to ensure the planned change happens.

Finally, the patron role of sustainability culture should encourage HR professionals to act as internal referees for pro-social conscience (i.e. one of the sustainable HRM performance outcomes) and develop that as a shared value of the organisational culture. Hence, HR professionals in this role must understand both the moral and the ethical rules of conducting a business so that they play an important role as a point of reference for all employees in the organisation to perform their actions in the business domain with a pro-social conscience. That is, HR professionals performing this role must develop the moral courage to identify and report actions by employees in the business domain that conflict with the sustainable HRM performance outcomes as they perceive them without any fear of repercussions. For example, identifying and reporting sustainable HRM performance outcomes such as occupational health harm of work and work–family restrictions or work–family imbalance issues (see Chapter 9), equal employment violations, sexual harassment, use of incentives for questionable business practices in supply chain management and so on. The pro-social conscience aspect of this role is essential because it will improve the organisation's sustainability reputation and provide ultimate value for both the organisation and the key stakeholders. Hence, *the patron role of sustainability culture is about HR professionals in operational HR roles to innovate HRM practices and facilitate change for pro-social culture in an organisation, and also act as social conscience to ensure employees' actions in the business domain are aligned with sustainable HRM performance outcomes for corporate sustainability.*

11.5.1.3 Standardised HR service role

Many HR administrative tasks are performed by standardising and centralising HRM functions through information technology (IT)-enabled service centres to improve cost efficiency for organisations and the speed and convenience of delivery to employees (Ulrich et al., 2008). Hence, the standardised HR service is about enacting traditional HRM functions such as payroll, employee leave, training and development administration through IT-enabled service centres. The standardised HR service is about catering to the basic requirements of employees to access HR administrative work at their convenience but it is not for adding value (i.e. strategic) to improve employee performance for achieving organisational goals. This role has an added dimension in using technology to capture and monitor the positive and negative impacts of business practices on the environment and human/social outcomes. For instance, technology can be used to reduce the impact of stress on individuals and families and of pollution based on environmental management systems. Furthermore, the use of technology for telecommuting or working from small office hubs can reduce travelling time and emissions in the environment.

In summary, the dedicated sustainable HRM positional roles include the strategic sustainable HR roles, the operational sustainable HR roles and the standardised HR service. The strategic sustainable HR roles are about HR professionals engaging with the top-level managers of an organisation to develop business strategies by incorporating the pro-social actions toward key stakeholders. Furthermore, as discussed, this strategic initiative will enhance the organisation's CSR reputation to create value for the organisation as well as for key stakeholders. The operational sustainable HR roles focus on providing services to HR professionals as well as to line managers in managing employees to translate initiatives of the strategic sustainable roles to operational HRM practices of an organisation. The HRM system of sustainability role and the patron of sustainability culture role are proposed as parts of the operational sustainable roles, and are used to translate the strategic sustainable HRM initiatives into operational HRM practices to benefit both the organisation and the key stakeholders. Finally, the standardised HR service is discussed to highlight IT-enabled systems that enhance convenience and speed in accessing the basic administrative HR needs for employees. All of these HR roles are discussed as dedicated roles for HR professionals to improve sustainable HRM performance outcomes for corporate sustainability. However, these dedicated roles are interdependent on each other for HR professionals to use in practice to achieve sustainable HRM performance outcomes. Hence, the next two identity-based sustainable HR roles include the interdependence and/or dynamic nature (overlap) of the dedicated sustainable HR roles using identity construction theory.

11.6 Rationale for the integration and fusion of sustainable HR roles

Contemporary and traditional HR theories on roles are biased towards having consistency in dedicated roles (e.g. Storey, 1992; Ulrich et al., 2008). However, evidence from Simpson and Carroll's (2008) study revealed that HR professionals experience conflict and tensions while practising these dedicated roles to achieve complex organisational goals because in reality the dedicated HR roles overlap with each other. Hence, the paradox-based understanding of sustainable HR roles will help reveal the conflicts and tensions created while engaging in roles that lead to achieving diverse sustainable HRM performance outcomes (i.e. improved organisational performance and pro-social organisational behaviour). The important characteristic of paradox in the organisational literature is the simultaneous existence of contradictory elements even when those elements are mutually exclusive (Clegg et al., 2002). Hence, in this chapter the paradox or tension that exists for HR professionals using multiple interdependent sustainable HR roles to engage in improving sustainable HRM performance outcomes is explained with reference to Figure 11.2.

In Figure 11.2 it is depicted that the currently dominant strategic HR roles (e.g. Ulrich et al., 2008) focus on improving organisational performance and that this focus has simultaneous (see dotted Arrow-A) unintended harm of work or negative impacts of work on employees (see Chapter 5 for more details) and the environment (Chapter 6). In the CSR literature the reciprocal stakeholder theory (Hahn, 2015) suggests that normative stakeholder demands associated with the harm of work (externalities) imposed on key stakeholders will have reciprocal negative impacts on the reputation of the organisation (see broken Arrow-B) and thus constrain organisational performance. The reciprocal stakeholder demands and the simultaneous constraints on organisational performance create tensions for HR professionals in engaging in roles for achieving sustainable HRM performance outcomes. In this context of role

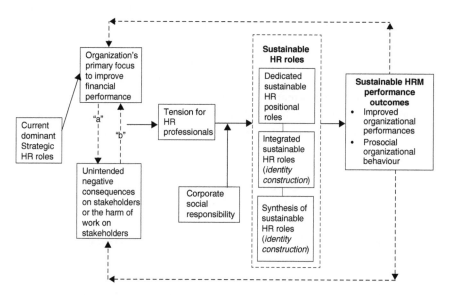

Figure 11.2   Rationale behind the role identity construction for sustainable HR

paradox/tension, the dedicated sustainable positional roles are less adaptable for HR professionals to improvise HR roles to handle the tension created by the reciprocal stakeholder–organisation relationship. The integration and fusion of sustainable HR roles are not 'planned or designed' behaviours such as with the dedicated HR roles but are the result of actions enacted (Clegg et al., 2002) in multiple interdependent roles. Hence, the integration and fusion of sustainable HR roles are explained using the identity construction so as to facilitate HR professionals in improvising dedicated sustainable HR roles to achieve the sustainable HRM performance outcomes.

11.6.1 Integrated sustainable HR roles

In the integrated sustainable HR roles, *HR professionals improvise and construct new knowledge through role identity construction by engaging in interdependent dedicated sustainable HR roles to achieve sustainable HRM performance outcomes.* HR professionals can use the integrated sustainable HR roles to manage the tension created by two different levels of roles (i.e. the strategic HR roles and the operational HR roles) and by multiple roles (i.e. the stakeholder custodian role and the sustainability business partner role) through identity construction to achieve sustainable HRM performance outcomes. The integration mechanism (Smith et al., 2010) used in the integrated sustainable HR roles can be treated as a solution to the role tension created by two or more dedicated roles or levels of sustainable HR to achieve sustainable HRM performance outcomes.

In the paradox perspective (Clegg et al., 2002) it is indicated that tension between roles is essential for continuous improvisation of future HR roles. Hence, integration from the paradox perspective is not an effective mechanism to achieve sustainable HRM performance outcomes because the role of tension is not maintained but rather the focus is to solve the tension. For example, HR professionals might construct a role identity by choosing to integrate 25 per cent of the stakeholder custodian role and 75 per cent of the sustainability business partner role as a political decision to resolve the role tension for achieving the outcomes of sustainable HRM performance. As indicated in the example discussed earlier in this paragraph the political reason for choosing a particular configuration of role identity in practice may reduce the role of tension. However, there will be limited opportunities to improvise role construction in this context to achieve sustainable HRM performance outcomes. Hence, the synthesis of HR roles for sustainability is discussed next to facilitate HR professionals in improvising their actions by performing contradictory and interdepended dedicated sustainable HR roles through identity construction to accept and maintain the role of tension in achieving sustainable HRM performance outcomes.

11.6.2 Fusion of sustainable HR roles

In the paradox perspective, a synthesis or fusion is bound to happen when extreme characteristics of a paradox exist simultaneously and have bidirectional relationships between the extreme characteristics (Clegg et al., 2002). That is, the existing strategic HR roles for improving organisational performance will have unintended negative consequences on the key stakeholders (dotted Arrow-A) and hence HR professionals will need to engage in the new proposed stakeholder custodian role to reduce the unintended negative impacts on the key stakeholders. Subsequently, the proposed strategic sustainable HR role must be used to engage with top-level management to highlight to them how unintended negative consequences for key stakeholders will have a reciprocal or reverse negative relationship on the organisational performance. In this situation, there will be a tension between the stakeholder custodian role and the sustainable business partner role if the top management is not convinced that the reciprocal negative impacts on organisational performance put forward by the sustainable business partner role will occur. A defensive response of avoiding engaging with the contradictions or integrating these two roles as part of a political decision are not effective. However, a fusion of the two roles based on pro-social conscience will facilitate engaging with the contradictions in the roles to create opportunities for role identity construction so as to improvise future management decisions and also main the role tension (Smith et al., 2010).

The fusion of sustainable HR roles is proposed for HR professionals *to develop innovative sustainable role identities by involving in multiple sustainable HR roles and continue to reframe and maintain the role tension based on pro-social conscience to achieve sustainable HRM performance outcomes.* Reframing the role tensions based on pro-social conscience will accommodate the emergent role tensions between two or more competing dedicated sustainable HR roles or levels contingent on managerial and key stakeholders' expectations for sustainable HRM performance outcomes. For example, demands for pro-social organisational behaviour may vary for different key stakeholders, and an organisation may choose to respond and adhere to one or a select few of key stakeholders' demands at a particular point in time and that might vary over a period of time. As indicated in the paradox literature, the improvisation of role identities happens as a result of real-time creativity while engaging in role tensions and it cannot be prescribed (e.g. Clegg et al., 2002). Hence, continuous reframing to maintain role tensions according to the stakeholder and managerial priorities will facilitate HR professionals in improvising their role identity construction while engaging in multiple inter-dependent roles to achieve sustainable HRM performance outcomes.

11.7 Competencies for sustainable HR roles

Competencies for sustainable HR roles are about the underlying attributes of HR professionals that are important for achieving sustainable HRM performance outcomes (i.e. improved organisational performance and pro-social organisational behaviour). In this section, we have explained the different sets of competencies for each of the proposed sustainable HR roles except for the standardised HR service role which is predominantly performed by IT and/or outsourced to a third-party service provider. However, it is important to note that the proposed HR competencies for each of the roles are not rigid and static but rather are dynamic and may need to be used in combination with other competencies to effectively perform the dedicated sustainable HR role as well as the integration and fusion of sustainable HR roles for achieving sustainable HRM performance outcomes (Table 11.1 and Table 11.2).

Table 11.1   Dedicated sustainable HR roles and Competencies

Sustainable HR roles	Competencies
Strategic sustainable HR role	
• Stakeholder custodian role	Ability to identify and engage with key stakeholders.
	Knowledge of the impact of HRM practices on the key stakeholders.
	Knowledge of social, environmental and ethical issues for the organisation and its supply chain.
	Ability to strategically think and align with future stakeholders' expectations.
• Sustainability business partner role	Promotes values with sustainability identity for the organisation.
	Moral values are embedded in business strategies and communication with stakeholders
	Ability to provide equal considerations to both a business case and a beyond business case for sustainability.
	Ability to envision alternative forms of organisations and business models to facilitate corporate sustainability.

Table 11.1 (Continued)

Sustainable HR roles	Competencies
Operational sustainable HR role	
• HR system of sustainability role	Systemic thinking to understand dynamic processes of a socially responsible organisation.
	Foster internally consistent bundle of HR roles to achieve positive outcomes for all the stakeholders.
	Be proactive in early identification of stakeholders' issues and business dilemma.
• Patron role of sustainability culture	Building and valuing relationships with different stakeholder groups.
	Acknowledgement of their role as a moral activity.
	Critically analyse decisions from both stakeholders' interests and financial business outcomes.
	Inspire critical reflection and active engagement with stakeholders in initiating organisational culture change processes to achieve corporate sustainability.
	Ability to think through issues, have patience and confidence to share knowledge and manage conflict while implementing organisational culture change for sustainability.
Standardized HR service role	Knowledge in operating varied systems for HRM functions.
	Ability to connect with key stakeholders for sustainability based on social network analyses.
	Skills to explore the use of technology to capture, monitor and evaluation variety of issues on sustainability.

11.7.1 Competencies for strategic sustainable HR roles

11.7.1.1 Competencies for stakeholder custodian role

The stakeholder custodian role relies on the ability to identify and engage with the key stakeholders involved in the achievement and impact of processes designed to achieve sustainable HRM performance outcomes. These include senior leadership, employees and other internal and also external stakeholders. This requires competencies such as knowledge of the impact of HR policies on key stakeholders, and the ability to communicate and involve a variety of stakeholders to ascertain the impact of the business on their health and well-being

Table 11.2 Integrated and fusion of sustainable HR roles and competencies

Sustainable HR roles	Competencies
Integrated and fusion of sustainable HR roles	A wide range of competencies required which includes the following competencies for these two roles; however, this is not an exhaustive list:
	Personal competencies:
	Courage, strong self-esteem, persistence, patience, emotional awareness, paradoxical mindset to cope with contradictory but complementary corporate sustainability outcomes.
	Specific knowledge:
	Ability to cultivate respect with senior management and stakeholders.
	Engagement with all stakeholders to develop a solution for paradoxical situation.
	Ability to accept, tolerate and find possible solutions for the tension created by competing outcomes.
	Ability to perceive decision choices not as an 'either/or' but to synthesise, integrate and demonstrate abstract thinking at a high level.

and on the ecological environment. These stakeholders could also be involved in participating in the exploration of a number of solutions to these issues.

Knowledge and empathy are required to develop methods of involving the stakeholders in revealing the potential impacts of present and planned policies on their well-being and capabilities. Knowledge of social, environmental and ethical issues for the organisation and its supply chain will be essential, as well as a knowledge of the changing stakeholders' demands, customer requirements, industry developments and competitive dynamics. Personal attributes such as the ability to question, explore, be inquisitive, accept feedback and question boundaries and assumptions are also needed. The role also requires the ability to develop a sustainable identity for the organisation. Furthermore, HR professionals must have the ability to imagine possible futures for the organisation and identify those futures which are consistent with the economic, social and ecological outcomes of the corporate sustainability business strategy.

11.7.1.2 Competencies for sustainability business partner role

HR professionals need to be aware of their pro-social values and assumptions about the key stakeholders, how organisations and management work, the role of organisations in society and the economy and realities of the way decisions are made in organisations, particularly their organisation. Such skills and knowledge enable a realistic assessment to be made about the intended integration of the desired values with senior and line management decisions and behaviour, and the actual dynamics of organisational life with the realities. The role promotes values associated with the sustainability identity and achievement or at the very least promotion of the organisation's three pillar outcomes. Consequently, moral decisions are made and will be embedded in business strategies, management policies, communication with stakeholders and behaviour in the workplace.

The competency requires the ability to evaluate potential alternative and actual decisions in terms of the dollar values associated with the costs and benefits for the organisation as well as to stakeholders. Furthermore, equal consideration will be given to the costs and benefits of decisions on employee health and social well-being and the impact on the ecological environment in the short term and longer term. This would require knowledge of systems and products which could be used to reduce resource consumption as well as knowledge of more effective means of organising work to enhance performance. In order to examine the future competencies required for the organisation to operate in a sustainable way it will require an ability to envision alternative forms of organisations and possibly even business models.

11.7.2 Competencies for operational sustainable HR role

11.7.2.1 Competencies for HRM system of sustainability role

HR professionals will require the competency of systemic thinking in order to integrate and synthesise information and build an understanding of the interconnectivity, relationships and dynamic processes involved in positioning the organisation in the future. Furthermore, HR professionals need to foster through policies mandating systems such as the selection, reward and performance management system consistent with the vision, strategy and values of the business which are concerned with achieving positive results for all stakeholders. HR professionals need to be proactive with stakeholders and anticipate future HR issues and business dilemmas. Essential to this is the knowledge of what line managers are really doing in the workplace and what their views are about particular issues and policies related to achieving sustainable HRM performance outcomes. Similarly, HR professionals need to know the real as well as the stated priorities of executives, and those with actual decision-making power. Without this knowledge, the influencing and persuading required to achieve sustainability outcomes will be unsuccessful.

11.7.2.2 Competencies for patron role of sustainability culture

HR professionals require competencies which are consistent with mindful leadership. Mindful leadership requires behaviour which is collaborative, a collective shared process (Fletcher 2004). It requires building and valuing relationships with other people and a sense of being connected to other people and their needs. This necessitates individuals having competencies of being able to see their decisions as part of stakeholders' interests and financial business outcomes. Such a competency requires the skills of critical reflection and an acknowledgement that their work is a moral activity. It also requires knowledge of their strengths and emotional responses to particular situations.

Some of the other essential competencies are to be able to inspire the development of organisational culture based on employees' commitment to positive human/social, financial and ecological outcomes and sense of belonging to an organisation that is able to further these outcomes. Critical to this is an environment of trust. If HR is concerned with facilitating positive outcomes from organisational activities, financial outcomes are important, but equally as important are the ecological and social and human outcomes. The case for change requires a business case for positive outcomes in all of these areas. This requires knowledge of the present and future potential impacts of the business on the key stakeholders. It also requires an ability to engage a variety of stakeholders in the process of identifying the areas for change, the potential resistance to change and the preferred results. Consistent with this approach to change is the view that change is regarded as an iterative, non-linear, continuing process. The role of change champion requires competencies such as critical reflection, an open mind and an ability to engage with a variety of stakeholders as well as an ability to listen and understand these stakeholders. This requires the skill of dialogue rather than debate. In addition, it requires the ability to think through issues with patience and confidence and to share knowledge and manage conflict.

11.7.2.3 Competencies for standardised HR service role

This role requires HR professionals to use technology to improve organisational efficiency and to reduce the impacts of business practices on human/social and environmental outcomes. Competencies required for this role include knowledge of the technology systems and products available for varied HRM functions, and knowledge of the advantages and disadvantages of using social media to stay connected with key stakeholders. The role will require knowledge and skills to explore the use of technology to capture, monitor and evaluate a variety of issues on sustainability that positively and negatively impact on the organisation and its stakeholders. Professionals in this role also require the ability to engage with and have a dialogue with a variety of stakeholders to evaluate the potential benefits and requirements of the use of technology in this way – for example, an ability to connect with key stakeholders for sustainability based on social network analyses. Finally, an ability to communicate the value of these technologies to senior management is also needed.

11.8 Competencies for integration and fusion of sustainable HR roles

A wide range of competencies are necessary to integrate and juggle multiple and interdependent sustainable HR roles. Personal competencies of courage, strong self-esteem, persistence, patience, emotional awareness and the coping abilities to deal with paradoxical situations are required. Specific knowledge is also required – for example, knowledge of the impact of conflicting outcomes, and knowledge of a variety of consequences resulting from actions. Certain abilities are also essential for the HR professionals undertaking multiple roles simultaneously. These include the ability to cultivate respect with senior management and stakeholders, engagement of all parties in developing a solution to a paradoxical situation, the ability to accept, tolerate and bear the tensions, or the ability to search for an accommodation of the tensions to achieve sustainable HRM performance outcomes. A central aspect of this role is the competency of seeing the HRM decision choices not as an 'either/or' choice, but rather as the reconciliation of paradoxes and if possible being able to dynamically balance these paradoxes. Competencies also include the ability to synthesise, integrate, and demonstrate abstract thinking at a high level.

11.9 Conclusion

Currently there is a growing trend towards socially responsible or pro-social organisational behaviour expectations by stakeholders and this has become an important disruptor for organisations. However, strategic HR roles and competencies provide very limited capabilities for HR professionals to facilitate organisations to cope with the disruption caused by stakeholders' expectations. Hence, in this chapter sustainable HR roles and competencies were explained to provide broader roles and competencies for HR professionals than the strategic HR roles to implement corporate sustainability business strategy. Three different sustainable HR roles were proposed, which include the dedicated sustainable HR positional roles, the identity construction for integrated sustainable HR roles, and the identity construction for the synthesising of sustainable HR roles. Different sets of competencies for each of the proposed sustainable HR roles were discussed to achieve sustainable HRM performance outcomes (i.e. improved organisational performances and prosocial organisational behaviour towards the key stakeholders). The proposed HR competencies for each of the roles are not rigid or static but rather are dynamic and may need to be used in combination with other competencies to perform effectively the dedicated, integrated and fusion of sustainable HR roles for achieving sustainable HRM performance outcomes. Sustainable HR roles and competencies were discussed to facilitate HR professionals in enabling organisations to achieve sustainable HRM performance outcomes for corporate sustainability as a competitive advantage.

References

Antonacopoulou, E. P. & FitzGerald, L. (1996). Reframing competency in management development. *Human Resource Management Journal*, 6(1), 27–48.

App, S., Merk, J. & Büttgen, M. (2012). Employer branding: Sustainable HRM as a competitive advantage in the market for high-quality employees. *Management Revue*, 23(3), 262–78.

Ashforth, B. (2000). *Role Transitions in Organizational Life: An Identity-Based Perspective.* New York: Routledge.

Barney, J. (1991). Firm resources and sustained competitive advantage. *Journal of Management*, 17(1), 99–120.

Baron, D. P. (2001). Private politics, corporate social responsibility, and integrated strategy. *Journal of Economics & Management Strategy*, 10(1), 7–45.

Baron, D. P., & Diermeier, D. (2007). Introduction to the special issue on nonmarket strategy and social responsibility. *Journal of Economics & Management Strategy*, 16(3), 539–45.

Batt, R. (2000). Strategic segmentation in front-line services: Matching customers, employees and human resource systems. *International Journal of Human Resource Management*, 11(3), 540–61.

Berger, P., & Luckmann, T. (1966). *The social construction of reality.* Garden City, NY: Doubleday.

Bowen, D. E. & Ostroff, C. (2004). Understanding HRM–Firm performance linkages: The role of the "strength" of the HRM system. *Academy of Management Review*, 29(2), 203–21.

Boyatzis, R. E. (1982). *The Competent Manager: A Model for Effective Performance.* New York: John Wiley & Sons.

Brockbank, W., Ulrich, D. & Beatty, R. W. (1999). HR professional development: Creating the future creators at the University of Michigan Business School. *Human Resource Management, 38*(2), 111–18.

Buckley, F. & Monks, K. (2004). The implications of meta-qualities for HR roles. *Human Resource Management Journal, 14*(4), 41–56.

Caldwell, R. (2003). The changing roles of personnel managers: Old ambiguities, new uncertainties. *Journal of Management Studies, 40*(4), 983–1004.

Cascio, W. F. (2005). From business partner to driving business success: The next step in the evolution of HR management. *Human Resource Management, 44*(2), 159–63.

Clegg, S. R., Da Cunha, J. V. & E Cunha, M. P. (2002). Management paradoxes: A relational view. *Human Relations, 55*(5), 483–503.

Dutton, J. E. & Ashford, S. J. (1993). Selling issues to top management. *Academy of Management Review, 18*(3), 397–428.

Fernández, E., Junquera, B. & Ordiz, M. (2003). Organizational culture and human resources in the environmental issue: A review of the literature. *International Journal of Human Resource Management, 14*(4), 634–56.

Fletcher, J. (2004). The paradox of postheroic leadership: An essay on gender, power and transformational change. *Leadership Quarterly, 15*(5), 647–61.

GRI (Global Reporting Initiative) (2017). *G4 Sustainability Reporting Guidelines.* https://www.globalreporting.org/information/g4/Pages/default.aspx. Accessed on 25 April 2017.

Hahn, T. (2015). Reciprocal stakeholder behavior: A motive-based approach to the implementation of normative stakeholder demands. *Business & Society, 54*(1), 9–51.

Hitchcock, D., & Willard, M. (2002). Sustainability: enlarging quality's mission. *Quality Progress, 35*(2), 43.

Hoffmann, T. (1999). The meanings of competency. *Journal of European Industrial Training, 23*(6), 275–86.

Johnson, C. D. & King, J. (2003). Are we properly training future HR/IR practitioners?: A review of the curricula. *Human Resource Management Review, 12*(4), 539–54.

Katz, D., & Kahn, R. L. (1966). *The Social Psychology of Organizations.* New York: Wiley.

Lado, A. A. & Wilson, M. C. (1994). Human resource systems and sustained competitive advantage: A competency-based perspective. *Academy of Management Review, 19*(4), 699–727.

Lau, C. M. & Ngo, H. Y. (2004). The HR system, organizational culture, and product innovation. *International Business Review, 13*(6), 685–703.

Legge, K. (1978). *Power, Innovation and Problem-Solving in Personnel Management,* London: McGraw Hill.

Long, C. S. & Ismail, W. K. W. (2011). An analysis of the relationship between HR professionals' competencies and firms' performance in Malaysia. *The International Journal of Human Resource Management, 22*(05), 1054–68.

McWilliams, A. & Siegel, D. (2001). Corporate social responsibility: A theory of the firm perspective. *Academy of Management Review, 26*(1), 117–27.

McWilliams, A. & Siegel, D. S. (2011). Creating and capturing value: Strategic corporate social responsibility, resource-based theory, and sustainable competitive advantage. *Journal of Management*, *37*(5), 1480–95.

Martell, K. & Carroll, S. J. (1995). How strategic is HRM? *Human Resource Management*, *34*(2), 253–67.

Ramlall, S. J. (2006). Identifying and understanding HR competencies and their relationship to organizational practices. *Applied HRM Research*, *11*(1), 27–38.

Rosen, S. (1974). Hedonic prices and implicit markets: Product differentiation in pure competition. *Journal of Political Economy*, *82*(1), 34–55.

Schein, E. H. (1990). Organizational Culture, *American Psychologist*, *45*(2), 109–19.

Schuler, R. S. (1990). Repositioning the human resource function: Transformation or demise? *The Executive*, *4*(3), 49–60.

Sharfman, M. P. & Fernando, C. S. (2008). Environmental risk management and the cost of capital. *Strategic Management Journal*, *29*(6), 569–92.

Siegel, D. S. & Vitaliano, D. F. (2007). An empirical analysis of the strategic use of corporate social responsibility. *Journal of Economics & Management Strategy*, *16*(3), 773–92.

Simpson, B. & Carroll, B. (2008). Re-viewing 'role' in processes of identity construction. *Organization*, *15*(1), 29–50.

Smith, W. K., Binns, A. & Tushman, M. L. (2010). Complex business models: Managing strategic paradoxes simultaneously. *Long Range Planning*, *43*(2), 448–61.

Steurer, R. (2006). Mapping stakeholder theory anew: From the 'stakeholder theory of the firm' to three perspectives on business–society relations. *Business Strategy and the Environment*, *15*(1), 55–69.

Steurer, R., Langer, M. E., Konrad, A. & Martinuzzi, A. (2005). Corporations, stakeholders and sustainable development. I: A theoretical exploration of business–society relations. *Journal of Business Ethics*, *61*(3), 263–81.

Storey, J. (1992). *Development in the Management of Human Resources*, Oxford: Blackwell.

Stryker, S., & Burke, P. J. (2000). The past, present, and future of an identity theory. *Social Psychology Quarterly*, *63*(4), 284–97.

Tebbel, C. (1999). Outsourcing the Road to Flexibility. *HR Monthly*, October, 18–22.

Ulrich, D. (1998). A new mandate for human resources. *Harvard Business Review*, *76*, 124–35.

Ulrich, D., & Beatty, D. (2001). From partners to players: Extending the HR playing field. *Human Resource Management*, *40*(4), 293–307.

Ulrich, D., Brockbank, W., Yeung, A. K. & Lake, D. G. (1995). Human resource competencies: An empirical assessment. *Human Resource Management*, *34*(4), 473–95.

Ulrich, D. & Dulebohn, J. H. (2015). Are we there yet? What's next for HR? *Human Resource Management Review*, *25*(2), 188–204.

Ulrich, D., Younger, J. & Brockbank, W. (2008). The twenty-first-century HR organization. *Human Resource Management*, *47*(4), 829–50.

Ulrich, D., Younger, J., Brockbank, W., & Ulrich, M. (2012). HR talent and the new HR competencies. *Strategic HR Review*, *11*(4), 217–22.

UN Global Compact (2014). *Overview of the UN Global Compact.* http://nbis.org/ nbisresources/sustainable_development_equity/un_global_compact.pdf. Accessed on 22 September 2015.

Wei, L. Q. & Lau, C. M. (2005). Market orientation, HRM importance and competency: Determinants of strategic HRM in Chinese firms. *The International Journal of Human Resource Management, 16*(10), 1901–18.

12

Global sustainable HRM practices

Robin Kramar and Sugumar Mariappanadar

12.1 Introduction

During recent decades manufacturing has been transferred from developed countries to Asian and Eastern European countries where labour costs are much lower than in developed countries. Even within these regions, there has been movement of production between higher cost and lower cost countries. For instance, the production of textiles and clothing has shifted from China to Bangladesh where labour costs remain cheaper than in China. The nature of the supply chain has, in some instances, developed to include subcontractors in a number of countries. This trend is also reflected in services, such as the transfer of contact centres to Asian countries and even professional and knowledge work, such as accounting, telecommunications support and other service work.

These changes in labour markets will act as a disrupter in the global context and this disruption will continue to have both positive and negative impacts on a variety of stakeholders in developed and developing countries. The quest for reductions in labour costs involves not only moving production and services between countries, but also substituting technology for human beings. Hence, these disruptions have impacts on organisational performances in the global context as well as on social and economic systems. For instance, the establishment of contact centres in the Philippines and India has been found to negatively impact the social lives of contact centre workers. The hours of work by contact centre employees are based on the business hours of the country to which their company is servicing. As a result, contact centre workers are required to work shifts which disrupt circadian rhythms, create psychological and physical problems, reduce employee safety and disrupt family life (Hechanove et al., 2016). These negative impacts on individuals detrimentally effect families, family life and the traditional way families function.

In the past decades organisations used strategic HRM in their global businesses to manage employees for the achievement of financial outcomes. Although the strategic HRM approach in the global context has improved economic benefits for stakeholders such as employees and their families, there is evidence in the literature that strategic HRM has imposed negative impacts on employees involved in subsidiaries of multinational enterprises (MNEs) as well as on the ecological system of the host countries. Hence, global sustainable HRM focuses on the requirement that MNEs ensure positive social, human, financial and ecological outcomes for key stakeholders in both home and host countries.

Sustainable HRM is by its very nature global. Sustainable HRM in a global context therefore moves beyond the realm of legal compliance and the complexities of accommodating the requirements of local or host country's expectations, with those consistent with the spirit of the parent company. This is done by using international conventions which establish principles relating to human/social and environmental standards as reference points for policies and decisions. It also involves the adaptation of fundamentally conflicting social norms and expectations of an organisation's workforce and the communities in which the organisation operates globally and this could result in a sustainability tension/paradox.

For example, in the broad Asian region (e.g. countries such as India, China, Japan, South Korea and Middle Eastern countries), socio-cultural influences were shaped by the values of creeds and ideologies such as Hinduism, Confucianism, Buddhism and Islam. These creeds and ideologies emphasised values such as social harmony, holistic living, that work is performed as a duty to achieve salvation, respect for authority, conflict avoidance and the importance of personal connections. These values were reflected in the operation and perception of the role of Asian firms and the responsibilities of employers and employees. Mutual loyalty was an integral part of the management of Asian organisations and this was reflected in an expectation of guaranteed lifetime employment for permanent employees (Debroux, 2014).

Global sustainable HRM is premised on an assumption that organisations, economies and markets are open systems. These open systems are interdependent and span geographic areas, cultural contexts and short-term time limitations. Furthermore, sustainable HRM requires equal emphasis be given to economic/financial, human/social and ecological outcomes resulting from the operation of an organisation in a global context. A variety of aspects of sustainable HRM was explored in previous chapters. For example, sustainable HRM include the longevity or endurance of HRM systems, the positive and negative impacts of HRM practices on the well-being of employees, their families and communities, the impact on ecological, human/social and financial outcomes of an organisation's activities and meeting the needs of a variety of stakeholders in the present and also in the future. Hence, this chapter examines the way sustainable HRM can be understood and implemented in varied geographical regions where MNEs and multinational corporations (MNCs) operate when the primary objective of the subsidiary operations is to reduce labour costs.

To achieve the aim of this chapter we initially discuss the nature of globalisation. Secondly, the need for global sustainable HRM is discussed based on the inability of strategic HRM to satisfy stakeholders' expectations in the global context. Thirdly, global sustainable HRM is explained using the values of global ethics informing CSR. Finally, the ways of transferring global sustainable HRM by MNEs/MNCs to their subsidiaries in diverse geographical locations is explained.

12.2 Globalisation and multinational enterprises

In different disciplines such as anthropology, media studies, ecology and business studies globalisation has distinct meanings (Clark & Knowles, 2003). In this chapter we explore globalisation from the business discipline perspective in order to have a comprehensive understanding of globalisation in the business management context. Globalisation highlights the closer integration of worldwide economies and countries through trade, technology and reduced transportation costs (Stiglitz, 2002). Globalisation also characterises the international setting of business transactions in which MNEs participate.

MNEs are the engine for globalisation and they use technological advancement to conduct businesses in order to integrate economies and countries. It is important to understand the difference between MNEs and MNCs from the global perspective because this is relevant for understanding global sustainable HRM. Reich (1998) indicated that MNEs are global companies that pursue a corporate strategy that strives for a worldwide intrafirm division of labour while MNCs are 'glocalising' companies which pursue an alternative strategy in which they seek to replicate production within several geographical regions. Glocalising is about companies seeking to generate a geographically concentrated inter-company division of labour. Therefore, global sustainable HRM is relevant for both MNEs and MNCs but the focus of this chapter is not about explaining the similarities and differences in sustainable

HRM practices in difference national cultures. However, it is about MNEs/MNCs and the tensions involved in attempting to transfer global sustainable HRM to their subsidiaries in other geographical regions and their need to explore the congruence between the values of global sustainable HRM practices and that of the dominant values in a national culture.

The annual revenue of some of the large MNEs such as Exxon Mobil Corporation exceeds the GDP of many nation states. Furthermore, MNEs in the global context are privileged in many ways, for instance they have limited state regulations. As a result of their international operation, these organisations are faced with pressures from their home country (i.e. head office of the organisation), host country (i.e. business operations in countries other than the home country) and international organisations (i.e. GRI and the UN Global Compact). In addition, they self-regulate their strategies that impact on the corporate sustainability outcomes. Specifically, these are the three pillar outcomes of economic/financial, human/social and environmental outcomes. MNEs are required to be managed in terms of acceptable global business ethics because of pressure from multiple stakeholders, many of which are global stakeholders. Consequently, MNEs need to move beyond all country- or region-specific business ethics differences and use globally acceptable ethical practices. That is, global business ethics is about the integration of home country and host country ethical standards and the identification of norms that will satisfy both countries, that is, the host country and the parent country (Carroll, 2004). Before we explore how global sustainable HRM can align with corporate sustainability business strategy of subsidiaries of MNEs, it is important to explore in the literature how strategic HRM practices were transferred by MNEs to their subsidiaries operating in varied national cultures. In addition, we will examine the value of developing and implementing global sustainable HRM practices in order to satisfy stakeholders' expectations.

12.3 Limitations of strategic HRM in addressing stakeholders' expectations

The strategic HRM approach to people management, with its emphasis on developing HRM policies that encouraged and rewarded employee behaviours contributing to organisational financial success, spread from the USA to other western developed countries during the last decades of the twentieth century. MNE and MNCs also adopted the strategic HRM approach and transferred some of the HRM policies consistent with strategic HRM to their subsidiaries in other developing countries.

The HRM policies which form part of a strategic HRM approach are based on assumptions that people are consistent, reasonable and can behave in a logical, rational way in line with the dominant western values of individualism, instrumentalism and utility. It is claimed the practice of strategic HRM is involved with 'distancing, depersonalizing and dissembling' in order to support the business not the people working for the organisation (De Gama et al., 2013, p. 97). People are referred to as 'assets' or 'human capital' or 'resources'. These terms objectify the employee and frame them in terms of their contribution to the achievement of organisational goals. This framing, and these terms, are also consistent with the free market capitalism model which underpins economies such as the USA, the UK and Australia. Although we have witnessed the development of HRM programmes, such as 'work–family balance', diversity, 'working from home' and 'personal leave arrangements', which appear to take into account employee needs, these arrangements have merely recognised the reality of needing to accommodate employee needs in order to further financial outcomes. They are not based on the fundamental premise of recognising the dignity of the individual person for their own sake (see Kramar, 2014).

The rights and responsibilities of large organisations, such as MNEs and MNCs, have developed within a legal framework which provides that the organisation primarily serves the interests of those providing the capital necessary to do business. Therefore, it is claimed that management decisions should serve the interests of the shareholders. Profit maximisation and increasing shareholder value are paramount, while the interests of other stakeholders, including employees, suppliers, distributors, customers and the community, are protected by contractual rights and laws. Proponents of this view argue that 'social welfare is maximized when all firms in the economy maximize the total firm value' (Jensen, 2002). Ertuna and Ertuna (2010) claim that this form of organisation evolved in western economies and has contributed to recent, significant technological and economic developments.

These assumptions about people and the rights and obligations of organisations, however, do not translate across cultures. Those assumptions that inform western organisations developed in the context of free market economics, in which there was limited or no state regulation, processes existed where buyers and sellers determined the price and cost of goods and services, and private ownership was paramount. Free market economies were also based on some of the philosophical traditions proposed by Adam Smith, Hegel and Ralph Waldo Emerson. The philosophical tradition of Adam Smith not only was concerned with the most efficient form of allocation of resources, but, like Emerson in the USA, was concerned with social good and the welfare of members of society. All three of these philosophers believed in the innate goodness of individuals, their need to care for other people and the idea of a common mind among members of societies. Hegel surprisingly inspired both Smith and Marx. Although these traditions were concerned with social good, emphasis was given to the efficient operation of the market. Smith gave emphasis to extraordinary individuals as drivers for change and to the importance of the rights of these individuals. Despite the importance of social good for these philosophers, the development of economic theory and management practices in western industrialised countries has been concerned with promoting the efficient operation of markets, including the labour market, rather than promoting social good.

It is assumed that strategic HRM practices such as HPWPs are globalised to promote labour efficiency in developing economies. However, Bae and Rowley (2001) have indicated that most of the organisations (i.e. subsidiaries) in developing economics have adopted HPWPs as part of a transfer of HRM practices from the parent company because of isomorphic institutional pressures. Also, there is evidence that convergence and divergence in international HRM are not black and white as perceived by HRM professionals Hence, MNEs, while transferring strategic HRM to their subsidiaries, include elements of 'best practices or universal HRM characteristics' as well as national and subnational diversity (Guillen, 2001). It is evident from the discussion here that strategic HRM practices were transferred by MNEs to their subsidiaries by recognising the divergence in cultural, social, institutional and legal systems and the impact this has on HRM practices. However, the negative impacts of strategic HRM on stakeholders (i.e. employees in subsidiaries, environment in host countries and the host community) are rarely explored in the literature. Hence, in this chapter global sustainable HRM extends the benefits and the negative impacts of sustainable HRM to stakeholders of a parent MNE as well as to their subsidiaries. This attempts to deal with the negative effects of global strategic HRM on stakeholders of the subsidiaries.

For instance, the offshoring of goods (e.g. manufacturing and service work) has been found to contribute to cost savings for the parent companies. However, this HR strategy has been found to reduce the demand for unskilled, skilled and professional workers in parent companies. This can contribute to lower morale and increased job insecurity and stress among workers in the parent company, while in subsidiary organisations workers have been exploited, subject to negative health impacts because of urbanisation, pollution and other damage to the local environment, and exposed to the possibility of employment insecurity as the parent company searches for cheaper sources of labour. At the same time, workers in the subsidiaries benefit from employment opportunities, wages which can be spent in the community, and contribute through the multiplier effect to increased expenditure, training and exposure to more sophisticated management systems.

12.4 Global sustainable HRM

12.4.1 Global business ethics and sustainable HRM

Business ethics goes beyond the legal requirements for common good. Business ethics also includes norms, standards and expectations that reflect a belief in what employees, consumers, shareholders and the global community regard as fair, just and consistent with the respect for and protection of stakeholders' moral rights. CSR goes beyond both legal requirements and business ethics. It includes economic, legal and philanthropic responsibilities (Gjølberg, 2009). In the global environment MNEs are the prime movers of the CSR phenomenon because these organisations need to secure human, environmental and organisational interests to achieve corporate sustainability. CSR is therefore a comprehensive concept to be explored because it includes business ethics, economic and legal responsibilities. For example, Gjølberg (2009) found that MNEs effectively used their CSR initiative along with post-materialist, rationalist, participatory national cultural values to achieve CSR performance (i.e. being recognised as one of the SustainAbility 100 best reports) in a strong regulatory context.

CSR was redefined by Porter and Kramer (2011) to suggest that corporate profits and societal interests are mutually dependent and need to be viewed from a long-term perspective. This was demonstrated by Blodgett and his colleagues (2014) who conducted a study to explore the relationship between ethical values indicated in CSR statements of US Fortune 250 companies and the ratings of company's social actions (e.g. Kinder, Lydenberg, Domini Research & Analytics, or KLD). In this study they found that there are significant differences between MNCs and non-MNCs on universal and other ethical values (Blodgett et al., 2011). In order to engage employees in the global context (i.e. subsidiaries in host countries) and to achieve the synthesis effect of economic/financial, human/social and environmental outcomes of MNEs, a number of ethical values of CSR are chosen for global sustainable HRM. These values include governance, environmentalism, human rights, social responsibility and organisational disclosure. The chosen ethical values for global sustainable HRM and definition are provided in Table 12.1.

The ethical value of social responsibility has a number of dimensions. The statement of social responsibility in Table 12.1 on the 'accountability

Table 12.1 Definition of ethical values relevant for global sustainable HRM

Ethical values relevant for global sustainable HRM	Definition and an example
Governance	A body of persons that constitutes the governing authority of an organisation to promote transparency. Example: *'For Chevron, good corporate governance means being transparent with and responsive to its stockholders while managing the company for long-term success.'*
Environmentalism	Organisational commitment to being green; an overt act; planning, anticipating; a sense of obligation to protect and sustain the natural environment. It includes environmental sustainability, renewable resources; preservation of species, green building; energy conservation; prevention of global warming; quality of life. Example: Sodexo/Montigny-le Bretonnes – *'Our mission is two folds: to "Improve the Quality of Daily Life" and to contribute to the economic, social and environmental development of the cities, regions and countries in which we operate.'*
Social responsibility	Recognising organisational obligation for oneself and accountability to societal and community well-being. It includes actions for sustainability. Example: Ford Motor Co – *'The conduct of our company worldwide must be pursued in a manner that is socially responsible and command respect and integrity for its positive contribution to society.'*
Human rights	Violation and potential risk of human rights violations that are fundamental to all employees. Human rights include freedom from unlawful imprisonment, torture and execution; care to employees by providing conducive working conditions; minimum wages; and employee health and safety. Example: Monsanto – *'Because our supply chain varies by country and seed crop, we conducted a global risk assessment with the help of outside experts to prioritize our human rights work. This assessment looked at the areas covered by the human rights policy and ranked our country operations in terms of potential for risk of specific human rights concerns.'*
Organisational disclosure	To expose organisational practices to stakeholders' view. Example: *'U.S. Steel was founded and built on principles of ethical business practice that foreshadowed the code of conduct which our directors and employees follow today. These include honesty and integrity, compliance with the law, fair dealing, protection and proper use of company assets, and full and accurate disclosure.'*

Definitions and examples are based on Blodgett, Hoitash and Markelevich (2014).

to societal and community well-being' covers many stakeholders, including individuals and groups within the organisation and across the broader industry. Social responsibility also involves understanding the impact of organisational practices, particularly HRM practices, on these stakeholders. Organisational practices can have positive impacts on individuals by enhancing human rights or reducing the negative impacts of 'harm' of work. Organisational practices can also have negative impacts on individuals by detracting from stakeholder well-being, producing negative effects on physical and mental health, and producing a lack of respect for religious customs and care responsibilities. Finally, organisational disclosure highlights the transparency of an organisation. That is, the organisation actively involves key stakeholders through consultation to ascertain their human/social and environmental expectations in the host countries where the subsidiaries operate and to disclose their management practices and economic/financial, human/social and environmental outcomes. Hence, these are the global business values that are relevant for global sustainable HRM to achieve corporate sustainability outcomes (i.e. economic/financial, human/social and natural environment) of subsidiaries of MNEs operating in varied host countries.

12.4.2 Characteristics of global sustainable HRM practices

An important component of international standards is the need to avoid harm resulting from work and/or negative impacts of HRM practices on key stakeholders (i.e. employees, host country, and society's sustainable environmental management expectations) accruing from the transfer of HRM by MNEs to a subsidiary company. In addition, global sustainable HRM is a way of reinforcing these international standards in global organisations with international supply chains and work locations. The Performance Standard 2 (PS2) is an example of a standard which furthers these sustainable HRM outcomes. This standard was established by the International Finance Corporation (IFC). The IFC is an international financial institution offering investment, advisory, and asset-management services seeking to encourage private sector development in developing countries and is a member of the World Bank Group. PS2 recognises the importance of pursuing economic growth through employment creation and income generation but only when this is balanced with the basic rights of workers. The overall objectives of PS2 are to:

- Establish, maintain and improve the worker–manager relationship
- Promote the fair treatment, non-discrimination and equal opportunity of workers, and compliance with national labour and employment laws

- Protect the workforce by addressing child labour and forced labour
- Promote safe and healthy working conditions, and to protect and promote the health of workers.

The requirements of this standard provide a means of specifying the need to practise management policies which enable positive outcomes throughout the production process, no matter what the nature of the engagement relationship is with the global organisation. It covers all workers in the supply chain and any workers conducting work for the organisation. The standard provides a means of dealing with tensions in HRM policies in emerging economies.

The operation of sustainable HRM in a global context provides an opportunity to meet CSR requirements. It also provides the means of managing paradoxes and tensions between conflicting desirable organisational outcomes and organisational operations, and to anticipate the human capital requirements. It moves beyond the boundaries of understanding global organisations in terms of cultural differences and the need to manage these differences, by identifying the broader matter of the tensions between different groups within the organisations. This provides a focus on process. The process of satisfying the economic/financial, human/social and environmental expectations of key stakeholders focuses on reducing harmful outcomes on a variety of stakeholders by using management decisions and actions of MNEs in their global business operations. Hence, *global sustainable HRM is about the universal values of HRM that are transferred by MNEs/MNCs to subsidiaries in varied host countries, based on congruence and divergence in culture, social and institutional systems, to improve organisational performances as well as reduce the negative human/social and natural environmental outcomes imposed on stakeholders (i.e. subsidiary employees, host country environment and society).*

The characteristics of global sustainable HRM are: firstly, to engage an MNE to effectively use governance to promote transparency, and improve employees' commitment to protect and sustain the natural environment in the host countries where their subsidiaries are located. Secondly, engaging employees in an MNE and in the subsidiaries to recognise organisational obligations for oneself and to be accountable for host country societal wellbeing. Thirdly, manage the potential risk of human rights violations, which is fundamental to all employees involved in the subsidiary business operations. Finally, use organisational disclosure to embody the requirement for the involvement, consideration and rights of a number of stakeholders in the formulation of HRM strategy and policies.

The characteristics of global sustainable HRM highlight the need for the collaboration of stakeholders with an organisation. It also requires the provision of an opportunity for the explicit recognition of values and customs in global organisations operating in countries outside the country of the parent organisation. For instance, in European countries such as Germany it was normal business practice to have a variety of stakeholders involved in decision making (Ireland & Pillay, 2010). This involvement was enshrined in legislation. Consequently, MNCs with subsidiaries operating in these countries are required to adhere to the legislation requiring employee representation through bodies such as works councils (Singe & Croucher, 2005). However, organisations in countries which are not members of the European Union are not required to abide by directives requiring employee representation.

Sustainable HRM provides an opportunity to move beyond the focus on cultural differences by emphasising universal ethical values that are congruent to national cultures. However, these universal ethical values are expressed in a variety of ways in many cultures. The following section explores the national values of a limited number of developing countries in which most of the subsidiaries of MNEs are located, and the transferability of global sustainable HRM based on congruence with the national cultures.

12.5 Transference and implementation of global sustainable HRM

Two important aspects of globalizing HRM are identified by Bae and Rowley's (2001) framework on the transfer of HRM by MNE to host country subsidiaries. These aspects are the alignment of 'best practices' or 'universal practices' with the host country's cultural values and the institutionalisation of best practices within the subsidiary company. Using Bae and Rowley's framework it is proposed that global sustainable HRM should attempt to simultaneously realise multiple business values (i.e. universal values and divergent or national culture-based values) towards sustainable outcomes (economic/financial, human/social and natural environment). Also, the framework indicates that an MNE should successfully internalise the hybrid culture based on universal values and the national cultural values of global sustainable HRM system for implementing a corporate sustainability business strategy through employee training, education, rewards and compensation. Hence, in this section the need to align the universal characteristics of global sustainable HRM and national culture in order to facilitate the transfer and implementation of sustainable HRM to subsidiaries is discussed first. Subsequently, the implementation of divergent business value aspects (i.e. national culture) of global sustainable HRM in subsidiaries is discussed.

12.5.1 National culturally congruent global sustainable HRM

The learnt behaviour of work is a product of national cultural factors. This occurs through historical processes. As society develops, certain attitudes to work and ways of working evolve, and these are passed on to the younger generations who, during education and other kinds of socialisation, develop these attitudes. Different civilisations in the past, and different nations (such as China, India, Japan, South Korea, etc.) in the contemporary world, have evolved very different work attitudes and types of organisation (Mariappanadar, 2005). In national cultures based on work values founded in Hinduism, Confucianism and Islamic beliefs, there was more concern with work organisations providing for the 'social good' (Micklethwaith & Wooldridge, 2003). The concept of 'social good' is much broader than the concern for the rights of stakeholders in their dealings with representatives of an organisation. Hence, environmentalism and social responsibility are the two characteristics of global sustainable HRM which are congruent with national cultures of developing economies in the Asian region. In order for MNEs to transfer and implement effectively sustainable HRM in their subsidiaries in the Asian region, it is important for MNEs to analyse the congruence between some of the characteristics of global sustainable HRM and the national culture of the host country.

This approach has two implications for the globalisation of business operations. Firstly, by analysing the congruence between the characteristics of sustainable HRM and national culture and recognising some of the tensions which arise, and adapting to these, the debilitating impact of the tensions can be limited. The minimised organisational culture and national culture tension will facilitate effective transfer and implementation of nationally congruent characteristics of sustainable HRM to achieve social good for the society. Secondly, the identification of nationally congruent characteristics of sustainable HRM will contribute to the development of a hybrid global HRM system of universal and nationally congruent values which is an essential requirement for effective transfer and implementation of global HRM practices by MNEs to subsidiaries (Bae & Rowley, 2001). The identification of tensions and the development of a hybrid global HR system for corporate sustainability are interrelated and are important factors in the transfer of sustainable HRM in a global context. The following discussion is concerned with explaining nationally congruent global sustainable HRM practices in terms of cultural values in developing economies in the Asian region where most of the subsidiaries of MNEs for production are located. Following this discussion, the transfer and implementation of universal values of global sustainable HRM are explained.

India is the birthplace of many dominant religions in the world, such as Buddhism, Hinduism, Jainism and Sikhism. Although, Buddhism originated from India, the majority of its followers live in Southeast Asian and Far East Asian countries. An attempt to generalise Indian cultural values is unrealistic and highly improbable because of the diversity. Hence, Arthasastra, has been used to explain the national culture that promotes social good. This is one of the old scriptures of India as indicated by the modern economist and Nobel laureate professor, Amartya Sen's commentary on *dharma* – work as a duty in Indian cultural values (cited in Budac, 2015) is used to explain the congruence of social responsibility with Indian values. *Dharma* highlights work as a duty for the 'social good' and is the means by which to acquire wealth through righteousness (i.e. social responsibility) for salvation, and this value of work as a duty highlights congruence between social responsibility as the characteristics of global sustainable HRM practices and an aspect of the Indian national culture.

Furthermore, regarding the environmentalist characteristics of global HRM, the holistic vision of work ethos in life as an Indian value indicated in the *Isa Upanishad* (a central scripture on the philosophical concepts and ideas of Hinduism and also shared by Buddhism, Jainism and Sikhism) highlights the connection between work and preserving the natural environment. In the holistic vision of this work ethos, it is highlighted that all work, be it physical or mental, is a manifestation of the essential divinity in man/woman. This divinity is achieved by working for the good of all beings, including the preservation of the natural environment for future generations.

In countries with cultures based on Confucian beliefs, personal relationships (guanxi), respect for hierarchies and centralised decision making are powerful influences. In economic systems in which social values of co-operation, harmony and respect are paramount, many strategic HRM policies are problematic. In these contexts, strategic HRM practices such as individual performance appraisals, merit selection and disciplinary practices have been shown to be incompatible because they fundamentally conflict with embedded social values. These social values could provide a sound basis for the development and implementation of sustainable HRM which seeks to create positive social and human outcomes using the characteristics of global sustainable HRM.

Similarly, in cultures framed within an Islamic tradition, decision making is based on 'hak', that is, promoting 'fairness'. Decisions made in this way can contribute to the social good. This concept is also reflected in the operation of organisations. Workers should be paid a 'fair' wage, people should be charged a 'fair' price and labour and capital should share the income generated by the organisation according to the predetermined 'mudaraba'. The 'mudaraba', or contract, provides for the sharing of the risks and the benefits of the operation of the organisation. According to this view, organisations should earn a fair profit, and consequently they compete with each other in order to serve the 'social good' (Ertuna & Ertuna, 2010). It has been argued that the Islamic approach to 'business ethics' is consistent with the values of CSR and that CSR could be a 'bridge between civilizations' (Williams & Zinkin, 2005). The characteristics of global sustainable HRM are developed based on the global business ethics of CSR, and hence the characteristics of global sustainable HRM are congruent with the Islamic tradition of social good for citizens.

As discussed in previous chapters, sustainable HRM takes a long-term view for the achievement of positive outcomes of organisational activity and the development of the capabilities of people doing the work of organisations. The principle of 'hak' (fairness) in Islamic cultures is embedded in economic transactions. For instance, as mentioned in the previous paragraph, in Islamic organisations, the income generated by an organisation is shared according to a predetermined agreement between those with the financial capital and the people providing the labour (Ertuna & Ertuna, 2010). It is evident from this section that characteristics of global sustainable HRM such as environmentalism and social responsibility are congruent to the 'social good' values of most of the developing countries whose national cultures are shaped by Hinduism, Confucianism and Islam. The national culturally congruent global sustainable HRM practices will facilitate transfer and implementation of sustainable HRM practices by MNEs to their subsidiaries to achieve economic/financial, human/social and environmental outcomes of corporate sustainability.

12.5.2 Divergent values of global sustainable HRM

Human dignity, respect, well-being and being valued as an individual are human rights and they indicate the importance of relationships between employees in the subsidiaries of MNEs and the importance of fair treatment in the workplace. Governance and organisational disclosure, which are characteristics of global sustainable HRM, are interlinked with protection of human rights. Although, protection of human rights is state-centric, in particular developing countries the protection of these rights is weaker in the subsidiaries than in the parent MNE because of the need for foreign direct investment (FDI) to facilitate economic growth (Deva, 2003). As a result, the protection of human rights is transferred and implemented in subsidiaries according to the voluntary codes of conduct based on universal values of MNEs (Campbell, 2006). Hence, characteristics of global sustainable

HRM such as the protection of human rights and the related governance and organisational disclosure for stakeholders are considered as divergent practices that are either incongruent to national culture and/or reflect the powerlessness of the state to enforce protection of human rights that are mandated by global labour organisations as international labour standards.

International standards exist for the protection of basic human rights in the context of work. Instruments, such as standards agreed to by parties, including governments, represent a minimum level of protection necessary for workers. This protection can include improvement of worker security, employment conditions, such as safety and health protection, and a fair wage. It also includes measures to ensure respect, equality and empowerment in the workplace. These standards are embodied in conventions and other instruments established by international bodies. For instance, the ILO advocates international standards which eradicate conditions producing injustice, hardship and privation.

These standards are also reflected in GRIs and the Universal Declaration of Human Rights. The labour codes and standards are reflected in national laws of ratifying countries. Consequently, these national laws and international standards provide the basis for the setting of standards for corporate governance and organisational disclosure on protections of human rights and they indicate these requirements are consistent with the characteristics of global sustainable HRM. As these divergent characteristics of sustainable HRM move beyond the focus of achieving financial outcomes, it is important that employees of MNEs as well as employees of their subsidiaries in other host countries are provided with training and development to accept the transference of divergent global HRM without resistance to the change. Hence, in the next section employee training on these divergent universal values is discussed.

12.5.3 Institutionalising global sustainable HRM

The second aspect of Bae and Rowley's (2001) framework highlights the importance of institutionalising the characteristics of global sustainable HRM using employee training and education. Hence, in this section employee training is explained as way of overcoming resistance to the divergent universal values of global sustainable HRM for corporate sustainability in subsidiaries.

12.5.3.1 Employee training on divergent universal values of global sustainable HRM

The development of human capital necessary for organisational success is at the heart of sustainable HRM. Sustainable HRM is particularly concerned with human capital/human capability/competencies for corporate sustainability. Human capital is regarded as critical for the transference and implementation of divergent universal values of global sustainable HRM. Human capital involves characteristics such as knowledge, skills, values, abilities and personal attributes, but other capabilities such as the capacity to work with, and utilise, many forms of technology and systems. Hence, it is important for MNEs to provide training to both parent company employees and subsidiary company employees on human rights, corporate governance and organisational disclosure on the prevention of human rights to stakeholders to all levels of employees. This initiative will enhance human capital of an MNE to effectively transfer and implement the characteristics of global sustainable HRM to subsidiaries and achieve corporate sustainability outcomes.

12.5.3.2 Educating prospective workforce on global sustainable HRM

A sustainable HRM approach suggests that other parties operating in the labour market, such as educational and training organisations and individuals, will have an active role in developing the human capital of employees, other people doing the work of organisations and potential entrants to the labour market. The development of an HRM strategy within the context of global sustainable HRM involves consideration of the human capital requirements of an organisation and then the influencing of external parties to enable the development and availability of this human capital with the global ethical values such as governance, environmental, social responsibility, human rights and organisational transparency. This could require collaboration between businesses and educational institutions and government policies which support this collaboration. Members of an existing and future workforce will require a positive attitude and expectations of learning new skills and developing global ethical values relating to sustainable HRM for corporate sustainability. Hence, this initiative will enhance the supply of quality human resources for MNEs and MNCs to implement global sustainable HRM practices in organisations in order to achieve corporate sustainability outcomes. For example, Nike as a transnational corporation sometimes partner with local civil society institutions and training authorities to train and educate members of the local population in a number of ways, including better governance practices and CSR.

12.5.4 Paradox of congruence and divergence

As mentioned earlier in the chapter, there is evidence that the use of the congruence/divergence debate is not a useful way of understanding the paradox of global sustainable HRM. Rather, markets are becoming globalised and subject to similar influences such as technological, financial, economic and ecological pressures. Managers need to adopt policies which can assist an organisation in adapting to the changes. These changes will be influenced by national policies. However, cultural and legal factors still influence the development of these policies. National context continues to influence HRM, despite the evidence of transfer of some HRM policies (Kramar & Parry, 2014).

The framing of global sustainable HRM in terms of divergence and convergence is a misleading way of framing the development of HRM globally. Hence, conceptualisation of a hybrid system of global sustainable HRM which includes the national culturally congruent universal values and divergent values of global sustainable HRM practices for corporate sustainability must be considered by MNEs while transferring and implementing such practices to subsidiaries in other host countries. The hybrid HRM system should be able to reconcile the paradox by acknowledging the national culture as well as the universal values in transferring and implementing sustainable HRM in the global context.

The use of a company code of conduct is one way of contributing to the reconciliation of this paradox of global sustainable HRM. For instance, the factories established in Vietnam by Nike were found to expose its female workers to unsafe working practices and toxic work environments which produced sickness and poor health among the workers. Following the activities of NGOs, Nike established a code of conduct which established guidelines for the type of working environment to be provided in its contracting factories.

12.6 Conclusion

MNEs are the engine for globalisation and hence in this chapter we have discussed how MNES could achieve effective transference and implementation of global sustainable HRM to subsidiaries to achieve corporate sustainability outcomes. Global sustainable HRM is about the universal values of HRM that are transferred by MNEs/MNCs to subsidiaries in varied host countries, based on congruence and divergence in culture, social and institutional systems, to improve organisational performances as well as reduce the negative human/social and natural environmental outcomes imposed on stakeholders (i.e. subsidiary employees, host country environment and society).

The universal values of global sustainable HRM include corporate governance, environmentalism, social responsibility, human rights and organisational disclosure of social and environmental outcomes to stakeholders. MNEs and MNCs will experience paradox/tension between congruence and divergent universal values while transferring and implementing global sustainable HRM practices to subsidiaries. To reconcile the paradox of congruence/divergence characteristics of global sustainable HRM, a hybrid HRM system is proposed. The hybrid sustainable HRM system includes two set of universal values, one set of national culturally congruent universal values and the other set is about divergent values of global sustainable HRM. The hybrid global sustainable HRM system is useful in engaging employees from both the parent company and subsidiaries to implement corporate sustainability business strategy in a global context. This chapter also discussed the importance of employee training and development on the universal values of global sustainable HRM practices in order to facilitate effective implementation of such practices in MNEs and MNCs so they can achieve human/social, economic/financial and environment outcomes of corporate sustainability.

References

Bae, J. & Rowley, C. (2001). The impact of globalization on HRM: The case of South Korea. *Journal of World Business*, *36*(4), 402–28.

Blodgett, M. S., Dumas, C. & Zanzi, A. (2011). Emerging trends in global ethics: A comparative study of US and international family business values. *Journal of Business Ethics*, *99*(1), 29–38.

Blodgett, M. S., Hoitash, R. & Markelevich, A. (2014). Sustaining the financial value of global CSR: Reconciling corporate and stakeholder interests in a less regulated environment. *Business and Society Review*, *119*(1), 95–124.

Budac, C. (2015). Mandala of power. *Procedia-Social and Behavioral Sciences*, *183*, 129–34.

Campbell, T. (2006). A human rights approach to developing voluntary codes of conduct for multinational corporations. *Business Ethics Quarterly*, *16*(2), 255–69.

Carroll, A. B. (2004). Managing ethically with global stakeholders: A present and future challenge. *The Academy of Management Executive*, *18*(2), 114–20.

Clark, T. & Knowles, L. L. (2003). Global myopia: Globalization theory in international business. *Journal of International Management*, *9*(4), 361–72.

De Gama, N., McKenna, S. & Peticca-Harris, A. (2013). Ethics and HRM: Theoretical and conceptual analysis. *Journal of Business Ethics*, *111*, 97–108.

Debroux, P. (2014), 'Sustainable HRM in East and Southeast Asia', In Ehnert, I., Harry, W. & Zink, K. J. (eds) *Sustainability and Human Resource Management: Developing Sustainable Business Organizations*, Berlin Heidelberg: Springer.

Deva, S. (2003). Human rights violations by multinational corporations and international law: Where from here. *Connecticut Journal of International Law*, *19*, 1–57.

Ertuna, O. & Ertuna, B. (2010). How globalization is affecting corporate social responsibility: Dynamics of the interaction between corporate social responsibility and globalization, In G. Aras & D. Crowther (eds), *A Handbook of Corporate Govern-ance and Social Responsibility* (pp. 323–40). Gower.

Gjølberg, M. (2009). Measuring the immeasurable?: Constructing an index of CSR practices and CSR performance in 20 countries. *Scandinavian Journal of Manage-ment, 25*(1), 10–22.

Guillén, M. (2001). Is globalization civilizing, destructive or feeble? A critique of five key debates in the social science literature. *Annual Review of Sociology, 27*, 235–60.

Hechanova, M. R. M., Alampay, R. B. A., & Franco, E. P. (2006). Psychological empow-erment, job satisfaction and performance among Filipino service workers. *Asian Journal of Social Psychology, 9*(1), 72–78.

Ireland, P. & Pillay, R. S. (2010). *Corporate Social Responsibility in a Neo-Liberal Age.* Berlin: Springer.

Jensen, M. (2002). Value maximization, stakeholder theory and the corporate objec-tive function. *Business Ethics Quarterly, 12*, 235–56.

Kramar, R. (2014). Beyond strategic human resource management: Is sustainable human resource management the next approach? *The International Journal of Human Resource Management, 25*(8), 1069–89.

Kramar, R. & Parry, E. (2014). Strategic human resource management in the Asia Pacific region: Similarities and differences. *Asia Pacific Journal of Human Resources, 52*(4), 400–19.

Mariappanadar, S. (2005). An emic approach to understand culturally indigenous and alien human resource management practices in global companies. *Research and Practice in Human Resource Management, 13*(2), 31–48.

Micklethwaith, J. & Wooldridge, A. (2003). *The Company: A Short History of a Revolu-tionary Idea.* New York: Modern Library Chronicles.

Porter, M. E. & Kramer, M. R. (2011). The big idea: Creating shared value. How to reinvent capitalism – and unleash a wave of innovation and growth. *Harvard Busi-ness Review, 89*(1–2).

Reich, S. (1998). *What Is Globalization?: Four Possible Answers.* Helen Kellogg Institute for International Studies Working paper series (Vol. 261), University of Notre Dame, Indiana.

Singe, I., & Croucher, R. (2005). US multi-nationals and the German industrial rela-tions system. *Management Revue, 16*(1), 123–127.

Stiglitz, J. (2002). *Globalisation and Its Discontents.* London: Allen Lane.

Index

Note: Page numbers with *f* indicate figures and those with *t* indicate tables.

ABC needs, 196
Ability–Motivation– Opportunities (AMO) theory, 11, 139–40
academic journals, 2
acceptance, to cope with paradox, 71–72, 71*f*
Accuracy, in GRI, 249
Action Transformation Collaboration (ACT), 253
AES, 208
Agenda 21. *See* Rio Declaration on Environment and Development
altruistic employee motivation, 84*t*
anthropocentric green HRM, 142–44, 143*f*, 149
anthropocentrism, 98, 129, 134–35, 142, 144, 147
anti-corruption, 42, 45*t*, 252, 263
aspect (GRI concept), 39*t*
attributes of negative externality of HRM practices
  avoidability of negative externality, 111–12
  impact of negative externality, 110–11
  level of negative externality, 109–10
  manifestation of negative externality, 110
attributes of sustainable HRM, 112–13
Australian Broadcasting Corporation (ABC), 171

autonomy, 196
avoidability of negative externality, 111–12

background for sustainable development, 34–37, 35*f*
Balance, in GRI, 249
Banco do Brasil (Bank of Brazil), 90
barriers to sustainable HRM, 22
  in implementing, overcoming, 177–80
  industry barriers, 178–79
  organisational barriers, 179–80
B-Corp, 264, 265–66*t*
B (Benefit)-Corp Movement, 264
Bellagio Sustainability Assessment and Measurement Principles (Bellagio STAMP), 261–62
belongingness, 196
benevolence (doing/being good), 171
BMW, 286
Brundtland Report, 33, 35, 35*f*, 36, 68
Buddhism, 308, 318, 319
bundles of sustainable HRM practices for corporate sustainability business strategy, 18
business case for sustainable HRM, 19–20
  beyond, 20–22
  defined, 19
business competitive condition, 50

business competitive conditions, 50–51
business strategy for sustainable development, characteristics of, 87–90, 88*t*
Buurtzorg, 207

capability oriented sustainable HRM strategy, 92
career development systems, 209–10
career ready for sustainability typology for OSCPQ-1, 160*f*, 163*t*, 165–66
category (GRI concept), 39*t*
challenges for strategic HRM in twenty-first century, 10–12
    critical HRM perspective, 12
    mutual benefits perspective, 11–12
Chartered Institute of Personnel and Development (CIPD), 63
civil society organisations
    as context for sustainable HRM, 45–47
    defined, 45
Clarity, in GRI, 249
Coal India, 259
collective agreements, 51, 255
collective bargaining, 36, 39*t*, 45*t*, 46, 52, 252, 254–56, 258–59, 263, 267
collective mindset, 199–200
common core processes, 290
Comparability, in GRI, 249
competence, 196
competencies for sustainable HR roles, 297–98*t*, 297–302, 299*t*
    for HRM system of sustainability role, 300
    for integration and fusion of sustainable HR roles, 302
    introduction to, 277–78
    for patron role of sustainability culture, 301
    for stakeholder custodian role, 298–99

for standardised HR service role, 301–2
strategic, 278–80
for sustainability business partner role, 299–300
competency and talent-based approach to sustainable HRM, 194–95
Completeness, in GRI, 248
compliance-based commitment, 173*f*, 174
compliance personnel category, 173*f*, 174
configurational model of job contexts, 158–64, 160*f*
    employee career life-cycle, 160*f*, 162
    processes of, 162–64
    simultaneous benefits dimension and its elements, 161–62
    structure of, 160–62
    work intensification as dimension and its elements, 160–61
Confucianism, 308, 318, 320
consultations, 36, 40, 255
Continental, 255–56
Continuity block in ROC model, approaches to implement, 205–11
    dare to co-create, 208–9
    encourage sustainable retention, 210–11
    optimise organisational structure and processes, 206–7
    strive for sustainable careers, 209–10
    theoretical background, 205–6
control and strategic HRM systems
    characteristics of, 85–87, 88–89*t*
    ethical issues of, 85–87
corporate social responsibility (CSR)
    actions/initiatives, 283–88
    civil society organisations and, 32
    defined, 86
    employment relations and, 51–52
    ethical value of, 313–15, 314*t*
    ethics of care and, 48–49, 86–87

corporate social responsibility (CSR)
(*Cont.*)
   multinational corporations and,
     48–56
   NGO activism in resolving issues
     in, 53
   reporting, 246–47
   socio-efficiency and, 19
   three 'Ps'of, 188
corporate sustainability
   assistance programme,
     characteristics of, 96–97
   assistance typology for OSCPQ-4,
     160*f*, 163*t*, 168–69
   reporting, 246–47
   scheme of classification of
     sustainable HRM for, 173–74
   in twenty-first century, 16–18
corporate sustainability assistance
   typology for OSCPQ-4, 160*f*,
   163*t*, 168–69
costs framework for harm of HRM
   practices, 117–21, 118*f*
   allocation of costs of harm to
     stakeholders, 119
   cost measures component of, 118–19
   valuation of costs of harm of HRM
     practices, 119–21
costs framework for harm of work,
   220–23
   allocation of costs of harm of work
     to stakeholders, 221–22
   valuation of costs of harm of HRM
     practices, 222–23
critical HRM perspective, 12
cultural values, 313, 317–19

dare to co-create, 208–9
dedicated sustainable HR positional
   roles, defined, 288–92
Department of Labour and National
   Service (DLNS), 9
descriptive aspects of paradox
   perspective, 66–67

design and process characteristics of
   sustainable HRM, organizational,
   90–91
developmental humanism, 84*t*
dharma, 319
disclosures and performance
   indicators, HRM-related GRI,
   249–62, 250–51*t*
   economic indicators related to
     HRM, 252–54
   general disclosures related to
     HRM, 252
   limitations of, 260–62
   social performance indicators
     related to HRM, 254–59
distributive justice, 171–72
diversity, 203–4
   sensitivity towards, 203–4
   social performance indicators
     regarding, 257–58
Diversity & Inclusion (D&I), 202
Dow Jones Sustainability Group
   Index (DJSI), 35*f*, 44, 47
dynamic business environment, 50

Earth Summit. *See* Rio Summit
ecocentric green HRM, 143*f*, 144–47
   for preserving health of ecosystem,
     characteristics of, 146–47
eco-efficiency, 19–20
ecological sustainability, 35*f*, 38, 145, 267
economic indicators related to HRM,
   252–54
Economic Standards, in GRI, 250*t*
Economy of the Common Good,
   264–67, 265–66*t*
ecosystem, health of, 8, 21–22, 98, 135,
   142, 144–50
educating workforce on global
   sustainable HRM, 322
education, social performance
   indicators regarding, 257
efficiency *versus* resilience paradox, 69
efficiency *versus* substance paradox,
   69–70

embedding characteristics of
    sustainable HRM typologies to
    HRM functions, 172–73
employee assistance programme
    (EAP), 97
employees
    competencies for sustainable HRM
        practices, characteristics of, 94
    educating on global sustainable
        HRM, 322
    employee assistance programme, 97
    employee career life-cycle, 160f, 162
    employment relations, 51–52
    empowerment for sustainable HRM
        practices, characteristics of, 95
    equal employment, 257–58
    health harm of work, 116–17
    level green behaviours, 140–41
    longitudinal relative deprivation
        of career growth opportunities,
        114–15
    motivation for sustainable HRM
        practices, characteristics of,
        94–95
    social performance indicators
        regarding, 254–55
    trade union associations and,
        52–53
    training on divergent universal
        values, 321–22
    vitality, 174–76
environmental awareness activities in
    the home, 204
environmental management system
    (EMS), 128–50. See also green
    HRM
    background of, 130–36
    characteristics of sustainable HRM
        for, 98
    ISO14001 and EMAS, 135–36
    perspectives of, 134–35
    role of HRM in, 136–37
    for sustainability, 132–35
environmental sustainability. See green
    HRM

environment performance indicators
    of HRM-related GRI, limitations
    of, 260–62
Environment Statement, 136
equal employment, 257–58
ethics
    of care and corporate social
        responsibility, 48–49
    developments in, 86–87
    in global sustainable HRM, 313–15,
        314t
    issues of control and strategic HRM
        systems, 85–87, 88–89t
ethics of care, 84t
European Union Eco-Management
    and Audit Scheme (EMAS),
    135–36, 149, 260, 268
Evonik Industries, 258
ExxonMobil, 255

Fairfax group, 171
family domain, 115, 234, 236, 241
Federal Ministry of Labour and Social
    Affairs (Germany), 219
financial market institutions as a
    context for sustainable HRM,
    44–45
forced proactivity category, 175f, 176
foreign direct investment (FDI), 320
Foundation, 248, 249
framework of synthesis of green HRM
    for environmental sustainability,
    142–48, 143f
    anthropocentric green HRM, 142–44
    ecocentric green HRM, 144–47
    synthesis of green HRM of
        environmental sustainability,
        147–48
FTSE4Good Index, 32, 35f, 44
functional HRM strategy, 91–92
fusion of sustainable HR roles, 294f,
    296–97
    competencies for, 302
Future Fit Foundation, 262
Future Fit Framework, 267

General Disclosures, in GRI, 250*t*
global reporting initiative (GRI)
  disclosures and performance
    indicators, 249–62, 250–51*t*
  framework, 247–62
  guidelines as a context for
    sustainable HRM, 38–42
  key definitions for understanding, 39*t*
  principles of, 248–49
  sample materiality matrix, 40, 40*f*
  stakeholder engagement and
    materiality related to HRM, 247–49
global sustainable HRM practices,
    307–24
  business ethics and, 313–15, 314*t*
  characteristics of, 315–17
  divergent values of, 320–21
  educating workforce on global
    sustainable HRM, 322
  ethics in, 313–15, 314*t*
  globalisation and multinational
    enterprises, 309–10
  institutionalising, 321–23
  national culturally congruent,
    318–20
  paradox of congruence and
    divergence, 322–23
  stakeholders' expectations,
    limitations of strategic HRM in
    addressing, 310–13
  transference and implementation of
    global sustainable HRM, 317–23
governance disclosure (GRI concept), 39*t*
green HRM, 137–41. *See also*
    environmental management
    system (EMS)
  defined, 139
  employee level green behaviours,
    140–41
  framework of synthesis for
    environmental sustainability,
    142–48, 143*f*
  greening of strategic HRM for
    environmental sustainability,
    137–39

institutional environmental
    sustainability leadership
    perspective for, 130–32
institutional level AMO framework
    for, 139–40
measure for practices, 237–39

harm of work measures, 228–36
  health harm of work, 229–33
  social harm of work, 234–36
harm of work theory, 106*f*, 113–17. *See
    also* costs framework for harm of
    HRM practices; stakeholder harm
    of work index
  aggregate social costs of, 226–27
  employee health harm of work,
    116–17
  measures for, 228–36
  psychological aspect of, 114–15
  social harm of work, 115–16
  stakeholder harm of work index,
    219–28
  sustainable HRM and, 117
health harm of work
  defined, 116
  employee, 116–17
  measures, 229–33
  scale, items for, 232*t*
  stress and, difference between,
    229–31
  usefulness of, 232–33
Henkel, 211
high-involvement HRM, 173*f*, 174
high performance work systems
    (HPWS), 122–23
Hinduism, 308, 318, 319, 320
honeybee leadership, 236, 241. *See also*
    sustainable leadership measure
HRM involvement classification,
    173*f*, 174
'human,' use of term, 8
human dignity, 37, 38, 54, 267
humanistic organisational values, 84*t*
humanity in mission and values,
    193–94

human potential index (HPI), 219
human resource (HR) competencies
    defined, 280
    introduction to, 277–78
    strategic, 279–80
    sustainable, 280–83
human resource management (HRM).
    See also sustainable HRM
    common core processes, 290
    defined, 10
    differentiation, 199–200
    system of sustainability role,
        289–91, 298*t*
human resource management (HRM)
        in twenty-first century, 7–23
    barriers to sustainable HRM, 22
    challenges for strategic HRM, 10–12
    corporate sustainability and
        sustainable HRM, 16–18
    human resources, defined, 8
    importance of sustainable HRM,
        19–22
    sustainable HRM, 12–16
    traditional human resource
        management, 9–10
human resource (HR) roles
    defined, 277
    introduction to, 277
    strategic, 278–79
    sustainable, 281–97
human resources (HR), defined, 8
human rights, 258–59

identity construction, 282–83, 293–97,
    294*f*
IKEA, 195
Ikuboss measures, 200
importance of sustainable HRM,
    19–22
    beyond business case for, 20–22
    business case for, 19–20
inclusive approach, 202–3
indicators (GRI concept), 39*t*
industrial ecosystems concept, 145
industrial relations (IR) category, 278

industry
    barriers, 178–79
    defined, 54
    meso-level, 49–54
    micro-level, 54–55
information technology (IT)-enabled
    service centres, 292–93
instantaneous negative externality of
    work, 110
institutional contexts for developing
    sustainable HRM, 31–56, 32*f*
    macro-level institutional contexts,
        32*f*, 33–47
    meso- and micro-level contexts,
        32*f*, 48–55
institutional environmental
    sustainability leadership (IESL)
    perspective for green HRM,
    130–32
institutionalising global sustainable
    HRM, 321–23
    educating workforce on global
        sustainable HRM, 322
    employee training on divergent
        universal values, 321–22
institutional level AMO framework for
    green HRM, 139–40
institutional theory
    defined, 31
    to explain the macro-, meso, and
        micro-level contexts, 31, 55
    in IESL, 130, 131, 149
    in individual and organisational
        actions, 175, 179, 181
    neo-, 130
    in societal embeddedness of HRM
        practices, 198
instrumental aspect, 67, 284
instrumental aspects of paradox
    perspective, 66–67
integrated sustainable HRM system
    model, 81–83, 82*f*
integrated sustainable HR roles, 294*f*,
    295
    competencies for, 302

integrity (adherence to a set of acceptable principles), 171
International Finance Corporation (IFC), 315
International Labour Organization (ILO), 8, 33–34, 35*f*, 196, 254, 321
International Standards Organization (ISO) 14001, 135–36, 149, 260, 268
intrinsic-based commitment, 173*f*, 174
irreversibility, 20, 21–22, 107, 145, 230–31
Isa Upanishad, 319
Islamic beliefs, 308, 318, 319–20
isomorphism *versus* change paradox, 68–69

Jainism, 319
JFE Steel, 255
Johnson & Johnson, 193–94

knowledge and skills abilities (KSA), 88*t*, 94, 165–66

labour conditions, 43, 45*t*
labour/management relations, social performance indicators regarding, 255–56
Labour Practices and Decent Work indicators, 92–93
Landesbank Baden-Wurttemberg (LBBW), 219
leader–member exchange (LMX), 196
legally abiding and benevolent organisation typology for OSCPQ-7 to OSCPQ-12, 160*f*, 163*t*, 170–72
legitimacy of HRM practices, 53–54
Likert scale, 232*t*, 235*t*, 237
Living Wage Foundation, 253
longitudinal relative deprivation of employees' career growth opportunities, 114–15
low health and social harm of work for sustainable HRM practices, characteristics of, 95–96

macro-level institutional contexts, 32*f*, 33–47
background for sustainable development, 34–37, 35*f*
civil society organisations as context for sustainable HRM, 45–47
financial market institutions as a context for sustainable HRM, 44–45
multilateral organisations for sustainability, 38–43
social sustainability and sustainable HRM, 37–38
UN Global Compact principles, 44–45, 45*t*
management approach (GRI concept), 39*t*
manifestation of negative externality, 110
material (GRI concept), 39*t*
material aspects (GRI concept), 39*t*
materiality matrix/analysis, 40, 40*f*
Materiality Principles, in GRI, 248
Matthew effect, 202–3
measurements for sustainable HRM practices, 216–41
for green HRM practices, 237–39
human potential index, 219
Likert scale used in, 232*t*, 235*t*, 237
measures for the harm of work, 228–36
role of, framework to understand, 217*f*
stakeholder harm of work index, 219–28
for sustainable leadership, 236–37
meso- and micro-level institutional contexts, 32*f*, 48–55
ethics of care and corporate social responsibility, 48–49
meso-level national context, 49–54
micro-level industry context, 54–55
meso-level national context, 49–54
business competitive conditions, 50–51

employment relations, 51–52
legitimacy of HRM practices, 53–54
regional/national NGOs, 53
trade union and employee
association, 52–53
micro-level industry context, 54–55
mission, humanity and sustainability
in, 193–94
mission statement, 64, 193–94
multilateral organisations for
sustainability, 38–43
GRI guidelines as a context for
sustainable HRM, 38–42
UN Global Compact guidelines
as a context, 42–43
multinational corporations (MNCs),
36
globalisation and, 309–11, 313,
316–17, 322
green HRM and, 138
institutional contexts and, 47–56
multinational enterprises (MNEs),
309–24. *See also* global
sustainable HRM practices
mutual benefits perspective, 11–12

national culturally congruent global
sustainable HRM practices,
318–20
negative externality of HRM practices
theory, 108–13. *See also* attributes
of negative externality of HRM
practices
negative side effects of work, HRM
attributes of, 95–98
low health and social harm of work
for sustainable HRM practices,
characteristics of, 95–96
regeneration of HR base for
sustainable HRM practices,
characteristics of, 97–98
sustainable corporate assistance
programme, characteristics of,
96–97
neo-institutional theory, 130

new environmental paradigm (NEP)
scale, 140
Nokia, 196
non-governmental organisations
(NGOs), 34–35
civil society organisations, 45–47
defined, 45–46
regional/national, 53
UN Global Compact and, 42–43
non-substitutability of capital, 20–21
normative aspects of paradox
perspective, 66–67

occupational health and safety,
social performance indicators
regarding, 256–57
occupational health performance,
indicators of, 116, 268
Openness block in ROC model,
approaches to implement,
198–204
aim for inclusive approach, 202–3
be sensitive to diversity and
environmental management, 203–4
combine HRM differentiation with
collective mindset, 199–200
invest in sustainable networks,
201–2
theoretical background, 198–99
operational sustainable HR roles,
288–92, 298*t*
HRM system of sustainability role,
289–91, 298*t*
patron role of sustainability culture,
291–92, 301
organisational barriers to
implementing sustainable HRM
practices, overcoming, 179–80
organisational paradoxes, 67–69
efficiency *versus* resilience, 69
isomorphism *versus* change, 68–69
personal *versus* organisational
sustainability agendas, 68
short-term *versus* long-term
orientation, 68

organisational performance, HRM
    attributes for improving, 94–95
  employee competencies for
    sustainable HRM practices,
    characteristics of, 94
  employee empowerment for
    sustainable HRM practices,
    characteristics of, 95
  employee motivation for sustainable
    HRM practices, characteristics
    of, 94–95
Organisation for Economic Co-
    operation and Development
    (OECD), 34, 35f
organisation-stakeholder care
    position quadrants (OSCPQs),
    160f, 164–73
  corporate sustainability assistance
    typology for OSCPQ-4, 168–69
  legally abiding and benevolent
    organisation typology for
    OSCPQ-7 to OSCPQ-12, 170–72
  sustainability awareness typology
    for OSCPQ-2, 166
  sustainability culture typology for
    OSCPQ-5, 169
  sustainability excellence typology
    for OSCPQ-3, 167
  sustainability veteran typology for
    OSCPQ-6, 169–70
organizational design and process
    characteristics of sustainable
    HRM, 88t, 90–91
organizational values for sustainable
    HRM, 83–85, 84t
Our Common Future report, 35. See
    also Brundtland Report

paradoxes
  acceptance to cope with, 71–72
  of congruence and divergence of
    global sustainable HRM practices,
    322–23
  descriptive aspects of, 66–67
  efficiency versus resilience, 69

efficiency versus substance, 69–70
  for HRM, key, 69–70
  of implementing strategic and
    sustainable HRM practices, 181–82
  isomorphism versus change, 68–69
  organisational, key, 67–69
  performance versus regeneration, 70
  personal versus organisational
    sustainability agendas, 68
  resolution to cope with, 72
  short-term versus long-term, 68, 70
  strategies to cope with, 70–73, 71f
  between using strategic and sustainable
    HRM practice, 98–99, 99f
paradox perspective for sustainable
    HRM, 61–73. See also paradoxes
  defining, 65–66
  descriptive aspect of, 67
  instrumental aspect of, 67
  key organisational paradoxes, 67–69
  key paradoxes for HRM, 69–70
  normative aspect of, 67
  strategies to cope with paradox,
    70–73, 71f
  tension between sustainability and
    HRM, 62–65
passivity category, 175f, 176
Patagonia's supply chain, 201
patron role of sustainability culture,
    291–92, 298t
  competencies for, 301
Performance Standard 2 (PS2), 315–16
performance versus regeneration
    paradox, 70
personal versus organisational
    sustainability agendas, 68
plan-do-check-act cycle, 132
+Power, 204
positional roles, 283–93
  operational sustainable HR roles,
    288–92
  standardised HR service, 292–93
  strategic sustainable HR roles,
    283–88
positive environmental deviance, 132

private provision of public goods, 284
pro-organisational-focused
    environmental management, 149
pro-social value orientation, 84t
psychological contract, 210

quality, principles for reporting, 260

Randstad Netherlands, 204
reduced family role facilitation
    dimension, 234
regeneration of HR base for
    sustainable HRM practices,
    characteristics of, 97–98
regional/national NGOs, 53
Reliability, in GRI, 249
religious customs, 315, 319
resolution, to cope with paradox, 71f, 72
resource regeneration strategy for
    sustainable work performance,
    174–77
    employee vitality as quality standard
        for sustainable HRM, 174–76
    framework, 175f
    sustainable HRM strategy to
        facilitate, 176–77
Respect, Openness, and Continuity
    (ROC) model, 188–212, 189f
    assumptions related to theoretical
        roots and foundations of,
        190, 191t
    Continuity, 205–11
    Openness, 198–204
    Respect, 192–98
    triple P translated into, 189–91
Respect block in ROC model,
    approaches to implement, 192–98
    act as transformational leader,
        196–98
    combine competency and talent-
        based approach to sustainable
        HRM, 194–95
    integrate humanity and
        sustainability in mission and
        values, 193–94

mainstream decent and meaningful
    work, 195–96
theoretical background,
    192–93
responsible personnel category, 173f,
    174
results oriented sustainable HRM
    strategy, 92–93
reversibility, 107, 110, 113, 145–46,
    161, 230–31
Rio Declaration on Environment and
    Development, 35, 42, 263
Rio Summit, 33, 34, 35, 36, 56

scheme of classification of sustainable
    HRM for corporate sustainability,
    173–74, 173f
self-managing teams, 207
short-term *versus* long-term paradox,
    68
Sikhism, 319
simultaneous benefits, 161–62
simultaneous effects of HRM
    practices. *See also* sustainable
    HRM theories
    benefits for organisations and
        stakeholders, 104–25, 106f
    perspectives of, 106–7
smart jobs, 209
social consciousness, 84t
social-constructivist concept, 190,
    209, 212
Social/Environmental Responsibility
    (SER), 201
social good, 86, 312, 318,
    319–20
social harm of work, 115–16
    measures, 234–36
    scale, items for, 234, 235t
    for sustainable HRM practices,
        characteristics of, 95–96
social justice, 37, 38, 54, 267
social performance indicators of
    HRM-related GRI, limitations of,
    260–62

social performance indicators of
HRM-related GRI, reporting
requirements, 254–59
in regard to diversity and equal
employment, 257–58
in regard to employment, 254–55
in regard to human rights, 258–59
in regard to labour/management
relations, 255–56
in regard to occupational health and
safety, 256–57
in regard to training and education,
257
social responsibility, corporate. *See*
corporate social responsibility
(CSR)
Social Standards, in GRI, 250–51*t*
social sustainability and sustainable
HRM, 37–38
socio-efficiency, 19
Southwest airlines, 202
stakeholder custodian role, 285–86,
297*t*
competencies for, 298–99
stakeholder harm of work index,
219–28
aggregate social costs of, 226–27
costs framework for, 220–23
defined, 220
for self-regulating system, 227–28
structure of, with illustrations,
223–26, 224–25*t*
usefulness of, for developing
sustainable HRM practices, 226–28
Stakeholder Inclusiveness, in GRI, 248
stakeholders. *See also* organisation-
stakeholder care position
quadrants (OSCPQs)
allocation of costs of harm to, 119
engagement and materiality related
to HRM, 247–49
expectations in global sustainable
HRM, limitations in addressing,
310–13

standardised HR service role, 292–93,
298*t*
competencies for, 301–2
strategic choice to overcome industry
barriers to implementing
sustainable HRM practices,
178–79
strategic HRM
characteristics of control and,
85–87, 88–89*t*
limitations of, in addressing
stakeholders' expectations,
310–13
in twenty-first century, challenges
for, 10–12
strategic sustainable HR roles,
283–88, 297*t*
stakeholder custodian role, 285–86,
298–99
sustainability business partner,
287–88, 299–300
structural changes, 211
subcategory (GRI concept), 39*t*
supply chain, 95–97, 201, 253, 258–59,
269, 276, 292, 307, 315
sustainability awareness typology for
OSCPQ-2, 160*f,* 163*t,* 166
sustainability business partner role,
287–88, 297*t*
competencies for, 299–300
Sustainability Context, in GRI, 248
sustainability culture typology for
OSCPQ-5, 160*f,* 163*t,* 169
sustainability excellence typology for
OSCPQ-3, 160*f,* 163*t,* 167
sustainability in mission and values,
193–94
sustainability performance, assessment
of, 262–67, 265–66*t*
B-Corp, 264
Economy of the Common Good,
264–67
Future Fit Framework, 267
UN Global Compact, 262–64

sustainability reporting, 245–69
  by corporations, 246–47
  global reporting initiative
    framework, 247–62
  from reporting standards to
    assessment of sustainability
    performance, 262–67
  sustainability reporting by
    corporations, 246–47
  sustainable HRM theories to enrich
    performance indicators of
    HRM-related GRI, 268–69
sustainability veteran typology for
  OSCPQ-6, 160f, 163t, 169–70
sustainable careers, 209–10
sustainable development
  background for, 34–37, 35f
  business strategy for, characteristics
    of, 87–90
  defined, 68
  institutional contexts for, 31–56, 32f
  stakeholder harm of work index in,
    226–28
sustainable HRM
  barriers to, 22
  challenges for strategic HRM, 10–12
  corporate sustainability and, 16–18
  defined, 13
  environmental management for,
    128–50
  human resources, defined, 8
  importance of, 19–22
  institutional contexts for
    developing, 31–56, 32f
  organizational design and process
    characteristics of, 90–91
  organizational values for, 83–85, 84t
  sustainable HRM, 12–16
  synthesis paradox perspective of,
    14–16, 14f
  traditional HRM, 9–10
  in twenty-first century, 7–23
sustainable HRM, implementing,
  157–83

embedding characteristics of
    sustainable HRM typologies to
    HRM functions, 172–73
  framework of typologies of
    sustainable HRM, 157–72
  overcoming barriers to
    implementing sustainable HRM
    practices, 177–80
  paradoxes in implementing strategic
    and sustainable HRM practices,
    181–82
  resource regeneration strategy for
    sustainable work performance,
    174–77
  scheme of classification of
    sustainable HRM for corporate
    sustainability, 173–74, 173f
  theoretical antecedents and
    overview of practical approaches
    to, 191t
sustainable HRM practices, 81–100,
    88–89t
  business strategy for sustainable
    development, characteristics of,
    87–90
  characteristics of, 93–98
  control and strategic HRM systems,
    characteristics of, 85–87, 88–89t
  for environmental management,
    characteristics of, 98
  implementing, 157–83
  integrated sustainable HRM system
    model, 81–83, 82f
  measurements for, 216–41
  negative side effects of work, HRM
    attributes of, 95–98
  organisational performance, HRM
    attributes for improving,
    94–95
  organizational design and process
    characteristics of sustainable
    HRM, 90–91
  organizational values for sustainable
    HRM, 83–85, 84t

sustainable HRM practices (*Cont.*)
  paradoxes or tensions between
    using strategic and sustainable
    HRM practice, 98–99, 99*f*
  ROC model, 188–212, 189*f*
  sustainability reporting, 245–69
  sustainable HRM strategies, 91–93
  typologies of, 157–72
  usefulness sustainable leadership
    indicators to develop, 237
sustainable HRM strategies, 91–93
  capability oriented, 92
  functional, 91–92
  results oriented, 92–93
sustainable HRM theories, 104–25, 106*f*
  costs framework for harm of HRM
    practices, 117–21
  to enrich performance indicators of
    GRI, 268–69
  harm of work, 113–17
  negative externality of HRM
    practices, 108–13
  perspectives of simultaneous effects
    of HRM practices, 106–7
  synthesis effects of HRM practices,
    106*f*, 121–23
sustainable HR roles, 275–303. *See also*
    competencies for sustainable HR
    roles
  integration and fusion of, rationale
    for, 293–97, 294*f*
  introduction to, 277–78
  link between sustainable HRM
    characteristics and, 276*f*
  need for, 281–82
  strategic, 278–80
  types of, 283–93 (*See also* dedicated
    sustainable HR positional roles)
sustainable leadership measure,
    236–37
sustainable networks, 201–2
sustainable organisational values,
    definitions, 84*t*
sustainable retention, 210–11

sustainable work performance
  comfortable energy category, 176
  forced proactivity category, 176
  framework, 175*f*
  passivity category, 176
  resource regeneration strategy for,
    174–77
  vitality category, 176
synthesis effects of HRM practices,
    theory of, 106*f*, 121–23
  empirical evidence of synthesis
    effects of HPWS, 122–23
synthesis of green HRM of
    environmental sustainability,
    147–48. *See also* framework
    of synthesis of green HRM for
    environmental sustainability
synthesis paradox perspective of
    sustainable HRM, 14–16, 14*f*
synthesis strategy, 71*f*, 72
system of sustainability role, 289–91,
    298*t*, 300

talent-based approach to sustainable
    HRM, 194–95
tensions
  strategies to manage, 71*f*
  between sustainability and HRM,
    62–65
  between using strategic and sustainable
    HRM practice, 98–99, 99*f*
theories. *See* sustainable HRM theories
three 'Ps' of CSR, 188, 191*t*
Timeliness, in GRI, 249
Toshiba, 209–10
Toyota, 200
trade union and employee association,
    52–53
traditional HRM, 9–10
training, social performance indicators
    regarding, 257
transcended HRM, 173*f*, 174
transference and implementation of
    global sustainable HRM, 317–23

transformational leader, 196–98
Tripartite Declaration of Principles concerning Multinational Enterprises and Social Policy, 36, 254
triple bottom line (TBL) concept, 2, 3, 16–17
triple P ('Planet, People and Profit') translated into ROC model, 189–91
typologies of sustainable HRM practices, 157–72
  career ready for sustainability typology, 165–66
  configurational model of job contexts, 158–64, 160*f*
  corporate sustainability assistance typology for OSCPQ-4, 160*f,* 163*t,* 168–69
  embedding characteristics of, to HRM functions, 172–73
  framework of, 157–72
  legally abiding and benevolent organisation typology for OSCPQ-7 to OSCPQ-12, 170–72
  list of, 163*t*
  sustainability awareness typology for OSCPQ-2, 166
  sustainability culture typology for OSCPQ-5, 169
  sustainability excellence typology for OSCPQ-3, 167
  sustainability veteran typology for OSCPQ-6, 169–70

UN Global Compact Communication on Progress (COP), 262–64
  guidelines as a context, 42–43
  principles, 44–45, 45*t*
UN Human Rights, 34, 35*f,* 36, 45*t*

United Nations Convention Against Corruption (UNGC), 42–43
Universal Standards, 248–50
utilitarian instrumentalism, 84*t*

valuation of costs of harm of HRM practices, 119–21
values
  cultural, 313, 317–19
  divergent, in ethics of care, 320–21
  employee training on divergent universal values, 321–22
  humanity and sustainability in, 193–94
  sustainability in, 193–94
  sustainable organizational, 83–85, 84*t*
vitality category, 175*f,* 176
voluntary workplace green behaviour (VWGB), 141
VOLVO, 197
Volvo Group Attitude Survey (VGAS), 197

Wells Fargo, 256
work, decent and meaningful, 195–96
workforce. *See* employees
work intensification, 160–61
World Business Council for Sustainable Development, 44
World Commission on Environment and Development (WCED), 17, 33, 34–35, 35*f,* 68, 113
World Summit on Sustainable Development (WSSD), 34–36

Yamaha Group, 204